T0330058

The Economics of Inaction

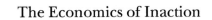

The Economics of Inaction
Stochastic Control Models with Fixed Costs

Nancy L. Stokey

Princeton University Press
Princeton and Oxford

Published by Princeton University Press, 41 William Street, Princeton, New Jersey 08540

In the United Kingdom: Princeton University Press, 6 Oxford Street, Woodstock, Oxfordshire OX20 1TW

Library of Congress Cataloging-in-Publication Data

Stokey, Nancy L.
    The economics of inaction : Stochastic control models with fixed costs / Nancy L. Stokey.
        p.   cm.
    Includes bibliographical references and index.
    ISBN-13: 978-0-691-13505-2
    ISBN-10: 0-691-13505-3
    1. Econometric models.   2. Brownian movements.   I. Title.
HB141.S853 2008
330.01′519233—dc22   2008062109

British Library Cataloging-in-Publication Data is available

This book was composed in New Baskerville using ZzTEX by Princeton Editorial Associates, Inc., Scottsdale, Arizona.

Printed on acid-free paper   ∞

press.princeton.edu

Printed in the United States of America

10 9 8 7 6 5 4 3 2 1

Contents

Preface   ix

1 Introduction   1
       Notes   12

I Mathematical Preliminaries   15

2 Stochastic Processes, Brownian Motions, and Diffusions   17
    2.1. Random Variables and Stochastic Processes   17
    2.2. Independence   18
    2.3. Wiener Processes and Brownian Motions   19
    2.4. Random Walk Approximation of a Brownian
           Motion   20
    2.5. Stopping Times   24
    2.6. Strong Markov Property   24
    2.7. Diffusions   25
    2.8. Discrete Approximation of an Ornstein-Uhlenbeck
           Process   27
           Notes   28

3 Stochastic Integrals and Ito's Lemma   30
    3.1. The Hamilton-Jacobi-Bellman Equation   31
    3.2. Stochastic Integrals   34
    3.3. Ito's Lemma   37
    3.4. Geometric Brownian Motion   38
    3.5. Occupancy Measure and Local Time   41
    3.6. Tanaka's Formula   43
    3.7. The Kolmogorov Backward Equation   47
    3.8. The Kolmogorov Forward Equation   50
           Notes   51

4   Martingales   **53**
   4.1.   Definition and Examples   53
   4.2.   Martingales Based on Eigenvalues   57
   4.3.   The Wald Martingale   58
   4.4.   Sub- and Supermartingales   60
   4.5.   Optional Stopping Theorem   63
   4.6.   Optional Stopping Theorem, Extended   67
   4.7.   Martingale Convergence Theorem   70
         Notes   74

5   Useful Formulas for Brownian Motions   **75**
   5.1.   Stopping Times Defined by Thresholds   78
   5.2.   Expected Values for Wald Martingales   79
   5.3.   The Functions ψ and Ψ 82
   5.4.   ODEs for Brownian Motions   87
   5.5.   Solutions for Brownian Motions When $r = 0$ 88
   5.6.   Solutions for Brownian Motions When $r > 0$ 93
   5.7.   ODEs for Diffusions   98
   5.8.   Solutions for Diffusions When $r = 0$ 98
   5.9.   Solutions for Diffusions When $r > 0$ 102
         Notes   106

II   Impulse Control Models   **107**

6   Exercising an Option   **109**
   6.1.   The Deterministic Problem   110
   6.2.   The Stochastic Problem: A Direct Approach   116
   6.3.   Using the Hamilton-Jacobi-Bellman Equation   119
   6.4.   An Example   125
         Notes   128

7   Models with Fixed Costs   **129**
   7.1.   A Menu Cost Model   130
   7.2.   Preliminary Results   133
   7.3.   Optimizing: A Direct Approach   136
   7.4.   Using the Hamilton-Jacobi-Bellman Equation   140
   7.5.   Random Opportunities for Costless Adjustment   145
   7.6.   An Example   146
         Notes   152

8   Models with Fixed and Variable Costs   **153**
   8.1.   An Inventory Model   154
   8.2.   Preliminary Results   157

8.3.	Optimizing: A Direct Approach	160
8.4.	Using the Hamilton-Jacobi-Bellman Equation	162
8.5.	Long-Run Averages	164
8.6.	Examples	166
8.7.	Strictly Convex Adjustment Costs	174
	Notes	175

9	**Models with Continuous Control Variables**	**176**
9.1.	Housing and Portfolio Choice with No Transaction Cost	178
9.2.	The Model with Transaction Costs	182
9.3.	Using the Hamilton-Jacobi-Bellman Equation	184
9.4.	Extensions	191
	Notes	196

III	**Instantaneous Control Models**	**197**

10	**Regulated Brownian Motion**	**199**
10.1.	One- and Two-Sided Regulators	201
10.2.	Discounted Values	205
10.3.	The Stationary Distribution	212
10.4.	An Inventory Example	218
	Notes	224

11	**Investment: Linear and Convex Adjustment Costs**	**225**
11.1.	Investment with Linear Costs	227
11.2.	Investment with Convex Adjustment Costs	232
11.3.	Some Special Cases	236
11.4.	Irreversible Investment	239
11.5.	Irreversible Investment with Two Shocks	243
11.6.	A Two-Sector Economy	247
	Notes	248

IV	**Aggregation**	**251**

12	**An Aggregate Model with Fixed Costs**	**253**
12.1.	The Economic Environment	256
12.2.	An Economy with Monetary Neutrality	259
12.3.	An Economy with a Phillips Curve	261
12.4.	Optimizing Behavior and the Phillips Curve	265
12.5.	Motivating the Loss Function	278
	Notes	280

A Continuous Stochastic Processes   **283**
    A.1.   Modes of Convergence   283
    A.2.   Continuous Stochastic Processes   285
    A.3.   Wiener Measure   287
    A.4.   Nondifferentiability of Sample Paths   288
            Notes   289

B Optional Stopping Theorem   **290**
    B.1.   Stopping with a Uniform Bound, $T \leq N$ 290
    B.2.   Stopping with $\Pr\{T < \infty\} = 1$ 292
            Notes   294

References   **295**

Index   **303**

Preface

THIS BOOK PROVIDES an introduction to stochastic control models in economics that feature fixed adjustment costs or other elements that lead to inaction regions. Such models arise in many areas, including monetary economics, where price-setting decisions are involved; business cycle theory, where investment decisions are central; and labor issues in macroeconomics, where hiring and firing decisions are critical.

The book arose from lecture notes for a course for advanced graduate students at the University of Chicago. The modeling techniques it presents are typically not covered in basic micro- or macroeconomics courses, although they are useful in a variety of areas. The goal of the book is to make these techniques accessible to a broad group of economists.

Consequently, an effort has been made to keep the mathematical prerequisites at a level that is comfortable for economists, while at the same time making the arguments rigorous enough to be useful in model building. Some background in probability theory is required, and familiarity with stochastic processes is useful, but the book is largely self-contained.

Many friends, colleagues, and students provided advice and support during the writing of this book. I am grateful to several cohorts of Chicago students, whose comments and feedback on successive drafts greatly improved both the substantive coverage and the exposition. Particular thanks go to Rubens P. Cysne and Jose Plehn-Dujowich, who provided detailed comments on early drafts, and to Yong Wang, who read the entire manuscript at a late stage. I thank Thomas Chaney, Willie Fuchs, Larry Jones, Patrick Kehoe, John Leahy, and Alessandro Pavan for many stimulating conversations and helpful comments, and I am especially grateful to Fernando Alvarez and Robert Shimer, who played the role of exceptionally probing, demanding, and inspiring students when they sat in the course. I am also grateful to the Federal Reserve Bank of Minneapolis, where early drafts were written and rewritten over the course of several visits. Finally, I thank Robert Lucas for his unfailing encouragement, advice, and support over the many years during which the book was in progress.

The Economics of Inaction

1
Introduction

IN SITUATIONS WHERE action entails a fixed cost, optimal policies involve doing nothing most of the time and exercising control only occasionally. Interest in economic models that exhibit this type of behavior has exploded in recent years, spurred by growing evidence that "lumpy" adjustment is typical in a number of important economic settings.

For example, the short-run effects of monetary policy are connected with the degree of price stickiness. Data from the U.S. Bureau of Labor Statistics on price changes at retail establishments for the period 1988–2003 suggest that price adjustment is sluggish, at least for some products. The average duration of a price varies greatly across different types of products, with some—gasoline, airfares, and produce—displaying frequent price changes, and others—taxi fares and many types of personal services—displaying much longer durations. The average duration across all products is about 5 months, but the range is wide, from 1.5 months at the 10th percentile to 15 months at the 90th percentile. The size distribution of adjustments is perhaps even more informative about price stickiness. Many adjustments are large, even after short-term sale prices have been removed. The average size is more than 8%. Moreover, 1988–2003 was a period of low inflation, so in the broad sample 45% of price changes are negative, and price cuts are almost as large as price increases. More detailed data for the largest three urban areas (New York, Los Angeles, and Chicago), show that about 30% of price changes are greater than 10% in magnitude, and the figure is about the same for increases and decreases.

The fact that many price changes are large suggests that there may be substantial fixed costs associated with changing a price. Otherwise it is difficult to explain why the changes are not carried out in series of smaller, more frequent increments.

Investment behavior provides a second example. Establishment-level data from the U.S. Census Bureau on 13,700 manufacturing plants for the period 1972–1988 show lumpy adjustment in two ways. First, more than half of the plants in the sample display an episode of large adjustment, at least 37%. In addition, a substantial fraction of aggregate investment, 25%, is concentrated in plants that are increasing their capital stock by more than 30%. At the other end of the distribution, over half of plants increase their capital stock by less than 2.5%, accounting for about 20% of total investment. Thus, for individual plants, changes in size come in substantial part from large one-year increases. From the aggregate point of view, a sizable share of total investment is devoted to these episodes of large increase. As with the price data, the evidence on investment suggests that fixed costs are important.

Evidence on job creation and destruction displays patterns similar to those in the investment data. The opening of a new establishment, the expansion of an old one, or the addition of a shift leads to concentrated job creation, while plant closings and mergers lead to concentrated destruction. Data from the U.S. Census Bureau on 300,000–400,000 manufacturing plants for the period 1972–88 show that two-thirds of total job creation and destruction occurs at plants where employment expands or contracts by more than 25% within a twelve-month period. One-quarter of job destruction arises from plant closings. Again, these adjustment patterns suggest that fixed costs are important.

For consumers, fixed costs are clearly important for durable goods such as housing and automobiles. U.S. Census Bureau data for 1996 show that among individuals aged 15 and older living in owner-occupied housing, the median tenure at the current residence is eight years, and about 40% have been at their current residence for more than eleven years. Although individuals have many motives for staying in their current residences, the substantial transaction costs—including time costs—involved in buying, selling, and moving clearly make frequent moves unattractive.

Evidence suggests that fixed costs are also important for explaining individual portfolio behavior. Absent fixed costs, it is hard to understand why so many households fail to participate in the stock market. The fact that lagged stock market participation increases the likelihood of current participation very strongly—by 32 percentage points, even after controlling for age, education, race, income, and other factors—strongly suggests that fixed entry costs are important. In addition, the fact that wealthier households are more likely both to own stocks and to trade suggests that fixed costs per period or per transaction are also important. In this context and others the costs of gathering and processing information are likely to be important components of the fixed cost.

These examples suggest that models using a representative firm and representative household may be inadequate for studying some questions. For example, the economic effects of an aggregate productivity shock or aggregate demand shock depend on the investment and hiring/firing response of firms. If fixed costs are important, describing the aggregate response requires averaging over a group of firms that are doing little or nothing and a group making substantial adjustments. Although it may happen that movements in the aggregate can be generated by a representative agent, it is difficult to confirm this—or to determine what the representative agent should look like—without explicitly carrying out the aggregation. Moreover, a representative agent that serves as an adequate proxy during periods of calm may be misleading during episodes when the economic environment becomes more turbulent. And on the household side, explicitly taking heterogeneity into account may have a substantial impact on conclusions about welfare.

In situations where fixed costs are important, continuous-time models in which the stochastic shocks follow a Brownian motion or some other diffusion have strong theoretical appeal. An optimal policy in this type of setting involves taking action when the state variable reaches or exceeds appropriately chosen upper and/or lower thresholds and doing nothing when the state lies inside the region defined by those thresholds. Continuous-time models permit a very sharp characterization of the thresholds that trigger an adjustment and the level(s) to which adjustment is made. Indeed, the thresholds and return points can often be characterized as the solution to a system of three or four equations in as many unknowns. The goal in this book is to develop the mathematical apparatus for analyzing models of this type. In the rest of this introduction the structure of typical models is briefly described and a few examples are discussed.

Suppose that in the absence of control the increments to a state variable $X(t)$ are those of a Brownian motion. The (flow) return to the decision maker at any date, $g(X(t))$, depends on the current state, where the function g is continuous and single peaked. Suppose the peak is at $x = a$, so that g is increasing on $(-\infty, a)$ and decreasing on $(a, +\infty)$. The decision maker can adjust the state by discrete amounts, and there is a fixed cost c associated with making any adjustment. For now suppose that the fixed cost is the only cost of adjustment. The decision maker's objective is to maximize the expected discounted value of returns net of adjustment costs, where future returns and costs are discounted at a constant interest rate r. The standard menu cost model has this structure, with $X(t)$ interpreted as the firm's price (in log form) relative to an industrywide or economywide price index that fluctuates stochastically.

The problem for the decision maker is to balance two conflicting goals: maintaining a high return flow by keeping the state in the region around a and avoiding frequent payment of adjustment costs. An optimal policy in this setting has the following form: the decision maker chooses threshold values b, B for the points where control will be exercised, with $b < a < B$, and a return point $S \in (b, B)$ to which the state is adjusted when control is exercised. As long as the state remains inside the open interval (b, B)—called the *inaction region*—the decision maker exercises no control: adjustment is not required. When the state falls to b or rises to B the fixed cost is paid and the state variable is adjusted to the return point S. If the initial state lies outside (b, B) an adjustment to S is made immediately. If the fixed cost c is sufficiently large relative to the range of the return function g, it is possible that $b = -\infty$, $B = +\infty$, or both.

Notice that in general an optimal policy does not involve returning to the point a where instantaneous returns are at a maximum. That is, in general $S \neq a$. For example, if the drift is positive, $\mu > 0$, the decision maker might choose $S < a$, anticipating that (on average) the state will rise. Or, if the return function g is asymmetric around a, he might skew the return point in the direction of higher returns.

Let $v(x)$ denote the expected discounted return from following an optimal policy, given the initial state $X(0) = x$. The first step in finding the optimum is to formulate a Bellman equation involving the function v. That equation can then be used to characterize the optimal policy. Indeed, it can be used in two different ways.

Suppose that thresholds b and B have been selected and that the initial state $X(0) = x$ lies between them, $b < x < B$. Let $\mathrm{E}_x [\cdot]$ and $\mathrm{Pr}_x [\cdot]$ denote expectations and probabilities conditional on the initial state x, and define the random variable $T = T(b) \wedge T(B)$ as the first time the process $X(t)$ reaches b or B. T is an example of a *stopping time*. It is useful to think of $v(x)$ as the sum of three terms:

$v(x) =$ expected returns over $[0, T)$

$\qquad +$ expected returns over $[T, +\infty)$ if b is reached before B

$\qquad +$ expected returns over $[T, +\infty)$ if B is reached before b.

Let $w(x, b, B)$ denote the first of these terms, the expected returns up to the stopping time T. The key to making this problem tractable is the fact that $w(x, b, B)$, which is the expected value of an integral over time up to the stopping time $T = T(b) \wedge T(B)$, can be written as an integral over states in the interval $[b, B]$. Specifically,

$$w(x, b, B) \equiv \mathrm{E}_x \left[\int_0^T e^{-rt} g(X(t)) dt \right]$$

$$= \int_b^B \hat{L}(\xi; z, b, B) g(\xi) d\xi,$$

where $\hat{L}(\cdot; x, b, B)$ is the *expected discounted local time* function. It is a weighting function—like a density—for each state ξ up to the stopping time $T(b) \wedge T(B)$, conditional on the initial state x. For the second and third terms it is useful to define

$$\psi(x, b, B) \equiv \mathrm{E}_x \left[e^{-rT} \mid X(T) = b \right] \mathrm{Pr}_x \left[X(T) = b \right],$$

$$\Psi(x, b, B) \equiv \mathrm{E}_x \left[e^{-rT} \mid X(T) = B \right] \mathrm{Pr}_x \left[X(T) = B \right].$$

Thus, $\psi(x, b, B)$ is the expected discounted value, conditional on the initial state x, of an indicator function for the event of reaching the lower threshold b before the upper threshold B is reached. The value $\Psi(x, b, B)$ has a similar interpretation, with the roles of the thresholds reversed. For any $r \geq 0$, clearly ψ and Ψ are bounded, taking values on the interval $[0, 1]$. With w, ψ, and Ψ so defined, the Principle of Optimality implies that v satisfies the Bellman equation

$$v(x) = \sup_{b, B, S} \{ w(x, b, B) + \psi(x, b, B) [v(S) - c]$$

$$+ \Psi(x, b, B) [v(S) - c] \}, \tag{1.1}$$

where the optimization is over the choice of the threshold values b and B and return point S.

If X is a Brownian motion or geometric Brownian motion, closed-form expressions can be derived for the functions $\hat{L}$, ψ, and Ψ, and (1.1) provides a direct method for characterizing the optimal policy. If X is a more general diffusion, closed forms for $\hat{L}$, ψ, and Ψ are not available, but fairly sharp characterizations can often be obtained. In either case, several properties of the solution are worth noting. First, it is immediate from (1.1) that the optimal return point S^* maximizes $v(S)$ and does not depend on x. Second, the Principal of Optimality implies that the thresholds b^* and B^* do not depend on x. That is, if b^*, B^* attain the maximum in (1.1) for any $x \in (b^*, B^*)$, then they attain the maximum for all $x \in (b^*, B^*)$. The rational decision maker does not alter his choice of thresholds as the state variable evolves. Finally, it is immediate from (1.1) that the value function is a constant function outside the inaction region, $v(x) = v(S^*) - c$, for all $x \notin (b^*, B^*)$.

An alternative method for characterizing the optimum involves an indirect approach based on (1.1). Notice that if x lies inside the open interval (b^*, B^*), then for Δt sufficiently small the probability of reaching either threshold can be made arbitrarily small. Hence it follows from (1.1) and the definition of v that

$$v(x) \approx g(x)\Delta t + \frac{1}{1+r\Delta t} E_x \left[v(x + \Delta X)\right],$$

where ΔX is the (random) increment to the state over Δt. As will be shown more formally in Chapter 3, if X is a Brownian motion with parameters (μ, σ^2), then a second-order Taylor series approximation gives

$$E_x \left[v(x + \Delta X)\right] \approx v(x) + v'(x)\mu\,\Delta t + \tfrac{1}{2}v''(x)\sigma^2\,\Delta t.$$

Using this fact, rearranging terms, and letting $\Delta t \to 0$ gives

$$rv(x) = g(x) + \mu v'(x) + \tfrac{1}{2}\sigma^2 v''(x). \tag{1.2}$$

This equation, a second-order ordinary differential equation (ODE), is called the *Hamilton-Jacobi-Bellman (HJB) equation*. The optimal value function v satisfies this equation on the inaction region, the interval $\left(b^*, B^*\right)$. To complete the solution of a second-order ODE two boundary conditions are needed. In addition, for this problem the thresholds b^* and B^* must be determined. Recall that v is known outside the inaction region, $v(x) = v(S) - c$, all $x \notin \left(b^*, B^*\right)$. The two boundary conditions for (1.2) and the thresholds b^* and B^* are determined by requiring that v and v' be continuous at b^* and B^*. These conditions, called *value matching* and *smooth pasting*, reproduce the solution obtained by maximizing in (1.1).

This approach can be applied to a variety of problems. For inventory or investment models it is natural to assume that there are proportional costs of adjustment as well as fixed costs, and that both types of costs can be different for upward and downward adjustments. Even with these changes, however, the overall structure of the solution is similar to the one for the menu cost model. The main difference is that there are two return points, $s^* < S^*$, where the former applies for upward adjustments, from b^*, and the latter for downward adjustments, from B^*.

Models with two state variables can sometimes be formulated in terms of a ratio so that they have this form as well. An example is a model of investment. Suppose that demand X follows a geometric Brownian motion. Suppose further that labor and raw materials can be continuously and costlessly adjusted, but that capital investment entails a fixed cost. Let revenue net of operating costs for labor and raw materials be $\Pi(X, K)$, and assume that Π displays constant returns to scale. Assume that the fixed cost of adjusting the capital stock, λK, is proportional to the size of the installed base. This cost can be interpreted as the time of managers and the disruption to current production. Assume the proportional cost $P\left(K' - K\right)$ is the price of investment goods multiplied by the size of the investment. Thus, $\lambda K/P$ can also be interpreted as the fraction of the existing capital stock that must be scrapped when new capital is installed.

Under either interpretation, the assumption that demand is a geometric Brownian motion and that Π is homogeneous of degree one together imply that the problem can be formulated in an intensive form that has only one state variable, the ratio $x = X/K$. The optimal policy for the problem so written then takes the form described above. There are thresholds b^*, B^* that define an inaction region and one or two return points inside that region. When the ratio x reaches either boundary of the inaction region, or if the initial condition lies outside that region, the firm immediately invests or disinvests. The return points are the same or different for upward and downward adjustments as the proportional costs are the same or different. Note that in this setting the investment decision involves, implicitly, taking into account the option to invest in the future. Thus, the rule of thumb "invest if the expected discounted returns exceed the cost of investment" does not hold. Instead the problem is one of judiciously choosing when and how much to invest, mindful that investing immediately in effect destroys the opportunity to invest in the near future.

Models with fixed adjustment costs for the state variables can also accommodate control variables that are continuously and costlessly adjustable. These controls affect the evolution of the state variable(s) and may affect the current return as well. An example is a model of portfolio choice and housing purchases. The goal in this model is to examine the effect of home ownership on other parts of the consumer's portfolio. Suppose that the consumer has total wealth Q and has a house of value K. Wealth grows stochastically, with a mean and variance that depend on the portfolio—the mix of safe and risky assets—held by the consumer. Suppose that when a house is sold the owner receives only the fraction $1 - \lambda$ of its value. The fraction λ can be thought of as representing agents' fees, time spent searching, moving costs, and so on. Thus, the fixed cost λK is proportional to the level of the state variable, as in the investment model described above. Assume that the consumer's preferences are homogeneous of some degree. That is, $U(K) = K^\theta/\theta$, where $\theta < 1$. Then the value function is homogeneous of degree θ, and the optimal policy functions are homogeneous of degree one. That is, the optimal policy for purchasing a new house involves only the ratio of total wealth to housing wealth, $q = Q/K$, and has the same form as the policy for the menu cost model.

The new element here is the portfolio, which can be continuously and costlessly adjusted. That is, the consumer can allow her mix of safe and risky assets to depend on her ratio q of total wealth to housing wealth. The question is whether her tolerance for risk varies with this ratio. For example, is her risk tolerance different when the ratio q is near a threshold, so that an adjustment in the near future is likely, and when it is near the return point, as it is just after a transaction? The key technical point is that her portfolio decisions affect the evolution of her wealth, so the state no longer follows an exogenously specified stochastic process between adjustments. Nondurable consumption can also be incorporated into the model as another control that can be continuously adjusted. In this case preferences must be assumed to have a form that preserves the required homogeneity property, but no other restrictions are needed.

In all of the examples considered so far the fixed cost is discrete, and the decision maker adjusts the state variable under his control by a discrete amount if he pays that cost. That is, the fixed cost is lumpy and so are the adjustments made by the decision maker. Models of this type are sometimes called *impulse control* models.

The last section of the book treats a somewhat different class of problems, called *instantaneous control* problems, in which adjustments are continuous. The decision maker chooses a rate of upward or downward adjustment in the state variable and pays a (flow) cost that depends on the rate of adjustment. The cost can have both proportional and convex components, and they can differ for upward and downward adjustments. Optimal policies in these settings share an important feature with the previous class of models, in the sense that there are typically upper and lower thresholds that define an inaction region. When the state is inside this region no adjustments are made. When the state reaches or exceeds either threshold control is exercised, with the optimal rate of adjustment depending on how far the state exceeds the threshold.

Instantaneous control models have an inaction region if the proportional costs are different for upward and downward control. For example, if the purchase price P for investment goods exceeds the sale price p, then investment followed quickly by disinvestment costs $P - p > 0$ per unit. An optimal policy involves avoiding adjustments of this type, creating an inaction region.

Instantaneous control models do not produce the lumpy adjustment that is characteristic of impulse control models, but their implications are similar if control is aggregated over discrete intervals of time. Once the state variable reaches or exceeds the threshold in a model with instantaneous control, it is likely to remain in that vicinity for some time. Consequently control is exercised for some time. Similarly, once the state is well inside the inaction region, there is likely to be a substantial interval of time during which no control is exercised. Hence when aggregated over discrete time intervals total control looks somewhat lumpy, with periods of substantial control and periods of little or no control.

An example is the following inventory problem. The state variable Z is the size of the stock, which in the absence of intervention is a Brownian motion. The manager's objective is to minimize total expected discounted costs. These costs have two components. First there is a (flow) holding cost $h(Z)$ that depends on the size of the stock. The function h is assumed to be continuous and U-shaped, with a minimum at zero. Negative stocks are interpreted as back orders. In addition there is a price $P > 0$ per unit for adding to the stock and a price $p \gtrless 0$ per unit for reducing it. If p is positive it is interpreted as the revenue per unit from selling off inventory, and otherwise it is interpreted as the unit cost of disposal. In this example there are no other costs of control. Clearly $p \leq P$ is required, so the system is not a money pump, and $p \neq P$ is required to avoid the trivial solution of keeping the stock identically equal to zero. The interest rate $r > 0$ is constant.

Suppose the manager chooses thresholds b, B, and adopts the policy of keeping the inventory inside the closed interval $[b, B]$. To do this, when the state is $Z = b$ he makes purchases that are just sufficient to keep the stock from falling below b, and when the state is $Z = B$ he sells off just enough inventory to keep the state from rising above B.

Let $v(z)$ denote the expected discounted total cost from following an optimal policy, given the initial state z. As before it is useful to think of $v(z)$ as the sum of three parts:

$$v(z) = \text{expected holding costs}$$

$$+ \text{ expected cost of control at } b$$

$$+ \text{ expected cost of control at } B.$$

Notice that each of these three terms is the expected value of an integral over the entire time horizon $t \in [0, +\infty)$. As before, the key to mathematical tractability is the fact that each of these terms can be written in a convenient way. In particular, the manager's problem can be written as

$$v(z) = \min_{b,B} \left[\int_b^B \pi(\zeta; z, b, B) h(\zeta) d\zeta \right.$$

$$\left. + \alpha(z, b, B) P - \beta(z, b, B) p \right], \quad z \in [b, B],$$

(1.3)

where $\pi(\zeta; z, b, B)$ is the expected discounted local time at each level $\zeta \in (b, B)$, given the initial state z, and

$$\alpha(z, b, B) \equiv \mathrm{E}_z \left[\int_0^\infty e^{-rs} dL \right],$$

$$\beta(z, b, B) \equiv \mathrm{E}_z \left[\int_0^\infty e^{-rs} dU \right],$$

represent the expected discounted control exercised at the two thresholds. If the underlying process is a Brownian motion explicit formulas are available for α, β, and π, and (1.3) provides a direct method for characterizing the optimal thresholds.

As before, there is also an indirect method for characterizing the optimum. Indeed, the first part of the argument is the same as before: if Z lies inside the interval (b, B), then over a sufficiently short period of time Δt the probability of reaching either threshold is negligible. Using the same second-order Taylor series approximation as before then produces the HJB equation, which in this case is

$$v(z) = h(z) + \mu v'(z) + \tfrac{1}{2}\sigma^2 v''(z).$$

As before, solving the HJB equation requires two boundary conditions, and in addition the optimal thresholds b^* and B^* must be determined. In the present case value matching holds automatically, so requiring v to be continuous at b^* and B^* provides no additional restrictions. Here the two constants and two thresholds required for the solution are determined by requiring that v' and v'' also be continuous at b^* and B^*. These conditions—smooth pasting and *super contact*—reproduce the solution obtained by maximizing (1.3).

Another example of this type of model is an investment problem in which demand $X(t)$ follows a geometric Brownian motion and investment is irreversible. Specifically, suppose that the unit cost of new investment is constant, $P > 0$, but capital has no scrap value, $p = 0$. Suppose, further, that there are no fixed costs and no other adjustment costs, and that the profit flow per unit of capital depends on the ratio of the capital stock to demand, $k = K/X$. The optimal policy in this setting involves choosing a critical value κ for the ratio k. When the ratio k falls to κ, the firm invests just enough to keep the ratio from falling below that threshold. When k exceeds κ, the firm does nothing. If the initial state k_0 is less than κ, the firm makes a one-time purchase of capital sufficient to bring the ratio up to the threshold. It is interesting to compare the optimal policy in this setting with optimal investment in a frictionless world, where the price P applies to sales of capital as well as to purchases. In the frictionless world the optimal policy involves maintaining the ratio k at a fixed level k^f. It can be shown that irreversibility makes the firm less willing to invest, in the sense that $\kappa < k^f$. Larger increases in demand are required to trigger investment, since subsequent reductions in demand cannot be accommodated by selling off installed capital.

The discussion so far has concerned problems faced by individual decision makers, firms, or households. For many questions, however, it is aggregates that are of interest. For example, to assess the role of sticky prices in generating short-run effects from monetary policy, the behavior of the aggregate price level must be determined, as well as the distribution of relative prices across firms. Similarly, to assess the role of hiring and firing rules, the impact on aggregate job creation and destruction is needed. And to assess the role of investment in propagating cyclical shocks, the effect on aggregate investment of a macroeconomic disturbance—such as a change in foreign demand—must be determined.

The difficulty of describing aggregates in models where individual agents face fixed adjustment costs depends largely on the nature of the exogenous shocks. Specifically, it depends on whether the shocks are idiosyncratic or aggregate. If the shocks that agents face are idiosyncratic and can be modeled as independently and identically distributed (i.i.d.) across agents, describing aggregates—at least in the long run—is fairly easy. In these cases the law of large numbers implies that the joint distribution of the shock and the endogenous state across agents converges to a stationary distribution in the long run. This stationary distribution, which also describes long-run averages for any individual agent, is easy to calculate. These distributions are described in Chapters 7, 8, and 10. Thus, describing aggregates is straightforward when the shocks are idiosyncratic.

If agents face an aggregate shock the situation is much more complicated. In settings of this type the law of large numbers is not helpful, and no general method is available for describing aggregates. The main issue is that the distribution of the endogenous states across agents varies over time, and at any point in time it depends on the history of realizations of the shock process. Thus, in general the cross-sectional distribution of the endogenous state does not converge.

For models of this sort there are two possible strategies. The first is to look for special assumptions that permit a stationary distribution. For example, for the menu cost model a uniform distribution of prices is compatible with individual adjustment behavior under certain assumptions about the money supply process. Consequently under these assumptions the model is tractable analytically. Alternatively, one can use computational methods that describe the evolution of the entire distribution. This approach is broadly applicable and it has been pursued successfully in several contexts. These applications are noted as they arise, and the references in these sections describe in more detail the methods they employ.

The goal in this book has been to keep the mathematical prerequisites at a level that is comfortable for builders of economic models. The discussion assumes some background in probability theory and stochastic processes, but an extensive knowledge of these areas is not required. Recursive arguments are used throughout, and familiarity with Bellman equations in discrete time is useful but not necessary.

The rest of the book is organized as follows. Chapters 2–5 introduce some basic mathematical tools. The goal is to provide enough background to permit a fairly rigorous treatment of the optimization problems under study, while keeping the entry barriers low. Thus, the coverage is deliberately selective and proofs are omitted if they play no role later. Chapter 2 introduces stochastic processes, focusing on continuous-time processes. Brownian motions and more general diffusions are defined, as well as stopping times. Chapter 3 treats stochastic integrals, Ito's lemma, occupancy measure, and local time, concepts that are used extensively later. Martingales are discussed in Chapter 4, and the optional stopping theorem is stated. Chapter 5 draws on this material to study the functions ψ, Ψ, and $\hat{L}$ defined above. Explicit formulas are derived for the case in which the underlying stochastic process is a Brownian motion or geometric Brownian motion, and sharp characterizations are provided for more general diffusions. Later chapters make repeated use of the explicit formulas developed in this chapter.

Chapters 6–9 treat a sequence of impulse control problems, displaying a range of applications—price adjustment, investment, and durable goods problems—as well as various modeling devices. These chapters provide a rigorous treatment of the value matching and smooth pasting conditions that describe optima, showing precisely the optimization problems that lead to those conditions.

Chapters 10 and 11 treat instantaneous control models. In Chapter 10 the notion of a regulated Brownian motion, the basis for these models, is introduced and is used to analyze a classic inventory problem. In Chapter 11 a variety of investment models are studied using similar techniques. Optimal control in these settings involves a super contact condition.

Chapter 12 treats two variations on an aggregate menu cost model. In one of them, an aggregate state variable is a regulated Brownian motion. On the substantive side, these models provide useful insights about the role of sticky prices as a source of short-run monetary non-neutrality. On the methodological side, they illustrate how specific assumptions can be used to make aggregate models with fixed costs analytically tractable.

Notes

Bils and Klenow (2004) look at detailed data on the frequency of price changes over 1995–97, and Klenow and Kryvtsov (2008) describe the magnitude of these changes over 1988–2003. Both use data from the U.S. Bureau of Labor Statistics. Doms and Dunne (1998) look at investment at the plant level, and Davis, Haltiwanger, and Schuh (1996) look at job creation and destruction at the plant level. Both use data from the U.S. Bureau of the Census on manufacturing plants for the period 1973–88. See Schachter and Kuenzi (2002) for data on the duration of residence. Vissing-Jorgensen (2002) and the references there discuss evidence on household portfolio behavior.

Many of the ideas developed in this book have appeared elsewhere, at various levels of mathematical rigor and with various emphases on techniques and economic questions. Dixit (1993) is an good introduction to impulse and instantaneous control models, with many examples and illustrations. Dixit and Pindyck (1994) treat a variety of investment problems, with excellent discussions of the economic issues these models address and the empirical predictions they lead to. Harrison (1985) has a detailed treatment of mathematical issues related to instantaneous control models, as well as many examples.

The methods developed here have many applications in finance. Excellent treatments of these problems are available elsewhere, however, as in Duffie (1988, 1996), so they have been neglected here.

The term *Principle of Optimality* was introduced by Richard Bellman. The idea was developed in Bellman (1957), which is still a rich source of applications and problems. See Stokey and Lucas (1989) for a discussion of recursive techniques in discrete time.

Part I

Mathematical Preliminaries

2
Stochastic Processes, Brownian Motions, and Diffusions

THIS CHAPTER CONTAINS background material on stochastic processes in general, and on Brownian motions and other diffusions in particular. Appendix A provides more detail on some of the topics treated here.

2.1. Random Variables and Stochastic Processes

To define a random variable, one starts with a *probability space* $(\Omega, \mathfrak{F}, P)$, where Ω is a set, $\mathfrak{F}$ is a σ-algebra of its subsets, and P is a probability measure on $\mathfrak{F}$. Each $\omega \in \Omega$ is an *outcome*, and each set $E \in \mathfrak{F}$ is an *event*. Given a probability space $(\Omega, \mathfrak{F}, P)$, a *random variable* is a measurable function $x : \Omega \to \mathbf{R}$. For each $\omega \in \Omega$, the real number $x(\omega)$ is the *realization* of the random variable. The probability measure for x is then

$$\mu(A) = P\left\{x^{-1}(A)\right\} = P\{\omega \in \Omega : x(\omega) \in A\}, \quad A \in \mathfrak{B},$$

where $\mathfrak{B}$ denotes the Borel sets. Since the function x is measurable, each set $x^{-1}(A)$ is in $\mathfrak{F}$, and the probability $\mu(A)$ is well defined. The distribution function for x is

$$G(a) = \mu((-\infty, a]), \quad a \in \mathbf{R}.$$

Probability measures or distribution functions for (measurable) functions of x can be constructed from μ or G.

To define a stochastic process one proceeds in a similar way, except that a time index t must be added. This index can be discrete or continuous, finite or infinite. In most of what follows the time index is continuous, starting at date 0 and having an infinite horizon; attention here will be focused on the case $t \in [0, \infty)$. Let Ω, $\mathfrak{F}$, and P be defined as before, but add an increasing family of σ-algebras $\mathbb{F} \equiv \{\mathfrak{F}_t, \ t \geq 0\}$ contained in $\mathfrak{F}$. That is,

$$\mathfrak{F}_s \subseteq \mathfrak{F}_t, \quad \text{all } s \leq t, \quad \text{and} \quad \mathfrak{F}_t \subseteq \mathfrak{F}, \quad \text{all } t,$$

where $\mathfrak{F} = \mathfrak{F}_\infty$ is the smallest σ-algebra containing all the $\mathfrak{F}_t$s. The family $\mathbb{F} \equiv \{\mathfrak{F}_t\}$ is called a *filtration*, and $(\Omega, \mathbb{F}, P)$ is called a *filtered probability space*. The interpretation of $\mathfrak{F}_t$ is that it is the set of events known at time t.

A stochastic process is a function on a filtered probability space with certain measurability properties. Specifically, let $(\Omega, \mathbb{F}, P)$ be a filtered probability space with time index $t \in [0, \infty) = \mathbf{R}_+$, and let $\mathfrak{B}_+$ denote the Borel subsets of $\mathbf{R}_+$. A *continuous-time stochastic process* is a mapping $x: [0, \infty) \times \Omega \rightarrow \mathbf{R}$ that is measurable with respect to $\mathfrak{B}_+ \times \mathfrak{F}$. That is, x is *jointly* measurable in (t, ω). Given a probability space $(\Omega, \mathfrak{F}, P)$ and a filtration $\mathbb{F} = \{\mathfrak{F}_t\}$, the stochastic process $x: [0, \infty) \times \Omega \rightarrow \mathbf{R}$ is *adapted* to $\mathbb{F}$ if $x(t, \omega)$ is $\mathfrak{F}_t$-measurable for all t.

For each fixed $t \in [0, \infty)$, the mapping $x(t, \cdot) : \Omega \rightarrow \mathbf{R}$ is an ordinary random variable on the probability space $(\Omega, \mathfrak{F}_t, P_t)$, where P_t is the restriction of P to $\mathfrak{F}_t$. That is, $x(t, \cdot)$ is an $\mathfrak{F}_t$-measurable function of ω. For each fixed $\omega \in \Omega$, the mapping $x(\cdot, \omega) : [0, \infty) \rightarrow \mathbf{R}$ is a Borel-measurable function of t. The mapping $x(\cdot, \omega)$ is called a *realization*, or *trajectory* or *sample path*.

For some purposes it is convenient to view a sample path $x(\cdot, \omega)$: $[0, +\infty) \rightarrow \mathbf{R}$ as a point in an appropriate space of functions. Here the focus is on stochastic processes that have continuous sample paths. Let $C = C[0, \infty)$ denote the space of continuous functions $x: [0, \infty) \rightarrow \mathbf{R}$. A stochastic process x is *continuous* if $x(\cdot, \omega) \in C$, almost every (a.e.) $\omega \in \Omega$. Stated a little differently, a continuous stochastic process is a mapping $x: \Omega \rightarrow C[0, \infty)$.

2.2. Independence

Let $(\Omega, \mathfrak{F}, P)$ be a probability space. Two events $D, E \in \mathfrak{F}$ are *independent* if

$$P(D \cap E) = P(D)P(E).$$

Two families of sets $\mathfrak{D}, \mathfrak{E} \subset \mathfrak{F}$ are *independent* if every pair of events chosen from the two families are independent, if

$$P(D \cap E) = P(D)P(E), \quad \text{all } D \in \mathfrak{D}, \ E \in \mathfrak{E}.$$

The random variables $x_1, x_2, \ldots, x_n$ (a finite collection) on $(\Omega, \mathfrak{F}, P)$ are *mutually independent* if for any Borel sets $A_1, A_2, \ldots, A_n$,

$$P(x_i \in A_i, \ i = 1, \ldots, n) = \prod_{i=1}^{n} P(x_i \in A_i),$$

where

$$P(x_i \in A_i) \equiv P(\omega \in \Omega : x_i(\omega) \in A_i).$$

The random variables $x_1, x_2, x_3, \ldots$ (an infinite collection) are mutually independent if any finite collection of them are mutually independent.

Exercise 2.1. Let $(\Omega, \mathfrak{F}, P)$ be a probability space; let $\mathfrak{D}$, $\mathfrak{E} \subset \mathfrak{F}$ be σ-algebras; and let x, y be random variables that are $\mathfrak{D}$-measurable and $\mathfrak{E}$-measurable, respectively. Show that if $\mathfrak{D}$ and $\mathfrak{E}$ are independent, then x and y are independent. Show that if x and y are independent, then the σ-algebras $\mathfrak{D}_x$ and $\mathfrak{E}_y$ generated by x and y are independent.

2.3. Wiener Processes and Brownian Motions

A *Wiener process* (or *standard Brownian motion*) is a stochastic process W having

  i. continuous sample paths,
 ii. stationary independent increments, and
iii. $W(t) \sim N(0, t)$, all t.

If $W(t)$ is a Wiener process, then over any time interval Δt, the corresponding (random) change is normally distributed with mean zero and variance Δt. That is,

$$\Delta W = \epsilon_t \sqrt{\Delta t}, \quad \text{where } \epsilon_t \sim N(0, 1).$$

As Δt becomes infinitesimally small, write $dW = \epsilon_t \sqrt{dt}$, so

$$\mathrm{E}\,[dW] = \mathrm{E}\left[\epsilon_t \sqrt{dt}\right] = 0,$$

$$\mathrm{E}\left[(dW)^2\right] = \mathrm{E}\left[\epsilon_t^2 dt\right] = dt.$$

A stochastic process X is a *Brownian motion* with *drift* μ and *variance* σ^2 if

$$X(t) = X(0) + \mu t + \sigma W(t), \quad \text{all } t, \tag{2.1}$$

where W is a Wiener process. Clearly, the state space for any Brownian motion, including a Wiener process, is all of **R**. Since $\mathrm{E}[W(t)] = 0$ and

$\mathrm{Var}[W(t)] = t$, it follows that

$$\mathrm{E}\,[X(t) - X(0)] = \mu t,$$

$$\mathrm{Var}\,[X(t) - X(0)] = \sigma^2 t, \quad \text{all } t.$$

Notice that the both the drift and variance of a Brownian motion increase linearly with the time interval.

The next result states that any continuous stochastic process $\{X(t),\ t \geq 0\}$ that has stationary independent increments is a Brownian motion.

Theorem 2.1. If the stochastic process $\{X(t),\ t \geq 0\}$ has continuous sample paths with stationary, independent, and identically distributed increments, then it is a Brownian motion. That is, there exists (μ, σ^2) such that for each $t \geq 0$, the random variable $[X(t) - X(0)]$ has a normal distribution with parameters $(\mu t, \sigma^2 t)$.

See Breiman (1968, Prop. 12.4) for a proof. The idea is to use the central limit theorem.

Theorem 2.1 says that to work in continuous time with a stochastic process that has continuous sample paths and i.i.d. increments, one must accept normality. The parameters (μ, σ^2) of the Brownian motion in (2.1) can be chosen, but nothing more. (Thus, part (iii) in the definition of a Wiener process is redundant.) In Section 2.7 a broader class of continuous stochastic processes is defined by dropping the requirement that the increments be identically distributed.

Since the mean of a Brownian motion grows like t and the standard deviation like $\sqrt{t}$, the standard deviation dictates the overall nature of the path in the short run and the drift—unless it is zero—dominates in the long run. Figure 2.1 displays the expected value and three confidence bands, at 66%, 95%, and 99%, for Brownian motions $X(t)$ with and without drift.

2.4. Random Walk Approximation of a Brownian Motion

A Brownian motion can be viewed as the limit of discrete-time random walks as the time interval and the step size shrink together in a certain way. Suppose that over each time increment Δt the process X increases by h with probability p and decreases by h with probability $(1 - p)$. Let

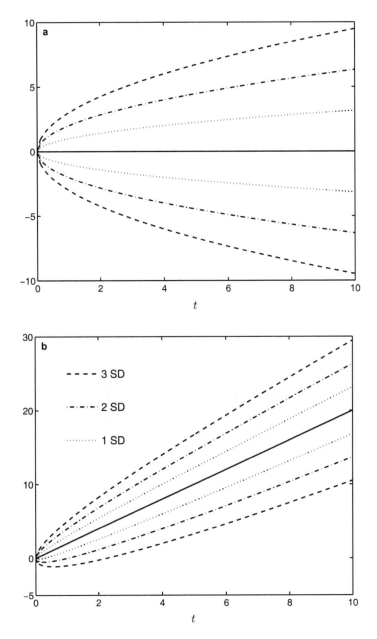

Figure 2.1. *Confidence bands for a Brownian motion with (a)* $\mu = 0$, $\sigma = 1$ *and (b)* $\mu = 2$, $\sigma = 1$.

$\Delta X = X(t + \Delta t) - X(t)$ denote the increment in X. Then

$$E[\Delta X] = ph - (1 - p)h$$
$$= (2p - 1)h,$$
$$\text{Var}[\Delta X] = E\left[(\Delta X)^2\right] - [E(\Delta X)]^2$$
$$= \left[1 - (2p - 1)^2\right]h^2.$$

Thus, to approximate the drift and variance of a Brownian motion with parameters (μ, σ^2), p and h must satisfy

$$\mu\Delta t = (2p - 1)h,$$
$$\sigma^2\Delta t = 4p(1 - p)h^2. \tag{2.2}$$

Eliminating h gives a quadratic in p,

$$p^2 - p + \frac{\sigma^2}{4(\sigma^2 + \mu^2\Delta t)} = 0.$$

Hence

$$p = \frac{1}{2}\left(1 + \sqrt{1 - \frac{\sigma^2}{\sigma^2 + \mu^2\Delta t}}\right)$$

$$= \frac{1}{2}\left(1 + \frac{\mu\sqrt{\Delta t}}{\sqrt{\sigma^2 + \mu^2\Delta t}}\right)$$

$$\approx \frac{1}{2}\left(1 + \frac{\mu}{\sigma}\sqrt{\Delta t}\right), \tag{2.3}$$

where the root is chosen so that $p \gtrless 1/2$ as $\mu \gtrless 0$, and the last line is a good approximation if Δt is small relative to σ^2/μ^2. For the step size h, use (2.2) to find that

$$h = \frac{\mu\Delta t}{2p - 1} = \sigma\sqrt{\Delta t}. \tag{2.4}$$

The idea is that since the drift and variance both have order Δt, if Δt is small relative to σ^2/μ^2, then $[E(\Delta X)]^2 = \mu^2(\Delta t)^2$ is negligible relative to $E\left[(\Delta X)^2\right] = \sigma^2\Delta t$. Hence $\text{Var}[\Delta X] \approx E\left[(\Delta X)^2\right]$ or $\sigma^2\Delta t \approx h^2$, as in (2.4).

In summary, to approximate a Brownian motion with parameters (μ, σ^2), choose Δt small relative to σ^2/μ^2, and choose h and p so that

$$(2p - 1)\, h = \mu \Delta t, \quad \text{and} \quad h^2 = \sigma^2 \Delta t,$$

as in (2.3) and (2.4). Notice that as the time increment Δt shrinks to zero, the step size h also shrinks to zero.

The following sequence of approximations, with decreasing time increment Δ_n, illustrates the idea behind Theorem 2.1 and also suggests methods for numerically approximating Brownian motions to any desired degree of accuracy. Fix a time interval $T > 0$, and define

$$\Delta_n \equiv T/n, \qquad h_n \equiv \sigma \sqrt{T/n}, \qquad p_n \equiv \frac{1}{2}\left(1 + \frac{\mu}{\sigma}\sqrt{T/n}\right),$$

$$\mathbf{X}_n \equiv \{-nh_n, \ldots, 0, \ldots, +nh_n\}$$
$$= \left\{-\sigma\sqrt{nT}, \ldots, 0, \ldots, +\sigma\sqrt{nT}\right\}, \quad n = 1, 2, \ldots.$$

For each n, let $\{\xi_i^n\}_{i=1}^n$ be a sequence of i.i.d. random variables taking values $\pm h_n$ with probabilities p_n and $(1 - p_n)$, and let

$$X_n = \xi_1^n + \xi_2^n + \cdots + \xi_n^n, \quad n = 1, 2, \ldots,$$

be their sum. Each of the random variables ξ_i^n has mean $\mu T/n$ and variance $\sigma^2 T/n$, so each of the random variables X_n has mean μT and variance $\sigma^2 T$. Moreover, each X_n takes values in the finite set $\mathbf{X}_n$ consisting of a grid of $2n + 1$ evenly spaced points centered around 0. The grid is on an interval of length $2\sigma\sqrt{nT}$, and the step size is $\sigma\sqrt{T/n}$. Thus, the number of grid points grows like n, with the interval length and the number of grid points on any subinterval both increasing like $\sqrt{n}$. Hence as $n \to \infty$ the number of points on any subinterval grows without bound, and the state space expands to cover all of $\mathbf{R}$. Moreover, by the central limit theorem the sequence $\{X_n\}$ converges in distribution to a normal random variable.

Exercise 2.2. Consider a (μ, σ^2) Brownian motion with initial state $x(0) = 0$. Fix $T > 0$ and $a > 0$. Use a sequence of discrete time approximations to calculate

$$\Pr\left\{\max_{0 \le t \le T} x(t) \ge a\right\}.$$

2.5. Stopping Times

A *stopping time* on a filtered probability space $(\Omega, \mathbb{F}, P)$ is a measurable function $T: \Omega \to [0, +\infty) \cup +\infty$ with the property that

$$\{\omega \in \Omega : T(\omega) \le t\} \in \mathfrak{F}_t, \quad \text{all } t \ge 0. \qquad (2.5)$$

The idea is that $T(\omega)$ is the (random) date when something happens, with $T(\omega) = +\infty$ interpreted as meaning it never happens. The measurability condition (2.5) states that it must be possible to tell at date t, given the available information $\mathfrak{F}_t$, whether the event has already happened. Notice that the filtration $\mathbb{F}$ is crucial for deciding whether a function T is a stopping time. If T takes values in $\mathbf{R}_+$ with probability one, then T is a random variable. Here $T < +\infty$ is used as a shorthand notation for $P\{T < +\infty\} = 1$.
The following are some standard examples of stopping times:

i. Any fixed date $T = \hat{T}$ is a stopping time.
ii. Suppose $\{X(t)\}$ is a stochastic process on $(\Omega, \mathbb{F}, P)$, and let A be any Borel set. Then the first date t for which $X(t) \in A$ is a stopping time. The kth date for which $X(t) \in A$ is also a stopping time, for any $k = 2, 3, 4, \ldots$.
iii. If S and T are stopping times, then $S + T$, $S \wedge T$, and $S \vee T$ are also stopping times, where $a \wedge b \equiv \min\{a, b\}$, and $a \vee b \equiv \max\{a, b\}$.

Exercise 2.3. Let $\{X(t)\}$ be a stochastic process on $(\Omega, \mathbb{F}, P)$. Explain briefly why each of the following is or is not a stopping time:

(a) $T - S$, where S and T are stopping times with $S \le T$.
(b) Let $\{a_j\}_{j=1}^n$ be a sequence of real numbers, and consider the first time X reaches a_n, after first reaching a_{n-1}, after first reaching $a_{n-2}, \ldots$, after first reaching a_1.
(c) Let $\{A_j\}_{j=1}^n$ be a sequence of measurable sets, and consider the first time X reaches A_n, after first reaching A_{n-1}, after first reaching $A_{n-2}, \ldots$, after first reaching A_1.
(d) $T - \Delta$, where T is any one of the stopping times above and $\Delta > 0$ is a constant.

2.6. Strong Markov Property

Let $\{X(t, \omega)\}$ be a stationary stochastic process on the filtered space $(\Omega, \mathbb{F}, P)$. Then X has the *strong Markov property* if, for any sequence of stopping times $T_0 < T_1 < \ldots < T_n$, any $s > 0$, any $x_0, x_1, \ldots, x_n$, and any measurable set A,

$$\Pr\{X(T_n + s) \subset A \mid X(T_0) = x_0, \ X(T_1) = x_1, \ldots, X(T_n) = x_n\}$$

$$= \Pr\{X(T_n + s) \subset A \mid X(T_n) = x_n\}. \tag{2.6}$$

That is, given the state at stopping time T_n, outcomes at earlier stopping times are not useful for predicting outcomes at later dates. Stated a little differently, (2.6) states that the evolution of the system after any stopping time T_n, given $X(T_n)$, is conditionally independent of the earlier outcomes. If the process is not stationary the condition is more complex but similar in essence.

The next theorem states that if a Brownian motion X is reinitialized at a stopping time T, the resulting process is also a Brownian motion, with the same mean and variance as the original. That is, Brownian motions have the strong Markov property.

Theorem 2.2. Let X be a (μ, σ^2) Brownian motion and $T < \infty$ a stopping time on the filtered space $(\Omega, \mathbb{F}, P)$, and let

$$X^*(t, \omega) = X(T + t, \omega) - X(T, \omega), \quad \text{all } t \geq 0, \quad \text{all } \omega \in \Omega.$$

Then X^* is a (μ, σ^2) Brownian motion with initial value zero, and for any $t > 0$, the random variables $X^*(t)$ and T are independent.

See Billingsley (1995, Theorem 37.5) for a proof. The idea is that since X has continuous sample paths and increments that are i.i.d. (and normally distributed), X^* also has these properties. Hence $\{X^*(t)\}$ satisfies the hypotheses of Theorem 2.1.

Since a constant value $T(\omega) = \hat{T}$ is a valid stopping time, the theorem implies that a Brownian motion that is reinitialized at a fixed date is itself a Brownian motion, with the same drift and variance.

Notice, however, that the filtration $\mathbb{F}$ is not appropriate for the process X^*. One that is can be constructed in the usual way. For each $t \geq 0$, let $\mathfrak{F}_t^*$ be the smallest σ-algebra for which the random variables $X^*(s, \omega)$, $0 \leq s \leq t$ are measurable; let $\mathfrak{F}^* = \mathfrak{F}_\infty^*$ be the smallest σ-algebra containing all of the $\mathfrak{F}_t^*$s; and define the filtration $\mathbb{F}^* = \{\mathfrak{F}_t^*, \ t \geq 0\}$. Then $(\Omega, \mathbb{F}^*, P)$ is a filtered space and, by construction, X^* is adapted to $\mathbb{F}^*$.

2.7. Diffusions

The term *diffusion* will be used here to refer to a continuous-time stochastic process that (i) has continuous sample paths and (ii) has the strong Markov property. The state space for a diffusion can be all of **R** or any open, closed, or half-open interval. That is, the state space is an interval of the form (ℓ, r), $[\ell, r)$, $(\ell, r]$, $[\ell, r]$, where $\ell = -\infty$ or $r = +\infty$ are allowed at open endpoints. Clearly, any Brownian motion is a diffusion, and its state space is all of **R**.

A diffusion is *regular* if, starting from any point in the interior of the state space, any other interior point is, with positive probability, reached in finite time. That is, if T_y denotes the first time the process reaches y, then

$$\Pr\left\{ T_y < \infty \mid X(0) = x \right\} > 0, \quad \text{all } \ell < x, y < r.$$

This assumption rules out the possibility of noncommunicating subsets. All of the diffusions considered in this book are regular.

Continuity implies that the probability of a large change in the state can be made arbitrarily small by making the time interval sufficiently short. Formally, let $\Delta > 0$ denote a time increment, and let

$$h(t, \Delta) \equiv X(t + \Delta) - X(t)$$

be the change in the level of the process during an interval of length Δ after date t. A diffusion has the property that for any $\varepsilon > 0$,

$$\lim_{\Delta \downarrow 0} \Pr\left\{ |h(t, \Delta)| > \varepsilon \mid X(t) = x \right\} = 0, \quad \text{all } x, \text{ all } t.$$

That is, the probability of a change of fixed size $\varepsilon > 0$ goes to zero as the time interval Δ gets arbitrarily short.

Any diffusion is characterized by its *infinitesimal parameters* $\mu(t, x)$ and $\sigma^2(t, x)$, defined by

$$\mu(t, x) \equiv \lim_{\Delta \downarrow 0} \frac{1}{\Delta} \mathrm{E}\left[h(t, \Delta) \mid X(t) = x \right],$$

$$\sigma^2(t, x) \equiv \lim_{\Delta \downarrow 0} \frac{1}{\Delta} \mathrm{E}\left[[h(t, \Delta)]^2 \mid X(t) = x \right], \quad \text{all } x, t, \tag{2.7}$$

where $h(t, \Delta)$ is the increment between t and $t + \Delta$, defined above. The function μ is called the *drift* or *infinitesimal mean*, and σ^2 is called the *diffusion parameter* or *infinitesimal variance*. The functions μ and σ^2 in (2.7) are assumed to be continuous, and the latter to be strictly positive on the interior of the state space. In most of applications of interest here, μ and σ are time-invariant, so the argument t does not appear.

All higher moments are usually zero:

$$\lim_{\Delta \downarrow 0} \frac{1}{\Delta} \mathrm{E}\left[[h(t, \Delta)]^r \mid X(t) = x \right] = 0, \quad \text{all } x, t, \ r = 3, 4, \dots$$

Although this is not required, it holds for all the diffusions considered in this book.

Two particular diffusions are widely used in economics.

Example 1. In many contexts it is useful to employ a stochastic process that has relative increments $\Delta X/X$ that are i.i.d. A stochastic process $X(t)$ is a *geometric Brownian motion* if

$$dX = \mu X dt + \sigma X dW,$$

so (with an obvious abuse of notation) $\mu(t, x) = \mu x$ and $\sigma^2(t, x) = \sigma^2 x$. The state space for a geometric Brownian motion is $\mathbf{R}_+$.

Example 2. In other contexts it is useful to employ a stochastic process that is *mean reverting*. A process with this property is the *Ornstein-Uhlenbeck* process, which has infinitesimal parameters $\mu(x) = -\alpha x$, where $\alpha > 0$, and $\sigma^2 > 0$. The state space for this process is all of $\mathbf{R}$, but the process has a central tendency toward zero: the drift is negative if the state exceeds zero and is positive if the state is less than zero, with the magnitude of the drift increasing with the distance from zero.

In contrast to a Brownian motion or geometric Brownian motion, the Ornstein-Uhlenbeck process has a stationary distribution. In particular, the stationary distribution is normal with mean zero and variance $\gamma = \sigma^2/2\alpha$. Hence it has the stationary density $\psi(x) = ce^{-\gamma x^2}$, where $c > 0$ is a constant that depends on the parameters (α, σ^2).

2.8. Discrete Approximation of an Ornstein-Uhlenbeck Process

An Ornstein-Uhlenbeck process can be approximated with a sequence of discrete-time, discrete-state processes in the same way that a Brownian motion can be. Fix the parameters (α, σ^2) and a time interval $T > 0$. For each $n = 1, 2, \ldots$, define the time increment Δ_n as before:

$$\Delta_n \equiv T/n.$$

Suppose, also as before, that during each time increment the process moves up or down one step. Notice that for an Ornstein-Uhlenbeck process, both the step size h_n and transition probabilities, p_n and $1 - p_n$, could, in principle depend on the current state x. It would be extremely awkward if the step size varied with x, however, since a fixed grid could no longer be used: one step up from x followed by one step down from $x + h_n(x)$ would bring the process to $x + h_n(x) - h_n[x + h_n(x)] \neq x$. Fortunately, this does not happen.

As before, the condition for the variance pins down the step size:

$$h_n = \sigma\sqrt{\Delta_n}, \quad \text{all } n.$$

Hence the step size is independent of x, and the state space

$$\mathbf{X}_n \equiv \{\ldots, -2h_n, -h_n, 0, +h_n, +2h_n, \ldots\}, \quad n = 1, 2, \ldots$$

can be used. Let

$$p_n(x) = \tfrac{1}{2} - \varepsilon_n(x), \quad x \in \mathbf{X}_n,$$

be the probability of an upward step. The transition probabilities must satisfy the drift condition,

$$
\begin{aligned}
-\alpha x \Delta_n &= p_n(x)h_n - [1 - p_n(x)]h_n \\
&= \left[\tfrac{1}{2} - \varepsilon_n(x)\right]h_n - \left[\tfrac{1}{2} + \varepsilon_n(x)\right]h_n \\
&= -2\varepsilon_n(x)h_n,
\end{aligned}
$$

so

$$
\begin{aligned}
\varepsilon_n(x) &= \frac{\alpha x}{2}\frac{\Delta_n}{h_n} \\
&= \frac{\alpha x}{2\sigma}\sqrt{\Delta_n}, \quad \text{all } x \in \mathbf{X}_n, \text{ all } n.
\end{aligned}
$$

It is straightforward to verify that all higher moments converge to zero as $n \to \infty$.

Notes

A good introduction to basic probability theory is Ross (1989). Feller (1968) is a classic treatment at a basic level, and Feller (1971) continues to more advanced material. Both contain many examples and helpful discussions. At an advanced level Breiman (1968), Chung (1974), and Billingsley (1995) are also excellent. Breiman includes a nice introduction to stochastic processes in general and to Brownian motion and Ornstein-Uhlenbeck processes in particular.

For an introduction to the basics of stochastic processes see Cinlar (1975) or Ross (1983). Karlin and Taylor (1975, 1981) provide an outstanding treatment at a more advanced level, with many applications and examples and an emphasis on problem solving. See Chapter 7 in the first volume for a discussion of many of the properties of Brownian motion. See chapters 14 and 15 in the second volume for a more detailed treatment of the strong Markov property and an excellent discussion of diffusions, including many examples and useful results.

If the stopping times in the definition of the strong Markov property are replaced with fixed dates, then X has the Markov property. For discrete-time processes the two concepts are equivalent, but for continuous-time processes they differ. See Chung (1974, Section 9.2) for a further discussion. Note that the definition here is for stationary processes only.

3

Stochastic Integrals
and Ito's Lemma

CONSIDER THE PRESENT discounted value of a stream of returns over an infinite horizon,

$$v(x_0) \equiv \int_0^\infty e^{-\rho t} \pi(x(t)) dt \qquad (3.1)$$

with $\dot{x}(t) = g(x(t)), \quad t \geq 0,$

$$x(0) = x_0,$$

where $\rho > 0$ is a discount rate, $\pi(x)$ is a return function, $x(t)$ is a state variable that evolves according to the law of motion $g(x)$, and x_0 is the initial state. For example, $v(x_0)$ might be the value of a firm, where ρ is the interest rate, $x(t)$ describes the size of the market for the firm's product, $\pi(x)$ is the profit flow as a function of market size, and $g(x)$ describes the evolution of market size. Since the horizon is infinite, ρ is constant, and π and g are stationary (time invariant), the function $v(x_0)$ representing the discounted value of the profit flow depends only on the initial state.

A standard and fairly simple argument, to be developed below, establishes that v satisfies the continuous-time Bellman equation

$$\rho v(x) = \pi(x) + v'(x) g(x). \qquad (3.2)$$

If v is the value of an asset, the interpretation of (3.2) is straightforward: the return on the asset, the term on the left, is the sum of the dividend and the capital gain, the terms on the right. A key step in deriving (3.2) from (3.1) involves using a first-order Taylor series approximation to the change in the value over a short interval of time Δt,

$$\Delta v \equiv v(x(t + \Delta t)) - v(x(t))$$
$$\approx v'(x(t)) \left[x(t + \Delta t) - x(t) \right]$$
$$\approx v'(x(t))g(x(t))\Delta t.$$

In many applications where value functions like v arise, it is natural to think of the exogenous state variable $x(t)$ as stochastic. Thus, instead of assuming that $x(t)$ is governed by a deterministic differential equation, as in (3.1), it is more accurately modeled as including a component that is a Brownian motion, a geometric Brownian motion, or some other diffusion. Then to develop the analog of (3.2), the analog of a Taylor series approximation is needed for the case where the state variable is a diffusion. Ito's lemma is the key ingredient for this task.

Ito's lemma and related results are developed in this chapter. In Section 3.1 the stochastic analog of (3.2) is derived using a heuristic approach. A brief discussion of stochastic integrals is provided in Section 3.2, and in Section 3.3 Ito's lemma is formally stated and used to obtain the stochastic analog of (3.2) more rigorously. In Section 3.4 Ito's lemma is used to derive some results about geometric Brownian motion. Occupancy measure and local time are defined in Section 3.5 and used in Section 3.6 to develop Tanaka's formula, an extension of Ito's lemma that applies to functions with kinks. Sections 3.7 and 3.8 develop the Kolmogorov backward and forward equations.

3.1. The Hamilton-Jacobi-Bellman Equation

Fix a filtered probability space $(\Omega, \mathbb{F}, P)$, and let $X(t, \omega)$ be a Brownian motion with initial value $X(0) = x_0$ and parameters (μ, σ^2). Then X can be written as

$$X(t) = X(0) + \mu t + \sigma W(t), \quad \text{all } t, \text{ all } \omega, \tag{3.3}$$

where W is a Wiener process, and where for notational simplicity the ω is suppressed. A shorthand notation for (3.3) is the differential form

$$dX(t) = \mu dt + \sigma dW(t), \quad \text{all } t, \text{ all } \omega. \tag{3.4}$$

Note that given the initial condition $X(0)$, (3.4) is simply an alternative way of writing (3.3).

More generally, suppose X is a diffusion with initial value $X(0) = x_0$ and infinitesimal parameters $(\mu(t, x), \sigma(t, x))$. Then the differential form, the analog of (3.4), is

$$dX(t) = \mu(t, X(t))dt + \sigma(t, X(t))dW(t), \quad \text{all } t, \text{ all } \omega. \qquad (3.5)$$

There is also an analog of (3.3), which will be developed later.

Let $F(t, x)$ be a function that is differentiable at least once in t and twice in x. The "total differential" of $F(t, X(t, \omega))$, call it dF, can be approximated with a Taylor series expansion. Use $F_t \equiv \partial F/\partial t$, $F_x \equiv \partial F/\partial x$, and so on, to denote the derivatives of F and substitute from (3.5) to find that

$$dF = F_t \, dt + F_x \, dX + \tfrac{1}{2} F_{xx} \, (dX)^2 + \cdots$$

$$= F_t \, dt + F_x \left[\mu \, dt + \sigma \, dW \right]$$

$$+ \tfrac{1}{2} F_{xx} \left[\mu^2 \, (dt)^2 + 2\mu\sigma \, dt \, dW + \sigma^2 \, (dW)^2 \right] + \cdots,$$

where the dots indicate higher order terms, and μ and σ are evaluated at $(t, X(t))$. Then rearrange terms and drop those of order higher than dt or $(dW)^2$ to obtain

$$dF = F_t dt + \mu F_x dt + \sigma F_x \, dW + \tfrac{1}{2}\sigma^2 F_{xx} \, (dW)^2. \qquad (3.6)$$

Notice that dF is the sum of four components, two in dt, one in dW, and one in $(dW)^2$.

Since $\mathrm{E}[dW] = 0$ and $\mathrm{E}\left[(dW)^2\right] = dt$, taking expectations in (3.6) gives

$$\mathrm{E}\,[dF] = \left[F_t + \mu F_x + \tfrac{1}{2}\sigma^2 F_{xx} \right] dt,$$

$$\mathrm{Var}\,[dF] = \mathrm{E}\,[\,dF - \mathrm{E}\,[dF]\,]^2$$

$$= \sigma^2 F_x^2 dt.$$

A case of particular interest is one in which the drift and variance $\mu(x)$ and $\sigma(x)$ are stationary and F is the discounted value of a stationary function. That is, $F(t, x) = e^{-rt} f(x)$, where $r \geq 0$ is the discount rate. For this case

$$\mathrm{E}\left[d\left(e^{-rt} f\right)\right] = \left[-rf + \mu f' + \tfrac{1}{2}\sigma^2 f'' \right] e^{-rt} dt, \qquad (3.7)$$

where μ, σ^2, f, f', and f'' are evaluated at $X(t)$. For $r = 0$ this equation is simply

$$\mathrm{E}\,[df] = \left[\mu f' + \tfrac{1}{2}\sigma^2 f'' \right] dt. \qquad (3.8)$$

One application of (3.7) is in deriving the analog of the Bellman equation (3.2). Consider an infinite stream of returns as in (3.1), but where X is a diffusion with infinitesimal parameters $\mu(x)$ and $\sigma(x)$. Let π and ρ be as before, with π bounded and continuous and $\rho > 0$. Define $v(x_0)$ to be the expected discounted value of the stream of returns given the initial state $X(0) = x_0$,

$$v(x_0) \equiv \mathrm{E}\left[\int_0^\infty e^{-\rho t} \pi(X(t,\omega)) dt \mid X(0) = x_0\right], \quad \text{all } x_0. \quad (3.9)$$

The integral on the right, an integral over time for a fixed sample path, is an ordinary Riemann integral. To see this note that since $X(\cdot,\omega)$ is the sample path of a diffusion, it is a continuous function. Since by assumption π is continuous, the integral over the horizon $[0, T]$ exists for any finite T. Moreover, since π is bounded and $\rho > 0$, the limit exists as $T \to \infty$, so the integral over the infinite horizon is also well defined. The integral is then a bounded random variable defined on Ω, so the expected value is well defined.

For any small interval of time Δt, (3.9) has the Bellman-type property

$$v(x_0) \approx \pi(x_0)\Delta t + \frac{1}{1+\rho\Delta t} \mathrm{E}\left[v(X(0+\Delta t)) \mid X(0) = x_0\right].$$

Multiply this equation by $(1+\rho\Delta t)$ and subtract $v(x_0)$ from each side to get

$$\rho v(x_0)\Delta t \approx \pi(x_0)\,(1+\rho\Delta t)\,\Delta t + \mathrm{E}\left[\Delta v \mid X(0) = x_0\right],$$

where

$$\Delta v \equiv v(X(\Delta t, \omega)) - v(x_0) \quad (3.10)$$

is the change in the value function over the interval Δt. Then divide by Δt and let $\Delta t \to 0$ to find that

$$\rho v(x_0) = \lim_{\Delta t \to 0}\left\{\pi(x_0)\,(1+\rho\Delta t) + \frac{1}{\Delta t}\mathrm{E}\left[\Delta v \mid X(0) = x_0\right]\right\}$$

$$= \pi(x_0) + \frac{1}{dt}\mathrm{E}\left[dv \mid X(0) = x_0\right].$$

The function v does not depend directly on time, so using (3.8) to evaluate $\mathrm{E}[dv]$ and dropping the subscript on the initial condition produces the *Hamilton-Jacobi-Bellman equation*

$$\rho v(x) = \pi(x) + \mu(x)v'(x) + \tfrac{1}{2}\sigma^2(x)v''(x), \quad \text{all } x. \quad (3.11)$$

This equation is the stochastic counterpart of the Bellman equation (3.2), and with $\mu(x) = g(x)$ and $\sigma^2(x) = 0$ the two are identical.

In the next section the differentials dX and dF in (3.5) and (3.6) are described in more detail. As with dX in (3.4), each is a shorthand notation for a more precise expression.

3.2. Stochastic Integrals

In this section the definition of the stochastic integral is first examined briefly. Doing so is useful because it shows why stochastic integrals have a certain fundamental property. Theorems 3.1 and 3.2 then characterize a class of integrable functions and state several properties of stochastic integrals.

All integrals are defined by first considering functions for which the integral of interest is an easily calculated sum and then extending the definition to a broader class of functions. For example, the Riemann integral is first defined for step functions. It is then extended to a broader class by approximating any other function of interest with a sequence of step functions, where the sequence is chosen so that the approximations become arbitrarily good. The integral of each function in the sequence is easily computed, and the integral of the function of interest is defined as the limit of the integrals of the approximating sequence. Similarly, integrals on measure spaces are defined first for simple functions, and the definition is then extended by approximating other measurable functions with sequences of simple functions.

The Ito integral is defined in a similar way. As with other integrals, the main issues are to show that the integral defined in this way exists and is unique: that there exists at least one approximating sequence, and that if there are many such sequences all have a common limit. Stated a little differently, the key step in defining an integral is to determine for which functions the approximation process leads to a uniquely defined value, that is, to determine what class of functions is integrable.

Fix a filtered probability space $(\Omega, \mathbb{F}, P)$, let W be a Wiener process on this space, and let Y be a stochastic process adapted to it. That is, $Y : [0, \infty) \times \Omega \to \mathbf{R}$ is jointly measurable in (t, ω). The goal is to define a *stochastic integral* of Y with respect to W:

$$I_Y(t, \omega) = \int_0^t Y(s, \omega) \, dW(s, \omega), \quad \text{all } t > 0, \text{ all } \omega. \tag{3.12}$$

Notice that $I_Y(t, \omega)$ is an integral of Y along a particular sample path ω up to date t. Since it is a function of (t, ω), assuming the required joint measurability condition holds, I_Y is itself a stochastic process adapted to $(\Omega, \mathbb{F}, P)$.

Since Y is jointly measurable, if it is also suitably bounded there is no problem integrating it with respect to t and then taking the expected value. To this end assume that

$$\mathrm{E}\left[\int_0^t Y^2(s,\omega)\,ds\right] < \infty, \quad \text{all } t > 0. \tag{3.13}$$

Let H^2 be the set of all stochastic processes Y satisfying (3.13). Any Brownian motion satisfies (3.13).

The stochastic integral in (3.12) is first defined in terms of sums for simple (step-type) functions and then extended to a broader class through approximating sequences. A stochastic process Y is called *simple* if there exists a countable sequence $\{t_k\}$ with $0 = t_0 < t_1 < \ldots < t_k \to \infty$, such that

$$Y(s,\omega) = Y(t_{k-1},\omega), \quad \text{all } s \in [t_{k-1}, t_k), \text{ all } \omega.$$

Note that the t_ks do not vary with ω. Let $S^2 \subset H^2$ be the set of all simple stochastic processes that satisfy (3.13).

It is easy to integrate functions in S^2 with respect to W over any finite time interval. Choose $Y \in S^2$, with steps at $\{t_k\}_{k=0}^\infty$. Fix $t > 0$ and $\omega \in \Omega$, and choose $n \geq 0$ such that $t_n < t \leq t_{n+1}$. Define the integral

$$\int_0^t Y(s,\omega)\,dW(s,\omega) \equiv \sum_{k=0}^{n-1} Y(t_k,\omega)\left[W(t_{k+1},\omega) - W(t_k,\omega)\right] \tag{3.14}$$

$$+ Y(t_n,\omega)\left[W(t,\omega) - W(t_n,\omega)\right].$$

The terms on the right side of (3.14) have a very important feature: the value of the state Y at date t_k is multiplied by the increment to W that comes *after* that date, the increment between t_k and t_{k+1}.

As noted above, the extension to a broader class of functions involves the use of approximating sequences, and the argument has two parts. First, it must be shown that for any function in the broader class there exists at least one sequence in S^2 that approximates it. Second, it must be shown that if there are many approximating sequences, all converge to a common value. The integral is then defined to be that common value. Both of these arguments are rather complicated, and they are not especially useful in the applications here. Therefore, several main results are simply stated.

The first part of Theorem 3.1 identifies a class of integrable functions, those in H^2. As noted above, the integral $I_Y(t,\omega)$ is a stochastic process. The second part of the theorem concerns the expected values of this process.

Theorem 3.1. (i) If $Y \in H^2$, then Y is integrable; that is, there exists a stochastic process $I_Y(t,\omega)$ satisfying (3.12).

(ii) If Y is integrable, then the expected value of $I_Y(t, \omega)$ is zero at all dates,

$$E\left[\int_0^t Y(s, \omega)dW(s, \omega)\right] = 0, \quad \text{all } t \geq 0.$$

Part (ii) of Theorem 3.1 asserts a remarkable property: the expected value of a stochastic integral is identically zero. Although this claim looks astonishing at first sight, the idea behind it is really very simple. Consider again the definition in (3.14) of the stochastic integral of a simple function. Each term in (3.14) involves $Y(t_k)$ multiplied by the increment to $W(t)$ over the *subsequent* interval, from t_k to t_{k+1}. The expected value of this increment at date t_k is zero, and the expected value of the integral is just the sum of these terms. Hence the zero expectation property holds for any simple function. But the stochastic integral of any other function is simply the limit of a sequence of integrals of simple functions, so the zero expectation property holds for all integrable functions.

The next result establishes two additional properties of stochastic integrals.

Theorem 3.2. If $X, Y \in H^2$, and $a, b \in \mathbf{R}$, then

    i. the stochastic integral of the weighted sum $(aX + bY)$ is the weighted sum of the stochastic integrals of X and Y:

$$\int_0^t (aX + bY)\, dW$$

$$= a \int_0^t X\, dW + b \int_0^t Y\, dW, \quad \text{all } \omega, \text{ all } t \geq 0; \text{ and}$$

    ii. the expected value of the product of the stochastic integrals of X and Y is the expected value of the (Riemann) integral of XY:

$$E\left[\int_0^t X\, dW \int_0^t Y\, dW\right] = E\left[\int_0^t X Y\, ds\right], \quad \text{all } t \geq 0.$$

The first part of Theorem 3.2 states that, like other types of integration, stochastic integration is a linear operator. The second part says that the expected value of the product of two stochastic integrals is equal to the expected value of the integral of their product. To see why this is so, consider approximating each of the integrals on the left with a finite sum. Since each of the increments dW over various subintervals has mean zero and all are mutually independent, all of the terms in the product have expected value zero except those that involve common time increments.

For these, $E\left[(dW)^2\right] = ds$, so the integral becomes an ordinary Riemann integral. Also note that since the integrals $\int_0^t X\, dW$ and $\int_0^t Y\, dW$ are random variables with means of zero, the expression in part (ii) of Theorem 3.2 is simply their covariance.

3.3. Ito's Lemma

Let W be a Wiener process on the filtered space $(\Omega, \mathbb{F}, P)$, let $\mu(t, x)$ and $\sigma(t, x) > 0$ be continuous functions, and let $X(0, \omega) = x_0(\omega)$ be a measurable function. The stochastic process X satisfying

$$X(t, \omega) = X(0, \omega) + \int_0^t \mu(s, X(s, \omega)) ds$$

$$+ \int_0^t \sigma(s, X(s, \omega))\, dW(s, \omega), \quad \text{all } t, \omega, \tag{3.15}$$

is a diffusion. Notice that the first integral in (3.15) is a Riemann integral, while the second is a stochastic integral of the type defined in the previous section. This equation is the integral form of the differential in (3.5), and a Brownian motion is simply the special case in which μ and σ are constant.

The next result, Ito's lemma, is the basis for calculating values of a function $F(t, x)$ that has a diffusion as its second argument.

Theorem 3.3 (Ito's lemma). Let $F: \mathbf{R}_+ \times \mathbf{R} \to \mathbf{R}$ be once continuously differentiable in its first argument and twice continuously differentiable in its second, and let X be the diffusion in (3.15). Then

$$F(t, X(t, \omega)) = F(0, X(0, \omega)) + \int_0^t F_t(s, X)\, ds$$

$$+ \int_0^t F_x(s, X)\mu(s, X)\, ds$$

$$+ \int_0^t F_x(s, X)\sigma(s, X)\, dW(s, \omega) \tag{3.16}$$

$$+ \tfrac{1}{2} \int_0^t F_{xx}(s, X)\sigma^2(s, X)\, ds, \quad \text{all } t, \omega,$$

where the arguments of $X(s, \omega)$ have been suppressed.

The right side of (3.16) contains four integrals. The third is a stochastic integral and the others are Riemann integrals. These four terms are the counterparts of the four terms in (3.6).

If μ and σ are stationary and $F(t, x) = e^{-rt}f(x)$, where $r \geq 0$ is a constant discount rate, then (3.16) takes the form

$$e^{-rt}f(X(t)) = f(X(0)) - r \int_0^t e^{-rs}f(X)\,ds$$

$$+ \int_0^t e^{-rs}f'(X)\mu(X)\,ds + \int_0^t e^{-rs}f'(X)\sigma(X)\,dW \qquad (3.17)$$

$$+ \frac{1}{2}\int_0^t e^{-rs}f''(X)\sigma^2(X)\,ds.$$

The expected value of the differential form of this equation is in (3.7).

These results can be used to derive the Hamilton-Jacobi-Bellman equation (3.11) more rigorously. Consider the term Δv in (3.10). Use (3.17) with $r = 0$, $X(0) = x_0$, and constant functions for μ and σ to get

$$\Delta v \equiv v(X(\Delta t)) - v(x_0)$$

$$= \mu \int_0^{\Delta t} v'(X(s))\,ds + \sigma \int_0^{\Delta t} v'(X(s))\,dW$$

$$+ \frac{1}{2}\sigma^2 \int_0^{\Delta t} v''(X(s))\,ds.$$

Then take the expected value, use the zero expectation property, and divide by Δt to obtain

$$\frac{1}{\Delta t}E\left[\Delta v\right] = \frac{1}{\Delta t}\left[\mu \int_0^{\Delta t} E\left[v'(X(s))\right]\,ds + \frac{1}{2}\sigma^2 \int_0^{\Delta t} E\left[v''(X(s))\right]\,ds\right].$$

Finally, take the limit to get

$$\lim_{\Delta t \to 0} \frac{1}{\Delta t}E\left[\Delta v\right] = \mu v'(x_0) + \frac{1}{2}\sigma^2 v''(x_0),$$

which agrees with the earlier result.

The next section shows how Ito's lemma can be used to characterize the moments of a geometric Brownian motion.

3.4. Geometric Brownian Motion

Recall from Chapter 1 that a *geometric Brownian motion* is a diffusion $X(t)$ with infinitesimal parameters $\mu(x) = \mu x$ and $\sigma(x) = \sigma x$. Thus, for a geometric Brownian motion

$$dX = \mu X dt + \sigma X dW, \tag{3.18}$$

so the relative increments dX/X are i.i.d. with fixed mean and variance. Several facts about this family can be proved using Ito's lemma.

Let X be as in (3.18), with $X(0) \equiv 1$, and consider the stochastic process $Y = \ln(X)$. Then (3.16) with $r = 0$ implies that

$$Y(t, \omega) = \ln(X(t, \omega))$$

$$= \ln(X(0)) + \int_0^t \left(\frac{1}{X} \mu X - \frac{1}{2} \frac{1}{X^2} \sigma^2 X^2 \right) ds + \int_0^t \frac{1}{X} \sigma X \, dW$$

$$= 0 + \int_0^t \left(\mu - \tfrac{1}{2}\sigma^2 \right) ds + \int_0^t \sigma \, dW$$

$$= \left(\mu - \tfrac{1}{2}\sigma^2 \right) t + \sigma W(t), \quad \text{all } t, \omega.$$

Thus, $Y = \ln(X)$ is an ordinary Brownian motion with drift and variance

$$\hat{\mu} = \mu - \tfrac{1}{2}\sigma^2, \quad \text{and} \quad \hat{\sigma}^2 = \sigma^2.$$

To understand the downward adjustment in the drift, notice that since the logarithm is a concave function, Jensen's inequality implies that $E[\ln(X(t))] < \ln(E[X(t)])$. Moreover, since the variance of $X(t)$ increases linearly with t, the difference between the two increases over time. Hence it is the drift that must be adjusted.

Exercise 3.1. (a) Let $Y(t)$ be a (μ, σ^2) Brownian motion. Use Ito's lemma to show that for any $\rho \neq 0$, $X(t) = \exp\{\rho Y(t)\}$ is a geometric Brownian motion with parameters $\left(\rho\mu + \tfrac{1}{2}(\rho\sigma)^2, \ (\rho\sigma)^2 \right)$.

(b) Let $X(t)$ be a geometric Brownian motion with parameters (m, s^2). Show that for any $\lambda \neq 0$, $p(t) = X^\lambda(t)$ is a geometric Brownian motion with parameters $\left(\lambda m + \tfrac{1}{2} s^2 \lambda(\lambda - 1), \ \lambda^2 s^2 \right)$.

The mean, variance, and higher moments of a geometric Brownian motion can be computed by using the fact that the expected values $E[X^k(t)]$, $k = 1, 2, \ldots$ are deterministic functions of time that satisfy simple ordinary differential equations.

Fix the initial value $X(0) = x_0$ and assume $|\mu|, \sigma^2 < \infty$. Then $E[X^2(t)]$ is bounded, for all t, so stochastic integrals involving X are well defined.

Integrate (3.18) to get

$$X(t) = x_0 + \mu \int_0^t X(s)ds + \sigma \int_0^t X(s)dW, \quad \text{all } t.$$

Then take the expected value and use the zero expectation property in part (ii) of Theorem 3.1 to find that

$$E\,[X(t)] = x_0 + \mu \int_0^t E\,[X(s)]\,ds, \quad \text{all } t. \tag{3.19}$$

Define $h(t) \equiv E\,[X(t)]$, and write (3.19) as

$$h(t) = x_0 + \mu \int_0^t h(s)ds, \quad \text{all } t.$$

Then h satisfies the differential equation

$$h'(t) = \mu h(t), \quad \text{all } t,$$

with the boundary condition $h(0) = x_0$. Hence

$$E\,[X(t)] \equiv h(t) = x_0 e^{\mu t}, \quad \text{all } t.$$

The argument also works for higher moments, with Ito's lemma providing a key step. For example, consider the second moment. Since $E[X^4(t)]$ is bounded for all t, stochastic integrals involving X^2 are well defined. Applying Ito's lemma to the function $f(x) = x^2$, one finds that (3.17) implies

$$X^2(t) = x_0^2 + \left(2\mu + \sigma^2\right) \int_0^t X^2(s)ds + 2\sigma \int_0^t X^2 dW, \quad \text{all } t, \omega.$$

Taking the expected value and using the zero expectation property then gives

$$E\left[X^2(t)\right] = x_0^2 + \left(2\mu + \sigma^2\right) \int_0^t E\left[X^2(s)\right] ds.$$

Define $h_2(t) \equiv E\left[X^2(t)\right]$. Then

$$h_2(t) = x_0^2 + \left(2\mu + \sigma^2\right) \int_0^t h_2(s)ds,$$

so h_2 satisfies the ordinary differential equation

$$h_2'(t) = \left(2\mu + \sigma^2\right) h_2(t), \quad \text{all } t,$$

with initial condition $h_2(0) = x_0^2$. Hence

$$E\left[X^2(t)\right] = h_2(t) = x_0^2 e^{\left(2\mu + \sigma^2\right)t}, \quad \text{all } t.$$

The variance of $X(t)$ can be computed by combining the formulas above,

$$\text{Var}\,[X(t)] = E\left[X^2(t)\right] - E\,[X(t)]^2$$

$$= x_0^2 e^{2\mu t}\left(e^{\sigma^2 t} - 1\right), \quad \text{all } t.$$

Note that if the drift is negative and sufficiently large relative to the variance, so $2\mu + \sigma^2 < 0$, then $E[X^2(t)]$ decreases over time. In this case $\lim_{t \to \infty} E[X^2(t)] = 0$ and $\lim_{t \to \infty} \text{Var}[X(t)] = 0$. For large t, the (non-negative) value $X(t)$ is, with high probability, very close to zero.

Higher moments of $X(t)$ can be computed in the same way.

Exercise 3.2. Calculate the skewness measure $E[X(t) - E\,[X(t)]]^3$.

3.5. Occupancy Measure and Local Time

Let $X(s)$ be a Brownian motion on the filtered space $(\Omega, \mathbb{F}, P)$. The *occupancy measure* of the process X is the function $m: \mathfrak{B} \times [0, \infty) \times \Omega \to \mathbf{R}_+$ defined by

$$m(A, t, \omega) = \int_0^t 1_A(X(s, \omega))ds, \quad \text{all } A \in \mathfrak{B}, \ t \geq 0, \ \omega \in \Omega, \quad (3.20)$$

where 1_A is the indicator function for the set A, and $\mathfrak{B}$ denotes the Borel sets. The value $m(A, t, \omega)$ is the total time the sample path $X(\cdot, \omega)$ has spent in the set A up to date t. Thus,

  i. for any fixed (t, ω), the mapping $m(\cdot, t, \omega): \mathfrak{B} \to [0, 1]$ is a measure (and hence the name) with total mass $m(\mathbf{R}, t, \omega) = t$;
  ii. for any fixed (A, t), the function $m(A, t, \cdot): \Omega \to \mathbf{R}_+$ is a random variable; and
  iii. for any fixed (A, ω), the function $m(A, \cdot, \omega): \mathbf{R}_+ \to \mathbf{R}$ is continuous and nondecreasing, and it is strictly increasing only when $X(t, \omega) \in A$.

The following result states that the function m defined above is absolutely continuous with respect to Lebesgue measure and has a continuous density. That is, it can be written as the integral of a continuous function.

Theorem 3.4. There exists a function $\ell : \mathbf{R} \times [0, \infty) \times \Omega \to \mathbf{R}_+$ with the property that $\ell(x, t, \omega)$ is jointly continuous in (x, t) for almost every (a.e.)

ω, and

$$m(A, t, \omega) = \int_A \ell(x, t, \omega) dx, \quad \text{all } A \in \mathcal{B}, \ t \geq 0, \ \omega \in \Omega. \quad (3.21)$$

See Chung and Williams (1990, Theorem 7.3) for a proof.

The process $\ell(x, \cdot, \cdot)$ is called the *local time* of X at level x. For fixed x, $\ell(x, \cdot, \cdot)$ is a continuous stochastic process with the property that it is positive if and only if $X(t, \omega) = x$. Thus, the local time $\ell(x, t, \omega)$ is a measure of the time that the process has spent at state x. Note that

$$\ell(x, t, \omega) = \lim_{\varepsilon \to 0} \frac{1}{2\varepsilon} m((x - \varepsilon, x + \varepsilon), t, \omega). \quad (3.22)$$

Theorem 3.4 suggests that ℓ can play the role of a density function. The following theorem shows that this conjecture is correct, leading to a useful fact about integrals along sample paths.

Theorem 3.5. Let $f : \mathbf{R} \to \mathbf{R}$ be a bounded, measurable function. Then

$$\int_0^t f(X(s, \omega)) ds = \int_{\mathbf{R}} f(x) \, \ell(x, t, \omega) \, dx, \quad \text{all } t \geq 0, \ \omega \in \Omega. \quad (3.23)$$

Theorem 3.5 says that an integral over time can be replaced with an integral over states, weighting outcomes by their local time ℓ. In this sense ℓ plays exactly the role of a density function.

For many economic applications these definitions and results must be extended in two ways: to allow final dates that are stopping times rather than fixed dates and to incorporate discounting. Both extensions are straightforward. For the former, it suffices to note that since (3.20)–(3.23) hold for all t and all ω, they also hold if t is replaced by a stopping time $\tau(\omega)$. To incorporate discounting, let $r > 0$ be an interest rate. At the risk of being tedious, the definitions and results so far are restated for this case.

Define the *discounted occupancy measure* of the process X, call it $\hat{m} \ (\cdot; r) :$ $\mathcal{B} \times \mathbf{R}_+ \times \Omega \to \mathbf{R}_+$ by

$$\hat{m}(A, t, \omega; r) \equiv \int_0^t e^{-rs} \, 1_A(X(s, \omega)) ds, \quad \text{all } A \in \mathcal{B}, \ t \geq 0, \ \omega \in \Omega. \quad (3.24)$$

The value $\hat{m}(A, t, \omega; r)$ is the total *discounted* time, discounted at the rate r, that the sample path $X(\cdot, \omega)$ has spent in the set A up to date t. Note that $\hat{m}$ has the same three properties as m, except that it has total mass $\hat{m}(\mathbf{R}, t, \omega; r) = (1 - e^{-rt})/r$. Note that $\hat{m}(\cdot; r)$ is continuous at $r = 0$: $\lim_{r \to 0} \hat{m}(A, t, \omega; r) = m(A, t, \omega)$.

Like m, the function $\hat{m}$ can be written as the integral of a continuous function.

Theorem 3.6. There exists a function $\hat{\ell}(\cdot; r) : \mathbf{R} \times [0, \infty) \times \Omega \to \mathbf{R}_+$ with the property that $\hat{\ell}(x, t, \omega; r)$ is jointly continuous in (x, t) for almost every ω, and

$$\hat{m}(A, t, \omega; r) = \int_A \hat{\ell}(x, t, \omega; r) dx, \quad \text{all } A \in \mathfrak{B}, \ t \geq 0, \ \omega \in \Omega. \quad (3.25)$$

The stochastic process $\hat{\ell}(x, \cdot, \cdot; r)$ is called the *discounted local time* of X at level x. As before, it follows from (3.24) and (3.25) that

$$\hat{\ell}(x, t, \omega; r) = \lim_{\varepsilon \to 0} \frac{1}{2\varepsilon} \hat{m}((x - \varepsilon, x + \varepsilon), t, \omega; r) \quad (3.26)$$

Like ℓ, $\hat{\ell}$ plays the role of a density function, giving the following analog of Theorem 3.5.

Theorem 3.7. Let $f : \mathbf{R} \to \mathbf{R}$ be a bounded, measurable function. Then

$$\int_0^t e^{-rs} f(X(s, \omega)) ds$$

$$= \int_{\mathbf{R}} f(x) \hat{\ell}(x, t, \omega; r) \, dx, \quad \text{all } t \geq 0, \ \omega \in \Omega. \quad (3.27)$$

Thus, an integral of discounted values over time can be written as an integral over states, weighting outcomes by their discounted local time $\hat{\ell}$. Equations (3.24)–(3.27) are the analogs, with discounting, of (3.20)–(3.23). In Chapter 5 explicit formulas for ℓ and $\hat{\ell}$ in (3.22) and (3.26) will be developed for the case where X is a Brownian motion.

3.6. Tanaka's Formula

In this section Tanaka's formula is derived, an extension of Ito's lemma that applies to functions with kinks, that is, those with discontinuous first derivatives.

Let $X(t)$ be a (μ, σ^2) Brownian motion, and recall that for any twice continuously differentiable function f, Ito's lemma states

$$f(X(t)) = f(X(0)) + \mu \int_0^t f'(X) \, ds$$

$$+ \sigma \int_0^t f'(X) \, dW(s) + \frac{1}{2} \sigma^2 \int_0^t f''(X) \, ds. \quad (3.28)$$

Consider the function

$$f(x) = \max\{0, cx\}, \quad c > 0. \tag{3.29}$$

This function is continuous, but it has a kink at $x = 0$, so

$$f'(x) = \begin{cases} 0, & x < 0, \\ \text{undefined}, & x = 0, \\ c, & x > 0, \end{cases}$$

and

$$f''(x) = \begin{cases} 0, & x < 0, \\ \text{undefined}, & x = 0, \\ 0, & x > 0. \end{cases}$$

Calculating the first and second integrals on the right side in (3.28) poses no problem: f' is discontinuous at $x = 0$, but a function with a finite number of jumps can be integrated in the usual way. The problem is the last term: f'' has an impulse at $x = 0$. This suggests that it may be helpful to think of f' as analogous to the cumulative distribution function (c.d.f.) for a (signed) measure. Tanaka's formula develops this observation more rigorously.

   To begin, note that the function in (3.29) can be approximated arbitrarily closely with functions having continuous first derivatives. For example, for any $\varepsilon > 0$, define the function

$$f_\varepsilon(x) = \begin{cases} 0, & x < -\varepsilon, \\ c\,(x + \varepsilon)^2/4\varepsilon, & -\varepsilon \leq x \leq +\varepsilon, \\ cx, & x > +\varepsilon. \end{cases}$$

This function is continuously differentiable, even at $x = \pm\varepsilon$:

$$f_\varepsilon'(x) = \begin{cases} 0, & x < -\varepsilon, \\ c\,(x + \varepsilon)/2\varepsilon, & -\varepsilon \leq x \leq +\varepsilon, \\ c, & x > +\varepsilon. \end{cases}$$

Hence $f_\varepsilon''(x)$ is also well defined and continuous, except at the points $x = \pm\varepsilon$:

$$f_\varepsilon''(x) = \begin{cases} 0, & x < -\varepsilon, \\ c/2\varepsilon, & -\varepsilon < x < +\varepsilon, \\ 0, & x > +\varepsilon. \end{cases}$$

For computing the last integral term in (3.28), it does not matter that f_ε'' is discontinuous at these two points. Figure 3.1 displays the functions f and f_ε and their first two derivatives, for two values of ε.

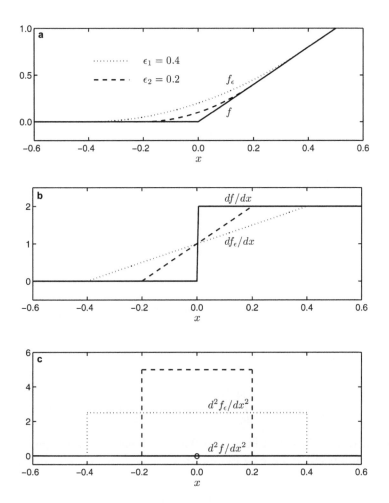

Figure 3.1. *For the functions f and f_ε, the (a) levels, (b) first derivatives, and (c) second derivatives.*

The idea is to approximate the last term in (3.28) using f_ε'' and then to take the limit as $\varepsilon \to 0$. The approximating functions f_ε'' take only two values, 0 and $c/2\varepsilon$. Therefore, using the definition of the occupancy measure in (3.20) one finds that

$$\int_0^t f_\varepsilon''(X(s))ds = \frac{c}{2\varepsilon}m((-\varepsilon,+\varepsilon),t,\omega).$$

Hence

$$\lim_{\varepsilon \to 0} \int_0^t f_\varepsilon''(X(s, \omega))ds = \lim_{\varepsilon \to 0} \frac{c}{2\varepsilon} m((-\varepsilon, +\varepsilon), t, \omega)$$

$$= c\ell(0, t, \omega),$$

where the second line uses the expression for local time in (3.22). Hence for the function in (3.29), the analog of (3.28) is

$$f(X(t)) = f(X(0)) + \mu \int_0^t f'(X)ds$$

$$+ \sigma \int_0^t f'(X)\, dW(s) + \frac{\sigma^2}{2} c\ell(0, t), \quad \text{all } \omega.$$

More generally, the following result holds.

Theorem 3.8 (Tanaka's formula). Let X be a (μ, σ^2) Brownian motion. Let f be a continuous function, with a derivative f' that is well defined and continuous except at a finite number of points. Define the signed measure ν on $(\mathbf{R}, \mathcal{B})$ by $\nu((a, b]) \equiv f'(b) - f'(a)$, for $-\infty < a < b < \infty$. Then

$$f(X(t)) = f(X(0)) + \mu \int_0^t f'(X)\, ds$$

$$+ \sigma \int_0^t f'(X)\, dW(s) + \frac{\sigma^2}{2} \int_{\mathbf{R}} \ell(x, t)\, \nu(dx).$$

See Harrison (1985) or Chung and Williams (1990) for more general versions of this result. In the example above the signed measure takes the simple form

$$\nu(A) = \begin{cases} c, & \text{if } 0 \in A, \\ 0, & \text{if } 0 \notin A. \end{cases}$$

Notice that if f is twice continuously differentiable, Tanaka's formula reverts to the expression in Ito's lemma. Specifically, the final term is

$$\frac{\sigma^2}{2} \int_{\mathbf{R}} \ell(x, t)\, \nu(dx) = \frac{\sigma^2}{2} \int_{\mathbf{R}} \ell(x, t)\, f''(x)\, dx$$

$$= \frac{\sigma^2}{2} \int_0^t f''(X(s))\, ds,$$

where the first line uses the definition of ν and the second uses Theorem 3.5. This expression agrees with the final term in (3.28).

3.7. The Kolmogorov Backward Equation

The Kolmogorov backward equation (KBE) is a second-order partial differential equation (PDE) satisfied by the densities at dates $t > 0$ generated by diffusions with different initial values x at date 0. The distribution functions corresponding to these densities also satisfy the KBE. The argument is as follows.

Let $\{X(t), t \geq 0\}$ be a regular diffusion on the open interval (ℓ, r), with infinitesimal parameters $(\mu(x), \sigma^2(x))$. Fix any bounded, piecewise continuous function g on (ℓ, r), and define

$$u(t, x) \equiv E[g(X(t)) \mid X(0) = x],$$

which is the expectation of $g(X)$ at date t, conditional on the initial value x at date 0. The first step is to show that u satisfies a certain PDE.

Fix any $t > 0$. By the law of iterated expectations, for any $h > 0$,

$$u(t + h, x) = E\left[g(X(t + h)) \mid X(0) = x\right]$$
$$= E\left\{E\left[g(X(t + h)) \mid X(h)\right] \mid X(0) = x\right\}$$
$$= E[u(t, X(h)) \mid X(0) = x],$$

where the second line inserts an inner expectation conditioned on information at date $h > 0$, and the third rewrites the second in term of u. It follows that for any $h > 0$,

$$\frac{1}{h}\left[u(t + h, x) - u(t, x)\right] = \frac{1}{h}E\left[u(t, X(h)) - u(t, x) \mid X(0) = x\right]. \quad (3.30)$$

Taking the limit in (3.30) as $h \to 0$ and using Ito's lemma on the right leads to

$$\frac{\partial u(t, x)}{\partial t} = \mu(x)\frac{\partial u(t, x)}{\partial x} + \frac{1}{2}\sigma^2(x)\frac{\partial^2 u(t, x)}{\partial x^2}. \quad (3.31)$$

The initial condition for this PDE is $u(0, x) = g(x)$, all x.

For the indicator function $g = 1_{(\ell, y]}$ this construction leads to $u(t, x) = P(t, x, y)$, where

$$P(t, x, y) \equiv \Pr\left[X(t) \leq y \mid X(0) = x\right]$$

is the probability that the process is below y at date t, given the initial condition x at date 0. In this case (3.31) implies

$$\frac{\partial P(t, x, y)}{\partial t} = \mu(x)\frac{\partial P(t, x, y)}{\partial x}$$

$$+ \frac{1}{2}\sigma^2(x)\frac{\partial^2 P(t, x, y)}{\partial x^2}, \quad t > 0, \ x \in (\ell, r). \tag{3.32}$$

Equation (3.32) is called the *Kolmogorov backward equation*. The boundary condition for P is

$$P(0, x, y) = \begin{cases} 1, & \text{if } x \le y, \\ 0, & \text{if } x > y. \end{cases}$$

Since X is a regular diffusion, for each $t > 0$ and $x \in (\ell, r)$, P has a density: $\partial P(t, x, y)/\partial y = p(t, x, y)$. Consequently (3.32) can be differentiated with respect to y to get

$$\frac{\partial p(t, x, y)}{\partial t} = \mu(x)\frac{\partial p(t, x, y)}{\partial x}$$

$$+ \frac{1}{2}\sigma^2(x)\frac{\partial^2 p(t, x, y)}{\partial x^2}, \quad t > 0, \ x \in (\ell, r). \tag{3.33}$$

That is, the transition density also satisfies the KBE. In this case the boundary condition is different, however: as $t \downarrow 0$, the density function $p(t, x, y)$ collapses to a mass point at $x = y$.

Notice that (3.32) and (3.33) do not involve y, which enters only through the boundary conditions. The KBE itself involves only the date t and the initial condition x. It describes, for fixed y, how the density at y, the value $p(t, x, y)$ varies with (t, x).

The PDE in (3.32) and (3.33) has many solutions. Indeed, there are many solutions that are c.d.f.s and densities. Thus, a boundary condition is needed to identify the one of interest in any particular context.

To illustrate more concretely what (3.32) and (3.33) imply, it is useful to look at specific examples: a Brownian motion, a geometric Brownian motion, and an Ornstein-Uhlenbeck (OU) process.

Recall that a normal distribution with mean and variance (m, v) has density

$$\phi(v, m, y) = \frac{1}{\sqrt{2\pi v}}\exp\left\{\frac{-(y - m)^2}{2v}\right\}, \quad y \in (-\infty, +\infty). \tag{3.34}$$

Example 1. For a Brownian motion the state space is **R** and the infinitesimal parameters are $\mu(x) = \mu$, $\sigma(x) = \sigma$. Hence (3.33) takes the form

$$\frac{\partial p}{\partial t} = \mu \frac{\partial p}{\partial x} + \frac{1}{2}\sigma^2 \frac{\partial^2 p}{\partial x^2}, \quad t > 0, \ x \in \mathbf{R}. \tag{3.35}$$

A normal distribution with parameters $(m, v) = (x + \mu t, \sigma^2 t)$ has density $\phi(\sigma^2 t, x + \mu t; y)$, where ϕ is as in (3.34). Thus, the claim is that the function

$$p(t, x, y) = \phi(\sigma^2 t, x + \mu t, y)$$

satisfies (3.35). Let $\phi_v = \partial \phi / \partial v$, $\phi_m = \partial \phi / \partial m$, and so on, denote the partial derivatives of ϕ. Then it follows from the chain rule for differentiation that p satisfies (3.35) if

$$\sigma^2 \phi_v + \mu \phi_m = \mu \phi_m + \frac{1}{2}\sigma^2 \phi_{mm},$$

or

$$\phi_v = \frac{1}{2}\phi_{mm}, \quad \text{all } v, m, y.$$

Using (3.34) it is straightforward to show that this condition holds.

Example 2. For a geometric Brownian motion the state space is $\mathbf{R}_+$ and the infinitesimal parameters are $\mu(x) = \mu x$, $\sigma(x) = \sigma x$. Hence (3.33) takes the form

$$\frac{\partial p}{\partial t} = \mu x \frac{\partial p}{\partial x} + \frac{1}{2}\sigma^2 x^2 \frac{\partial^2 p}{\partial x^2}, \quad t > 0, \ x \in \mathbf{R}_+. \tag{3.36}$$

It is straightforward to verify that

$$p(t, x, y) = \phi \left[\sigma^2 t, \ln x + \left(\mu - \tfrac{1}{2}\sigma^2 \right) t, \ln y \right]$$

satisfies (3.36).

Example 3. For an OU process the state space is $\mathbf{R}$ and the infinitesimal parameters are $\mu(x) = -\alpha x$, $\sigma(x) = \sigma$. Hence (3.33) takes the form

$$\frac{\partial p}{\partial t} = -\alpha x \frac{\partial p}{\partial x} + \frac{1}{2}\sigma^2 \frac{\partial^2 p}{\partial x^2}, \quad t > 0, \ x \in \mathbf{R}_+. \tag{3.37}$$

An OU process has increments that are Gaussian but not independent, and it is straightforward to verify that the transition density

$$p(t, x, y) = \phi \left(\frac{\sigma^2}{2\alpha} \left(1 - e^{-2\alpha t} \right), x e^{-\alpha t}, y \right)$$

satisfies (3.37).

3.8. The Kolmogorov Forward Equation

The backward equation involves time t and the initial condition x, with the current state y held fixed. A similar PDE, the Kolmogorov forward equation (KFE), involves t and y, with the initial state x fixed. The forward equation is useful for characterizing the limiting distribution, if one exists. It is worth emphasizing that while the backward equation holds for all regular diffusions, the forward equation does not. For example, it may not hold if the state space is bounded and probability accumulates at the boundaries. It does hold for Brownian motions (both ordinary and geometric) and for OU processes.

To derive the forward equation, start by considering any smooth function η satisfying

$$\eta(t + s, y) = \int \eta(t, \xi) p(s, \xi, y) d\xi, \quad \text{all } t, s, y. \tag{3.38}$$

For example, the density $p(t, x, \xi)$ satisfies (3.38), for any initial value x. The stationary density $\psi(\xi)$ also satisfies (3.38), if one exists.

For diffusions that are well behaved in the sense noted above, it can be shown that for any function η satisfying (3.38),

$$\frac{\partial \eta(t, y)}{\partial t} = -\frac{\partial}{\partial y} \left[\mu(y)\eta(t, y) \right] + \frac{1}{2} \frac{\partial^2}{\partial y^2} \left[\sigma^2(y)\eta(t, y) \right]. \tag{3.39}$$

For the density $p(t, x, \xi)$, (3.39) takes the form

$$\frac{\partial p(t, x, y)}{\partial t} = -\frac{\partial}{\partial y} \left[\mu(y)p(t, x, y) \right] + \frac{1}{2} \frac{\partial^2}{\partial y^2} \left[\sigma^2(y)p(t, x, y) \right], \tag{3.40}$$

where x is fixed. Equation (3.40) is called the *Kolmogorov forward equation*.

Perhaps the most important use of (3.39) is to characterize the stationary density $\psi(y)$, if one exists. If it does exist, (3.39) implies that it satisfies

$$0 = -\frac{d}{dy} \left[\mu(y)\psi(y) \right] + \frac{1}{2} \frac{d^2}{dy^2} \left[\sigma^2(y)\psi(y) \right]. \tag{3.41}$$

Exercise 3.3. Use (3.41) to show that a Brownian motion does not have a stationary density.

If there is a stationary density, it can be found as follows. Integrate (3.41) once to get

$$c_1 = \frac{d}{dy} \left[\sigma^2(y)\psi(y) \right] - 2\mu(y)\psi(y),$$

where c_1 is a constant that must be determined. Then use the integrating factor

$$s(y) = \exp\left\{-\int^y \frac{2\mu(\xi)}{\sigma^2(\xi)}d\xi\right\}$$

to write this equation as

$$\frac{d}{dy}\left[s(y)\sigma^2(y)\psi(y)\right] = c_1 s(y),$$

and integrate again to get

$$\psi(x) = \frac{1}{s(x)\sigma^2(x)}\left[c_1\int^x s(y)dy + c_2\right].$$

The constants c_1, c_2 must be chosen so that $\psi(x) \geq 0$, all x, and

$$\int \psi(x)dx = 1.$$

Example 4. For an OU process $\sigma(x) = \sigma$ and $\mu(x) = -\alpha x$, so the integrating factor is

$$s(y) = \exp\left\{\frac{\alpha}{\sigma^2}\int^y 2\xi d\xi\right\}$$

$$= \exp\left\{\gamma y^2\right\},$$

where $\gamma \equiv \alpha/\sigma^2$. Hence

$$\psi(x) = \hat{c}_1\int_0^x e^{\gamma\left(y^2 - x^2\right)}dy + \hat{c}_2 e^{-\gamma x^2},$$

where the variance has been absorbed into the constants. If $\hat{c}_1 \neq 0$, the first term diverges as $|x|$ gets large, and $\psi(x)$ cannot be a density. Hence $\hat{c}_1 = 0$, and the stationary density has the form $\psi(x) = \hat{c}_2 e^{-\gamma x^2}$, where $\hat{c}_2$ is chosen so that $\int \psi = 1$. Thus, from (3.34) we see that $\psi(x) = \phi(1/2\gamma, 0, x)$, and the limiting distribution is a normal with mean $m = 0$ and variance $v = 1/2\gamma$.

Notes

Fleming and Rishel (1975), Harrison (1985), Fleming and Soner (1993), and Krylov (1995) all provide good treatments of stochastic integration. Karatzas and Shreve (1991), which is very complete, is useful as a reference.

The discussion of geometric Brownian motion in Section 3.4 follows Karlin and Taylor (1975, Section 7.4). See Chung and Williams (1990, Chapter 7) for a rigorous development of occupancy measure and local time. The discussion of Tanaka's formula in Section 3.6 follows Harrison (1985, Section 4.6). There are many good treatments of the Kolmogorov backward and forward equations. The discussion in Sections 3.7 and 3.8 is based on Karlin and Taylor (1981, Section 15.5).

4

Martingales

MARTINGALES ARE AN example of mathematics at its best, sublimely elegant and at the same time enormously useful. Initially developed to study questions that arise in gambling, the theory of martingales has subsequently been used to study a wide array of questions.

The treatment here is only an introduction, covering the key concepts and major results. Section 4.1 provides a formal definition and illustrates the idea with some examples. Section 4.2 shows how martingales can be constructed from the (stationary) transition function for a discrete-time Markov process, using an eigenvector of the transition matrix if the state space is discrete and an eigenfunction if the state space is continuous. Section 4.3 shows a systematic way to carry out the construction if the Markov process is the sum of i.i.d. random variables and extends the method to continuous-time processes, both Brownian motions and more general diffusions. Sub- and supermartingales are defined in Section 4.4, and two results are proved. The first describes two important ways that submartingales arise, and the second provides an extension of Kolmogorov's inequality. The optional stopping theorem, a fundamental result for stopping times applied to martingales, is presented in Section 4.5 and extended in Section 4.6. Section 4.7 provides a statement and proof of the martingale convergence theorem.

4.1. Definition and Examples

Let $(\Omega, \mathfrak{F}, P)$ be a probability space, $\mathbb{F} = \{\mathfrak{F}_t, \ t \geq 0\}$ a filtration contained in $\mathfrak{F}$, and $\{Z(t), \ t \geq 0\}$ a stochastic process adapted to $\mathbb{F}$. Then $[Z, \mathbb{F}]$ is a *martingale* (or Z is a *martingale with respect to* $\mathbb{F}$) if for all $t \geq 0$,

$$E\left[\,|Z(t)|\,\right] < \infty, \tag{4.1}$$

and with probability one,

$$E\left[Z(t) \mid \mathfrak{F}_s\right] = Z(s), \quad \text{all } 0 \leq s < t. \tag{4.2}$$

Note that the time index t may be discrete or continuous, and the horizon may be finite or infinite. Also note that the definition involves the filtration $\mathbb{F}$ in a fundamental way. If the filtration is understood, however, one may say simply that Z is a martingale.

It is useful to consider a few examples, which illustrate some of the many ways that martingales arise. In each case, to establish that a process is a martingale requires verifying that it is adapted to an appropriate filtered space and that it satisfies (4.1) and (4.2).

The first and most obvious way to construct a martingale is as the sum of independent random variables with mean zero. Indeed, the idea originated as the stochastic process describing the wealth of a gambler playing games of chance at fair odds.

Example 1 (gambler's wealth). Let $X_1, \ldots, X_i, \ldots$ be a (finite or infinite) sequence of independent random variables on the probability space $(\Omega, \mathfrak{F}, P)$, each with mean zero and with finite absolute deviation: $E[X_i] = 0$ and $E[|X_i|] < \infty$, all i. Let $Z_0 = 0$, and for each $k = 1, 2, \ldots,$ define the random variable $Z_k = \sum_{i=1}^{k} X_i$ to be the partial sum of the first k elements in the sequence. For each k let $\mathfrak{F}_k \subset \mathfrak{F}$ be the smallest σ-algebra for which $\{Z_j\}_{j=1}^{k}$ are measurable, and let $\mathbb{F} = \{\mathfrak{F}_k\}$ be the filtration consisting of this (increasing) sequence. Then the stochastic process Z is a martingale on the filtered space $(\Omega, \mathbb{F}, P)$.

To see this, first note that by construction Z is adapted to $\mathbb{F}$. Then note that for any k,

$$E\left[|Z_k|\right] = E\left[\left|\sum_{i=1}^{k} X_i\right|\right] \leq E\left[\sum_{i=1}^{k} |X_i|\right]$$

$$= \sum_{i=1}^{k} E\left[|X_i|\right] < \infty,$$

so (4.1) holds. Finally, to see that (4.2) holds, note that for any $j < k$,

$$E\left[Z_k \mid \mathfrak{F}_j\right] = E\left[\sum_{i=1}^{k} X_i \,\middle|\, \mathfrak{F}_j\right]$$

$$= \sum_{i=1}^{j} X_i + \sum_{i=j+1}^{k} E\left[X_i \mid \mathfrak{F}_j\right]$$

$$= Z_j,$$

where the second line uses the fact that X_i is $\mathfrak{F}_j$-measurable for $i \leq j$, and the third uses the fact that the X_is are mutually independent and all have mean zero.

An analogous argument establishes that a Brownian motion without drift is a martingale. The following exercise identifies some other useful martingales connected with Brownian motions.

Exercise 4.1.   (a) Show that if X is $(0, \sigma^2)$ Brownian motion, then $X^2 - \sigma^2 t$ and $(X/\sigma)^2 - t$ are martingales.
(b) Show that if X is (μ, σ^2) Brownian motion, then $X - \mu t$, $(X - \mu t)^2 - \sigma^2 t$, and $\left[(X - \mu t)/\sigma\right]^2 - t$ are martingales.

The key feature of a martingale is that it has increments, at every point along every sample path, with (conditional) mean zero. Thus, martingales can be created from other stochastic processes by repeatedly (in discrete time) or continuously adjusting for the (conditional) expected increment along each sample path, as in part (b) of the previous exercise. The next examples illustrate other situations in which martingales arise.

Example 2 (family composition).   Consider a society in which each family has exactly N children. Children are born in succession (no twins), and the probability is $\pi = 1/2$ that any new addition is a girl.
To analyze various questions about family composition in this society, an appropriate probability space is needed. To construct one, note first that an outcome in this setting is a vector of length N of the form $\omega = (b, g, \ldots, g, b, \ldots, b)$ describing the sequence of births. Let Ω be the set consisting of all such vectors. Note that Ω is a discrete space containing 2^N elements. Let $\mathfrak{F}$ be the complete σ-algebra for Ω, that is, the σ-algebra consisting of all subsets. Each outcome is equally likely, so let P be the probability measure on $\mathfrak{F}$ that assigns probability $1/2^N$ to each point. Then $(\Omega, \mathfrak{F}, P)$ is a probability space.
Define a filtration on this space by the sequence of births. Specifically, let ω_i, $i = 1, \ldots, N$, denote the ith component of the vector ω; for each k,

let $\mathfrak{F}_k \subset \mathfrak{F}$ be the smallest σ-algebra for which $\omega_1, \ldots, \omega_k$ are measurable; and let $\mathbb{F} = \{\mathfrak{F}_k\}$ be the filtration defined by this (increasing) sequence.

A number of different stochastic processes can be defined on the filtered space $(\Omega, \mathbb{F}, P)$. For example, let $g_0 = 0$ and for $k = 1, \ldots, N$, let g_k be the number of girls among the first k children. Notice that each g_k is a random variable on $(\Omega, \mathfrak{F}, P)$. Other processes can be constructed from $\{g_k\}$.

Let $X_0 = 0$ and

$$X_k = g_k - (k - g_k), \quad k = 1, 2, \ldots, N,$$

be the excess of girls over boys in the first k births. Let $Y_0 = 0$ and

$$Y_k = g_k - \frac{k}{2}, \quad k = 1, 2, \ldots, N,$$

be the excess of girls over $k/2$ in the first k births. Let $Z_0 = 0$ and

$$Z_k = \frac{g_k}{k} - \frac{1}{2}, \quad k = 1, 2, \ldots, N,$$

be the deviation from $1/2$ of the fraction of girls in the first k births.

Exercise 4.2. (a) Verify that $\{g_k\}$, $\{X_k\}$, $\{Y_k\}$, and $\{Z_k\}$ in Example 2 are stochastic processes on $(\Omega, \mathbb{F}, P)$.

(b) Show that $\{X_k\}$ and $\{Y_k\}$ are martingales and that $\{Z_k\}$ is not.

The next example illustrates the very general principle that in a learning context, the sequence of Bayesian posteriors is a martingale. The intuition for this fact is clear: if this were not so the observer would want to revise his current beliefs to incorporate the expected change next period.

Example 3 (Bayesian learning). Consider an experimenter trying to determine whether an urn is of type A or type B. Both types of (outwardly identical) urn contain a large number of black and white balls, but in different proportions. In the former the proportion of black balls is a and in the latter it is b, where $0 \leq a, b \leq 1$, with $a \neq b$. The urn the experimenter faces was drawn randomly from a population in which the proportion of type A urns is $p_0 \in (0, 1)$. To determine more precisely which type it is, he samples balls (with replacement), updating his beliefs by using Bayes' rule after each draw. Let p_k, $k = 1, 2, \ldots$, denote his posterior probability after k balls have been drawn. Notice that each p_k is a random variable that takes $k + 1$ possible values. (Why?)

Exercise 4.3. (a) Define an appropriate probability space for the situation described in Example 3.

(b) Define a filtration that makes the sequence of posteriors $\{p_k\}_{k=0}^{\infty}$ a stochastic process.

(c) Show that $\{p_k\}_{k=0}^{\infty}$ is a martingale.

4.2. Martingales Based on Eigenvalues

The next two examples show how martingales can be constructed from the (stationary) transition function for a discrete-time Markov process. If the state space is discrete the construction uses an eigenvector of the transition matrix. If the state space is continuous it uses the continuous analog, an eigenfunction associated with the transition function.

Example 4 (based on eigenvectors). Consider a Markov chain with state space $i \in \{1, 2, \ldots, I\}$ and the $I \times I$ transition matrix $\Pi = [\pi_{ij}]$, where π_{ij} is the probability of a transition from state i to state j.

Any function of the state is represented by a vector $f^T = (f_1, \ldots, f_I)$ containing the values for the function in states $1, \ldots, I$, and the vector Πf contains the conditional expected values for the function next period, given the possible states $1, \ldots, I$ this period. Recall that the pair (λ, v), with $\lambda \neq 0$ and $v \in \mathbf{R}^k$, is an eigenvalue and associated right eigenvector of Π if $\Pi v = \lambda v$.

Let (λ, v) be such a pair, q_0 be a probability vector describing the distribution of the initial state, and $\{i_k\}_{k=0}^{\infty}$ with $i_k \in \{1, 2, \ldots, I\}$ be the integer-valued stochastic process indicating the outcomes. Define the stochastic process $\{V_k\}_{k=0}^{\infty}$ by $V_k = v_{i_k}$, all k. Then

$$\mathrm{E}\left[V_{k+1} \mid i_k\right] = \mathrm{E}\left[v_{i_{k+1}} \mid i_k\right]$$

$$= e_{i_k} \Pi v$$

$$= \lambda v_{i_k}$$

$$= \lambda V_k, \quad k = 0, 1, \ldots,$$

where $e_i = (0, \ldots, 0, 1, 0, \ldots, 0)$ is a vector with a one in the ith position and zeros elsewhere, and the third line uses the eigenvector property. If $\lambda = 1$ then V is a martingale. Otherwise, the stochastic process Z defined by

$$Z_k = \lambda^{-k} V_k = \lambda^{-k} v_{i_k}, \quad k = 0, 1, \ldots,$$

is a martingale. In either case the filtration is the one generated by $\{i_k\}$. This filtration is strictly finer than the one generated by $\{v_{i_k}\}$ if v has two elements that are identical, $v_i = v_j$, for $i \neq j$.

Note that the argument in Example 4 continues to hold if the state space is infinite, if $I = \infty$.

The next example provides an analogous construction for Markov chains taking values in all of **R**.

Example 5 (based on eigenfunctions). Let F be the (stationary) transition function for a Markov chain $Y = \{Y_k\}$ with a continuous state space. That is,

$$\Pr \{Y_{k+1} \leq b \mid Y_k = a\} = F(b \mid a), \quad k = 1, 2, \ldots.$$

Let $\lambda \neq 0$ be a real number and $v(\cdot)$ a function such that

$$\mathrm{E}\left[|v(Y_k)|\right] < \infty, \quad \text{all } k,$$

and

$$\int v(y) dF(y \mid a) = \lambda v(a), \quad \text{all } a.$$

Then v is called an *eigenfunction* of F, with associated eigenvalue λ. An argument like the one above establishes that the stochastic process

$$Z_k = \lambda^{-k} v(Y_k), \quad k = 0, 1, 2, \ldots,$$

is a martingale.

4.3. The Wald Martingale

An important class of Markov processes are those constructed as sequences of partial sums of i.i.d. random variables. In this case there is a systematic way to construct eigenfunctions, and the associated martingales are called *Wald martingales*. The next three examples show how they are constructed for discrete-time processes, Brownian motions, and general diffusions, respectively,

Example 6 (discrete time). Let $\{X_k\}_{k=1}^{\infty}$ be a sequence of i.i.d. random variables with a common c.d.f. G. Then the partial sums $Y_0 = 0$ and $Y_k = Y_{k-1} + X_k$, $k = 1, 2, \ldots$, form a Markov process with stationary increments, and the transition function is $F(b \mid a) = G(b - a)$, all a, b.

Suppose that for $\eta \neq 0$ the expected value

$$\lambda(\eta) = \int e^{\eta x} dG(x)$$

exists. Then the function $v(y; \eta) = e^{\eta y}$ is an eigenfunction of F with associated eigenvalue $\lambda(\eta)$. To see this, note that

$$\int v(y; \eta) dF(y \mid a) = \int e^{\eta y} dG(y - a)$$

$$= \int e^{\eta(a+x)} dG(x)$$

$$= v(a; \eta)\lambda(\eta).$$

Hence the argument in Example 5 implies that the stochastic process

$$Z_k = \lambda^{-k}(\eta) v(Y_k; \eta), \quad \text{all } k,$$

is a martingale.

A family of martingales can be constructed by varying the parameter η in Example 6. In particular, if η can be chosen so that $\lambda(\eta) = 1 + r$, where r is a discount rate, then $\lambda(\eta)^{-k} = 1/(1 + r)^k$ plays the role of a discount factor.

The next two examples show that a similar argument can be used to construct martingales for Brownian motions and other diffusions. These martingales are used extensively in later chapters.

Example 7 (Brownian motion). Let X be a (μ, σ^2) Brownian motion. Recall (see Exercise 3.1) that for any $\rho \neq 0$, the stochastic process $Y(t) = \exp\{\rho X(t)\}$ is a geometric Brownian motion with parameters $\left(q(\rho), (\rho\sigma)^2\right)$, where

$$q(\rho) \equiv \rho\mu + \tfrac{1}{2}(\rho\sigma)^2. \tag{4.3}$$

Consequently,

$$E\left[\exp\{\rho X(t)\}\right] = E\left[Y(t)\right]$$

$$= Y(0) e^{q(\rho)t}$$

$$= \exp\{\rho X(0) + q(\rho)t\}, \quad \text{all } t.$$

Hence the stochastic process

$$M(t; \rho) \equiv \exp\{\rho X(t) - q(\rho)t\}, \quad \text{all } t, \tag{4.4}$$

is a martingale.

Similarly, if Y is a geometric Brownian motion with parameters $(\hat{\mu}, \sigma^2)$, then for any $\rho \neq 0$ the stochastic process

$$M(t; \rho) \equiv Y^\rho(t) e^{-\hat{q}(\rho)t}, \quad \text{all } t,$$

is a martingale, where

$$\hat{q}(\rho) \equiv \rho \left(\hat{\mu} - \tfrac{1}{2}\sigma^2 \right) + \tfrac{1}{2}(\rho\sigma)^2.$$

Example 8 (diffusions).   More generally, let X be a diffusion with stationary infinitesimal parameters $\mu(\cdot)$ and $\sigma(\cdot)$. Suppose the function $F(t, x)$ satisfies

$$F_t(t, x) + \mu(x)F_x(t, x) + \tfrac{1}{2}\sigma^2(x)F_{xx}(t, x) = 0, \quad \text{all } t, x. \qquad (4.5)$$

Then the stochastic process

$$M(t) = F(t, X(t)), \quad \text{all } t, \omega,$$

is a martingale. To see this, note that

$$\text{E}[dM] = \text{E}\left[F_t dt + F_x \mu(X)dt + F_x \sigma(X)dW + \tfrac{1}{2}F_{xx}\sigma^2(x)dt \right]$$

$$= 0,$$

where the first line uses Ito's lemma, and the second uses (4.5) and the zero expectation property of stochastic integrals (Theorem 3.1).

In particular, the stochastic process

$$M(t) = e^{-rt}f(X(t)), \quad \text{all } t, \omega,$$

is a martingale if the pair (r, f) satisfies

$$-rf(x) + \mu(x)f'(x) + \tfrac{1}{2}\sigma^2(x)f''(x) = 0, \quad \text{all } x. \qquad (4.6)$$

For a Brownian motion, μ and σ^2 are constants, and (4.6) holds for any (r, f) defined by

$$r = q(\rho), \ f(x) = e^{\rho x}, \quad \text{all } x,$$

where $\rho \neq 0$ and the function $q(\cdot)$ is defined in (4.3).

4.4. Sub- and Supermartingales

Submartingales and supermartingales are defined by replacing condition (4.2) with an inequality. A stochastic process Z on the filtered space $(\Omega, \mathbb{F}, P)$ is a *submartingale* if for all $t \geq 0$, (4.1) holds and with probability one,

$$\text{E}\left[Z(t) \mid \mathfrak{F}_s \right] \geq Z(s), \quad \text{all } 0 \leq s < t. \qquad (4.7)$$

It is a *supermartingale* if the inequality in (4.7) is reversed. Thus, on average a submartingale rises over time and a supermartingale falls. Notice that

- Z is a submartingale if and only if $-Z$ is a supermartingale;
- Z is a martingale if and only if it is both a submartingale and a supermartingale;
- Z is a martingale if and only if both Z and $-Z$ are submartingales.

Exercise 4.4. Consider a modified version of Example 1: suppose the gambler is playing at less than fair odds. That is, suppose that each of the X_is has a nonpositive mean, $\mathrm{E}[X_i] \leq 0$, all i. For $k = 1, 2, \ldots$, let $Y_k = -Z_k$ denote the gambler's net *loss* after k rounds of play. Show that Z_k is a submartingale.

Exercise 4.5. Consider a modified version of the society in Example 2. Suppose that at each birth the probability of a girl is $\pi < 1/2$. Define the sequences g_k, X_k, and Y_k as before. Show that X_k and Y_k are supermartingales.

Exercise 4.6. Consider a modified version of the Bayesian learning in Example 3. Suppose that the experimenter is mistaken about the fraction of type A urns in the population from which the urn under study was drawn. The experimenter believes that the fraction of type A urns is $\hat{p}_0$, with $0 < \hat{p}_0 < p_0$. As before the experimenter draws balls from the urn sequentially, with replacement, and updates his beliefs after each draw by using Bayes' rule. Let $\{\hat{p}_k\}$ denote his sequence of posteriors. Show that $\{\hat{p}_k\}$ is a submartingale.

Exercise 4.7. Show that if X is a Brownian motion with positive (negative) drift, then it is a submartingale (a supermartingale).

The following theorem describes two ways that submartingales arise.

Theorem 4.1. (i) If Z is a martingale on the filtered space $(\Omega, \mathbb{F}, P)$, ϕ is a measurable convex function, and $\phi(Z(t))$ is integrable, all t, then the stochastic process $\phi(Z)$ is a submartingale.

(ii) If Z is a submartingale on the filtered space $(\Omega, \mathbb{F}, P)$; ϕ is a measurable, increasing, convex function; and $\phi(Z(t))$ is integrable, all t, then the stochastic process $\phi(Z)$ is a submartingale.

Proof. In each case it must be shown that $\phi(Z)$ is adapted to $(\Omega, \mathbb{F}, P)$ and that it satisfies (4.1) and (4.7), for all t.

(i) For each t, since $Z(t)$ is $\mathfrak{F}_t$-measurable and ϕ is a measurable function, it follows immediately that $\phi(Z(t))$ is also $\mathfrak{F}_t$-measurable. Hence $\phi(Z)$ is adapted to $(\Omega, \mathbb{F}, P)$. By assumption $\phi(Z(t))$ is integrable, so it satisfies (4.1), for all t, and since Z is a martingale it satisfies (4.2), for all t. Then since ϕ

is convex, it follows from Jensen's inequality that with probability one,

$$\phi(Z(s)) = \phi(\mathrm{E}[Z(t) \mid \mathfrak{F}_s])$$
$$\leq \mathrm{E}[\phi(Z(t) \mid \mathfrak{F}_s)] \quad \text{all } 0 \leq s < t, \tag{4.8}$$

so $\phi(Z)$ satisfies (4.7), for all t.

(ii) Most of the argument for part (i) applies. For the last step notice that since Z is a submartingale, it satisfies (4.7) for all t. Hence, since ϕ is increasing,

$$\phi(Z(s)) \leq \phi(\mathrm{E}[Z(t) \mid \mathfrak{F}_s]), \quad \text{all } 0 \leq s < t,$$

The inequality in (4.8) then follows from convexity, as before. ∎

Part (i) of Theorem 4.1 implies that if Z is a martingale, then $|Z|$ and Z^2 are submartingales. In particular, if X is a (μ, σ^2) Brownian motion then $X - \mu t$ is a martingale, so $|X - \mu t|$ and $[X - \mu t]^2$ are submartingales.

The following result, an extension of Kolmogorov's inequality, provides a useful bound.

Theorem 4.2. If $\{Z_k\}_{k=1}^n$ is a submartingale, then for any $\alpha > 0$,

$$P\left[\max_{1 \leq k \leq n} |Z_k| \geq \alpha\right] \leq \frac{1}{\alpha} \mathrm{E}\left[|Z_n|\right].$$

Proof. Fix $\alpha > 0$ and define the (disjoint) sets A_k by

$$A_k = \{\omega \in \Omega : Z_k \geq \alpha \text{ and } Z_j < \alpha, j = 1, 2, \ldots, k-1\}.$$

Then

$$\mathrm{E}\left[|Z_n|\right] \geq \sum_{k=1}^n \int_{A_k} |Z_n| \, dP$$
$$\geq \sum_{k=1}^n \int_{A_k} Z_k \, dP$$
$$\geq \sum_{k=1}^n \alpha \, P(A_k)$$
$$= \alpha P(\cup_{k=1}^n A_k)$$
$$= \alpha P\left[\max_{1 \leq k \leq n} |Z_k| \geq \alpha\right],$$

where the first line uses the fact that the A_ks are disjoint, with $\cup_{k=1}^n A_k \subseteq \Omega$; the second line uses the fact that $\{Z_k\}$ is a submartingale; and the last three lines use the definition of the A_ks. ∎

For an application of this result, let $\{X_i\}_{i=1}^n$ be a sequence of random variables, each with zero mean and finite variance, and let $S_k = \sum_{i=1}^k X_i$, $k = 1, \ldots, n$, be the sequence of their partial sums. Clearly $\{S_k\}$ is a martingale, and hence by Theorem 4.1, $Z_k = |S_k|$ is a submartingale. In this case Theorem 4.2 asserts that

$$P\left[\max_{1 \le k \le n} |S_k| > \alpha\right] = P\left[\max_{1 \le k \le n} S_k^2 > \alpha^2\right] \le \frac{1}{\alpha} E\left[|S_n|\right],$$

which is Kolmogorov's inequality.

4.5. Optional Stopping Theorem

The optional stopping theorem is a powerful and extremely useful result about stopping times for martingales and submartingales. (To avoid excessive duplication, the results will not be stated separately for supermartingales.) The theorem applies to a wide class of stochastic processes, including discrete-time processes and diffusions, so it applies for all of the processes considered in this book. The theorem has many forms. The one below is presented for its simplicity, and its implications for some of the examples are discussed. A stronger form is presented in Section 4.6.

For any two dates s and t, let $s \wedge t \equiv \min\{s, t\}$ denote the earlier of the two. Then, if Z is a stochastic process and T is a stopping time, let $Z(T \wedge t)$ denote the "stopped" process defined by

$$Z(T \wedge t, \omega) = \begin{cases} Z(t, \omega), & \text{if } t < T(\omega), \\ Z(T(\omega), \omega), & \text{if } t \ge T(\omega). \end{cases}$$

Along each sample path the stopped process replaces the fluctuating path after date T with the constant value $Z(T)$.

The optional stopping theorem assets that if Z is a (sub)martingale and T is a stopping time, then the stopped process $Z(T \wedge t)$ is also a (sub)martingale. Moreover, the expected value of the stopped process at any date t (is bounded below by) is equal to the expectation of the initial value $Z(0)$ and (is bounded above by) is equal to the expected value of the unstopped process at t. Finally, if the stopping time is bounded, then the expected terminal value for the stopped process (is greater than) is equal to the expected value at the initial date.

Theorem 4.3 (optional stopping theorem).   Let Z be a (sub)martingale on
the filtered space $(\Omega, \mathbb{F}, P)$ and T a stopping time. Then
    (i) $Z(T \wedge t)$ is also a (sub)martingale, and it satisfies

$$\mathrm{E}\,[Z(0)]\,(\leq) = \mathrm{E}\,[Z(T \wedge t)]\,(\leq) = \mathrm{E}\,[Z(t)], \quad \text{all } t; \tag{4.9}$$

    (ii) if there exists $N < \infty$ such that $0 \leq T(\omega) \leq N$, all ω, then

$$\mathrm{E}\,[Z(0)]\,(\leq) = \mathrm{E}\,[Z(T)]\,(\leq) = \mathrm{E}\,[Z(N)]. \tag{4.10}$$

See Appendix B for a proof.

The intuition for part (i) of this result is clear. For a martingale, the constant value along the sample path after date $T(\omega)$ in the stopped process
is equal to the expected value of the original process at all subsequent
dates, $\mathrm{E}\big[Z(t) \mid Z(T)\big] = Z(T)$, all $t \geq T(\omega)$. Consequently, replacing the original (fluctuating) path with the (constant) stopped value does not change
expectations taken at earlier dates. For a submartingale, the same reasoning produces the stated inequalities. If the stopping time T is uniformly
bounded, then (4.10) follows immediately: set $t = N$ in (4.9) and note that
$T \wedge N = T$.
    To see more concretely what Theorem 4.3 states, it is useful to look again
at the examples in Section 4.1.

Example 1′ (gambler's wealth).   Recall the gambler. We saw in Example 1
that if the game has fair odds and the gambler simply plays without stopping,
the stochastic process $\{Z_k\}$ describing his net gain is a martingale. Hence
for any fixed k, his expected net gain after k rounds of play is zero: $\mathrm{E}[Z_k] =$
0, $k = 1, 2, \ldots$. Theorem 4.3 says something even stronger.
    Suppose that the gambler has a "system" that involves stopping when
he is ahead. Any such system defines a stopping time T. We must now
distinguish between potential rounds and rounds actually played. Part (i)
of Theorem 4.3 says that if the gambler uses his system, then his sequence
of net gains $\big\{Z_{T \wedge k}\big\}_{k=1}^{\infty}$ is still a martingale. Hence his expected net gain after
k potential rounds is zero, as it would have been if he had simply played all
k rounds. That is,

$$0 = Z_0 = \mathrm{E}\,\big[Z_{T \wedge k}\big] = \mathrm{E}\,\big[Z_k\big], \quad k = 1, 2, \ldots.$$

Part (ii) says that if his stopping rule puts a finite upper bound N on the
number of rounds actually played, then his expected net gain at the end of
play is also zero. That is, no stopping rule can alter the martingale property
of the net gains, and none can lead to an expected net gain (or loss).
    Similarly, as shown in Exercise 4.4, if the gambler is playing at unfair
odds, the stochastic process $\{Y_k\} = \{-Z_k\}$ describing his net loss is a sub-

martingale: his expected losses increase with each round of play. Part (i) of Theorem 4.3 states that the same is true if he uses a stopping rule: his sequence of net losses $\{Y_{T \wedge k}\}$ is still a submartingale. Its expected value after k rounds of potential play is bounded below by zero and bounded above by the expected value of the net loss if all k rounds are actually played. Thus, using a stopping rule can reduce his expected net loss but cannot produce an expected gain. Part (ii) says that if there is a finite bound on the stopping time, then his expected net loss at the end of play is bounded below by zero and bounded above by the expected loss he would incur if he simply played all N rounds.

Example 2′ (family composition). Recall the model of family composition. Suppose parents value sons over daughters and would like to tilt their expected family composition toward sons. Suppose that every family has at least one child and that there is an upper bound N on family size. The only tool parents have at their disposal is their decision about when to stop having children. For example, they might use the rule: keep having children until a son is born or there are N daughters, and then stop.

We saw in Example 2 that if the probability of a girl is $\pi = 1/2$ at each birth, and if the family has N children, then the stochastic processes X_k describing the excess of girls over boys after k births, and Y_k describing the excess of girls over $k/2$ after k births, are martingales. Part (i) of Theorem 4.3 implies that if the family uses a stopping rule T, with $T \leq N$, then the corresponding stopped processes are also martingales. Part (ii) implies that the expected values for these two variables are zero for completed families under the stopping rule, just as they are if every family has N children.

Similarly, as shown in Exercise 4.5, if the probability of a girl is $\pi < 1/2$ at each birth and the family has N children, then X_k and Y_k are supermartingales. Part (i) of Theorem 4.3 then implies that if families use a stopping rule T, the corresponding stopped sequences are also supermartingales. Parts (i) and (ii) together imply that

$$\mathrm{E}\left[X_N\right] \leq \mathrm{E}\left[X_T\right] \leq \mathrm{E}\left[X_0\right] = 0,$$

and similarly for Y_k. That is, by either measure family composition is tilted toward boys (because of the uneven birth ratio) and is more heavily tilted for the unstopped process.

Exercise 4.8. Consider the family composition example with $\pi = 1/2$.

(a) Suppose all families have exactly N children, and let G be the fraction of girls in completed families. What are the possible values for the random variable G? What is the probability distribution over these outcomes?

(b) Suppose families use the stopping rule: continue having children until a son is born or there are N daughters, and then stop. Let H be the fraction of girls in completed families. What are the possible values for the random variable H? What is the probability distribution over these outcomes? What is average family size in this society?

Example 3′ (Bayesian learning).   Recall the example of Bayesian learning. Suppose that an outside observer is watching the experiments, and that the experimenter wants to manipulate the observer's beliefs. For concreteness suppose that he would like to convince her that the urn is likely to be of type A. The only tool the experimenter can use to manipulate the observer's beliefs is a stopping rule. If the experimenter draws a ball, the outcome is seen by the observer. But the experimenter can stop sampling at any time, that is, he can choose a stopping rule T.

Consider first the case where the observer's prior is p_0, the (correct) ex ante probability that the urn is type A. As the sampling progresses her sequence of posteriors is the stochastic process $\{p_k\}$ described in Example 3. As shown in that example, this process is a martingale. Part (i) of Theorem 4.3 implies that if the experimenter uses a stopping rule T, the stochastic process $\{p_{k\wedge T}\}$ describing the observer's posteriors is still a martingale. Thus, even a devious experimenter cannot design a sampling rule that destroys the martingale property of the posteriors. (Neither can a clumsy one.)

Part (ii) of Theorem 4.3 implies that if there is an upper bound N on the sample size under the stopping rule, then the expected value of the observer's posterior after sampling has stopped is equal to her prior before sampling begins, regardless of the stopping rule chosen by the experimenter. That is, $\mathrm{E}[p_T] = p_0$, for any stopping rule.

If the observer's prior is incorrect, with $0 < \hat{p}_0 < p_0$, then her sequence of posteriors as sampling proceeds is the stochastic process $\{\hat{p}_k\}$ in Exercise 4.6. We saw there that this process is a submartingale. In this case part (i) of Theorem 4.3 implies that if the experimenter uses a stopping rule T, the process $\{\hat{p}_{k\wedge T}\}$ describing the observer's posteriors is still a submartingale, and it satisfies the inequalities in (4.9). If the sample size is uniformly bounded above by N, part (ii) puts bounds on the observer's final beliefs $\hat{p}_T$.

Now suppose the experimenter can choose the stopping rule and is interested in convincing the observer that the urn is likely to be of type A. That is, he wants to choose a stopping rule T that maximizes the observer's final posterior $\mathrm{E}[\hat{p}_T]$. Since $\{\hat{p}_k\}$ is a submartingale, part (ii) of Theorem 4.3 implies that the experimenter can do no better than to set $T = N$, always using the largest allowable sample. The idea behind this result is clear: since the observer's initial beliefs are biased downward, providing her with more information moves them, on average, further upward (closer to the true value).

If the observer's initial prior is biased in the other direction, if $p_0 < \hat{p}_0 < 1$, then the stochastic process $\{\hat{p}_k\}$ describing her posteriors is a supermartingale. In this case an analogous argument shows that an experimenter who wants to maximize $E[\hat{p}_T]$ should choose the stopping rule $T = 0$, giving the observer no information.

4.6. Optional Stopping Theorem, Extended

Part (ii) of Theorem 4.3 requires that the stopping time T be uniformly bounded. Here the result is extended to cases in which $T < \infty$, but there is no uniform upper bound on the stopping time. An example is then used to illustrate what can go wrong if a key assumption does not hold.

The main idea is as follows. Let $S_t \subseteq \Omega$ denote the set where the process has stopped by date t:

$$S_t = \{\omega \in \Omega : T(\omega) \le t\}.$$

Then the expected value of the stopped process can be written as the sum of two parts:

$$
\begin{aligned}
E\left[Z_0\right] &= E\left[Z_{T \wedge t}\right] \\
&= \int_\Omega Z_{T \wedge t}(\omega)dP(\omega) \\
&= \int_{S_t} Z_T(\omega)dP(\omega) + \int_{S_t^c} Z_t(\omega)dP(\omega), \quad \text{all } t,
\end{aligned}
$$

where the first line uses part (i) of Theorem 4.3. To insure that the expression in the last line converges to $E[Z_T]$ as $t \to \infty$, several restrictions are needed. First, the probability accounted for by the first term must converge to one: $\lim_{t \to \infty} P(S_t) = 1$. This holds if (and only if) $\Pr\{T < \infty\} = 1$. In addition, to insure that the first term has a well defined limit, the positive and negative parts of Z_T must have bounded integrals, that is, Z_T must be integrable. Finally, the second term must converge to zero as $t \to \infty$. The next result states these requirements more formally.

Theorem 4.4 (extension of optional stopping theorem). Let Z be a (sub) martingale on the filtered space $(\Omega, \mathbb{F}, P)$ and T a stopping time. If

$$\text{i.} \quad \Pr[T < \infty] = 1,$$

$$\text{ii.} \quad \mathrm{E}\left[|Z(T)|\right] < \infty,$$

$$\text{iii.} \quad \lim_{t \to \infty} \mathrm{E}\left[\left|Z(t)I_{\{T > t\}}\right|\right] = 0,$$

then

$$\mathrm{E}\left[Z(0)\right](\le) = \mathrm{E}\left[Z(T)\right].$$

See Appendix B for a proof.

The following example illustrates why condition (iii) is needed. Consider a gambler playing at fair odds in a game where the bet is \$1 in the first round and is doubled at each subsequent round. That is, at each round $k = 1, 2, \ldots$, the gambler wins or loses $X_k = \pm 2^{k-1}$, and the probability of winning is $1/2$. Let $Z_0 = 0$ and $Z_k = \sum_{i=1}^{k} X_i$, $k = 1, 2, \ldots$, so $\{Z_k\}$ is the sequence of his net gains. Clearly $\{Z_k\}$ is a martingale, and $\mathrm{E}[Z_k] = 0$, $k = 1, 2, \ldots$.

Suppose the gambler uses the following system to try to win: he stops playing when his net gain is positive and continues otherwise. Under this stopping rule T the evolution of his net wealth $\{Z_{T \wedge k}\}$ is described by

	0	1	2	3	4	5	6
1		1/2	3/4	7/8	15/16	31/32	63/64
0	1						
−1		1/2					
−3			1/4				
−7				1/8			
−15					1/16		
−31						1/32	. . .

Each column represents a time period $k = 0, 1, 2, \ldots$, and each row represents a possible value for $Z_{T \wedge k} \in \{1, 0, -1, -3, -7, \ldots, 1 - 2^k, \ldots\}$. The entries in column k constitute the probability vector for the outcomes $Z_{T \wedge k}$. Notice that the stopped process $\{Z_{T \wedge k}\}$ satisfies

$$\mathrm{E}\left[Z_{T \wedge k}\right] = 0 = Z_0, \quad k = 0, 1, 2, \ldots,$$

in accord with part (i) of Theorem 4.3.

It is clear that for any $\varepsilon > 0$ there exists $n > 1$ such that $\Pr\{T > n\} < \varepsilon$. Hence $\Pr\{T < \infty\} = 1$. In addition, there is no problem integrating the constant function Z_T. But clearly

$$\mathrm{E}\left[Z_T\right] = 1 \neq 0 = Z_0.$$

To see why Theorem 4.4 does not apply, note that the gambler's total loss conditional on continued betting, multiplied by the probability that he is still betting, is

$$\mathrm{E}\left[Z_k I_{\{T>k\}}\right] = \frac{1}{2^k} \sum_{i=1}^{k} X_i$$

$$= 2^{-k} \left[-2^0 - 2^1 - \cdots - 2^{k-1}\right]$$

$$= -\sum_{i=1}^{k} 2^{-i} \to -1 \quad \text{as } k \to \infty.$$

(This fact can also be read directly from the table above.) Hence condition (iii) of Theorem 4.4 does not hold: the gambler's losses increase fast enough to offset the declining probability that he is still playing.

Exercise 4.9. Let $\{X_i\}_{i=1}^{\infty}$ be a sequence of random variables, each taking values ± 1 with equal probability. Let $Z_k = \sum_{i=1}^{k} X_i$ be the sequence of their partial sums. Fix an integer $M \geq 1$, and let T be the stopping time defined as the first time the process reaches M. By Theorem 4.3 the stopped process $Z_{T \wedge k}$ satisfies

$$0 = Z_0 = \mathrm{E}\left[Z_{T \wedge k}\right] = \mathrm{E}\left[Z_k\right], \quad \text{all } k \geq 0.$$

In addition, $\Pr\{T < \infty\} = 1$. But clearly

$$\mathrm{E}\left[Z_T\right] = M \neq 0 = \mathrm{E}\left[Z_0\right].$$

Evidently Theorem 4.4 does not apply.
    Show that $\{Z_k\}$ violates the condition

$$\lim_{k \to \infty} \mathrm{E}\left[\left|Z_k I_{\{T>k\}}\right|\right] = 0.$$

The next result is a further extension of the optional stopping results in Theorems 4.3 and 4.4. The new feature here is that the expectation is conditioned on the information at a stopping time rather than a fixed date.

Theorem 4.5. If $\{Z_k\}_{k=1}^n$ is a (sub)martingale, and τ_1, τ_2 are stopping times with $1 \le \tau_1 \le \tau_2 \le n$, then

$$\mathrm{E}\left[Z_{\tau_2} \mid \mathfrak{F}_{\tau_1}\right] (\ge) = Z_{\tau_1}.$$

For a proof see Billingsley (1995, Theorem 35.2). Theorem 4.5 is used to establish a preliminary result that in turn will be used to prove the martingale convergence theorem.

4.7. Martingale Convergence Theorem

The martingale convergence theorem is one of the most famous results for stochastic processes. It has a wide array of uses, so its fame is justified. In this section it is stated in a general form and proved for discrete time processes. A few of its implications are then discussed.

The proof draws on a preliminary result, a crossing property. If $\{Z_k\}_{k=1}^n$ is a submartingale, then in expectation it is nondecreasing. Fix any two numbers $\alpha < \beta$. An *upcrossing* occurs whenever the sample path rises from α to β. To count the upcrossings, define the sequence of stopping times $\{\tau_i\}$ as follows. For $i = 1$,

$$\tau_1 = \begin{cases} \min\{k \ge 1 : Z_k \le \alpha\}, & \text{if } Z_k \le \alpha, \text{ some } k \ge 1, \\ n, & \text{otherwise.} \end{cases}$$

Thereafter, if i is even,

$$\tau_i = \begin{cases} \min\{k > i - 1 : Z_k \ge \beta\}, & \text{if } Z_k \ge \beta, \text{ some } k > i - 1, \\ n, & \text{otherwise;} \end{cases}$$

and if i is odd,

$$\tau_i = \begin{cases} \min\{k > i - 1 : Z_k \le \alpha\}, & \text{if } Z_k \le \alpha, \text{ some } k > i - 1, \\ n, & \text{otherwise.} \end{cases}$$

Define M by $\tau_M = n$, and let U be the number of upcrossings. The broken line in Figure 4.1 depicts a sample path $Z_k(\omega)$ with two upcrossings. The small circles indicate the stopping times $\tau_i, i = 1, \dots, 6$.

The following result bounds the expected number of upcrossings.

Lemma 4.6. If $\{Z_k\}_{k=1}^n$ is a submartingale, then

$$\mathrm{E}\,[U] \le \frac{\mathrm{E}\left[|Z_n|\right] + |\alpha|}{\beta - \alpha}. \tag{4.11}$$

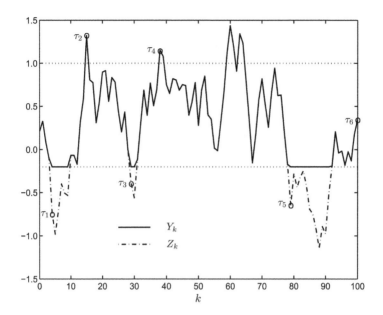

Figure 4.1. *Upcrossings, for $\alpha = -0.2$ and $\beta = 1.0$.*

Proof. Define $Y_k = \max\{\alpha, Z_k\}$. Figure 4.1 shows how Y_k, the solid line, alters the sample path for Z_k. Since Y_k is an increasing convex function of Z_k, by Theorem 4.1 the stochastic process $\{Y_k\}$ is also a submartingale. Moreover, $\{Y_k\}$ and $\{Z_k\}$ have the same stopping times $\{\tau_{i_k}\}$ and the same number of upcrossings, call it U, between α and β.

Note that

$$Y_n = Y_{\tau_1} + \sum_{i=2}^{M} \left[Y_{\tau_i} - Y_{\tau_{i-1}} \right].$$

Let Σ_e be the sum for i even, and Σ_o be the sum for i odd. Then take expectations and use the fact that $Y_{\tau_1} = \alpha$ to find that

$$\mathrm{E}\left[Y_n - \alpha \right] = \mathrm{E}\left[\Sigma_e \right] + \mathrm{E}\left[\Sigma_o \right].$$

Since Y_k is a submartingale and the τ_js are stopping times, Theorem 4.5 implies that

$$\mathrm{E}\left[\Sigma_o \right] = \mathrm{E}\left[\sum_{j=3,5,\ldots}^{M \text{ or } M-1} \left(Y_{\tau_j} - Y_{\tau_{j-1}} \right) \right] \geq 0.$$

The same holds for Σ_e, but something stronger is needed. The term Σ_e includes all the upcrossings plus, possibly, a remainder term. That is,

$$\Sigma_e \geq \begin{cases} (\beta - a)U + \left[Y_{\tau_M} - Y_{\tau_{M-1}}\right], & \text{if } M \text{ is even and } Y_{\tau_M} < \beta, \\ (\beta - a)U, & \text{otherwise.} \end{cases}$$

Since Y is a submartingale, $\mathrm{E}\left[Y_{\tau_M} - Y_{\tau_{M-1}} | Y_{\tau_{M-1}}\right] \geq 0$. Hence

$$\mathrm{E}\left[\Sigma_e\right] \geq (\beta - \alpha)\,\mathrm{E}\,[U],$$

and summing the two pieces gives

$$\mathrm{E}\left[|Y_n|\right] + |\alpha| \geq \mathrm{E}\left[Y_n - \alpha\right]$$
$$= \mathrm{E}\left[\Sigma_e\right] + \mathrm{E}\left[\Sigma_o\right]$$
$$\geq (\beta - a)\,\mathrm{E}\,[U]. \quad \blacksquare$$

Since Σ_o appears to be the sum of downcrossings, the conclusion that $\mathrm{E}[\Sigma_o] \geq 0$ may seem surprising. The idea is that if i is odd, having reached $Z_{\tau_{i-1}} \geq \beta$, there are two possibilities for τ_i. The process can fall back to α, or it can stay above α, in which case $\tau_i = \tau_M = n$. Since $\{Z_k\}$ is a submartingale, the expected increment, conditional on any state, is nonnegative. Hence conditional on $Z_{\tau_{i-1}}$, in expectation these two possibilities contribute a positive increment. In the sum Σ_o the positive contribution appears in the remainder terms, terms of the form $\left[Z_{\tau_M} - Z_{\tau_{M-1}}\right]$, which in expectation outweigh the others.

The final result is the famous martingale convergence theorem. It states that if Z is a submartingale and is bounded in a certain sense, then with probability one it converges to a random variable Z^*. Thus, the result has two parts. First, for a.e. $\omega \in \Omega$, the sample path $Z(t, \omega)$ converges pointwise. That is, there exists $Z^*(\omega) = \lim_{t \to \infty} Z(t, \omega)$. In addition, Z^* is integrable, so

$$\lim_{t \to \infty} \mathrm{E}\left[|Z_t - Z^*|\right] = 0.$$

Theorem 4.7 (Martingale convergence). Let Z be a submartingale with

$$\sup_{t \geq 0} \mathrm{E}\,[|Z(t)|] = D < +\infty.$$

Then $Z(t) \to Z^*$ with probability one, where Z^* is a random variable with $\mathrm{E}\left[|Z^*|\right] \leq D$.

Proof. (For discrete time) Let $\{Z_k\}$ be a submartingale and fix any $\alpha < \beta$. By Lemma 4.6 the expected number of upcrossings of $Z_1, \ldots, Z_n$, call it U_n, satisfies (4.11):

$$\mathrm{E}\left[U_n\right] \leq \frac{\mathrm{E}\left[|Z_n|\right] + |\alpha|}{\beta - \alpha}.$$

The random variable U_n is nondecreasing and is bounded above by $(D + |\alpha|)/(\beta - \alpha)$, so it follows from the monotone convergence theorem that $\lim_{n\to\infty} U_n$ is integrable, and consequently is finite-valued a.e.

For each ω, define

$$Z^{\mathrm{sup}}(\omega) = \lim_{k\to\infty} \sup \, Z_k(\omega),$$

$$Z_{\mathrm{inf}}(\omega) = \lim_{k\to\infty} \inf \, Z_k(\omega).$$

If $Z_{\mathrm{inf}}(\omega) < \alpha < \beta < Z^{\mathrm{sup}}(\omega)$, then $U_n(\omega)$ diverges as $n \to \infty$. Hence

$$P\left[Z_{\mathrm{inf}} < \alpha < \beta < Z^{\mathrm{sup}}\right] = 0.$$

But the set where $Z_{\mathrm{inf}} < Z^{\mathrm{sup}}$ can be written as

$$\left[Z_{\mathrm{inf}} < Z^{\mathrm{sup}}\right] = \bigcup \left[Z_{\mathrm{inf}} < \alpha < \beta < Z^{\mathrm{sup}}\right],$$

where the union is over all rational pairs $\alpha < \beta$. Since each set on the right side has probability zero, so does their sum. Hence $P\left[Z_{\mathrm{inf}} < Z^{\mathrm{sup}}\right] = 0$. That is, $P\left[Z_{\mathrm{inf}} = Z^{\mathrm{sup}}\right] = 1$. Call their common value Z^*. By Fatou's lemma

$$\mathrm{E}\left[|Z^*|\right] \leq \lim_{k\to\infty} \inf \, \mathrm{E}\left[|Z_k|\right] \leq D,$$

so Z^* is integrable. Hence Z^* is finite with probability one. ∎

It is essential for the result that $\mathrm{E}\left[|Z_k|\right]$ be bounded by some finite D. To see why, consider the following example. Let $\{X_i\}$ be a sequence of i.i.d. random variables taking values ± 1 with equal probability, and let $Z_k = \sum_{i=1}^k X_i$ be the sequence of partial sums. Clearly $\{Z_k\}$ is a martingale. For large k, the distribution of Z_k is well approximated by a normal with mean zero and a standard deviation that grows like $\sqrt{k}$. Hence $Z_k \nrightarrow Z^*$, for any Z^*. Theorem 4.7 does not apply here: for any finite D there exists k sufficiently large so that $\mathrm{E}\left[|Z_k|\right] > D$.

Exercise 4.10.   For each of the following examples either show that Theorem 4.7 applies and calculate Z^*, or explain why Theorem 4.7 does not apply.

   (a) Let $\{Z_k\} = \{p_k\}$ be the sequence of posteriors for the Bayesian learning problem in Example 3, where the prior p_0 is correct.
   (b) Let $\{Z_k\} = \{\hat{p}_k\}$ be the sequence of posteriors for the Bayesian learning problem in Exercise 4.6, where the prior $\hat{p}_0 < p_0$ is too low.
   (c) Let $\{Z_k\}$ be the sequence of net gains defined in Section 4.6, for the gambler who stops if he wins and doubles his bet if he loses.
   (d) Let $Z = M(t; \rho)$ be a Wald martingale of the type defined in (4.4).

Notes

Karlin and Taylor (1975, Chapters 6 and 7) provide an excellent introductory discussion of stopping times and martingales, with many helpful examples. Breiman (1968) and Billingsley (1995) also have excellent discussions, including treatments of the martingale convergence theorem and various forms of the optional stopping theorem.

5

Useful Formulas
for Brownian Motions

IN SITUATIONS WHERE action involves a fixed cost, optimal policies have the property that control is exercised only occasionally. Specifically, optimal policies involve taking action when a state variable reaches an appropriately chosen threshold value. In this chapter methods are developed for analyzing models of this type.

To fix ideas, consider the following example. Suppose the profit flow $g(X)$ of a firm depends on its relative price $X = p - \overline{p}$, where p is the firm's own price and $\overline{p}$ is an aggregate price index, both in log form. Assume that $\overline{p}$ evolves as a Brownian motion. Then in the absence of action by the firm X also evolves as a Brownian motion, with a drift of opposite sign. But at any time the firm also has the option of changing its nominal price p, altering X by a discrete amount. Suppose that the firm adopts a policy of doing so when the relative price reaches either of two critical thresholds, a lower value b or an upper value B. Assume the initial condition $X(0) = x$ lies between the two thresholds, and let $v(x)$ denote the expected discounted return from following the stated policy, discounted at a constant rate r, conditional on the initial state.

Define the stopping time $T = T(b) \wedge T(B)$ as the first time the stochastic process X reaches b or B. The firm's policy involves doing nothing before T, and at T taking an action that may depend on whether b or B has been reached. Hence $v(x)$ can be written as the sum of three terms:

$v(x) = $ expected returns over $[0, T)$

$\qquad +$ expected returns over $[T, +\infty)$ if b is reached before B

$\qquad +$ expected returns over $[T, +\infty)$ if B is reached before b.

Recall from Theorem 3.7 that for a function $f(\cdot)$ that has a Brownian motion X as its argument, the integral of $e^{-rt} f(X)$ along any sample path

75

up to a stopping time T can be written as an integral over states, where the latter integral uses the discounted local time $\hat{\ell}$ as a weighting function. For the first term in $v(x)$ above, the expectation of $\hat{\ell}$ is needed. For the discussion here it is useful to indicate the initial condition for the process X. Let $\hat{\ell}(\xi; x, T; r)$ denote the discounted local time at level ξ, given the initial state x. In addition the stopping times of interest here always take the form $T = T(b) \wedge T(B)$, so it is convenient to write $\mathrm{E}[\hat{\ell}]$ in terms of b and B rather than T. For any $b < B$ let

$$\hat{L}(\xi; x, b, B; r) \equiv \mathrm{E}\left[\hat{\ell}(\xi; x, T(b) \wedge T(B); r)\right], \quad \xi, x \in (b, B), \quad (5.1)$$

denote the expected local time at ξ before either threshold b or B is reached, given the initial state x.

Let $\mathrm{E}_x[\cdot]$ and $\mathrm{Pr}_x[\cdot]$ denote expectations and probabilities conditional on the initial state x, and let $w(x, b, B)$ denote the first term in $v(x)$, the expected returns before T. Then w can be written in terms of $\hat{L}$:

$$w(x, b, B) \equiv \mathrm{E}_x\left[\int_0^T e^{-rt} g(X(t)) dt\right] \tag{5.2}$$

$$= \mathrm{E}\left[\int_{\mathbf{R}} \hat{\ell}(\xi; x, T; r)\, g(\xi)\, d\xi\right]$$

$$= \int_b^B \hat{L}(\xi; x, b, B; r)\, g(\xi)\, d\xi.$$

For the second and third terms define

$$\psi(x, b, B) \equiv \mathrm{E}_x[e^{-rT} \mid X(T) = b]\,\mathrm{Pr}_x[X(T) = b]$$
$$\Psi(x, b, B) \equiv \mathrm{E}_x[e^{-rT} \mid X(T) = B]\,\mathrm{Pr}_x[X(T) = B] \tag{5.3}$$

Thus, $\psi(x, b, B)$ is the expected discounted value of an indicator function for the event of reaching b before B is reached, given the initial state x. The value $\Psi(x, b, B)$ has a similar interpretation, with the roles of b and B reversed.

The functions $\hat{L}$, ψ, and Ψ in (5.1) and (5.3) can be used to describe the expected discounted profits of the firm for arbitrary thresholds b and B. Consequently they can also be used to characterize the optimal policy—the thresholds and the value to which the relative price is adjusted—and the associated value function $v(x)$.

Probabilities and long-run averages can be characterized as well, by using an interest rate of zero in the expressions above. For example, setting $r = 0$ in (5.3) gives

$$\theta(x, b, B) \equiv \Pr_x[X(T) = b]$$
$$\Theta(x, b, B) \equiv \Pr_x[X(T) = B] \tag{5.4}$$

For an interpretation, consider a firm that operates over a long period with a fixed price adjustment policy. That is, for some S, b, B, with $b < S < B$, the firm always sets its relative price at $x = S$ when it makes an adjustment and always adjusts when the relative price reaches b or B. Then $\theta(S, b, B)$ is the fraction of adjustments from b in the long run, and $\Theta(S, b, B)$ is the fraction from B.

Other features of the long run can also be described. For example, to calculate the average length of time between adjustments consider the function

$$\tau(x, b, B) \equiv \mathrm{E}_x[T(b) \wedge T(B)] \tag{5.5}$$

the expected time until the next adjustment conditional on the current state x. For a firm using the adjustment policy described above, $\tau(S, b, B)$ is the average length of time between adjustments. Then note that setting $r = 0$ in (5.1) gives

$$L(\xi; x, b, B) \equiv \mathrm{E}\left[\ell(\xi; x, T(b) \wedge T(B)\right], \quad \xi, x \in (b, B),$$

the (undiscounted) expected local time at level ξ. Normalizing this function by the expected time between adjustments gives $L(\cdot; S, b, B)/\tau(S, b, B)$, a density function for the time the firm's price is at each level $\xi \in (b, B)$ in the long run.

In settings with a large number of such agents and idiosyncratic shocks, the undiscounted functions also describe cross-sectional averages. In particular, suppose that there is a continuum of agents with total mass one and that the shocks are i.i.d. across agents. (This assumption makes no sense for the shock in the menu cost model, but it is reasonable in other settings.) A setting of this type has a stationary cross-sectional distribution for the state variable, and the system converges to that distribution in the long run. Individual agents experience fluctuations as their own state rises and falls, but aggregates—the cross-sectional distribution of the state and the arrival rates at the two thresholds—are constant. That is, $\theta(S, b, B)$ and $\Theta(S, b, B)$ describe the fractions of adjustments at each threshold, $L(\cdot; S, b, B)/\tau(S, b, B)$ is the cross-sectional density for price, $1/\tau(S, b, B)$ is the aggregate adjustment rate, and so on.

In this chapter closed-form solutions are derived for the functions $\hat{L}$, ψ, Ψ, and so on, for Brownian motions and geometric Brownian motions. For more general diffusions, sharp characterizations of these functions are obtained. In Section 5.1 conditions are provided under which the stopping time T is finite with probability one, and in Section 5.2 this result is used to apply the optional stopping theorem to Wald martingales associated with X. In Section 5.3 the resulting relationship is used to obtain solutions for ψ, Ψ, θ, and Θ, and properties of those functions are developed.

In Section 5.4 a different approach is developed for Brownian motions, one that involves analyzing ordinary differential equations (ODEs) of a certain form. In Section 5.5 the ODE is solved for $r = 0$ to obtain L, θ, Θ, and τ, and in Section 5.6 it is solved for $r > 0$ to obtain ψ, Ψ, and $\hat{L}$. In Sections 5.7–5.9 the argument is extended to cover general diffusions, including geometric Brownian motions and Ornstein-Uhlenbeck processes. For the former closed-form solutions are obtained.

5.1. Stopping Times Defined by Thresholds

Let X be a Brownian motion with parameters (μ, σ^2) and finite initial value $X(0) = x$, and let b, B be threshold values satisfying $-\infty \le b \le x \le B \le +\infty$. As above, let E_x and Pr_x denote expectations and probabilities conditional on the initial value x. In this section conditions are described under which the stopping time $T = T(b) \wedge T(B)$ is finite with probability one.

The following assumption, which puts restrictions on b, B, and σ^2 for any μ is needed for the result.

Assumption 5.1.

    i. If $\mu > 0$, then $B < \infty$;
    ii. if $\mu < 0$, then $b > -\infty$;
    iii. if $\mu = 0$, then $\sigma^2 > 0$ and either $B < \infty$, or $b > -\infty$, or both.

The logic behind these restrictions is as follows. Suppose the drift is positive, $\mu > 0$. As $b \to -\infty$ with B fixed, the probability that the lower threshold is reached first goes to zero, but the probability that the upper threshold is reached approaches unity. Hence T is finite with probability one. Moreover, the argument applies even if $\sigma^2 = 0$. However, if $B = +\infty$ with b finite, there are outcome paths for which b is never reached, so $T = \infty$ with positive probability. An analogous argument applies for $\mu < 0$ with b and B reversed.

If $\mu = 0$, clearly the variance σ^2 must be strictly positive. Thus, limits as $\sigma^2 \downarrow 0$ are well behaved if and only if $\mu \ne 0$. With $\mu = 0$ it suffices if one threshold is finite.

Theorem 5.1. Let X be a (μ, σ^2) Brownian motion; μ, σ^2, b, B satisfy Assumption 5.1; the initial condition x satisfy $b \le x \le B$; and T be the stopping time $T = T(b) \wedge T(B)$. Then $\Pr_x [T < \infty] = 1$.

Proof. If $\mu > 0$ then $B < \infty$, so

$$\Pr_x[T > t] \le \Pr_x[X(t) < B] \quad \text{all } t \ge 0.$$

If $\sigma = 0$, the right side is zero for all $t > (B - x)/\mu$. If $\sigma > 0$,

$$\Pr_x[X(t) < B] = F_N(B; x + \mu t, \sigma^2 t),$$

where $F_N(\cdot; m, s^2)$ denotes the c.d.f. for a normal distribution with parameters (m, s^2). Since $\mu > 0$, the term on the right goes to zero as $t \to \infty$.

If $\mu < 0$ then $b > -\infty$, and a symmetric argument applies.

If $\mu = 0$ then $\sigma^2 > 0$, and $|b| < \infty$, $|B| < \infty$, or both. Suppose both thresholds are finite. Then

$$\Pr_x[T > t] \le \Pr_x[b < X(t) < B]$$

$$= F_N(B; x, \sigma^2 t) - F_N(b; x, \sigma^2 t).$$

Since $\sigma^2 > 0$, the right side goes to zero as $t \to \infty$.

Suppose $|B| < \infty$ and $b = -\infty$. As will be shown in Section 5.3, for any finite b and $T = T(b) \wedge T(B)$,

$$\Pr_x [X(T) = B] = \frac{x - b}{B - b}.$$

As $b \to -\infty$ this probability goes to one. Hence $\Pr_x[T < \infty] = 1$ for $b = -\infty$. A similar argument hold if $|b| < \infty$. ∎

5.2. Expected Values for Wald Martingales

Recall from Chapter 4 that for any $\rho \ne 0$ and

$$q(\rho) \equiv \rho\mu + \tfrac{1}{2}(\rho\sigma)^2, \tag{5.6}$$

the stochastic process

$$M(t; \rho) \equiv \exp\{\rho X(t) - q(\rho)t\}, \quad \text{all } t, \tag{5.7}$$

is a *Wald martingale* with parameter ρ. For $\rho = 0$ let

$$M(t; 0) \equiv \lim_{\rho \downarrow 0} \frac{1}{\rho}[M(t; \rho) - 1]$$

$$= X(t) - \mu t, \quad \text{all } t. \tag{5.8}$$

In economic applications a discount rate $r \geq 0$ is typically given, and the issue is to find values ρ for which $q(\rho) = r$. From (5.6), these values are roots of the quadratic

$$\tfrac{1}{2}\sigma^2 R^2 + \mu R - r = 0. \tag{5.9}$$

If $\sigma^2 > 0$, these roots are

$$R_1 = \frac{-\mu - J}{\sigma^2} \leq 0, \qquad R_2 = \frac{-\mu + J}{\sigma^2} \geq 0, \tag{5.10}$$

where

$$J \equiv \left(\mu^2 + 2r\sigma^2\right)^{1/2} \geq |\mu|. \tag{5.11}$$

The associated Wald martingale is then given by (5.7) and (5.8) as $R_i \neq 0$ or $R_i = 0$. There are three cases:

  i. if $r > 0$, the roots are of opposite sign, $R_1 < 0 < R_2$;
  ii. if $r = 0$ and $\mu \neq 0$, the roots are $R_i = -2\mu/\sigma^2$ and $R_j = 0$, with the allocation depending on the sign of μ; and
  iii. if $r = 0$ and $\mu = 0$, then $R_1 = R_2 = 0$ is a repeated root.

If $\sigma^2 = 0$, then (5.9) has one root, $R = r/\mu$. Corresponding to this fact, one root in (5.10) converges to a finite limit as $\sigma \downarrow 0$, and the other diverges. Hence for $\sigma^2 = 0$,

$$R_1 = \frac{r}{\mu} \leq 0, \text{ and } R_2 \text{ is undefined,} \quad \text{if } \mu < 0,$$

$$R_2 = \frac{r}{\mu} \geq 0, \text{ and } R_1 \text{ is undefined,} \quad \text{if } \mu > 0. \tag{5.12}$$

(If $\sigma^2 = \mu = 0$, a case excluded by Assumption 5.1, then (5.9) has no solution. Correspondingly, for $\mu = 0$ both of the roots in (5.10) diverge as $\sigma \downarrow 0$.)

Notice that the roots depend on r, μ, and σ^2 only through their ratios. Since changing the time unit—for example, measuring time in months rather than years—requires proportional changes in (μ, σ^2, r), such a change leaves the roots unaltered.

Exercise 5.1. Describe the effect on $|R_1|$, $|R_2|$, and $R_2 - R_1$ of changes in r, μ, and σ^2.

The next result shows that if both b and B are finite then the optional stopping theorem applies to M. The assumption that both thresholds are finite is strong, but it simplifies the proof. Cases with $b = -\infty$ or $B = +\infty$ are treated in Sections 5.4–5.7 with a different approach.

Theorem 5.2. Let the hypotheses of Theorem 5.1 hold, and in addition assume $|b|, |B| < \infty$. Then

$$\mathrm{E}_x \left[M(T; R_i) \right] = M(0; R_i) \tag{5.13}$$

in the following cases:

    a. if $\sigma^2 > 0, r > 0$, and R_i, $i = 1, 2$, are as defined in (5.10);
    b. if $\sigma^2 > 0, r = 0$, and $R_i = -2\mu/\sigma^2$;
    c. if $\sigma^2 = 0, r \geq 0$, and $R_i = r/\mu$.

Proof. It has been shown already that M is a martingale and T is a stopping time, so it suffices to show that the hypotheses of Theorem 4.4 hold:

    i. $\Pr\{T < \infty\} = 1$,
    ii. $\mathrm{E}_x \left[|M(T; R_i)| \right] < \infty$,
    iii. $\lim_{t\to\infty} \mathrm{E}_x \left[|M(t; R_i)| \, I_{\{T > t\}} \right] = 0$.

Theorem 5.1 establishes (i). For the other hypotheses there are several cases.

If $\sigma^2 = 0$ then Assumption 5.1 requires $\mu \neq 0$. $X(t)$ is deterministic, $M(t; R_i) = x$ is constant, and (ii)–(iii) follow immediately.

If $\sigma^2 > 0$ and $R_i \neq 0$, let

$$A_i = \max \left\{ e^{R_i b}, e^{R_i B} \right\}.$$

Then

$$\left| M(T; R_i) \right| \leq A_i e^{-rT} \leq A_i, \quad \text{all } \omega,$$

so (ii) holds. In addition $\left| M(t; R_i) \right| < A_i$, all $t < T$, so

$$\lim_{t\to\infty} \mathrm{E}_x \left[|M(t; R_i)| \, I_{\{T > t\}} \right] \leq A_i \lim_{t\to\infty} \Pr_x \left[T > t \right]$$

$$= 0,$$

where the second line uses Theorem 5.1. Hence (iii) holds.

If $\sigma^2 > 0$ and $R_i = 0$, then $\mu = 0$. Hence $M(t; 0) = X(t)$, and

$$|M(T; 0)| = |X(T)| \leq A_i = \max\{|b|, |B|\}, \quad \text{all } \omega,$$

so (ii) holds. In addition $|M(t; 0)| < A_i$, all $t < T$, and the argument for (iii) is as before. ∎

5.3. The Functions ψ and Ψ

Recall the functions $\psi(x, b, B; r)$ and $\Psi(x, b, B; r)$ defined in (5.3), the expected discounted values of indicator functions for reaching the lower threshold before the upper one (ψ) and the reverse (Ψ), and the functions $\theta(x, b, B)$ and $\Theta(x, b, B)$, the probabilities of these events, respectively. In this section explicit formulas are derived for these functions, and some of their properties are established. The proofs here use Theorem 5.2, so they require $|b|, |B| < \infty$. The results hold even without that assumption, however, as will be seen later.

The following result characterizes ψ and Ψ for $r > 0$.

Proposition 5.3. Let X be a (μ, σ^2) Brownian motion with initial condition $x \in [b, B]$, T be the stopping time $T = T(b) \wedge T(B)$, and $r > 0$. If $\sigma^2 > 0$, then

$$\psi(x, b, B; r) = \frac{e^{R_1 x} e^{R_2 B} - e^{R_2 x} e^{R_1 B}}{e^{R_1 b} e^{R_2 B} - e^{R_2 b} e^{R_1 B}},$$

$$\Psi(x, b, B; r) = \frac{e^{R_1 b} e^{R_2 x} - e^{R_2 b} e^{R_1 x}}{e^{R_1 b} e^{R_2 B} - e^{R_2 b} e^{R_1 B}},$$

(5.14)

where R_1 and R_2 are defined in (5.10).

If $\sigma^2 = 0$ and $\mu \neq 0$, then

$$\psi(x, b, B; r) = 0, \qquad \Psi(x, b, B; r) = e^{R_2(x-B)}, \quad \text{if } \mu > 0,$$

$$\psi(x, b, B; r) = e^{R_1(x-b)}, \quad \Psi(x, b, B; r) = 0, \qquad \text{if } \mu < 0,$$

where R_1 and R_2 are defined in (5.12).

Proof. Suppose $\sigma^2 > 0$. Since $r > 0$, the roots in (5.10) are $R_1 < 0 < R_2$. Let $M(t; R_i)$, $i = 1, 2$, be as in (5.7). Theorem 5.2 implies (5.13) holds for $i = 1, 2$. Break the expression on the left in (5.13) into two parts corresponding to stops at the lower and upper thresholds, and substitute from (5.7) to find that

$$e^{R_i x} = \mathrm{E}_x \left[M(T; R_i) \mid X(T) = b \right] \mathrm{Pr}_x \left[X(T) = b \right]$$

$$+ \mathrm{E}_x \left[M(T; R_i) \mid X(T) = B \right] \mathrm{Pr}_x \left[X(T) = B \right]$$

$$= \mathrm{E}_x \left[\exp \left\{ R_i X(T) - q(R_i) T \right\} \mid X(T) = b \right] \mathrm{Pr}_x \left[X(T) = b \right]$$

$$+ \mathrm{E}_x \left[\exp \left\{ R_i X(T) - q(R_i) T \right\} \mid X(T) = B \right] \mathrm{Pr}_x \left[X(T) = B \right]$$

$$= e^{R_i b} \mathrm{E}_x \left[e^{-rT} \mid X(T) = b \right] \mathrm{Pr}_x \left[X(T) = b \right]$$

$$+ e^{R_i B} \mathrm{E}_x \left[e^{-rT} \mid X(T) = B \right] \mathrm{Pr}_x \left[X(T) = B \right]$$

$$= e^{R_i b} \psi(x, b, B) + e^{R_i B} \Psi(x, b, B), \quad i = 1, 2, x \in [b, B]. \tag{5.15}$$

This pair of linear equations in $\psi(x)$ and $\Psi(x)$ has the solution in (5.14).

If $\sigma^2 = 0$, let R_1 or R_2 be the one root in (5.12). Apply the argument above to the one (relevant) threshold to get the solution. ∎

Figure 5.1 displays the function $\psi(x, b, B)$ for $b = 0$, $B = 2$, $r = 0.05$, $\mu = 0.2$, and $\sigma = 1$, and also shows the effect of changes in the parameters r, μ, and σ. The function is in all cases decreasing, with $\psi(b) = 1$ and

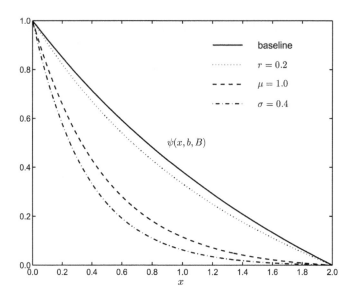

Figure 5.1. *The expected discounted indicator for $T = T(b)$, for $b = 0$ and $B = 2$. The baseline parameter values are $r = 0.05$, $\mu = 0.2$, and $\sigma = 1$.*

$\psi(B) = 0$. Notice that parameter changes alter $\psi(x)$ through three channels: by changing the probability that b is reached before B, by changing the time elapsed before b is reached, and by changing the discounting before b is reached. An increase in the interest rate r bends the curve downward by increasing the discounting. An increase in μ reduces the probability that the lower threshold is reached first, and on paths where b is still reached first, it increases the time. A reduction in σ has similar effects.

For $r = 0$, the functions ψ and Ψ are simply the probabilities that the lower and upper thresholds are reached first, the functions $\theta(x, b, B)$ and $\Theta(x, b, B)$ defined in (5.4). An analogous argument provides closed forms for these functions.

Proposition 5.4. Let X be a (μ, σ^2) Brownian motion with initial condition $x \in [b, B]$, and let T be the stopping time $T = T(b) \wedge T(B)$. If $\sigma^2 > 0$, then

$$\theta(x, b, B) = \frac{e^{-\delta B} - e^{-\delta x}}{e^{-\delta B} - e^{-\delta b}},$$

$$\Theta(x, b, B) = \frac{e^{-\delta x} - e^{-\delta b}}{e^{-\delta B} - e^{-\delta b}}, \quad \text{if } \mu \neq 0, \tag{5.16}$$

where $\delta \equiv 2\mu/\sigma^2$, and

$$\theta(x, b, B) = \frac{B - x}{B - b},$$

$$\Theta(x, b, B) = \frac{x - b}{B - b}, \quad \text{if } \mu = 0.$$

If $\sigma^2 = 0$ and $\mu \neq 0$, then

$$\theta(x, b, B) = 0, \quad \Theta(x, b, B) = 1, \quad \text{if } \mu > 0,$$

$$\theta(x, b, B) = 1, \quad \Theta(x, b, B) = 0, \quad \text{if } \mu < 0.$$

Proof. In all cases Theorem 5.1 implies

$$1 = \theta(x, b, B) + \Theta(x, b, B). \tag{5.17}$$

If $\sigma^2 = 0$, the result is immediate. If $\sigma^2 > 0$, recall that for $r = 0$ the roots in (5.10) are $R_i = -\delta$ and $R_j = 0$. Theorem 5.2 applies to the root $R_i = -\delta$, so

$$e^{-\delta x} = e^{-\delta b}\theta(x, b, B) + e^{-\delta B}\Theta(x, b, B), \quad \text{if } \mu \neq 0,$$

$$x = b\theta(x, b, B) + B\Theta(x, b, B), \quad \text{if } \mu = 0.$$

This equation and (5.17) are a linear pair whose solution is in (5.16). ∎

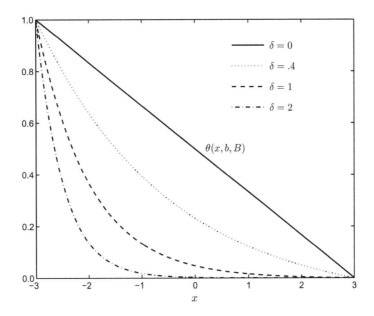

Figure 5.2. *The probability that* $T = T(b)$, *for* $b = -3$, $B = 3$, *and various* $\delta = 2\mu/\sigma$.

Figure 5.2 displays the function $\theta(x, b, B)$ for $b = -3$, $B = +3$, and various values for δ. The function is decreasing, with $\theta(b) = 1$ and $\theta(B) = 0$. For $\delta = 0$ the function is linear. Positive values for δ bow the function ever more strongly downward, and negative values (not shown) bow it upward. The function $\Theta(x, b, B) = 1 - \theta(x, b, B)$ is the complement of the one displayed.

The functions ψ and Ψ have several important properties. All of these hold for $r = 0$, so θ and Θ have these properties as well. First, notice that they can be written in terms of just the differences $(x - b)$ and $(x - B)$ (and their difference, $(B - b)$):

$$\psi(x, b, B) = \frac{e^{R_1(x-B)} - e^{R_2(x-B)}}{e^{R_1(b-B)} - e^{R_2(b-B)}},$$

$$\Psi(x, b, B) = \frac{e^{R_1(x-b)} - e^{R_2(x-b)}}{e^{R_1(B-b)} - e^{R_2(B-b)}}, \quad x \in [b, B]. \tag{5.18}$$

Since X is a Brownian motion, its increments do not depend on its current level, so translating x, b, and B leaves ψ and Ψ unchanged. Thus, it is clear from (5.18) that

$$\psi_b + \psi_x + \psi_B = 0, \quad \Psi_b + \Psi_x + \Psi_B = 0. \tag{5.19}$$

Next, note that $\psi_b(x)$ is the effect of an increase in the threshold b on the expected discounted value of an indicator function for reaching the threshold b before B is reached, given the initial state x. Proposition 5.5 shows that $\psi_b(x)$ is equal to the effect of the change conditional on arriving at b, $\psi_b(b)$, multiplied by the conditioning factor $\psi(x)$, which adjusts for the probability that this event occurs and the appropriate discounting. It also shows that conditional on $x = b$, increasing x and b together has no effect on ψ. Similar conclusions hold for Ψ and at B.

Proposition 5.5. For any $r \geq 0$, the functions ψ and Ψ satisfy

$$\psi_b(x) = \psi(x)\psi_b(b), \quad \Psi_b(x) = \psi(x)\Psi_b(b),$$

$$\psi_B(x) = \Psi(x)\psi_B(B), \quad \Psi_B(x) = \Psi(x)\Psi_B(B),$$

$$\psi_b(b) + \psi_x(b) = 0, \quad \Psi_b(b) + \Psi_x(b) = 0,$$

$$\psi_B(B) + \psi_x(B) = 0, \quad \Psi_B(B) + \Psi_x(B) = 0, \quad x \in (b, B).$$

Proof. Suppose $r > 0$ and consider the claims for ψ, those in the first column. The first follows immediately from (5.14) or (5.18). For the second note that

$$\psi(x, b, B) = \frac{e^{R_1 x} e^{(R_2 - R_1)B} - e^{R_2 x}}{e^{R_1 b} e^{(R_2 - R_1)B} - e^{R_2 b}},$$

so

$$\psi_B(x) = \frac{(R_2 - R_1) e^{(R_2 - R_1)B}}{e^{R_1 b} e^{(R_2 - R_1)B} - e^{R_2 b}} \left[e^{R_1 x} - \psi(x)e^{R_1 b} \right].$$

Since $\psi(B) = 0$, it follows that

$$\psi_B(B) = \frac{(R_2 - R_1) e^{R_2 B}}{e^{R_1 b} e^{(R_2 - R_1)B} - e^{R_2 b}}.$$

Using the latter expression and (5.15) in the expression for $\psi_B(x)$ establishes the second claim. Since $\psi(b) = 1$, it follows from the expression above that $\psi_B(b) = 0$. Hence the third claim follows from (5.19). A similar argument establishes the fourth. Analogous arguments establish the claims for Ψ and those when $r = 0$. ∎

The arguments in this section apply when the underlying process is a Brownian motion, and similar arguments can be made for a geometric

Brownian motion. But for more general diffusions a different approach is needed, and cases with only one threshold are also treated more easily by this second approach. This approach is developed for Brownian motions in Sections 5.4–5.6, where it is used to derive the functions τ, L, and $\hat{L}$, and is extended to general diffusions in Sections 5.7–5.9.

5.4. ODEs for Brownian Motions

Let X be as in Section 5.3 and consider the function $\psi(x)$. Fix an initial state in the interior of the interval of interest, $x \in (b, B)$, and consider an increment of time $h > 0$ sufficiently small so that the probability of reaching b or B is negligible. Then

$$\psi(x) \approx e^{-rh} E_x \left[\psi(X(h)) \right], \quad x \in (b, B),$$

where $X(h)$ is the value of the state variable at date h. Use Ito's lemma and the approximation $e^{rh} \approx (1 + rh)$ to find that

$$(1 + rh)\, \psi(x) \approx E_x \left[\psi(x) + \psi'(x)\Delta X + \tfrac{1}{2}\psi''(x)\, (\Delta X)^2 \right]$$

$$\approx \psi(x) + \psi'(x)\mu h + \tfrac{1}{2}\psi''(x)\sigma^2 h,$$

where $\Delta X = X(h) - x$ denotes the (random) increment to the state over the time increment h. The approximation is arbitrarily good as $h \to 0$, so

$$r\psi(x) = \mu\psi'(x) + \tfrac{1}{2}\sigma^2\psi''(x), \quad x \in (b, B).$$

The boundary conditions are obviously $\psi(b) = 1$ and $\psi(B) = 0$. Use this argument with $r = 0$ for $\theta(x)$, and use a similar construction with the boundary conditions reversed for $\Psi(x)$ and $\Theta(x)$.

For the function $w(x)$ defined in (5.2) an analogous argument establishes that

$$w(x) \approx g(x)h + \frac{1}{1+rh} \left[w(x) + w'(x)\mu h + \tfrac{1}{2}w''(x)\sigma^2 h \right],$$

so the relevant ODE is

$$rw(x) = g(x) + \mu w'(x) + \tfrac{1}{2}\sigma^2 w''(x), \quad x \in (b, B).$$

Clearly the boundary conditions are $w(b) = w(B) = 0$. For $r = 0$ and $g(x) = 1$, $w(x)$ is the expected value of the stopping time, the function

$$\tau(x, b, B) \equiv E_x \left[T(b) \wedge T(B) \right]$$

defined in (5.5).

Thus, each example leads to an equation of the form

$$\tfrac{1}{2}\sigma^2 f''(x) + \mu f'(x) - rf(x) = -g(x), \quad x \in (b, B), \qquad (5.20)$$

where the function $g(x)$ is given. This equation, which is a second-order linear ODE with fixed coefficients, is called a Hamilton-Jacobi-Bellman equation. Equations of this type appear in many applications, with the solution depending on the function g and the boundary conditions.

If $\sigma^2 = 0$ and $\mu \neq 0$, this equation is first order, with solution

$$f(x)e^{-(r/\mu)x} = c_0 - \frac{1}{\mu}\int^x g(\xi)d\xi,$$

and if $\sigma^2 = \mu = 0$, the solution is $f(x) = g(x)/r$. The arguments in the rest of this chapter assume $\sigma^2 > 0$. It is also assumed throughout that g is piecewise continuous, so it can be integrated.

5.5. Solutions for Brownian Motions When $r = 0$

If $r = 0$, (5.20) can be written as a first-order equation in the function $\phi \equiv f'$,

$$\phi'(x) + \delta\phi(x) = -\frac{2g(x)}{\sigma^2}, \quad x \in (b, B),$$

where as before $\delta \equiv 2\mu/\sigma^2$. Clearly solutions have the form

$$\phi(x)e^{\delta x} = c_1 - \frac{2}{\sigma^2}\int^x g(\xi)e^{\delta\xi}d\xi.$$

Integrate again to obtain f, and find that if $r = 0$ any solution to (5.20) has the form

$$f(x) = c_0 + \int^x \left[e^{-\delta z}c_1 - \frac{2}{\sigma^2}\int^z g(\xi)e^{\delta(\xi-z)}d\xi \right] dz, \quad x \in [b, B]. \quad (5.21)$$

As usual, the lower limits of integration in (5.21) can be chosen for convenience, and the constants c_0 and c_1 are determined by boundary conditions.

Using b for both limits, reversing the order of integration, and using the boundary condition at b to eliminate c_0 gives

$$f(x) = f(b) - \frac{1}{\delta}\left(e^{-\delta x} - e^{-\delta b}\right)c_1 \tag{5.22}$$

$$-\frac{1}{\mu}\int_b^x \left[1 - e^{\delta(\xi - x)}\right]g(\xi)d\xi, \qquad\qquad \text{if } \mu \neq 0,$$

$$f(x) = f(b) + (x - b)\,c_1 - \frac{2}{\sigma^2}\int_b^x (x - \xi)\,g(\xi)d\xi, \quad \text{if } \mu = 0,$$

where c_1 is determined by the boundary condition at B. Reversing the roles of b and B produces similar expressions.

For the function θ use $g(\cdot) \equiv 0$ and the boundary conditions $\theta(b) = 1$ and $\theta(B) = 0$. For Θ reverse the boundary conditions.

Exercise 5.2. Verify that the solutions for θ and Θ obtained from (5.22) agree with those in Proposition 5.4.

Notice that the argument here requires $\sigma^2 > 0$ but it does not require Assumption 5.1. The results must be interpreted carefully if Assumption 5.1 fails, however. For example, suppose $\mu > 0$. Then $\delta > 0$, and Assumption 5.1 allows $b = -\infty$ but not $B = +\infty$. Consider both cases. Since $\lim_{b \to -\infty} e^{-\delta b} = +\infty$, (5.16) implies

$$\lim_{b \to -\infty} \theta(x, b, B) = 0$$

$$\lim_{b \to -\infty} \Theta(x, b, B) = 1, \quad \text{if } \mu > 0,$$

in agreement with Theorem 5.1. On the other hand $\lim_{B \to +\infty} e^{-\delta B} = 0$, so (5.16) implies

$$\lim_{B \to +\infty} \theta(x, b, B) = e^{-\delta(x - b)} > 0,$$

$$\lim_{B \to +\infty} \Theta(x, b, B) = 1 - e^{-\delta(x - b)} > 0, \quad \text{if } \mu > 0.$$

Here $\Theta(x, b, +\infty) > 0$ is the probability that the lower threshold is never reached. The situation is symmetric for $\mu < 0$. If $\mu = 0$ the probabilities go to zero and one.

For the function τ defined in (5.5) use $g(\cdot) \equiv 1$ and the boundary conditions $\tau(b) = \tau(B) = 0$ to obtain

$$\tau(x, b, B) = \frac{1}{\mu}\frac{e^{-\delta x}(B - b) - e^{-\delta b}(B - x) - e^{-\delta B}(x - b)}{e^{-\delta B} - e^{-\delta b}}, \quad \text{if } \mu \neq 0,$$

$$\tag{5.23}$$

$$\tau(x, b, B) = \frac{1}{\sigma^2}(B - x)(x - b), \qquad\qquad\qquad \text{if } \mu = 0.$$

Exercise 5.3.   Use (5.21) or (5.22) to obtain (5.23).

Again, this expression holds even if one of the thresholds diverges. For example, suppose the drift is positive. If the lower threshold diverges

$$\lim_{b \to -\infty} \tau(x) = \frac{1}{\mu}(B - x), \quad \text{if } \mu > 0,$$

so the expected first hitting time for B is finite. If the upper threshold diverges

$$\lim_{B \to +\infty} \tau(x) = \lim_{B \to +\infty} \frac{1}{\mu}\left[1 - e^{-\delta(x-b)}\right] B = +\infty, \quad \text{if } \mu > 0.$$

Since the probability that b is never reached is positive, the expected time is infinite. If $\mu = 0$ then $\tau(x) \to +\infty$ as either threshold diverges.

Figure 5.3 displays $\tau(x, b, B)$ for $b = -3$, $B = +3$, and various values for δ. In each case τ is hump shaped, and higher values for δ flatten the hump.

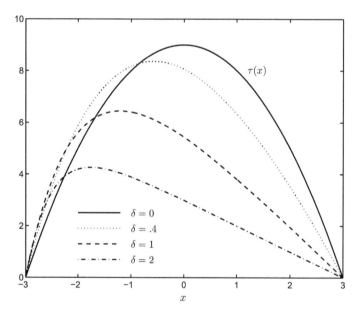

Figure 5.3. *The expected duration* $\mathrm{E}_x[T]$, *for* $b = -3$, $B = 3$, *and various* $\delta = 2\mu/\sigma$.

Finally, recall from Section 3.5 the function

$$m(A, T, \omega) = \int_0^T 1_A\,(X\,(s, \omega))\,ds, \quad \text{all } A \in \mathcal{B}, \ t \geq 0, \ \omega \in \Omega,$$

the undiscounted occupancy measure for the set A up to the stopping time T. Here we are interested in the expected value of this occupancy measure for sets of the form $[b, z]$, for the stopping time $T = T(b) \wedge T(B)$, conditional on the initial state $X(0) = x$. Call this function

$$M(z; x, b, B) \equiv \mathrm{E}_x \left[\int_0^{T(b) \wedge T(B)} 1_{[b,z]}(X(t))\,dt \right]$$

$$= \mathrm{E}_x[m([b, z], T(b) \wedge T(B))]$$

For fixed x, $M(\cdot\,; x, b, B)$ is like a c.d.f., with $M(B; x, b, B) = \tau(x, b, B)$.

To construct M, however, one must proceed the other way around, with a fixed function $g = 1_{[b,z]}$. That is, fix z, b, and B and apply (5.22) with $g = 1_{[b,z]}$ and the boundary conditions $M(z; b) = M(z; B) = 0$. Doing so gives

$$M(z; x) = \frac{1}{\mu}\Theta(x) \left[(z - b) - \frac{1}{\delta}e^{-\delta B}\left(e^{\delta z} - e^{\delta b}\right) \right]$$

$$- \frac{1}{\mu} \int_b^{\min\{x,z\}} \left[1 - e^{\delta(\xi - x)} \right]d\xi, \quad \text{if } \mu \neq 0,$$

$$M(z; x) = \frac{1}{\sigma^2}\Theta(x)\,(z - b)\,[(B - z) + (B - b)]$$

$$- \frac{2}{\sigma^2} \int_b^{\min\{x,z\}} (x - \xi)\,d\xi, \qquad \text{if } \mu = 0.$$

Note that M is continuous and is differentiable except at $z = x$.

The expected local time function $L(\cdot\,; x, b, B)$ is found by differentiating M with respect to z. Hence

$$L(z; x, b, B) = \frac{1}{\mu}\left\{ \Theta(x)\left[1 - e^{-\delta(B-z)} \right] - \left[1 - e^{\delta \min\{(z-x),0\}} \right] \right\}, \quad \mu \neq 0,$$

$$L(z; x, b, B) = \frac{2}{\sigma^2}\,[\Theta(x)\,(B - z) + \min\,\{(z - x), 0\}], \qquad \qquad \mu = 0.$$

Note that L is continuous but has a kink at $z = x$. Figure 5.4a displays $L(\cdot\,; x, b, B)$ for the thresholds $b = -3$ and $B = 3$ and initial conditions

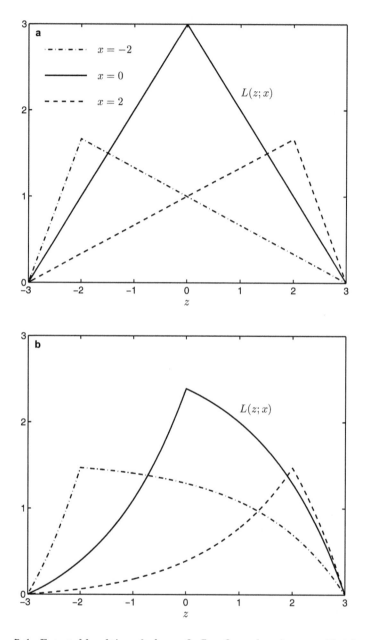

Figure 5.4. *Expected local time, for b = −3, B = 3, and various x, with (a) μ = 0, σ = 1, and (b) μ = 0.3, σ = 1.*

$x = -2, 0$, and 2, for the parameters $\mu = 0$ and $\sigma = 1$. Figure 5.4b is a similar plot for a positive drift parameter, $\mu = 0.3$.

5.6. Solutions for Brownian Motions When $r > 0$

Similar constructions can be used when the discount rate is positive, when $r > 0$. The main difference is that the differential equation (5.20) is second order and requires a slightly different argument. Recall that all the solutions of a second-order linear ODE can be written as

$$f(x) = f_P(x) + a_1 h_1(x) + a_1 h_1(x),$$

where f_P is any particular solution, h_1, h_2 are homogeneous solutions, and a_1, a_2 are constants determined by the boundary conditions.

    If $r > 0$ the homogeneous equation corresponding to (5.20) is

$$\tfrac{1}{2}\sigma^2 f''(x) + \mu f'(x) - rf(x) = 0.$$

Recall the constants R_1, R_2, and J defined in (5.10) and (5.11). With $r, \sigma^2 > 0$ they satisfy $R_1 < 0 < R_2$ and $J > 0$. Clearly the functions

$$f_i(x) = e^{R_i x}, \quad i = 1, 2,$$

are solutions of the homogeneous equation. In addition, since

$$\tfrac{1}{2}\sigma^2 \left(R_2 - R_1 \right) = J,$$

it follows that

$$f_P(x) = \frac{1}{J}\left[\int^x e^{R_1(x-z)} g(z)dz + \int_x e^{R_2(x-z)} g(z)dz \right]$$

is a particular solution of (5.20). Consequently, if $\sigma^2 > 0$ and $r > 0$, any solution of (5.20) has the form

$$f(x) = \frac{1}{J}\left[\int^x e^{R_1(x-z)} g(z)dz + \int_x e^{R_2(x-z)} g(z)dz \right] + c_1 e^{R_1 x} + c_2 e^{R_2 x}. \quad (5.24)$$

This equation can be solved—with different choices for g and the boundary conditions—to obtain ψ, Ψ, and $\hat{L}$.

    For the function ψ, use $g(x) \equiv 0$ and the boundary conditions $\psi(b) = 1$ and $\psi(B) = 0$. For Ψ, reverse the boundary conditions.

Exercise 5.4. Verify that the solutions obtained from (5.24) for ψ and Ψ agree with those in Proposition 5.3.

For the function $w(x, b, B)$ defined in (5.2), $g(\cdot)$ is arbitrary and the boundary conditions are $w(b) = w(B) = 0$. Use b and B for the limits of integration in (5.24) to find that

$$w(x) = \frac{1}{J} \left[\int_x^B e^{R_2(x-z)} g(z) dz + \int_b^x e^{R_1(x-z)} g(z) dz \right. \tag{5.25}$$

$$\left. - \Psi(x) \int_b^B e^{R_1(B-z)} g(z) dz - \psi(x) \int_b^B e^{R_2(b-z)} g(z) dz \right].$$

Since (5.25) holds for any return function g, the expected discounted local time function $\hat{L}(z; x, b, B; r)$ is

$$\hat{L}(z; x, b, B; r) = \frac{1}{J} \left[e^{R_i(x-z)} - \Psi(x) e^{R_1(B-z)} - \psi(x) e^{R_2(b-z)} \right],$$

$$\text{where } i = \begin{cases} 1, & \text{if } b \le z \le x, \\ 2, & \text{if } x \le z \le B. \end{cases}$$

Figure 5.5 shows the function $\hat{L}(z; x, b, B; r)$ for $x = 0$, $b = -4$, and $B = +4$, for the baseline parameters $r = 0.05$, $\mu = 0.3$, and $\sigma = 1$. It also shows the effects of parameter changes.

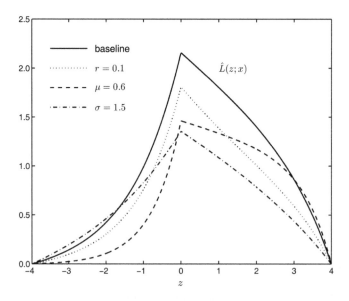

Figure 5.5. *Expected discounted local time, for $x = 0$, $b = -4$, and $B = 4$. The baseline parameter values are $r = 0.05$, $\mu = 0.3$, and $\sigma = 1$.*

The next result shows that the functions $\hat{L}$ and w have the properties established for ψ and Ψ in Proposition 5.5. The interpretation here is also the same. For example, the effect on w of a change in the threshold b, conditional on the current state x, is the product of $\psi(x)$ and the effect of the change conditional on the state b. That is, $w_b(x) = \psi(x)w_b(b)$. In addition, conditional on $x = b$, increasing x and b together has no effect on w. Similar conclusions hold for $\hat{L}(z; \cdot)$, for any z, and at B.

Proposition 5.6.   The functions $\hat{L}$ and w satisfy

$$\hat{L}_b(z; x) = \psi(x)\hat{L}_b(z; b), \quad \hat{L}_B(z; x) = \Psi(x)\hat{L}_B(z; B),$$

$$\hat{L}_x(z; b) + \hat{L}_b(z; b) = 0, \quad \hat{L}_x(z; B) + \hat{L}_B(z; B) = 0, \quad z, x \in [b, B],$$

and

$$w_b(x) = \psi(x)w_b(b), \quad w_B(x) = \Psi(x)w_B(B),$$

$$w_x(b) + w_b(b) = 0, \quad w_x(B) + w_B(B) = 0, \quad x \in [b, B].$$

Proof.   Since

$$\hat{L}_b(z; x) = -\frac{1}{J}\left[\Psi_b(x)e^{R_1(B-z)} + \psi_b(x)e^{R_2(b-z)} + R_2\psi(x)e^{R_2(b-z)}\right],$$

the first claim follows immediately from Proposition 5.5. And for $x = b < z$,

$$\hat{L}_x(z; b) = \frac{1}{J}\left[R_2 e^{R_2(b-z)} - \Psi_x(b)e^{R_1(B-z)} - \psi_x(b)e^{R_2(b-z)}\right],$$

so the second claim is also immediate from Proposition 5.5. Similar arguments hold at B.

The claims for w then follow immediately from the fact that

$$w(x, b, B) = \int_b^B \hat{L}(z; x, b, B)g(z)dz. \quad \blacksquare$$

Next consider expected discounted returns over an infinite time horizon. If $r > 0$ and $|g|$ is bounded, then the integral in (5.2) is bounded as $T \to \infty$. Taking the limit in (5.25) as $b \to -\infty$ and $B \to \infty$ gives

$$V_P(x) \equiv E_x\left[\int_0^\infty e^{-rt}g(X(t))\,dt\right]$$

$$= \frac{1}{J}\int_x^{+\infty} e^{R_2(x-z)}g(z)dz + \frac{1}{J}\int_{-\infty}^x e^{R_1(x-z)}g(z)dz. \quad (5.26)$$

Equation (5.26) provides an interpretation for the roots R_1 and R_2. Given the initial state x, states $z < x$ in (5.26) are weighted by $e^{R_1(x-z)}/J$ and states

$z > x$ by $e^{R_2(x-z)}/J$. Both exponential terms have negative signs, so $|R_1|$ and $|R_2|$ measure how sharply more distant states are downweighted. Of course, the weights satisfy

$$\frac{1}{J}\left[\int_0^\infty e^{-R_2\zeta}d\zeta + \int_{-\infty}^0 e^{-R_1\zeta}d\zeta\right] = \frac{1}{J}\left(\frac{1}{R_2} - \frac{1}{R_1}\right)$$

$$= \frac{1}{r},$$

reflecting the fact that for $g(x) \equiv 1$, (5.26) implies $V_P(x) = 1/r$.

Figure 5.6 displays $\hat{L}(z; 0, -\infty, +\infty) = e^{-R_i z}/J$ for the parameters $r = 0.05$, $\mu = 0.3$, and $\sigma = 1$. It also shows the effects of parameter changes. Note that, in accord with the results in Exercise 5.1,

— an increase in the interest rate r downweights all states, and the effect is greater for states farther from x;

— an increase in the variance σ^2 shifts weight away from states closer to x toward states that are farther away; and

— if $\mu > 0$, an increase in μ shifts weight away from states below x toward states above it.

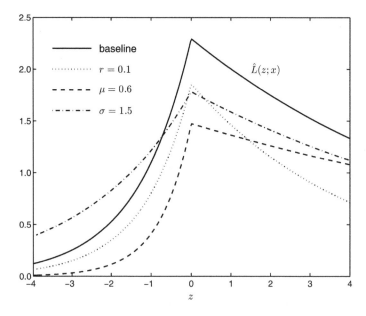

Figure 5.6. *Expected discounted local time, for $x = 0$, $b = -\infty$, and $B = \infty$. The baseline parameter values are $r = 0.05$, $\mu = 0.3$, and $\sigma = 1$.*

The assumptions $r > 0$ and $|g| < M$ together insure that the integrals in (5.26) are finite, so V_P is well defined. With an infinite horizon $r = 0$ cannot be allowed, for obvious reasons, but the restriction on g can be relaxed. The next exercise shows that if $V_P(x)$ is finite for any x, then it is finite everywhere.

Exercise 5.5. Let $\sigma^2 > 0$ and $r > 0$. Show that if $\left|V_P(\hat{x})\right| < \infty$, for any $\hat{x}$, then $\left|V_P(x)\right| < \infty$, all x.

In addition, it is easy to show that if g is continuous, then V_P is twice continuously differentiable. Differentiate (5.26) to find that

$$V'_P(x) = \frac{R_1}{J} \int_{-\infty}^{x} e^{R_1(x-z)} g(z)dz + \frac{R_2}{J} \int_{x}^{+\infty} e^{R_2(x-z)} g(z)dz$$

$$+ \frac{1}{J}\left[\lim_{z\uparrow x} g(x) - \lim_{z\downarrow x} g(x)\right].$$

If g is continuous at x, then the last term is zero, and

$$V''_P(x) = \frac{R_1^2}{J} \int_{-\infty}^{x} e^{R_1(x-z)} g(z)dz + \frac{R_2^2}{J} \int_{x}^{+\infty} e^{R_2(x-z)} g(z)dz + \frac{R_1 - R_2}{J} g(x).$$

The next result is useful in applications, where it is convenient to know that V_P has a unique local maximum.

Proposition 5.7. If g is continuous and single peaked and $\left|V_P(x)\right| < \infty$, then V_P is single peaked.

Proof. Note that V_P satisfies (5.20):

$$g(x) = r V_P(x) - \mu V'_P(x) - \tfrac{1}{2}\sigma^2 V''_P(x), \quad \text{all } x.$$

Suppose there exist values $x_1 < x_2 < x_3$ such that x_1 and x_3 are local maxima and x_2 is a local minimum. Then

$$V'_P(x_i) = 0, \quad i = 1, 2, 3,$$

and

$$V''_P(x_2) \geq 0, \quad V''_P(x_i) \leq 0, \quad i = 1, 3,$$

so

$$g(x_2) \leq r V_P(x_2) \leq r V_P(x_i) \leq g(x_i), \quad i = 1, 3,$$

contradicting the assumption that g is single peaked. ∎

5.7. ODEs for Diffusions

For more general diffusions the approach in Sections 5.4–5.6 can be used to characterize the functions ψ, Ψ, w, and so on, rather sharply, even if closed-form solutions are not generally available. Geometric Brownian motions and Ornstein-Uhlenbeck processes provide useful examples. Not surprisingly, the former deliver closed-form solutions that are closely related to those for Brownian motions.

Assume that $X(t)$ is a regular, stationary diffusion. That is,

   i. its domain is an interval of the form (ℓ, r), $[\ell, r)$, $(\ell, r]$, or $[\ell, r]$, where $\ell = -\infty$ and $r = +\infty$ are allowed if the endpoint is open;
  ii. its infinitesimal parameters $\mu(x)$ and $\sigma(x)$ are continuous functions, with $\sigma^2(x) > 0$, all x; and
 iii. for any points x, y in the interior of the state space,

$$\Pr_x\left[T(y) < \infty\right] > 0.$$

First note that the arguments leading to the ODE in (5.20) still apply. The only change is that $\mu(x)$ and $\sigma^2(x)$ are functions of the state. Thus, ψ, Ψ, θ, Θ, w, and τ satisfy ODEs of the form

$$\tfrac{1}{2}\sigma^2(x)f''(x) + \mu(x)f'(x) - rf(x) = -g(x), \quad x \in (b, B), \quad (5.27)$$

where property (iii) for a diffusion insures $\sigma^2(x) > 0$, all x.

5.8. Solutions for Diffusions When $r = 0$

As before, if $r = 0$ (5.27) becomes a first-order equation:

$$\phi'(x) + \delta(x)\phi(x) = -\hat{g}(x), \quad x \in (b, B), \quad (5.28)$$

where $\phi = f'$, and

$$\delta(x) \equiv \frac{2\mu(x)}{\sigma^2(x)}, \qquad \hat{g}(x) \equiv \frac{2g(x)}{\sigma^2(x)}.$$

For a Brownian motion $\delta(x)$ is constant and (5.28) has solutions of the form

$$\phi(x)e^{\delta x} = -\int^x \hat{g}(\xi)e^{\delta\xi}d\xi.$$

More generally,

$$s(x) = \exp\left\{\int^x \delta(\xi)d\xi\right\} \quad (5.29)$$

is an integrating factor for (5.28). That is, (5.28) can be written as

$$\frac{d}{dx}\left[\phi(x)s(x)\right] = \left[\phi'(x) + \delta(x)\phi(x)\right]s(x)$$

$$= -\hat{g}(x)s(x),$$

where $s(x)$ is in (5.29). Integrating and multiplying by $1/s(x)$ gives the
particular solution

$$\phi_p(x) = -\int^x \hat{g}(\xi)\frac{s(\xi)}{s(x)}d\xi.$$

In addition, solutions of the homogeneous equation corresponding to
(5.28) have the form

$$\phi_h(x) = \frac{c_1}{s(x)}.$$

Hence any solution of (5.28) can be written as

$$\phi(x) = \frac{c_1}{s(x)} - \int^x \hat{g}(\xi)\frac{s(\xi)}{s(x)}d\xi, \quad x \in (b, B).$$

Integrating again gives the function of interest. Thus, if $r = 0$, any solution
of (5.27) can be written as

$$f(x) = c_0 + \int^x \left[\frac{c_1}{s(z)} - \int^z \hat{g}(\xi)\frac{s(\xi)}{s(z)}d\xi\right]dz, \quad x \in [b, B]. \quad (5.30)$$

Note that (5.30) is a generalization of (5.21). As before, the lower limits of
integration can be chosen for convenience, and the constants c_0 and c_1 are
determined by boundary conditions.

Using b for both limits and reversing the order of integration gives

$$\int_b^x \int_b^z \hat{g}(\xi)\frac{s(\xi)}{s(z)}d\xi\, dz = \int_b^x \hat{g}(\xi)s(\xi)\, H(\xi, x)d\xi,$$

where

$$H(x, y) \equiv \int_x^y s^{-1}(\xi)d\xi, \quad b \le x \le y \le B.$$

Thus, if $r = 0$, any solution of (5.27) can be written as

$$f(x) = f(b) + c_1 H(b, x) - \int_b^x g(\xi)\frac{2s(\xi)}{\sigma^2(\xi)} H(\xi, x)d\xi, \quad (5.31)$$

where g is returned to its original form and c_1 is determined by the boundary condition at B. Reversing the roles of b and B produces a similar expression.

It follows from (5.31) that

$$\theta(x) = \frac{H(x, B)}{H(b, B)}, \qquad \Theta(x) = \frac{H(b, x)}{H(b, B)},$$

$$\tau(x) = \frac{H(b, x)}{H(b, B)} \int_b^B \frac{2s(\xi)}{\sigma^2(\xi)} H(\xi, B)d\xi - \int_b^x \frac{2s(\xi)}{\sigma^2(\xi)} H(\xi, x)d\xi \qquad (5.32)$$

$$= \Theta(x) \int_x^B \frac{2s(\xi)}{\sigma^2(\xi)} H(\xi, B)d\xi + \theta(x) \int_b^x \frac{2s(\xi)}{\sigma^2(\xi)} H(b, \xi)d\xi.$$

To determine the undiscounted expected occupancy measure and local time, use the same procedure as in Section 5.5. Let $M(z; x, b, B)$ denote the expected occupancy measure for the set $[b, z]$ up to the stopping time $T = T(b) \wedge T(B)$, conditional on the initial state $X(0) = x$. Recall that M is calculated by fixing z, b, B, and using (5.31) with $g = 1_{[b,z]}$ and the boundary conditions $M(z, b) = M(z, B) = 0$. Hence

$$M(z; x) = \frac{H(b, x)}{H(b, B)} \int_b^z \frac{2s(\xi)}{\sigma^2(\xi)} H(\xi, B)d\xi - \int_b^{\min\{x,z\}} \frac{2s(\xi)}{\sigma^2(\xi)} H(\xi, x)d\xi$$

$$= \theta(x) \int_b^{\min\{x,z\}} \frac{2s(\xi)}{\sigma^2(\xi)} H(b, \xi)d\xi + \Theta(x) \int_{\min\{x,z\}}^z \frac{2s(\xi)}{\sigma^2(\xi)} H(\xi, B)d\xi.$$

The expected local time function is the derivative of M with respect to z:

$$L(z; x, b, B) = \frac{2s(z)}{\sigma^2(z)} \times \begin{cases} \theta(x)H(b, z), & \text{if } z < x, \\ \Theta(x)H(z, B), & \text{if } z \geq x. \end{cases}$$

Notice that L is continuous at $z = x$, but it has a kink at that point.

Exercise 5.6. (a) Verify that for a Brownian motion the expressions in (5.32) for θ, Θ, and τ agree with those in (5.16) and (5.23).

(b) Verify that the expression above for L also agrees with the one obtained earlier.

5.8.1. Geometric Brownian Motion

If X is a geometric Brownian motion with parameters $\hat{\mu}, \hat{\sigma}^2$, then $\delta(x) = 2\hat{\mu}/\hat{\sigma}^2 x$ and $\sigma^2(x) = (\hat{\sigma}x)^2$. If $\hat{\mu} \neq \hat{\sigma}^2/2$, then

$$s(x) = x^{1-\omega}, \qquad H(x, y) = \frac{y^\omega - x^\omega}{\omega},$$

where $\omega \equiv 1 - 2\hat{\mu}/\hat{\sigma}^2$. Hence

$$\theta(x) = \frac{B^\omega - x^\omega}{B^\omega - b^\omega}, \qquad \Theta(x) = \frac{x^\omega - b^\omega}{B^\omega - b^\omega},$$

$$\tau(x) = \frac{1}{\hat{\mu} - \hat{\sigma}^2/2} \left[\theta(x) \ln b + \Theta(x) \ln B - \ln x\right],$$

and

$$L(z; x, b, B) = \frac{1}{\hat{\mu} - \hat{\sigma}^2/2} \frac{1}{z} \times \begin{cases} \theta(x)\left[(b/z)^\omega - 1\right], & \text{if } z < x, \\ \Theta(x)\left[1 - (B/z)^\omega\right], & \text{if } z \geq x. \end{cases}$$

If $\hat{\mu} = \hat{\sigma}^2/2$, then $\delta(x) = 1/x$, $\omega = 0$, and

$$s(x) = x, \qquad H(x, y) = \ln y - \ln x.$$

Hence

$$\theta(x) = \frac{\ln B - \ln x}{\ln B - \ln b}, \qquad \Theta(x) = \frac{\ln x - \ln b}{\ln B - \ln b},$$

$$\tau(x) = \frac{1}{\hat{\sigma}^2} (\ln B - \ln x)(\ln x - \ln b),$$

and

$$L(z; x, b, B) = \frac{1}{\hat{\sigma}^2/2} \frac{1}{z} \times \begin{cases} \theta(x)(\ln z - \ln b), & \text{if } z < x, \\ \Theta(x)(\ln B - \ln z), & \text{if } z \geq x. \end{cases}$$

Exercise 5.7. Let $Y = \ln X$, where X is as above. Show that the expressions above for θ, Θ, τ, and L agree with the corresponding functions for the process Y.

5.8.2. Ornstein-Uhlenbeck Processes

For an Ornstein-Uhlenbeck process $\mu(x) = -\alpha x$, where $\alpha > 0$, and $\sigma^2 > 0$ is constant. Hence $\delta(x) = -2\eta x$, where $\eta = \alpha/\sigma^2 > 0$. An integrating factor is

$$s(x) = \exp\left\{-\int^x 2\eta\xi d\xi\right\}$$

$$= \exp\left\{-\eta x^2\right\},$$

so

$$H(x, y) = \int_x^y e^{\eta\xi^2} d\xi.$$

Hence

$$\theta(x) = \frac{\int_x^B e^{\eta\xi^2}d\xi}{\int_b^B e^{\eta\xi^2}d\xi}, \qquad \Theta(x) = \frac{\int_b^x e^{\eta\xi^2}d\xi}{\int_b^B e^{\eta\xi^2}d\xi}, \qquad \text{and so on.}$$

5.9. Solutions for Diffusions When $r > 0$

If $r > 0$, solutions to (5.27) can be characterized by using the "variation of parameters" method. Suppose that two linearly independent solutions f_1, f_2 of the homogeneous equation

$$\frac{1}{2}\sigma^2(x)f''(x) + \mu(x)f'(x) - rf(x) = 0 \tag{5.33}$$

have already been obtained. The ease or difficulty of this step depends on the infinitesimal parameters $\mu(x)$ and $\sigma(x)$.

If f_1 and f_2 are available, conjecture that (5.27) has a particular solution of the form

$$f_p(x) = \sum_{i=1}^2 \gamma_i(x)f_i(x),$$

where the γ_is are functions that must be determined. The key step is an additional conjecture that γ_1 and γ_2 satisfy

$$\sum_{i=1}^2 \gamma_i'(x)f_i(x) = 0. \tag{5.34}$$

If this conjecture is correct, then

$$f_p'(x) = \sum_{i=1}^2 \gamma_i(x)f_i'(x),$$

$$f_p''(x) = \sum_{i=1}^2 \left[\gamma_i'(x)f_i'(x) + \gamma_i(x)f_i''(x)\right].$$

Substitute f_p and its derivatives into (5.27) and use the fact that f_i, $i = 1, 2$, satisfy (5.33). Most of the terms cancel, and what remains is

$$\frac{1}{2}\sigma^2(x)\sum_{i=1}^2 \gamma_i'(x)f_i'(x) = -g(x). \tag{5.35}$$

Hence the conjecture is correct if functions γ_1 and γ_2 satisfying (5.34) and (5.35) can be found. That is, γ_1' and γ_2' must satisfy

$$\begin{pmatrix} f_1(x) & f_2(x) \\ f_1'(x) & f_2'(x) \end{pmatrix} \begin{pmatrix} \gamma_1'(x) \\ \gamma_2'(x) \end{pmatrix} = \begin{pmatrix} 0 \\ -\hat{g}(x) \end{pmatrix}, \qquad x \in (b, B),$$

where as before $\hat{g}(x) \equiv 2g(x)/\sigma^2(x)$. Hence

$$\gamma_1'(x) = \frac{f_2(x)\hat{g}(x)}{W(f_1, f_2)(x)}, \qquad \gamma_2'(x) = -\frac{f_1(x)\hat{g}(x)}{W(f_1, f_2)(x)},$$

where

$$W(f_1, f_2)(x) \equiv f_1(x)f_2'(x) - f_1'(x)f_2(x), \quad x \in (b, B),$$

is the Wronskian. Integrate to get

$$\gamma_1(x, b) = \int_b^x \frac{f_2(z)\hat{g}(z)}{W(f_1, f_2)(z)} dz,$$

$$\gamma_2(x, B) = \int_x^B \frac{f_1(z)\hat{g}(z)}{W(f_1, f_2)(z)} dz,$$

(5.36)

where the limits of integration have been chosen in a specific way. Sum the particular and homogeneous solutions to find that if f_1, f_2 satisfy (5.33), then any solution to (5.27) can be written as

$$f(x, b, B) = [\gamma_1(x, b) + c_1] f_1(x)$$
$$+ [\gamma_2(x, B) + c_2] f_2(x), \quad x \in (b, B),$$

(5.37)

where γ_1, γ_2 are defined in (5.36), and c_1, c_2 incorporate the constant terms from (5.36). Note that while f_1 and f_2 are functions of x only, γ_1 and γ_2 each depend in addition on one threshold.

For the function ψ use $\hat{g}(\cdot) \equiv 0$ and the boundary conditions $\psi(b) = 1$ and $\psi(B) = 0$, and for Ψ reverse the boundary conditions. In either case $\gamma_1 = \gamma_2 = 0$, so (5.37) implies

$$\psi(x, b, B) = \frac{1}{D} [f_1(x)f_2(B) - f_1(B)f_2(x)],$$

$$\Psi(x, b, B) = \frac{1}{D} [f_1(b)f_2(x) - f_1(x)f_2(b)],$$

(5.38)

where

$$D \equiv f_1(b)f_2(B) - f_1(B)f_2(b).$$

For the function $w(x)$, $\hat{g}(\cdot)$ in (5.36) is arbitrary, and the boundary conditions are $w(b) = w(B) = 0$. Hence c_1 and c_2 satisfy

$$\begin{pmatrix} f_1(b) & f_2(b) \\ f_1(B) & f_2(B) \end{pmatrix} \begin{pmatrix} c_1 \\ c_2 \end{pmatrix} = \begin{pmatrix} -\gamma_2(b, B)f_2(b) \\ -\gamma_1(B, b)f_1(B) \end{pmatrix}.$$

Solve for the constants and use the expressions above for ψ and Ψ to find that

$$w(x, b, B) = \gamma_1(x, b) f_1(x) + \gamma_2(x, B) f_2(x)$$
$$- \Psi(x, b, B) \gamma_1(B, b) f_1(B) - \psi(x, b, B) \gamma_2(b, B) f_2(b). \tag{5.39}$$

The next result shows that for any regular diffusion ψ, Ψ, $\hat{L}$, and w have the properties established in Propositions 5.5 and 5.6 for a Brownian motion. The interpretations are as before.

Proposition 5.8. The functions $f = \psi$, Ψ, $\hat{L}$ $(z; \cdot)$, and w satisfy

$$f_b(x) = \psi(x) f_b\ (b), \quad f_B(x) = \Psi(x) f_B(B), \quad x \in (b, B),$$
$$f_b(b) + f_x(b) = 0, \quad f_B(B) + f_x(B) = 0.$$

Proof. Use (5.36) and evaluate the derivatives in (5.38) and (5.39). ∎

Exercise 5.8. Show that

$$f_i(x) = f_i(b) \psi(x, b, B) + f_i(B) \Psi(x, b, B), \quad i = 1, 2.$$

The expected value over an infinite horizon can be found by taking limits in (5.39) as $b \to -\infty$ and $B \to +\infty$:

$$V_P(x) \equiv E_x \left[\int_0^\infty e^{-rt} g\ (X(t))\, dt \right]$$

$$= f_1(x) \int_{-\infty}^x \frac{f_2(z) \hat{g}(z)}{W(f_1, f_2)(z)} dz + f_2(x) \int_x^\infty \frac{f_1(z) \hat{g}(z)}{W(f_1, f_2)(z)} dz.$$

5.9.1. Geometric Brownian Motion

For a geometric Brownian motion with parameters $\hat{\mu}$ and $\hat{\sigma}^2 > 0$, the solutions of the homogenous equation (5.33) are

$$f_i(x) = x^{R_i}, \quad i = 1, 2,$$

where $R_1 < 0 < R_2$ are the roots of the quadratic

$$\frac{1}{2} \hat{\sigma}^2 R^2 + \left(\hat{\mu} - \frac{1}{2} \hat{\sigma}^2 \right) R - r = 0.$$

Hence

$$R_1 = -\frac{1}{2}\left[\left(\hat{\mu} - \hat{\sigma}^2/2\right) + J\right] < 0,$$

$$R_2 = \frac{1}{2}\left[-\left(\hat{\mu} - \hat{\sigma}^2/2\right) + J\right] > 0,$$

where

$$J \equiv \sqrt{\left(\hat{\mu} - \hat{\sigma}^2/2\right)^2 - 2\hat{\sigma}^2 r},$$

and

$$\psi(x) = \frac{x^{R_1}B^{R_2} - B^{R_1}x^{R_2}}{b^{R_1}B^{R_2} - B^{R_1}b^{R_2}},$$

$$\Psi(x) = \frac{b^{R_1}x^{R_2} - x^{R_1}b^{R_2}}{b^{R_1}B^{R_2} - B^{R_1}b^{R_2}}.$$

The Wronskian in this case is

$$W(f_1, f_2)(x) \equiv \left(R_2 - R_1\right) x^{R_1 + R_2 - 1},$$

and $\hat{g}(z) = 2g(z)/\left(\hat{\sigma}z\right)^2$, so

$$\gamma_1(x, b) = \frac{1}{J}\int_b^x z^{-R_1 - 1}g(z)dz,$$

$$\gamma_2(x, B) = \frac{1}{J}\int_x^B z^{-R_2 - 1}g(z)dz,$$

where

$$\frac{1}{J} = \frac{1}{R_2 - R_1}\frac{1}{\hat{\sigma}^2/2}.$$

Hence for a geometric Brownian motion

$$w(x) = \frac{1}{J}\left[\int_b^x \left(\frac{x}{z}\right)^{R_1} g(z)\frac{dz}{z} + \int_x^B \left(\frac{x}{z}\right)^{R_2} g(z)\frac{dz}{z}\right.$$

$$\left. - \Psi(x)\int_b^B \left(\frac{B}{z}\right)^{R_1} g(z)\frac{dz}{z} - \psi(x)\int_b^B \left(\frac{b}{z}\right)^{R_2} g(z)\frac{dz}{z}\right].$$

Since this holds for any return function g, it follows that the expected discounted local time function $\hat{L}$ is

$$\hat{L}(z; x, b, B; r) = \frac{1}{z}\frac{1}{J}\left[\left(\frac{x}{z}\right)^{R_i} - \Psi(x)\left(\frac{B}{z}\right)^{R_1} - \psi(x)\left(\frac{b}{z}\right)^{R_2}\right],$$

$$\text{where} \quad i = \begin{cases} 1, & \text{if } b \leq z \leq x, \\ 2, & \text{if } x < z \leq B. \end{cases}$$

Exercise 5.9.   Let $Y = \ln X$, where X is a geometric Brownian motion. Show that the expressions for ψ, Ψ, and w above agree with those in (5.18) and (5.25). What is the relationship between the roots for the two processes?

5.9.2. Ornstein-Uhlenbeck Processes

An Ornstein-Uhlenbeck process has drift $\mu(x) = -\alpha x$ and variance $\sigma^2 > 0$, so (5.33) takes the form

$$\tfrac{1}{2}\sigma^2 f''(x) - \alpha x f'(x) - r f(x) = 0. \tag{5.40}$$

Although this equation does not have a closed-form solution, it is easy to verify that if h satisfies

$$\tfrac{1}{2}\sigma^2 h''(x) + \alpha x h'(x) + (\alpha - r) h(x) = 0,$$

then

$$f(x) = h(x)e^{\eta x^2},$$

where $\eta = \alpha/\sigma^2$, is a solution of (5.40).

Notes

The arguments in Section 5.1–5.3 follow Harrison (1985, Sections 1.5 and 3.2), where the term *Wald martingale* is introduced, and the arguments in Sections 5.4–5.9 follow Karlin and Taylor (1981, Section 15.3). Borodin and Salminen (2002) is a useful compendium of a vast number of formulas related to Brownian motion.

Part II

Impulse Control Models

6

Exercising an Option

IN THE PRESENCE of a fixed cost of adjustment, optimally exercising control has two aspects: deciding at what point(s) action should be taken and choosing what the action(s) should be. In this chapter the simplest example of this sort is studied, the problem of exercising a one-time option of infinite duration. The option problem is simple because action is taken only once and the action itself is fixed, so the only issue is timing—deciding when, if ever, to exercise the option. Its simplicity makes this problem a useful introduction to methods that are applicable more broadly.

Two approaches are studied. The first uses the functions $\hat{L}$ and ψ defined in Chapter 5. Recall that $\hat{L}(z; x, b, B)$ is the expected discounted local time of a stochastic process at level z before the stopping time $T = T(b) \wedge T(B)$, given the initial state $x \in [b, B]$, and $\psi(x, b, B)$ is the expected discounted value of an indicator function for the event $T = T(b)$. The option problem involves only a lower threshold, so $B = +\infty$ and stops at an upper threshold are not involved. The expected discounted return from an arbitrary threshold policy can be written in terms $\hat{L}$ and ψ, and finding the optimal policy then involves a straightforward maximization over the threshold value b.

The second approach uses the Hamilton-Jacobi-Bellman (HJB) equation for the firm's problem. Recall from Chapter 3 that the HJB equation is the stochastic analog to a continuous-time Bellman equation. The difference is that the variance term makes the HJB equation a second-order ordinary differential equation (ODE), while the Bellman equation is first order. The second approach involves determining appropriate boundary conditions for this ODE and solving it.

While mechanically quite different from each other, the two approaches are closely related. The connections between them are discussed after both have been studied in detail.

The rest of the chapter is organized as follows. In Section 6.1 a deterministic version of the problem is studied using several approaches: as a control problem formulated in terms of the date when action should be taken, as a control problem formulated in terms of a threshold value for the state where action should be taken, and in terms of a Bellman equation. The second and third approaches are analogs of those used for the stochastic problem studied next. In Section 6.2 the stochastic problem is analyzed using the functions $\hat{L}$ and ψ, and in Section 6.3 it is studied using the HJB equation. The connections between the two are then discussed, and Section 6.4 concludes with an example.

6.1. The Deterministic Problem

Consider a plant that generates a profit flow as long as it is operated. Profits depend on a state variable $X(t)$ that can reflect demand or plant capacity or both. The state has a stationary law of motion, which for now is assumed to be deterministic and linear,

$$X(t) = x_0 + \mu t, \quad \text{all } t \geq 0, \tag{6.1}$$

where the initial state $X(0) = x_0$ is given. $X(t)$ could be interpreted as the log of the capital stock, with depreciation at the constant rate $\delta = -\mu > 0$, in a setting with time-invariant demand. Or $X(t)$ could be interpreted as a measure of demand, which falls at the rate $|\mu|$.

Let $\pi(x)$ be the net profit flow from operating the plant if the current state is x. The function π is time invariant, and it is defined net of operating costs for labor, materials, and other inputs. Let $r > 0$ be the (constant) interest rate.

The plant can be shut down at any time, and it cannot be reopened after it has been closed. When the plant is shut down it has a salvage value S, which might represent the scrap value of the capital stock. For now suppose that this value is independent of the state $X(t)$ at the time of the closing. The objective of the firm is to choose a shutdown policy that maximizes the discounted value of total returns: the profits from operating the plant plus the salvage value when it is shut down. Thus, the value from following an optimal policy, given the initial state x_0, is

$$V(x_0) \equiv \sup_{T \geq 0} \left[\int_0^T e^{-rt} \pi(X(t)) dt + e^{-rT} S \right], \tag{6.2}$$

where $X(t)$ is as in (6.1), and $T = +\infty$ if the firm chooses to operate the plant forever.

The primitives for the problem are the constants r, μ, and S and the function π. The following assumption will be used throughout the chapter.

Assumption 6.1.   (i) $r > 0$, $\mu < 0$, $S > 0$;
   (ii) $\pi(\cdot)$ is bounded, continuous, and strictly increasing, with

$$\lim_{x \to -\infty} \pi(x) < rS < \lim_{x \to +\infty} \pi(x).$$

Part (ii) of the assumption insures that it is optimal to shut down immediately if the initial state is sufficiently low and to continue operating—at least for a while—if it is sufficiently high.

The restriction $\mu < 0$ is needed to avoid corner solutions of the following sort. If $\mu > 0$ the incentive to continue operating grows over time, so it is never optimal to operate for a finite length of time and then shut down. The following exercise shows that the optimal shutdown time is $T^* = 0$ or $+\infty$ if $\mu > 0$.

Exercise 6.1.   Let r, π, and S satisfy Assumption 6.1, and consider the problem in (6.2). Show that if $\mu \geq 0$ there is a critical value x_c with the following property:

   if $x < x_c$, the unique optimal policy is to shut down immediately, $T^* = 0$;
   if $x > x_c$, the unique optimal policy is to operate the plant forever, $T^* = +\infty$;
   if $x = x_c$, then both $T^* = 0$ and $T^* = \infty$ are optimal policies, and
      if $\mu > 0$ there are no others;
      if $\mu = 0$ any choice of T is optimal.

Under Assumption 6.1 the optimal policy is unique and involves operating for a finite length of time. To see this, note that the first-order condition for an optimum in (6.2) is

$$e^{-rT^*} \left[\pi(X(T^*)) - rS \right] \leq 0, \quad \text{with equality if } T^* > 0. \qquad (6.3)$$

The expression in brackets in (6.3) represents the effects of operating a little longer: the additional profit flow less the foregone interest on the salvage value. At an interior optimum the two are equal. Under Assumption 6.1 there is a unique value b^* satisfying

$$\pi(b^*) - rS = 0, \qquad (6.4)$$

and since π is increasing and $\mu < 0$, the problem is concave. Hence for any initial state x the unique optimal shutdown date is

$$T^* = \begin{cases} 0, & \text{if } x < b^*, \\ (b^* - x)/\mu, & \text{if } x \geq b^*, \end{cases}$$

and the value function V is

$$V(x) = \begin{cases} S, & \text{if } x < b^*, \\ \int_0^{(b^*-x)/\mu} e^{-rt}\pi(X(t))dt + e^{-(b^*-x)r/\mu}S, & \text{if } x \geq b^*, \end{cases}$$

where for notational simplicity the subscript on the initial state x has been dropped.

The approach above involves using the shutdown date T as the control variable, but the form for the optimal policy suggests that it may be simpler to formulate the problem in terms of a critical value b for the state variable. To start, note that since π is increasing and $\mu < 0$, the optimal policy is a threshold policy. For the threshold b, call the interval $(-\infty, b]$ the *action (or shutdown) region* and $(b, +\infty)$ the *inaction (or continuation) region*.

Fix the initial state x and suppose the firm uses a threshold policy with critical value $b \leq x$. Let $F(x, b)$ denote the returns from this policy, and use the change of variable $\xi = x + \mu t$ to write the problem in (6.2) as

$$V(x) \equiv \max_{b \leq x} F(x, b)$$

$$= \max_{b \leq x} \left[\frac{1}{-\mu} \int_b^x e^{(x-\xi)r/\mu}\pi(\xi)d\xi + e^{(x-b)r/\mu}S \right]. \tag{6.5}$$

The following result characterizes the solution.

Proposition 6.1. Let r, μ, S, and π satisfy Assumption 6.1 and let X be as in (6.1). The solution to the problem in (6.5) is

$$b = \min\{x, b^*\},$$

where b^* is defined in (6.4). The associated value function is

$$V(x) = \begin{cases} S, & \text{if } x < b^*, \\ -\mu^{-1} \int_{b^*}^x e^{(x-\xi)r/\mu}\pi(\xi)d\xi + e^{(x-b^*)r/\mu}S, & \text{if } x \geq b^*. \end{cases} \tag{6.6}$$

Proof. The first-order condition for an optimum in (6.5) is

$$\frac{\partial F(x, b)}{\partial b} = \frac{1}{\mu}e^{(x-b)r/\mu}[\pi(b) - rS] \geq 0, \quad \text{with equality if } b < x. \tag{6.7}$$

If $x \geq b^*$, then $b = b^*$ and this condition holds with equality. If $x < b^*$, then $b = x$ and it holds with strict inequality. ∎

Thus, the optimal policy is

    i. if $x \leq b^*$, shut down immediately; and
    ii. if $x > b^*$, operate until the state reaches b^* and then shut down.

There is a third approach to this problem as well, which uses the Bellman equation. As before, begin by noting that the policy takes the form of a threshold. Let x be the initial state and fix a threshold $b \leq x$. If $b < x$ then the firm continues operating for a while, so for any sufficiently small time interval h the value from this policy, call it $F(x, b)$, satisfies

$$F(x, b) = \int_0^h e^{-rt} \pi(X(t)) dt + e^{-rh} F(X(h), b)$$

$$\approx \pi(x)h + \frac{1}{1+rh} \left[F(x, b) + \mu h F_x(x, b) \right],$$

where $X(t)$ in the first line is as in (6.1), the second line uses a first-order Taylor series approximation to $F(X(h), b)$, and $F_x(x, b) \equiv \partial F(x, b)/\partial x$. Rearrange terms, divide by h, and let $h \to 0$ to get the Bellman equation,

$$r F(x, b) = \pi(x) + \mu F_x(x, b). \tag{6.8}$$

Since b is fixed, (6.8) is a first-order ODE. In addition $F(\cdot, b)$ satisfies

$$\lim_{x \downarrow b} F(x, b) = S. \tag{6.9}$$

Integrate (6.8) and use the boundary condition in (6.9) to obtain the function $F(x, b)$ in (6.5).

In the preceding argument b is fixed and arbitrary. An optimal policy involves choosing b to maximize $F(x, b)$, which as before leads to the first-order condition in (6.7) involving $\partial F/\partial b$. But notice from (6.5) that

$$-F_b(x, b) = -e^{(x-b)r/\mu} \frac{1}{\mu} [\pi(b) - rS]$$

$$= -e^{(x-b)r/\mu} F_b(b, b)$$

$$= +e^{(x-b)r/\mu} F_x(b, b), \quad \text{all } b \leq x, \text{ all } x. \tag{6.10}$$

The interpretation is as follows. Suppose the firm uses the threshold policy b. For the first line in (6.10), note that a small negative perturbation of the threshold, by $-\varepsilon < 0$, delays the closing of the plant by $\varepsilon/(-\mu) > 0$ units of time. Over this interval the firm collects profits at the rate $\pi(b)$ but loses interest on the salvage value at the rate rS. If the initial state is $x > b$, the threshold b is reached at date $t = (x - b)/(-\mu) > 0$, and these changes in the firm's revenue must be appropriately discounted.

For the second line in (6.10), the interpretation is the same, except that the initial state is at the boundary, $x = b$. The discount factor must be appended to equate the second line with the first.

For the third line, suppose again that the initial state is $x = b$. A small positive perturbation of the state, by $\varepsilon > 0$, also delays the closing of the firm by $\varepsilon/(-\mu) > 0$ units of time, changing net revenue in the same way as a negative perturbation to the threshold.

Thus, conditional on $x = b$, positive perturbations of the state and negative perturbations of the threshold have identical effects. If $x > b$, a negative perturbation of the threshold also has the same effect, except that it is discounted.

It follows from (6.10) that the critical value b^* in (6.4) satisfies

$$\frac{\partial F(x, b^*)}{\partial x}\Big|_{x=b^*} = \frac{1}{\mu}\left[\pi(b^*) - rS\right] = 0, \tag{6.11}$$

In contrast to (6.7), which involves a derivative with respect to the threshold b holding the state x fixed, (6.11) involves a derivative with respect to the state x, evaluated at $x = b^*$, holding the threshold fixed. Hence, among all solutions $F(\cdot, b)$ to the ODE in (6.8) with the boundary condition in (6.9), the optimized value function $V = F(\cdot, b^*)$ is the one that in addition has the property in (6.11): $F_x(b^*, b^*) = V'(b^*) = 0$. The following result formalizes this conclusion.

Proposition 6.2. Let r, μ, S, and π satisfy Assumption 6.1 and let X be as in (6.1). The function V and threshold b^* defined in (6.6) and (6.7) have the following properties:

  i. V satisfies

$$rV(x) = \pi(x) + \mu V'(x), \quad x > b^*, \tag{6.12}$$

$$V(x) = S, \qquad\qquad\qquad x \le b^*;$$

 ii. V is continuous at b^*:

$$\lim_{x \downarrow b^*} V(x) = S; \tag{6.13}$$

iii. V' is continuous at b^*:

$$\lim_{x \downarrow b^*} V'(x) = 0. \tag{6.14}$$

Proof. There is a family of solutions to (6.12) and (6.13) indexed by b, the functions $F(\cdot, b)$ in (6.5). The unique member of this family that in addition satisfies (6.14) is the one with $b = b^*$, where b^* is defined by (6.4). ∎

To summarize, there are two ways to arrive at the function $F(x, b)$ in (6.5), which describes the expected discounted value from using the arbitrary threshold policy b, given the initial state x. The first begins with the integral over time in (6.2) and converts it into the integral over states in (6.5). The second uses the fact that for any b, the function $F(\cdot, b)$ satisfies the Bellman equation in (6.8) on $(b, +\infty)$, with the boundary condition in (6.9).

There are also two ways to characterize the optimal threshold b^*. The first involves maximizing $F(x, b)$ with respect to b, as in (6.5), to get the first-order condition in (6.7), a condition on $\partial F/\partial b$. The second involves using (6.10) to replace (6.7) with (6.11), a condition on the derivative $\partial F/\partial x$, evaluated at $x = b$.

Proposition 6.1 uses the first methods and Proposition 6.2 the second.

The following exercise extends the model to allow the salvage value $S(x)$ to depend on the state.

Exercise 6.2. Let r, μ, and π satisfy Assumption 6.1, and assume in addition that

i. $S(x)$ is bounded and continuously differentiable, and
ii. the function

$$\phi(x) \equiv \pi(x) + \mu S'(x) - r S(x)$$

is strictly increasing in x, with

$$\lim_{x \to -\infty} \phi(x) < 0 < \lim_{x \to +\infty} \phi(x).$$

Use all three approaches to characterize the value function and optimal policy for the shutdown problem

$$V(x) \equiv \sup_{T \geq 0} \left[\int_0^T e^{-rt} \pi(X(t)) dt + e^{-rT} S(X(T)) \right],$$

where $X(t)$ is as in (6.1), with $X(0) = x$. What is the interpretation of the inequality restriction in (ii)?

6.2. The Stochastic Problem: A Direct Approach

Next, suppose that r, μ, S, and π satisfy Assumption 6.1, but that the state variable $X(t)$ is a Brownian motion with parameters μ and $\sigma^2 > 0$. The methods used in Propositions 6.1 and 6.2 to solve the deterministic problem can be applied in this case as well, requiring only modest modification to accommodate the fact that $X(t)$ is a stochastic process.

Begin by noticing that an optimal policy for the stochastic model has two basic properties. First, since the problem is stationary, it is clear that if an optimal policy requires (allows) shutting down in state b, it requires (allows) shutting down the first time the process reaches state b. Hence we can limit our attention to threshold policies. For any b, let $T(b)$ be the stopping time defined as the first time $X(t)$ takes the value b.

Second, since π is increasing and $\mu < 0$, an optimal policy cannot involve waiting for the state to increase and then shutting down. Thus, as in the deterministic case, the optimal policy is characterized by a single threshold b, a lower bound on the region in the state space where the plant continues operating. As before this threshold divides the state space into an action region $(-\infty, b]$ and an inaction region (b, ∞). Hence the firm's problem can be written as

$$v(x) = \sup_{b \leq x} \mathrm{E}_x \left[\int_0^{T(b)} e^{-rt} \pi(X(t))dt + e^{-rT(b)}S \right], \qquad (6.15)$$

where $\mathrm{E}_x[\cdot]$ denotes an expectation conditional on the initial state.

Consider the expected return from an arbitrary policy. Let $f(x, b)$ be the total expected discounted return, given the initial state $X(0) = x$, from a policy of operating until the first time the state reaches $b \leq x$ and then shutting down,

$$f(x, b) \equiv \mathrm{E}_x \left[\int_0^{T(b)} e^{-rt} \pi(X(t))dt + e^{-rT(b)}S \right]$$

$$= \int_b^\infty \hat{L}(\xi; x, b, \infty)\pi(\xi)d\xi + \psi(x, b, \infty)S$$

$$= \frac{1}{J} \left[\int_b^x e^{R_1(x-\xi)}\pi(\xi)d\xi + \int_x^\infty e^{R_2(x-\xi)}\pi(\xi)d\xi \right. \qquad (6.16)$$

$$\left. - e^{R_1(x-b)} \int_b^\infty e^{R_2(b-\xi)}\pi(\xi)d\xi \right] + e^{R_1(x-b)}S, \quad \text{all } b \leq x,$$

where the second line uses the expected discounted local time function $\hat{L}$ to replace the expectation of the integral over time with an integral over states and uses ψ in place of $E_x\left[e^{-rT(b)}\right]$; the third line uses the expressions for $\hat{L}$ and ψ in Sections 5.3 and 5.6; and the constants $J > 0$ and $R_1 < 0 < R_2$, which depend on the parameters r, μ, and σ^2, were defined in Section 5.2. The first two terms in brackets in (6.16) represent the expected returns from operating the plant forever, neglecting profits that accrue when the state is below b, and the third subtracts the portion of those expected returns that accrues after b has been reached for the first time. The last term is the salvage value.

The firm's problem is then

$$v(x) = \max_{b \leq x} f(x, b),$$

so the first-order condition for a maximum at $b \leq x$ is

$$0 \leq \frac{\partial f(x, b)}{\partial b}$$

$$= \int_b^\infty \hat{L}_b(\xi; x, b, \infty)\pi(\xi)d\xi + \psi_b(x, b, \infty)S,$$

$$= \psi(x, b, \infty)\left[\int_b^\infty \hat{L}_b(\xi; b, b, \infty)\pi(\xi)d\xi + \psi_b(b, b, \infty)S\right]$$

$$= e^{R_1(x-b)}\left[(R_1 - R_2)\frac{1}{J}\int_b^\infty e^{R_2(b-\xi)}\pi(\xi)d\xi - R_1 S\right], \qquad (6.17)$$

with equality if $b < x$,

where the second line uses the fact that $\hat{L}(b; x, b, \infty) = 0$, and the third uses Propositions 5.5 and 5.6. Note that $\hat{L}_b < 0$ and $\psi_b > 0$, since raising the threshold decreases the expected discounted local time at every level and advances the time when the threshold is reached. Correspondingly, the first term in brackets in (6.17) is negative, representing the reduction in expected operating profits from increasing the shutdown threshold. These are profits that would have accrued along sample paths where the state fell almost to b but not quite. Along these paths, the state variable can rise to any level before falling again to b, so a small increase in the threshold strictly reduces the expected discounted local time at every level exceeding b. The second term, which is positive, represents the increase in the expected salvage revenue from shutting down earlier.

For the stochastic problem, b^* is the value for which the term in square brackets in (6.17) is equal to zero. To establish the existence of a solution, note that

$$\frac{R_1 - R_2}{R_1}\frac{1}{J} = \left(\frac{1}{R_2} - \frac{1}{R_1}\right)\frac{R_2}{J} = \frac{R_2}{r},$$

and define

$$\Pi(b) \equiv R_2 \int_b^\infty e^{R_2(b-\xi)}\pi(\xi)d\xi$$

$$= R_2 \int_0^\infty e^{-R_2\zeta}\pi(b+\zeta)d\zeta.$$

Then (6.17) can be written as

$$-\Pi(b) + rS \geq 0, \quad \text{with equality if } b < x, \tag{6.18}$$

and the critical value b^* satisfies

$$\Pi(b^*) - rS = 0. \tag{6.19}$$

Under Assumption 6.1, Π is increasing, since π is, and in addition

$$\lim_{b \to -\infty} \Pi(b) < rS < \lim_{b \to +\infty} \Pi(b).$$

Hence (6.19) has a unique solution and f is concave in b at b^*. Then (6.18) implies that if the initial state x exceeds b^*, the constraint $b \leq x$ is slack and $b = b^*$. Otherwise the constraint binds and $b = x$. The following proposition summarizes these arguments.

Proposition 6.3.   Let r, μ, S, and π satisfy Assumption 6.1, and let X be a Brownian motion with parameters μ and $\sigma^2 > 0$. Then there exists a unique value b^* satisfying (6.19), and the optimal policy for the problem in (6.15) is

$$b = \min\{x, b^*\}.$$

The value from this policy is

$$v(x) = S, \qquad\qquad\qquad\qquad\qquad\qquad\qquad\qquad\qquad x \leq b^*,$$

$$v(x) = \frac{1}{J}\int_x^\infty e^{R_2(x-\xi)}\pi(\xi)d\xi + \frac{1}{J}\int_{b^*}^x e^{R_1(x-\xi)}\pi(\xi)d\xi$$

$$- e^{R_1(x-b^*)}\frac{1}{J}\int_{b^*}^\infty e^{R_2(b^*-\xi)}\pi(\xi)d\xi + e^{R_1(x-b^*)}S, \quad x > b^*. \tag{6.20}$$

Thus, the optimal policy is

    i. if $x \leq b^*$, shut down immediately;

    ii. if $x > b^*$, operate until the first time the state reaches b^* and then shut down.

The following exercise looks at the relationship between the stochastic and deterministic problems.

Exercise 6.3. Show that the function f in (6.16) and the first-order condition (6.17) for the stochastic problem converge to their respective deterministic counterparts (6.5) and (6.7) as $\sigma^2 \to 0$.

6.3. Using the Hamilton-Jacobi-Bellman Equation

The stochastic problem, like the deterministic one, can also be analyzed by solving an appropriate ODE. As before, begin by noting that the optimal shutdown region has the form $(-\infty, b]$. Fix any initial state x and any candidate threshold $b \leq x$, and let $f(x, b)$ be the return from the policy of operating until b is reached and then shutting down. If $x > b$ the policy requires that operation be continued, at least for a while. In this case let h be a time interval that is short enough so that the probability of shutting down before h is negligible. Then

$$f(x, b) \approx \mathrm{E}_x \left[\int_0^h e^{-rt} \pi(X(t)) dt + e^{-rh} f(X(h), b) \right]$$

$$\approx \pi(x)h + \frac{1}{1+rh} \left[f(x, b) + f_x(x, b)\mu h + \frac{1}{2} f_{xx}(x, b)\sigma^2 h \right],$$

where the second lines uses a second-order Taylor series approximation to $f(X(h), b)$ and an application of Ito's lemma, as in Section 5.4. The argument is like the one for the deterministic problem, except that a second-order approximation is needed to capture the variance term in ΔX. Rearrange terms, divide by h, and let $h \to 0$ to get

$$rf(x, b) = \pi(x) + \mu f_x(x, b) + \tfrac{1}{2}\sigma^2 f_{xx}(x, b), \quad \text{all } x > b. \quad (6.21)$$

With b fixed, this equation is a second-order linear ODE with constant coefficients, and it has exactly the same form as those in Section 5.6.

Recall from Chapter 5 the function

$$v_P(x) \equiv \mathrm{E}_x \left[\int_0^\infty e^{-rt} \pi(X(t)) dt \right], \quad \text{all } x,$$

the expected discounted value if the plant is operated forever. Under Assumption 6.1, π is bounded and $r > 0$, so v_P is bounded. As shown in Chapter 5, the function v_P is a particular solution of (6.21), and the functions $h_i(x) = e^{R_i x}$, $i = 1, 2$, are homogeneous solutions. Hence any solution has the form

$$f(x, b) = v_P(x) + c_1 e^{R_1 x} + c_2 e^{R_2 x}, \tag{6.22}$$

where c_1, c_2 are constants that must be determined from boundary conditions. For the upper boundary, note that as $x \to \infty$ the stopping time $T(b)$ diverges to $+\infty$. Hence for any b

$$\lim_{x \to \infty} \left[f(x, b) - v_P(x) \right] = 0. \tag{6.23}$$

Since $R_2 > 0$ it follows that $c_2 = 0$. For the lower boundary, note that for $x \le b$ the policy involves stopping immediately, so

$$f(x, b) = S, \quad x \le b. \tag{6.24}$$

Use this fact at $x = b$ to conclude that

$$c_1 = e^{-R_1 b} \left[S - v_P(b) \right].$$

Hence for any b,

$$f(x, b) = \begin{cases} S, & x \le b, \\ v_P(x) + e^{R_1(x-b)} \left[S - v_P(b) \right], & x > b. \end{cases} \tag{6.25}$$

When the firm shuts down it receives the salvage value S but loses the remaining profit stream $v_P(b)$. Hence for any fixed b the value of a firm that uses b for its threshold can be written as the value of operating forever, the term $v_P(x)$, plus the expected discounted net gain from shutting down.

So far the threshold b has been arbitrary. Given x, the firm's problem is to choose the threshold b to maximize $f(x, b)$,

$$v(x) = \max_{b \le x} f(x, b)$$

$$= v_P(x) + \max_{b \le x} e^{R_1(x-b)} \left[S - v_P(b) \right]. \tag{6.26}$$

Hence the condition for a maximum at b is

$$0 \le \frac{\partial f(x, b)}{\partial b}$$

$$= -e^{R_1(x-b)} \left\{ v_P'(b) + R_1 \left[S - v_P(b) \right] \right\}, \quad \text{with equality if } b < x. \tag{6.27}$$

Substituting the expressions in Section 5.6 for v_P and v'_P in (6.27) reproduces (6.17). As before b^* is the value for which (6.27) holds with equality.

Note that the maximized value of the second term in (6.26) is the value of the option to shut down in the present context or the value of exercising control in more general settings. Clearly for $x \geq b^*$,

$$p(x) = e^{R_1(x-b^*)} \left[S - v_P(b^*) \right]$$

is the price of the option in an appropriate market setting. Note that the term $\left[S - v_P(b^*) \right]$ is positive, reflecting the fact that the firm has the option to remain open. That is, a necessary condition for exercising control is that doing so raises the total return. The following exercise verifies that the approach in (6.26) leads to the solution obtained earlier.

Exercise 6.4. (a) Verify that substituting for v_P and v'_P in (6.27) produces (6.17).
 (b) Show that $\left[S - v_P(b^*) \right] > 0$.

Note that

$$e^{R_1(x-b)} = \psi(x, b, \infty) = \mathrm{E}_x \left[e^{-rT(b)} \right],$$

so f can be written as

$$f(x, b) = v_P(x) + \psi(x, b, \infty) \left[S - v_P(b) \right], \quad \text{all } b \leq x, \text{ all } x. \quad (6.28)$$

Recall from Proposition 5.5 that for any b, B,

$$-\psi_x(b, b, B) = \psi_b(b, b, B),$$
$$\psi_b(x, b, B) = \psi(x, b, B)\psi_b(b, b, B), \quad x \in (b, B). \quad (6.29)$$

Use (6.28) and the first line in (6.29) to find that, as in the deterministic model,

$$-\frac{\partial f(x, b)}{\partial b}\Big|_{x=b} = +\frac{\partial f(x, b)}{\partial x}\Big|_{x=b}, \quad \text{all } b. \quad (6.30)$$

The interpretation of this fact is as before. Fix a threshold b, suppose that the state is at the threshold, $x = b$, and consider the effect of a small increase h in the state. The firm operates longer and receipt of the salvage value is delayed. Alternatively, reducing the threshold by h has exactly the same effect.

Then use (6.28) again with the second line in (6.29) to find that

$$\frac{\partial f(x, b)}{\partial b} = \psi_b(x, b, \infty) \left[S - v_P(b) \right] - \psi(x, b, \infty) v'_P(b)$$

$$= \psi(x, b, \infty) \left\{ \psi_b(b, b, \infty) \left[S - v_P(b) \right] - v'_P(b) \right\}$$

$$= \psi(x, b, \infty) \frac{\partial f(x, b)}{\partial b} \big|_{x=b}, \quad \text{all } b \le x, \text{ all } x. \qquad (6.31)$$

In the stochastic environment the function ψ plays the role of a discount factor: the effect of a change in the threshold b if the current state is x is the change it has when b is reached, adjusted for the expected discounted time until that event occurs.

Combine (6.30) and (6.31) to conclude that

$$f_b(x, b^*) = 0, \quad \text{all } x \ge b^* \iff f_x(b^*, b^*) = 0.$$

Hence the condition $f_x(b^*, b^*) = 0$ provides a convenient method for characterizing b^*. Specifically, among all functions $f(x, b)$ satisfying (6.23) and (6.24), the optimized value function $v = f(\cdot, b^*)$ is the one that has the additional property $f_x(b^*, b^*) = 0$. The following result summarizes these conclusions.

Proposition 6.4. Let r, μ, S, and π satisfy Assumption 6.1, and let X be a Brownian motion with parameters μ and $\sigma^2 > 0$. The threshold b^* and function v defined in (6.19) and (6.20) have the following properties:

i. v satisfies

$$rv(x) = \pi(x) + \mu v'(x) + \tfrac{1}{2}\sigma^2 v''(x), \quad x > b^*, \qquad (6.32)$$

$$v(x) = S, \qquad\qquad\qquad\qquad x \le b^*;$$

ii. v has the limiting property

$$\lim_{x \to \infty} \left[v(x) - v_P(x) \right] = 0; \qquad (6.33)$$

iii. v is continuous at b^*,

$$\lim_{x \downarrow b^*} v(x) = S; \quad \text{and} \qquad (6.34)$$

iv. the derivative of v is continuous at b^*,

$$\lim_{x \downarrow b^*} v'(x) = 0. \qquad (6.35)$$

Proof. There is a family of solutions to (6.32)–(6.34), indexed by b, and they are as in (6.25). The only member of this family that in addition satisfies (6.35) is the one with $b = b^*$, where b^* is defined by (6.19). ∎

Condition (6.34) is called the *value matching* condition and (6.35) is called the *smooth pasting* condition. Call (6.33) the *no bubble* condition. Thus, an alternative way to solve for the optimal value function v and threshold b^* is by using the HJB equation (6.32) together with the boundary conditions in (6.33)–(6.35).

For a heuristic argument that leads to the smooth pasting condition, suppose the threshold b has been chosen and the state is $x = b$, and consider the expected returns from two strategies: (i) shutting down immediately, and (ii) continuing to operate for a short interval of time h and then deciding what to do. The return from the first strategy is simply $\Pi_1 = S$. The return from the latter can be calculated using the random walk approximation described in Section 3.4. The payoff $\pi(b)$ is collected over the time interval h, and then a decision is made. The increment to the state over h is

$$\Delta X = \pm \sigma \sqrt{h},$$

and the probability of an upward jump is

$$p = \frac{1}{2}\left[1 + \frac{\mu\sqrt{h}}{\sigma}\right].$$

Assume that at the end of the time interval h, the firm keeps the plant open if X has increased and shuts it down if X has decreased. Then the expected return from the second strategy is approximately

$$\Pi_2 = \pi(b)h + (1 - rh)\left[pf(b + \sigma\sqrt{h}, b) + (1 - p)S\right].$$

Use a Taylor series expansion to evaluate f and find that

$$pf\left(b + \sigma\sqrt{h}, b\right) + (1 - p)S \approx p\left[f(b, b) + f_x(b, b)\sigma\sqrt{h}\right] + (1 - p)S$$

$$= S + pf_x(b, b)\sigma\sqrt{h},$$

where the second line uses the value matching condition $f(b, b) = S$. Hence the difference between the two payoffs is approximately

$$\Pi_2 - \Pi_1 = \pi(b)h + (1 - rh)\left[S + pf_x(b, b)\sigma\sqrt{h}\right] - S$$

$$\approx [\pi(b) - rS]h + pf_x(b, b)\sigma\sqrt{h}$$

$$\approx \tfrac{1}{2}f_x(b, b)\sigma\sqrt{h},$$

where the second line drops terms of order higher than h and the third drops those of order higher than $\sqrt{h}$. If the threshold b is optimal, the firm is indifferent between the two strategies. This is true if and only if the threshold satisfies

$$f_x(b^*, b^*) = 0,$$

which is exactly the smooth pasting condition (6.35).

As in the deterministic model, there are two ways to characterize the function f. For the stochastic model the first uses the functions $\hat{L}$ and ψ, while the second starts with the HJB equation.

There are also two methods for characterizing the optimal threshold b^*. The first involves a derivative of $f(x, b)$ with respect to b. The second uses Proposition 5.5 to replace $f_b(x, b^*)$ with the smooth pasting conditions $f_x(b^*, b^*) = 0$.

The next two exercises look at the effects of parameters changes in the shutdown problem and at a start-up problem that is the mirror image of the one studied here.

Exercise 6.5. (a) Describe the qualitative effects of small changes in the parameters μ, σ^2, S, and r on the optimal threshold b^* and the maximized value function v.

(b) Describe the qualitative effect of each of these parameters on the expected length of time until the option is exercised, conditional on a fixed initial condition $x_0 > b$.

Exercise 6.6. Consider an unemployed worker who continuously receives wage offers. Suppose that the stochastic process $\{X(t)\}$ describes these offers. The worker can accept a job at any time. When he does accept an offer, his wage remains constant forever afterward. The worker receives an unemployment benefit s (a flow) as long as he remains unemployed. The worker lives forever and is interested in maximizing the expected discounted value of his lifetime income, discounted at the constant rate $r > 0$.

(a) Describe his optimal strategy when $X(t)$ is a Brownian motion with parameters (μ, σ^2). What restrictions (if any) are needed to make the problem well behaved?

(b) Repeat (a) assuming that $X(t)$ is an Ornstein-Uhlenbeck process with parameters (α, σ^2).

6.4. An Example

Suppose the profit function is

$$\pi(x) = ae^{\eta x},$$

with $a > 0$ and $0 < \eta < R_2$. Then Assumption 6.1 holds for any salvage value $S > 0$. In addition

$$v_P(x) = \frac{a}{J}\left[\int_0^\infty e^{-R_2 z}e^{\eta(x+z)}dz + \int_{-\infty}^0 e^{-R_1 z}e^{\eta(x+z)}dz\right]$$

$$= aCe^{\eta x},$$

where the restriction on η insures that

$$C \equiv \frac{1}{J}\left[\frac{1}{R_2 - \eta} - \frac{1}{R_1 - \eta}\right] > 0$$

is finite.

Hence for an arbitrary threshold b, the value function is

$$f(x, b) = v_P(x) + e^{R_1(x-b)}\left[S - v_P(b)\right]$$

$$= aCe^{\eta x} + e^{R_1(x-b)}\left[S - aCe^{\eta b}\right].$$

Figure 6.1 displays the function $f(x, b)$ for $x \in [31, 41]$ and $b \in [30, 40]$, for the parameter values

$$\mu = -.001, \quad \sigma = 10, \quad r = .045,$$

$$a = .03, \quad \eta = .02, \quad S = 4.$$

For high values of x, $f(x, b)$ exceeds S and is strictly concave in b over the displayed range. For intermediate values of x it exceeds S, is strictly concave in b for $b < x$, and is constant at $f(x, b) = S$ for $b > x$. For low values of x and b, with $b < x$, the function lies below S, rising to S at $b = x$.

The optimal threshold b^* solves

$$0 = (R_1 - \eta) aCe^{\eta b^*} - R_1 S,$$

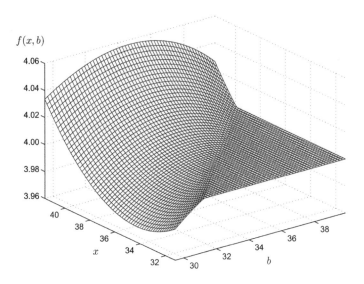

Figure 6.1. *The value function* $f(x, b)$, *for* $\mu = -0.001$, $\sigma = 10$, $r = 0.045$, $a = 0.03$, $\eta = 0.02$, *and* $S = 4$.

so

$$b^* = \frac{1}{\eta} \ln\left(\frac{S}{aC} \frac{R_1}{R_1 - \eta}\right)$$

$$= \frac{1}{\eta} \ln\left(\frac{rS}{a} \frac{R_2 - \eta}{R_2}\right) = 34.69.$$

The restriction on η insures that there is a solution, and the value function is

$$v(x) = f(x, b^*) = aCe^{\eta x} + e^{R_1(x - b^*)}\left[S - aCe^{\eta b^*}\right].$$

Figure 6.2 displays three cross sections of f, for $b_1 < b^* < b_2$. Notice that $f(\cdot, b^*)$ lies above the other two curves and is smooth at $x = b^*$, that $f(\cdot, b_1)$ falls below S and has a kink at $x = b_1$, and that $f(\cdot, b_2)$ has a kink at $x = b_2$.

Figure 6.3 displays v_P, v, and two additional functions. Note that v approaches v_P from above as x gets large. If the no bubble condition (6.33) is ignored, then for any threshold b, the constants c_1 and c_2 in (6.22) can be chosen so that the value matching and smooth pasting conditions (6.34) and

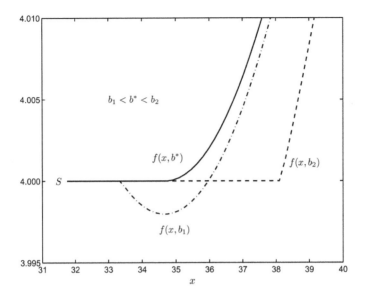

Figure 6.2. *Cross sections of $f(x, b)$, for thresholds $b_1 < b^* < b_2$.*

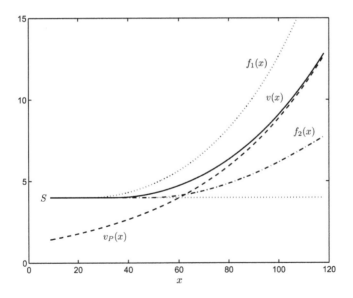

Figure 6.3. *Solutions to the Hamilton-Jacobi-Bellman equation for various boundary conditions.*

(6.35) hold. Figure 6.3 displays two such "pseudo-value functions" f_1 and f_2, for $b_1 < b^* < b_2$. Both are similar to v except that neither approaches v_P as $x \to +\infty$.

Notes

The literature on option pricing in financial markets is vast. See Duffie (1988, 1996) and the references there for an introduction. Cox and Ross (1976) and Cox, Ross, and Rubinstein (1979) are early and highly readable treatments based on discrete approximations to a Brownian motion.

Option theory has been employed in a wide variety of other areas as well. For example, see MacDonald and Siegel (1985, 1986) for applications to the timing of entry and exit—investment and shutting down; see Weisbrod (1964), Arrow and Fisher (1974), and Henry (1974) for applications to environmental protection; and see Brennan and Schwartz (1985) for the role of option values in assessing natural resource projects.

7

Models with Fixed Costs

IN THE OPTION problem of Chapter 6 the fact that the option can be exercised only once acts like a fixed cost. In other settings action can be taken many times, but there is an explicit fixed cost of adjustment. The methods used to analyze the option problem can readily be extended to this class. The problem of optimally exercising control is then more complicated in two respects, however. First, the size of the adjustment must be chosen. In addition, because action is taken repeatedly, decisions must be forward looking in a more complex sense, anticipating future actions by the decision maker as well as changes in the economic environment. A stochastic version of the menu cost model studied by Sheshinski and Weiss (1977, 1983) and others provides an example.

In the menu cost model the profit flow of a firm depends on the price of its own product relative to a general price index. The general price index follows a geometric Brownian motion, and the firm's problem is to choose a policy for changing the nominal price of its own product. Changing the price is assumed to entail a fixed cost, interpreted as the time cost of managerial decision making as well as the cost of printing a new menu, but no variable costs. As will be shown below, under fairly mild restrictions the optimal policy has the following form: there is an inaction region (b, B) and a return point $S \in (b, B)$. While the relative price remains inside the inaction region the firm does nothing. When the relative price leaves this region the firm immediately adjusts its nominal price so that the relative price is equal to the return value S.

Action is taken repeatedly in the menu cost model, and long-run averages under the optimal policy can also be described. For example, the fraction of adjustments at each threshold, the average time between adjustments, and the long-run density for relative price can all be calculated. In similar settings with a large number of agents experiencing i.i.d. shocks (not

129

a sensible assumption for the menu cost model) these averages can also be interpreted as cross-sectional averages in the stationary distribution.

The model can also be extended to allow the occasional arrival of opportunities to adjust without paying the fixed cost. The method for incorporating such shocks, which are modeled as having Poisson arrivals, is also described.

The rest of the chapter is organized as follows. In Section 7.1 the model is set up, feasible policies are described, the problem is formulated in a recursive way that exploits stationarity, and the optimized value function is shown to be bounded. Section 7.2 develops two more preliminary results, providing conditions under which the optimal policy involves exercising control and showing that there is a single inaction region. In Section 7.3 the expected discounted local time function $\hat{L}$ and the expected discounted indicator functions ψ and Ψ are used to characterize the optimal policy and value function. In Section 7.4 the Hamilton-Jacobi-Bellman equation is used to obtain the solution, and long-run averages are described. In Section 7.5 exogenous opportunities for costless adjustment are discussed. Section 7.6 contains an example.

7.1. A Menu Cost Model

Consider a firm whose profit flow at any date t depends on the ratio of its own nominal price to an aggregate (industrywide or economywide) price index, where the latter is a geometric Brownian motion. It is convenient to work with the prices in log form. Let $p(t)$ be the log of the firm's nominal price and $\overline{p}(t)$ the log of the aggregate price index. The latter is a Brownian motion with initial value $\overline{p}(0) = \overline{p}_0$ on a filtered space $(\Omega, \mathbb{F}, Q)$. All of the stochastic processes for prices, profits, and so on developed below are defined on this space.

The initial value for the firm's (log) nominal price p_0 is given. The firm can change its nominal price at any time, but to do so it must pay a fixed adjustment cost $c > 0$. This cost is constant over time and measured in real terms. Because control entails a fixed cost, the firm adjusts the price only occasionally and by discrete amounts. That is, it chooses an increasing sequence of stopping times $0 \le T_1 \le_2 < \ldots \le T_i < \ldots$, the (random) dates at which it adjusts its nominal price.

Since the profit flow at any date depends only on the firm's relative price, the problem can be formulated in terms of that one state variable. Doing so streamlines the notation and focuses attention on the economically interesting aspects of the problem. Let

$$Z(t) \equiv p(t) - \overline{p}(t), \quad \text{all } t \ge 0, \text{ all } \omega,$$

with initial value $z_0 \equiv p_0 - \overline{p}_0$, be the log of the firm's relative price at date t. At each stopping time T_i when the firm adjusts its nominal price, it in effect chooses a value z_i for its relative price. Thus, in addition to the sequence of stopping times the firm chooses a sequence of random variables $\{z_i\}_{i=1}^{\infty}$, where $z_i(\omega)$ is the (log) relative price set at $T_i(\omega)$.

Formally, $\gamma = \{(T_i, z_i)\}_{i=1}^{\infty}$ is an *impulse control policy* if

    i. $0 \leq T_1 \leq T_2 < \cdots \leq T_i < \cdots$ are stopping times, and
    ii. each z_i is $\mathfrak{F}_{T_i}$−measurable.

Note that these requirements involve the filtration $\mathbb{F}$. The first states that at any date t it must be possible for the decision maker to tell whether T_i has occurred, and the second states that the price set at $T_i(\omega)$ can depend only on information available at that date. Let Γ be the set of all impulse control policies.

At each stopping time $T_i(\omega)$, the firm's relative price $Z(t)$ jumps to the targeted level $z_i(\omega)$, and during the subsequent (random) time interval $[T_i, T_{i+1})$ the increments to $Z(t)$ mirror—with a sign change—the increments to $\overline{p}(t)$. Thus, given the initial value $Z(0) = z_0$ and an impulse control policy $\gamma = \{(T_i, z_i)\}_{i=1}^{\infty}$, the stochastic process for the firm's relative price is

$$Z(t) = z_i - \left[\overline{p}(t) - \overline{p}(T_i)\right], \quad t \in [T_i, T_{i+1}), \quad i = 0, 1, 2, \ldots, \quad \text{all } \omega, \quad (7.1)$$

where $T_0 \equiv 0$. Requirements (i) and (ii) on γ insure that $Z(t)$ satisfies the measurability conditions for a stochastic process. Since $\overline{p}(t)$ is a Brownian motion, over each interval $[T_i, T_{i+1})$ the relative price $Z(t)$ also behaves like a Brownian motion. Let $(-\mu, \sigma^2)$ be the parameters of the process $\overline{p}$, so that Z has parameters (μ, σ^2).

The profit flow of the firm, $\pi(z)$, is a stationary function of its relative price z, and profits are discounted at a constant interest rate r. The following restrictions on π, r, c and the parameters μ, σ^2 insure that the problem is well behaved.

Assumption 7.1.   (i) $r, c, \sigma^2 > 0$;
    (ii) π is continuous and is strictly increasing on $(-\infty, 0)$ and strictly decreasing on $(0, \infty)$.

The assumption that π is single peaked insures that the optimal policy is unique and involves only one inaction region. The assumption that the peak is at $z = 0$ is simply a convenient normalization.

Given an initial state z_0 and an impulse control policy $\gamma \in \Gamma$, let $H(z_0; \gamma)$ be the expected discounted value of total returns:

$$H(z_0; \gamma) \equiv E_{z_0} \left\{ \int_{T_0}^{T_1} e^{-rt} \pi[Z(t)]dt + \sum_{i=1}^{\infty} \left[-e^{-rT_i}c + \int_{T_i}^{T_{i+1}} e^{-rt} \pi[Z(t)]dt \right] \right\},$$

where $Z(t)$ is as in (7.1). Under the stated assumptions on γ and r, c, π, the integrals in this expression are well defined and the expected value exists (although it may be $-\infty$).

The firm's problem is to maximize discounted returns net of adjustment costs. Let $v(z)$ be the maximized value for discounted returns, given the initial state z. Then

$$v(z) \equiv \sup_{\gamma \in \Gamma} H(z; \gamma), \quad \text{all } z.$$

The following proposition establishes an important fact about v.

Proposition 7.1. Under Assumption 7.1 v is bounded.

Proof. Clearly H and v are bounded above by $\pi(0)/r$. For a bound from below define the policy $\hat{\gamma}$ as follows. Choose any $a < s < A$ and let

$$z_i(\omega) = s, \quad \text{all } i, \omega,$$

$$T_1 = 0,$$

$$T_{i+1} = \min\{t > T_i : Z(t) \notin (a, A)\}, \quad i = 1, 2, \ldots.$$

Then

$$H(z; \hat{\gamma}) = E_z \left\{ \sum_{i=1}^{\infty} \left[-e^{-rT_i}c + \int_{T_i}^{T_{i+1}} e^{-rt} \pi(Z(t))dt \right] \right\} \equiv h_0,$$

is finite and independent of z, so $v \geq h_0$. ∎

With Proposition 7.1 established the firm's problem can be stated in a way that exploits recursivity. Since the environment is stationary, the Principle of Optimality suggests that the value function v (and only v) satisfies the Bellman equation

$$v(z) = \sup_{T \geq 0, s} E_z \left\{ \int_0^T e^{-rt} \pi(Z(t))dt + e^{-rT}[v(s) - c] \right\}, \quad \text{all } z, \quad (7.2)$$

where T is a stopping time.

Note that the recursive approach in (7.2), where v does not depend directly on time, depends critically on the assumption that $\bar{p}$ is a Brownian motion. Under this assumption the process

$$x_i(s) = \bar{p}(T_i + s) - \bar{p}(T_i), \quad s \in [0, T_{i+1} - T_i),$$

has the same distribution for all i, ω, so the increments to Z in (7.1) have the same distribution for any choice of stopping times. This would not be true if $\bar{p}$ were a more general diffusion.

7.2. Preliminary Results

The optimal policy does not necessarily involve exercising control, and it is useful to begin by describing conditions under which no control is exercised. Let $v_P(z)$ be the expected returns over an infinite horizon if no control is exercised,

$$v_P(z) \equiv E_z \left[\int_0^\infty e^{-rt} \pi \left(Z(t) \right) dt \right]$$

$$= \int_{-\infty}^\infty \hat{L}(\zeta; z, -\infty, \infty) \pi(\zeta) d\zeta$$

$$= \frac{1}{J} \left[\int_z^\infty e^{R_2(z-\zeta)} \pi(\zeta) d\zeta + \int_{-\infty}^z e^{R_1(z-\zeta)} \pi(\zeta) d\zeta \right], \quad \text{all } z,$$

where $R_1 < 0 < R_2$ and $J > 0$ are as defined in Section 5.2 and the second line uses the results from Section 5.6. The next result provides necessary and sufficient conditions for $v = v_P$, for no control to be an optimal policy.

Proposition 7.2. Under Assumption 7.1, $v = v_P$ if and only if $v_P > -\infty$ and

$$\inf_z v_P(z) \geq \sup_z v_P(z) - c. \tag{7.3}$$

Proof. Suppose $v_P > -\infty$ and (7.3) holds. Then

$$v(z) = \sup_{T \geq 0, s} E_z \left\{ \int_0^T e^{-rt} \pi(Z(t)) dt + e^{-rT} \left[v_P(s) - c \right] \right\}$$

$$= v_P(z) + \sup_{T \geq 0} E_z \left\{ e^{-rT} \left[\sup_s v_P(s) - c - v_P(Z(T)) \right] \right\}$$

$$= v_P(z),$$

where T is a stopping time, the second line uses the fact that since v_P is bounded, expected returns up to the stopping time T can be written as $v_P(z) - E_z\left[e^{-rT}v_P(Z(T))\right]$, and the last line uses (7.3).

Conversely, suppose $v = v_P$. Then by Proposition 7.1 v_P is bounded, and in addition v_P satisfies (7.2). Since $T = 0$ is feasible, it follows that (7.3) holds. ∎

The idea behind this result is straightforward. If (7.3) holds, then the function v_P is very flat, varying by less than c between its minimum and its maximum. Thus, the fixed cost is too large to justify even a single adjustment. For the rest of the analysis the following assumption is used.

Assumption 7.2.   Either $v_P = -\infty$ or

$$c < \sup_z v_P(z) - \inf_z v_P(z).$$

The next result establishes that under Assumptions 7.1 and 7.2 there exist unique critical values b^*, B^*, with $b^* < 0 < B^*$, that characterize the optimal stopping times. Specifically, an optimal policy requires adjusting immediately if the current state lies outside (b^*, B^*) and adjusting at $T(b^*) \wedge T(B^*)$ otherwise. Notice that Assumption 7.2 rules out cases in which $b^* = -\infty$ *and* $B^* = \infty$, but it allows cases in which only one threshold is finite.

Proposition 7.3.   Under Assumptions 7.1 and 7.2 there exist $b^* < 0 < B^*$, with $|b^*| < \infty$, $B^* < \infty$, or both, with the following property: the unique optimal stopping time in (7.2) is $T = 0$ for $z \notin (b^*, B^*)$ and is $T = T(b^*) \wedge T(B^*)$ for $z \in (b^*, B^*)$.

Proof.   Adjusting at every point is not an optimal policy, so there is at least one interval in **R** that is an inaction region. And by Proposition 7.2, $T = \infty$ is not an optimal policy, so there is at least one interval in **R** where the firm adjusts immediately. Hence the optimal policy divides the real line into alternating action and inaction regions. That is, there exist

$$\ldots < b_{i-1} < B_{i-1} < b_i < B_i < b_{i+1} < B_{i+1} < \ldots$$

with the property that for all i,

$$T = \begin{cases} T(b_i) \wedge T(B_i), & \text{all } z \in (b_i, B_i), \\ 0, & \text{all } z \in [B_i, b_{i+1}]. \end{cases}$$

Define

$$M \equiv \sup_s v(s) - c,$$

and note that since $\pi(z)$ has its maximum at $z = 0$,

$$M < \frac{\pi(0)}{r} - c.$$

Suppose the initial state is $z_0 = 0$. Adjusting immediately would give a payoff of M, while waiting for $h > 0$ units of time, for h small, gives an expected payoff of approximately $\pi(0)h + (1 - rh)\,M$. The difference between the two returns is

$$\Delta = h\,[\pi(0) - rM] > hrc > 0.$$

Hence $z = 0$ is inside an inaction region. Let $b_0 < 0 < B_0$ be the optimal thresholds for $z_0 = 0$.

Suppose there were another inaction region above B_0. That is, suppose the interval (b_1, B_1) is an inaction region, for some $0 < B_0 < b_1 < B_1$. Consider an initial condition $z \in (b_1, B_1)$. By using the stopping time $T = T(b_1) \wedge T(B_1)$ the firm gets the expected payoff

$$E_z\left[\int_0^T e^{-rs}\pi(Z(s))ds + e^{-rT}M\right]$$

$$< E_z\left[\frac{1}{r}\left(1 - e^{-rT}\right)\pi(b_1) + e^{-rT}M\right]$$

$$= \frac{1}{r}\pi(b_1) + \left[M - \frac{1}{r}\pi(b_1)\right]E_z\left[e^{-rT}\right],$$

where the second line uses the fact that π is decreasing for $z > 0$. The return from this policy exceeds the return M from adjusting immediately only if

$$\frac{1}{r}\pi(b_1) - M > \left[\frac{1}{r}\pi(b_1) - M\right]E_z\left[e^{-rT}\right].$$

Since $E_z\left[e^{-rT}\right] < 1$, this inequality holds if and only if $\pi\,(b_1) > rM$. But consider an initial condition $z \in (B_0, b_1)$. Since adjusting immediately delivers a higher return than operating for a small increment of time $h > 0$ and then adjusting,

$$h\pi(z) + (1 - rh)\,M < M, \quad \text{all } z \in (B_0, b_1),$$

or $\pi(z) < rM$. Since $\pi(z)$ is strictly decreasing for $z > 0$, these two conclusions contradict each other.

A similar argument applies for intervals below b_0. Hence there is a single inaction region (b^*, B^*), and $b^* < 0 < B^*$. ∎

Having established that there is a unique inaction region, the remaining task is to characterize the critical values b^*, B^*, S^*. The next sections examine two methods for doing so.

7.3. Optimizing: A Direct Approach

One method for characterizing the optimal policy is a direct approach like the one used for the option problem. This method, which uses the functions $\hat{L}$, ψ, and Ψ defined in Chapter 5, involves describing the expected value from following an arbitrary policy b, B, S and then maximizing that value in the usual way.

Fix any b, B, S with $b < S < B$, and let $F(z, b, B, S)$ be the expected discounted return from using the policy defined by these critical values. Note that for $z \in (b, B)$ the expected return from this policy can be written as the sum of three parts: expected returns before the stopping time $T = T(b) \wedge T(B)$ and the expected continuation values after stops at b and B. Hence F satisfies the Bellman-type equation

$$F(z, b, B, S) = \begin{cases} w(z, b, B) + \left[\psi(z, b, B) + \Psi(z, b, B)\right] \\ \quad \times \left[F(S, b, B, S) - c\right], & \text{if } z \in (b, B) \\ F(S, b, B, S) - c, & \text{if } z \notin (b, B), \end{cases}$$

(7.4)

where

$$w(z, b, B) \equiv \mathrm{E}_z \left[\int_0^T e^{-rs}\pi(Z(s))ds\right]$$

$$= \int_b^B \hat{L}(\zeta; z, b, B)\pi(\zeta)d\zeta,$$

$$\psi(z, b, B) \equiv \mathrm{E}_z \left[e^{-rT} \mid Z(T) = b\right] \mathrm{Pr}_z \left[Z(T) = b\right],$$

$$\Psi(z, b, B) \equiv \mathrm{E}_z \left[e^{-rT} \mid Z(T) = B\right] \mathrm{Pr}_z \left[Z(T) = B\right],$$

are as defined in Chapter 5, and $\mathrm{E}_z [\cdot]$ denotes an expectation conditional on the initial value z. The firm's problem is to choose b, B, and S to maximize F, so

$$v(z) = \max_{b, B, S} F(z, b, B, S). \tag{7.5}$$

The optimal critical values b^*, B^*, and S^* are characterized by first order conditions obtained from (7.5). The following lemma establishes an important fact about the first order conditions for the thresholds b^* and B^*.

Lemma 7.4. Let Assumptions 7.1 and 7.2 hold.

 i. Fix any M and $\hat{b} < B$. If

$$w_b(z, \hat{b}, B) + \left[\psi_b(z, \hat{b}, B) + \Psi_b(z, \hat{b}, B)\right] M = 0 \qquad (7.6)$$

holds for some $z \in [\hat{b}, B)$, then it holds for all $z \in [\hat{b}, B)$ and in addition

$$w_z(\hat{b}, \hat{b}, B) + \left[\psi_z(\hat{b}, \hat{b}, B) + \Psi_z(\hat{b}, \hat{b}, B)\right] M = 0.$$

 ii. Fix any M and $\hat{B} > b$. If

$$w_B(z, b, \hat{B}) + \left[\psi_B(z, b, \hat{B}) + \Psi_B(z, b, \hat{B})\right] M = 0 \qquad (7.7)$$

holds for some $z \in (b, \hat{B}]$, then it holds for all $z \in (b, \hat{B}]$ and in addition

$$w_z(\hat{B}, b, \hat{B}) + \left[\psi_z(\hat{B}, b, \hat{B}) + \Psi_z(\hat{B}, b, \hat{B})\right] M = 0.$$

Proof. i. Fix any M and $\hat{b} < B$. If (7.6) holds for $\hat{z} \in [\hat{b}, B)$, then

$$0 = w_b(\hat{z}, \hat{b}, B) + \left[\psi_b(\hat{z}, \hat{b}, B) + \Psi_b(\hat{z}, \hat{b}, B)\right] M$$

$$= \psi(\hat{z}) \left\{w_b(\hat{b}, \hat{b}, B) + \left[\psi_b(\hat{b}, \hat{b}, B) + \Psi_b(\hat{b}, \hat{b}, B)\right] M\right\}$$

$$= -\psi(\hat{z}) \left\{w_z(\hat{b}, \hat{b}, B) + \left[\psi_z(\hat{b}, \hat{b}, B) + \Psi_z(\hat{b}, \hat{b}, B)\right] M\right\},$$

where the second and third lines use Propositions 5.5 and 5.6. Since $\psi(\hat{z}) > 0$ for $\hat{z} \in [\hat{b}, B)$, the term in braces in the last line must be equal to zero. Reversing the argument then implies (7.6) holds for all $z \in [\hat{b}, B)$.

 ii. A similar argument establishes the claims here. ∎

Lemma 7.4 implies that if the first-order condition $F_b(z, b^*, B^*, S^*) = 0$ holds for any $z \in (b^*, B^*)$, then it holds for all $z \in (b^*, B^*)$. That is, the optimal threshold b^* does not vary with z. The same is true for B^*. In addition, the same is clearly true for the optimal return point: since S^* maximizes the last term in (7.4), which is simply $F(S)$, it is independent of the current state. The fact that the optimal critical values do not vary with the current state is an immediate consequence of the Principle of Optimality. Suppose that decision maker chooses b^*, B^*, and S^* when the state is $z \in (b^*, B^*)$. Suppose further that some time passes and neither threshold has been reached. If the decision maker re-optimizes he should choose the same thresholds and return point.

The next result uses Lemma 7.4 to characterize the optimal policy.

Proposition 7.5.   Let Assumptions 7.1 and 7.2 hold. If b^*, B^*, S^* attain the maximum in (7.5), with b^* and B^* finite, then

$$w_z(b^*, b^*, B^*) + \left[\psi_z(b^*, b^*, B) + \Psi_z(b^*, b^*, B^*)\right] M^* = 0, \quad (7.8)$$

$$w_z(B^*, b^*, B^*) + \left[\psi_z(B^*, b^*, B^*) + \Psi_z(B^*, b^*, B^*)\right] M^* = 0, \quad (7.9)$$

$$w_z(S^*, b^*, B^*) + \left[\psi_z(S^*, b^*, B^*) + \Psi_z(S^*, b^*, B^*)\right] M^* = 0, \quad (7.10)$$

where

$$M^* = \frac{w(S^*, b^*, B^*) - c}{1 - \psi(S^*, b^*, B^*) - \Psi(S^*, b^*, B^*)}. \quad (7.11)$$

If $b^* = -\infty$, then

$$\lim_{z \to -\infty} \pi(z) \geq r M^* \quad (7.12)$$

replaces (7.8). If $B^* = \infty$, then

$$\lim_{z \to \infty} \pi(z) \geq r M^* \quad (7.13)$$

replaces (7.9).

Proof.   Suppose both b^* and B^* are finite. Then

$$v(z) = \begin{cases} w(z, b^*, B^*) + \left[\psi(z, b^*, B^*) + \Psi(z, b^*, B^*)\right] M^*, & z \in (b^*, B^*), \\ M^*, & z \notin (b^*, B^*), \end{cases}$$

$$(7.14)$$

where $M^* \equiv v(S^*) - c$. Then

$$M = w(S^*, b^*, B^*) + \left[\psi(S^*, b^*, B^*) + \Psi(S^*, b^*, B^*)\right] M^* - c,$$

so (7.11) holds. Clearly v is differentiable, so a necessary condition for a maximum at S^* is $v'(S^*) = 0$. Hence (7.10) holds. A necessary condition for the optimality of b^* is (7.6), and by Lemma 7.4 it implies (7.8). Similarly, (7.7) is necessary for the optimality of B^*, and it implies (7.9).

If $b^* = -\infty$, then for any $y > -\infty$,

$$0 > w_b(z, y, B^*) + \left[\psi_b(z, y, B^*) + \Psi_b(z, y, B^*)\right] M^*$$
$$= -\psi(z) \left\{w_z(y, y, B^*) + \left[\psi_z(y, y, B^*) + \Psi_z(y, y, B^*)\right] M^*\right\}, \quad \text{all } z > y.$$

Taking the limit as $y \to -\infty$, this condition implies

$$0 \le \lim_{y \to -\infty} \left\{w_z(y, y, B^*) + \left[\psi_z(y, y, B^*) + \Psi_z(y, y, B^*)\right] M^*\right\}. \quad (7.15)$$

Consider the three terms in (7.15). Recall the constant J and roots R_1, R_2 defined in Section 5.2. Since

$$\lim_{y \to -\infty} w_z(y, y, B^*) = \frac{R_2 - R_1}{J} \lim_{y \to -\infty} \int_y^{B^*} e^{R_2(y-\xi)} \pi(\xi) d\xi,$$

$$\lim_{y \to -\infty} \psi_z(y, y, B^*) = R_1,$$

$$\lim_{y \to -\infty} \Psi_z(y, y, B^*) = 0,$$

it follows that (7.15) holds if and only if

$$0 \le \frac{R_2 - R_1}{J} \lim_{y \to -\infty} \int_y^{B^*} e^{R_2(y-\xi)} \pi(\xi) d\xi + R_1 M^*.$$

Since $(R_1 - R_2)/R_1 J = R_2/r$, this condition holds if and only if

$$r M^* \le \lim_{y \to -\infty} \int_y^{B^*} R_2 e^{R_2(y-\xi)} \pi(\xi) d\xi,$$

which in turn holds if and only if (7.12) is satisfied.

A similar argument establishes that (7.13) holds if $B^* = \infty$. ∎

Proposition 7.5 uses a direct approach to the firm's problem, characterizing the expected payoff from arbitrary policies and then optimizing. Moreover, since the functions w, ψ, and Ψ are known, (7.8)–(7.11) is simply a system of four equations in the unknowns b^*, B^*, S^*, M^*. That system can be used to study the effects of parameter changes analytically, and computing solutions numerically with it is relatively simple. There is an alternative, however, which is examined next.

7.4. Using the Hamilton-Jacobi-Bellman Equation

The Hamilton-Jacobi-Bellman (HJB) equation provides another approach for studying value functions, both the optimized function v and the functions $F(\cdot, b, B, S)$ that describe expected returns from arbitrary policies. Specifically, they all satisfy the HJB equation, differing only in their boundary conditions. In each case the boundary conditions involve the continuity of the value function at the thresholds b and B. The function v satisfies three additional optimality conditions, one each for b, B, and S. Thus, the HJB equation together with the appropriate boundary conditions provides a way to construct any of these functions. This approach is perhaps less transparent than the one employing $\hat{L}$, ψ, and Ψ, but it has the advantage of being more flexible. This additional flexibility is exploited in Chapter 8.

The HJB equation is derived, as usual, by looking at the value of a firm with initial state $Z(0) = z$ in the interior of the inaction region. Consider the function v. For a sufficiently short interval of time h the value of the firm can be written as

$$v(z) \approx \pi(Z(0))h + \frac{1}{1+rh} E_z \left[v(Z(0) + \Delta Z) \right]$$

$$\approx \pi(z)h + \frac{1}{1+rh} \left[v(z) + \mu v'(z)h + \frac{1}{2}\sigma^2 v''(z)h \right], \qquad (7.16)$$

where ΔZ denotes the (random) change in $Z(t)$ over the time interval $[0, h]$, and the second line uses a second-order Taylor series approximation and Ito's lemma. Rearranging terms and taking the limit as $h \to 0$ produces the HJB equation.

The HJB equation is a second-order ODE, so two boundary conditions are required to complete the solution. Three additional conditions are then needed to determine b^*, B^*, and S^*. The following result describes these boundary and optimality conditions.

Proposition 7.6. Let Assumptions 7.1 and 7.2 hold. Let v be the function in (7.14) and let b^*, B^*, S^* be the optimal policy. If b^* and B^* are finite, then

    i. v satisfies

$$rv(z) = \pi(z) + \mu v'(z) + \tfrac{1}{2}\sigma^2 v''(z), \quad z \in \left(b^*, B^* \right), \qquad (7.17)$$

$$v(z) = v(S^*) - c, \qquad\qquad\qquad\qquad z \notin \left(b^*, B^* \right); \qquad (7.18)$$

    ii. v and v' are continuous at b^*,

$$\lim_{z \downarrow b^*} v(z) = v(S^*) - c, \quad \text{and} \quad \lim_{z \downarrow b^*} v'(z) = 0; \qquad (7.19)$$

iii. v and v' are continuous at B^*,

$$\lim_{z \uparrow B^*} v(z) = v(S^*) - c, \quad \text{and} \quad \lim_{z \uparrow B^*} v'(z) = 0; \tag{7.20}$$

iv. S^* satisfies

$$v'(S^*) = 0. \tag{7.21}$$

If $b^* = -\infty$, then instead of (7.19)

$$\lim_{z \to -\infty} v(z) = \lim_{z \to -\infty} v_P(z) \geq v(S^*) - c; \tag{7.22}$$

and if $B^* = \infty$, then instead of (7.20)

$$\lim_{z \to \infty} v(z) = \lim_{z \to \infty} v_P(z) \geq v(S^*) - c, \tag{7.23}$$

where v_P is as defined in Section 7.2.

Remark. Equation (7.17) is the HJB equation, which holds on the inaction region, and (7.18) extends the value function outside that region. The first conditions in (7.19) and (7.20), which state that v is continuous at the thresholds b^* and B^*, are the *value matching* conditions. The second conditions in (7.19) and (7.20), which state that v' is continuous at the thresholds b^* and B^*, are the *smooth pasting* conditions. The *optimal return* condition in (7.21) characterizes the point S^*. The value matching and smooth pasting conditions are as in the option problem of Chapter 6, except that here there is an upper threshold as well as a lower one. The optimal return condition is new. Since exercising the option was a one-time event, it did not involve a return point.

Proof. Multiply (7.16) by $(1 + rh)$, divide by h, and let $h \to 0$ to find that v satisfies (7.17). It is clear from (7.14) that (7.18) holds.

If both b^* and B^* are finite, then it is immediate from (7.14) that the value matching conditions in (7.19) and (7.20) hold. In addition, since (7.8)–(7.10) are satisfied, it follows that the smooth pasting conditions in (7.19) and (7.20) and the optimal return condition in (7.10) also hold.

Suppose $b^* = -\infty$. Then (7.14) implies

$$\lim_{z \to -\infty} v(z) = \lim_{z \to -\infty} \{ w(z, -\infty, B^*)$$

$$+ \left[\psi(z, -\infty, B^*) + \Psi(z, -\infty, B^*) \right] \left[v(S^*) - c \right] \}$$

$$= v_P(z) + (0 + 0) \left[v(S^*) - c \right],$$

so the first claim in (7.22) holds. The second follows immediately from the hypothesis that $b^* = -\infty$ is the optimal policy.

A similar argument establishes the claims in (7.23). ∎

The following corollary shows that some of these claims also hold for the value functions $F(\cdot, b, B, S)$ associated with arbitrary policies.

Corollary. Let $b < S < B$, with b and B finite, be an arbitrary policy, and let $F(\cdot, b, B, S)$ be the function in (7.4). Then F satisfies (7.17) and (7.18), and it is continuous in z at b and B. If $b = -\infty$ then the first condition in (7.22) replaces continuity at b. If $B = +\infty$ then the first condition in (7.23) replaces continuity at B.

Proof. The arguments in the proof of Proposition 7.6 hold for any $b < S < B$. ∎

It is not surprising that F satisfies the HJB equation and value matching conditions. The logic leading to the HJB equation does not involve optimization, only inaction in a fixed region, and the value matching conditions hold if any fixed adjustment policy is used outside that inaction.

Note, too, that the functions v and F can be constructed by reversing the arguments. Recall from Chapter 5 that $h_i(z) = e^{R_i z}$, $i = 1, 2$, are homogeneous solutions of (7.17). Hence all solutions have the form

$$\hat{v}(z) = f_P(z) + d_1 e^{R_1 z} + d_2 e^{R_2 z},$$

where f_P is any particular solution, and d_1, d_2 are arbitrary constants. For example, recall from Chapter 5 that v_P is a particular solution, and so is $w(\cdot, b, B)$, for any b, B. Therefore, using w as the particular solution one finds that for any $b < B$, solutions to (7.17) have the form

$$\hat{v}(z) = w(z, b, B) + d_1 e^{R_1 z} + d_2 e^{R_2 z}, \quad \text{all } z \in (b, B). \tag{7.24}$$

Fix any policy $b < S < B$, with b and B finite. Let $\hat{v}$ be as in (7.24) on (b, B) and as in the second line of (7.17) for $z \notin (b, B)$. Value matching requires that the two expressions agree at b and B. Since $w(b, b, B) = w(B, b, B) = 0$, this requires

$$d_1 e^{R_1 b} + d_2 e^{R_2 b} = \hat{v}(S) - c,$$

$$d_1 e^{R_1 B} + d_2 e^{R_2 B} = \hat{v}(S) - c.$$

Solving this pair of equations and substituting for d_1 and d_2 in (7.24) gives

$$\hat{v}(z) = w(z, b, B) + \left[\psi(z, b, B) + \Psi(z, b, B) \right] \left[\hat{v}(S) - c \right], \tag{7.25}$$

which is the function $F(\cdot, b, B, S)$ in (7.4).

For $b = -\infty$, value matching at b is replaced with the first condition in (7.22). Since $R_1 < 0$, this condition requires $d_1 = 0$. Value matching at B then implies

$$d_2 = e^{-R_2 B} \left[\hat{v}(S) - c \right].$$

Hence for any $z \leq B$,

$$d_1 e^{R_1 z} + d_2 e^{R_2 z} = 0 + e^{R_2(z-B)} \left[\hat{v}(S) - c \right]$$

$$= \psi(z, -\infty, B) + \Psi(z, -\infty, B) \left[\hat{v}(S) - c \right],$$

so (7.25) is unaltered. A similar argument holds if $B = \infty$.

The argument thus far does not involve optimization. Hence for any choice of $b < S < B$, the construction above produces the function $\hat{v} = F(\cdot, b, B, S)$. The optimized function v is found by choosing, among all these solutions, the one that satisfies the smooth pasting and optimal return conditions as well, $F_z(b) = F_z(B) = F_z(S) = 0$, to determine the critical values b^*, B^*, S^*. By Lemma 7.4, these three conditions are equivalent to the first-order conditions $F_b = F_B = F_S = 0$. If $b^* = -\infty$, then smooth pasting at b is replaced with

$$\lim_{z \to -\infty} \hat{v}(z) \geq v(S^*) - c,$$

and similarly if $B^* = \infty$.

If the function v_P is bounded, then it provides another convenient choice for the particular solution. Since v_P is the expected discounted value of returns if no control is exercised, for this choice the term $d_1 e^{R_1 z} + d_2 e^{R_2 z}$ represents the value of exercising control.

Exercise 7.1. Suppose that v_P is bounded, and consider the function

$$F(z, b, B, S) = v_P(x) + d_1(b, B, S) e^{R_1 z} + d_2(b, B, S) e^{R_2 z},$$

where $b < S < B$ are arbitrary and the constants d_1 and d_2 are chosen so that the value matching conditions hold. Show that the optimal policy b^*, B^*, S^* maximizes the sum $d_1(b, B, S) e^{R_1 z} + d_2(b, B, S) e^{R_2 z}$.

If v_P is not bounded, the return function π can be altered in the extreme regions to make it so. To see this, suppose that v is the optimized value function and b^*, B^*, S^* is the associated policy for the return function π. Notice that π appears in (7.17)–(7.23) only in the HJB equation, which holds only on (b^*, B^*). Consider any function $\hat{\pi} \geq \pi$ that coincides with π on (b^*, B^*) and satisfies Assumption 7.1. Clearly v and b^*, B^*, S^* are also the solution for $\hat{\pi}$.

Thus to construct the solution when $v_P = -\infty$, one can proceed the other way around. Choose $\hat{\pi} \geq \pi$ satisfying Assumption 7.1 so that (i) it coincides with π on an interval (a, A) that is large enough to contain the inaction region, and (ii) it has the property that $\hat{v}_P$ is bounded. Solve the firm's problem for $\hat{\pi}$. If the optimal inaction region (b^*, B^*) is contained in (a, A), then the solution for $\hat{\pi}$ is also the solution for π.

Since the profit function π in the menu cost model is single peaked, it is reasonable to suppose that the value function v is also single peaked. Proposition 7.7 shows that this conjecture is correct. (Recall that it has already been shown, in Proposition 7.3, that the peak of the return function lies inside the inaction region, $b^* < 0 < B^*$.)

Proposition 7.7. Under Assumptions 7.1 and 7.2 the value function v is single peaked.

Proof. Proposition 7.3 shows that there is a single inaction region (b^*, B^*), and Proposition 7.6 states that the value function v satisfies (7.17) on this interval. Hence the argument in the proof of Proposition 5.7 applies, and it implies that v is single peaked on (b^*, B^*). Since v is continuous and is constant for $z \notin (b^*, B^*)$, it is single peaked on all of **R**. ∎

After the optimal policy b^*, B^*, S^* has been determined it is straightforward to calculate various statistics that describe long-run behavior. Since the firm always sets a relative price of S^* when it adjusts, long-run averages are calculated with S^* as the initial condition. Recall the functions θ, Θ, τ, and L defined in Section 5.5. If the firm operates over a long period, the fraction of adjustments at the lower boundary is $\theta(S^*, b^*, B^*)$, the fraction at the upper boundary is $\Theta(S^*, b^*, B^*)$, the expected time between adjustments is $\tau(S^*, b^*, B^*)$, and the long-run density for the firm's relative price is $L(\cdot; S^*, b^*, B^*)/\tau(S^*, b^*, B^*)$.

The exogenous shock in the menu cost model studied here is a shock to an aggregate price index. Thus if there were a large number of firms, they would all experience the same shocks. But the arguments above can be adapted to study price adjustment in the presence of shocks to the demand for the firm's product or the costs of its inputs. In this case assuming i.i.d. shocks across firms is sensible, and the averages described above also represent the cross-sectional averages in the stationary distribution.

The next exercise, which involves entry and exit, looks at the long-run stationary distribution in a setting where firms follow an arbitrary decision rule.

Exercise 7.2. Consider an economy with a large number of firms. Each firm i is characterized by its stochastic productivity level X_i, and the productivity level for each firm is a Brownian motion with parameters (μ, σ^2). These processes are independent across firms, and $\mu < 0$.

There is entry and exit in this economy. Specifically, new firms enter at the rate $\gamma > 0$ per unit time, and each enters with a productivity level of $x_0 > 0$. A firm exits when its productivity level reaches $\underline{x} = 0$.

Describe the stationary cross-sectional distribution of productivity levels and the total mass of firms for this economy.

7.5. Random Opportunities for Costless Adjustment

The model above can easily be extended to allow the possibility that occasionally, at randomly occurring times, the firm can change its price without paying the fixed cost. Specifically, suppose that opportunities of this sort have Poisson arrival times, and consider a firm with current state z that is inside the inaction region. Consider a small increment of time $h > 0$. Over this interval the firm earns returns in the usual way, and at the end of the interval there are two possibilities. With probability λh the shock has arrived and the firm can change its price without incurring the adjustment cost, and with probability $1 - \lambda h$ it receives the usual expected continuation value. Hence the firm's current value $v(z)$ can be written as

$$v(z) \approx \pi(z)h + \frac{\lambda h}{1 + rh} \max_{z'} v(z') + \frac{1 - \lambda h}{1 + rh} E_z \left[v(z + \Delta Z) \right].$$

Using the optimal return point $z' = S^*$ and proceeding in the usual way, one obtains the modified HJB equation

$$(r + \lambda) v(z) \approx \pi(z) + \lambda v(S^*) + \left[\mu v'(z) + \tfrac{1}{2}\sigma^2 v''(z) \right]. \tag{7.26}$$

Note that $v(S^*) - v(z)$ is the capital gain the firm enjoys if the shock arrives when the state is z, so $\lambda \left[v(S^*) - v(z) \right]$ is the expected (flow) return from the arrival of the shock. The modified HJB equation in (7.26) adds this term to the usual current return.

The next exercise shows that the possibility of costless adjustment reduces the firm's incentive to pay the fixed cost, widening the inaction region at both ends.

Exercise 7.3. Show that the optimal lower threshold b^* is decreasing in λ and the upper threshold B^* is increasing in λ.

The next exercise looks at a version of a classic cash management problem.

Exercise 7.4. Consider an individual who holds cash to carry out transactions. Suppose she uses the following rule of thumb for cash management.

When her cash holdings reach zero she pays a fixed cost $c > 0$, goes to the ATM and withdraws M units of cash, where $M > 0$ is fixed. Between withdrawals her cash holdings are a (μ, σ^2) Brownian motion with $\mu < 0$.

Let $F(z)$ be the expected discounted value of the total fixed costs she pays, given current cash balances z, where the interest rate $r > 0$ is constant.

(a) Derive the HJB equation for this problem. What is a particular solution to this equation? What are the boundary conditions?

(b) Suppose that in addition to the fixed cost, the individual counts the foregone interest on her cash balances as a holding cost. Let $\hat{F}$ be the expected discounted value of the total fixed costs plus holding costs that she pays. Repeat part (a).

(c) Suppose that the individual gets utility $u(z)$ from holding cash balances z, where u is strictly increasing, strictly concave, continuously differentiable, and satisfies the Inada conditions $u'(0) > \infty$ and $\lim_{z \to \infty} u'(z) = 0$. The costs are as in part (b), so her net return from holding cash balances z is $u(z) - rz$. What is her optimal cash management strategy?

(d) Suppose that the individual is sometimes near the ATM by chance and can make withdrawals for free. These opportunities to get additional cash without paying the fixed cost have Poisson arrivals at rate $\lambda > 0$. What is the HJB equation for the individual, otherwise like the one in part (c), who gets these opportunities?

7.6. An Example

Let

$$\pi(z) = \begin{cases} \pi_0 e^{\eta z}, & z \geq 0, \\ \pi_0 e^{\delta z}, & z < 0, \end{cases}$$

where $\eta < 0 < \delta$ and $\pi_0 > 0$. Clearly Assumption 7.1 holds, and for fixed η, δ, Assumption 2 holds if π_0 is large enough. It is clear that the optimal policy depends on π_0 and c only through the ratio c/π_0, and in addition the parameters r, μ, σ^2 enter only as ratios. Thus, without loss of generality π_0 and r can be fixed and attention limited to changes in c, μ, and σ.

For baseline values let

$$\mu = 0, \qquad \sigma = 1, \qquad c = 1,$$
$$\eta = -0.4, \qquad \delta = 2.0, \qquad \pi_0 = 1, \qquad r = 0.05.$$

Figure 7.1 displays the annualized profit function π/r, the expected discounted return if no adjustment is ever made v_P, and the optimized value function v, as well as the optimal thresholds b^* and B^* and return point S^*. The profit function is asymmetric, falling off more sharply for negative values than for positive ones. Hence v_P is also asymmetric, with its peak at a

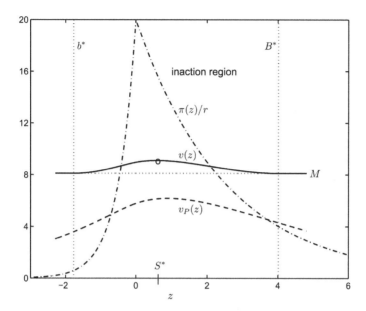

Figure 7.1. *The functions π/r, v, and v_P for the menu cost model, for the baseline parameter values $r = 0.05$, $\mu = 0$, $\sigma = 1$, $\eta = -0.4$, $\delta = 2$, $\pi_0 = 1$, and $c = 1$. The optimal policy is $b^* = -1.77$, $S^* = 0.59$, $B^* = 4.02$.*

positive value, even though the Brownian motion has zero drift. In addition v_P is much flatter than π/r and for z near zero is much lower, reflecting the fact that over time the state drifts away from its initial value.

The optimized value function v is also asymmetric, with its peak at a positive value, $S^* = 0.59$. In addition, the upper threshold $B^* = 4.02$ is looser than the lower one, $b^* = -1.77$, also a reflection of the asymmetry in π.

Figure 7.2 displays the long-run density for relative price $q(z; S^*, b^*, B^*)$ $\equiv L(\cdot; S^*, b^*, B^*)/\tau(S^*, b^*, B^*)$. It has a slightly asymmetric tent shape, with a peak at S^*.

Figures 7.3–7.5 display the effects of changing the parameters c, μ, and σ on the critical values b^*, B^*, S^*, the continuation value M, the expected time between adjustments $\tau(S^*)$, and the share of adjustments at the lower threshold, $\theta(S^*)$.

Figure 7.3 displays the effects as the adjustment cost c varies on $[0, 6]$. Since v_P takes values on $[0, 6.17]$, by Proposition 7.2, $c = 6.17$ is the highest fixed cost for which making price adjustments is worthwhile. Increasing c changes the return point S^* very little, but it makes the inaction region (b^*, B^*) broader. The continuation value M falls to zero and the expected

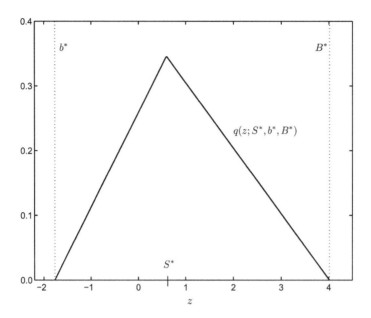

Figure 7.2. *The stationary density for relative price under the optimal policy, for the baseline parameter values.*

time between adjustments $\tau(S^*)$ grows rather sharply, but the fraction of adjustments at the lower threshold $\theta(S^*)$ does not change much.

Figure 7.4 displays the effects as the drift parameter μ varies on $[-1, +1]$. The return point S^* decreases with μ, as one would expect. The band (b^*, B^*) is narrowest for μ near zero and becomes broader as $|\mu|$ increases. In particular, for $\mu < 0$, B^* increases sharply as the drift becomes stronger, and for $\mu > 0$, b^* decreases sharply as the drift becomes stronger. This is also as one would expect. In both regions the drift is likely to move the state back toward the region with higher returns. The continuation value M is hump shaped, the expected time between adjustments $\tau(S^*)$ is single-peaked, with a maximum near $\mu = 0$, and the fraction of adjustments at the lower boundary $\theta(S^*)$ decreases with μ.

Figure 7.5 displays the effects as the diffusion parameter σ varies on $[0, 8]$. Increasing σ has little effect on S^*, but it makes the inaction region (b^*, B^*) broader. It reduces the continuation value M, since less time is spent in the region of high profits. The expected time between adjustments $\tau(S^*)$ rises as the inaction region gets broader, reflecting the fact that the firm

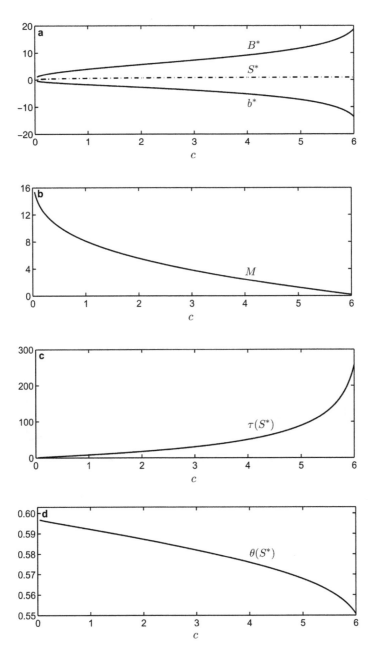

Figure 7.3. *The effects of changing the adjustment cost c, with baseline values for the other parameters, on (a) the optimal thresholds b^*, B^*, and return point S^*, (b) the normalized continuation value M, (c) the expected time between adjustments $\tau(S^*)$, and (d) the share of adjustments at the lower threshold $\theta(S^*)$.*

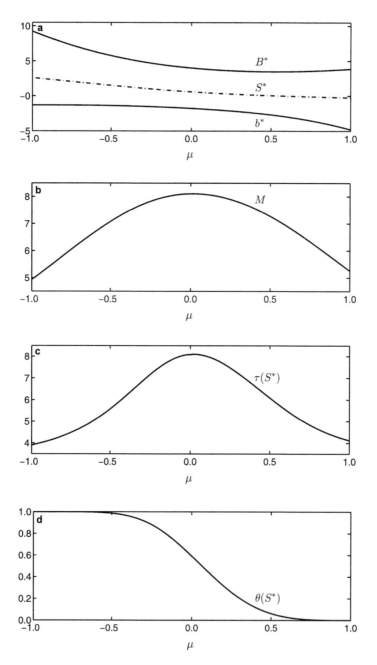

Figure 7.4. *The effects of changing the drift parameter* μ, *with baseline values for the other parameters, on (a) the optimal thresholds* b^*, B^*, *and return point* S^*, *(b) the normalized continuation value* M, *(c) the expected time between adjustments* $\tau(S^*)$, *and (d) the share of adjustments at the lower threshold* $\theta(S^*)$.

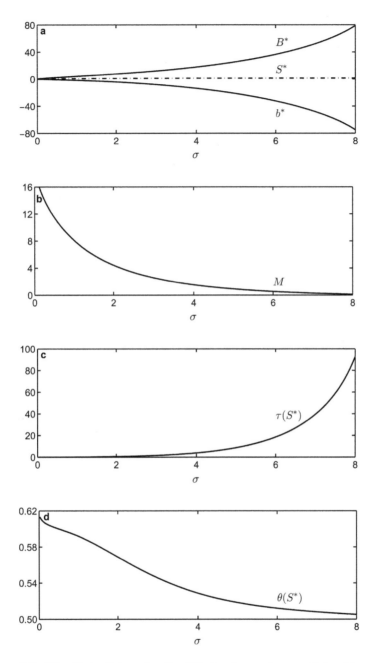

Figure 7.5. *The effects of changing the diffusion parameter σ, with baseline values for the other parameters, on (a) the optimal thresholds b^*, B^*, and return point S^*, (b) the normalized continuation value M, (c) the expected time between adjustments $\tau(S^*)$, and (d) the share of adustments at the lower threshold $\theta(S^*)$.*

adjusts on both margins. Because of the asymmetry in the return function, it also causes a slight decrease in $\theta(S^*)$, the share of adjustments at the lower boundary.

Notes

Sheshinski and Weiss (1977, 1983) were among the first to study pricing with fixed adjustment costs, and Sheshinski and Weiss (1993) draws together much of the early work—both theoretical and empirical—on menu costs. See Plehn-Dujowich (2005) for a discussion of sufficient conditions to insure that the optimal policy takes the form of a control band. See Ahlin (2001) for an example where the exogenous stochastic process is not a Brownian motion, and the optimal policy takes a different form. See Lach and Tsiddon (1991), Kashyap (1995), Bils and Klenow (2004), Klenow and Kryvtsov (2008), and Nakamura and Steinsson (2007) for empirical evidence on the size and frequency of price adjustments.

Dixit (1991b) has a simple treatment of impulse and instantaneous control based on discrete approximations, and Dumas (1991) has an approach based on HJB equations. Dixit (1991a) develops a method for approximating the effects of fixed costs and shows why even small fixed costs can lead to large inaction regions.

8

Models with Fixed and Variable Costs

IN MANY CONTEXTS exercising control involves variable costs of adjustment as well as fixed costs. The presence of a variable cost means that the decision about how much control to exercise is slightly more complicated than in the menu cost model, but the overall character of the solution is similar nevertheless: an optimal policy still involves doing nothing most of the time and exercising control only occasionally.

A standard inventory model of the type studied by Scarf (1960), Harrison, Selke, and Taylor (1983), and others provides an example. Suppose there is a plant that produces output, and there are customers who place orders. Both supply and demand are flows, both may be stochastic, and the difference between the two is the net inflow into a buffer stock. When left unregulated the stock behaves like a Brownian motion, with negative stocks interpreted as back-orders. Control is exercised by a manager who can add to the stock by purchasing the good elsewhere and can reduce it by selling on a secondary market.

The manager's problem involves cost minimization (as opposed to profit maximization), and there are three types of costs. Holding costs, which depend on the size of the stock, are the analog of profits in the menu cost model. They can be interpreted as interest, storage, and depreciation costs on positive stocks, and as the loss of goodwill from the delays on back-orders. The fixed cost of adjustment is also as in the menu cost model.

The variable cost of adjustment is a new feature. It is proportional to the size of the adjustment, and it represents the unit cost of purchasing goods from an outside source or the unit revenue from disposing of goods on a secondary market. Thus it may be different for upward and downward adjustments. The manager's problem is to choose a policy for managing the inventory that minimizes the expected discounted value of total costs: holding costs plus fixed and variable adjustment costs.

153

The optimal policy for the inventory model is qualitatively similar to the one for the menu cost model. The manager chooses two critical thresholds, b and B, where control is exercised. While the stock remains in the open interval (b, B) the manager does nothing, so this interval is still an inaction region. When the stock reaches either threshold an adjustment is made. Specifically, when it reaches the lower threshold b, the manager adjusts the stock upward to a return point q; when it reaches the upper threshold B, he adjusts it downward to a return point Q. Thus, in contrast to the menu cost model there are two return points q, Q, with $b < q \leq Q < B$. If the initial value for the state variable lies outside (b, B) the manager exercises control immediately, adjusting the state variable to q or Q. Thereafter the state remains in the interval $[b, B]$. In some applications one threshold may be exogenously fixed. For example, in an inventory model where negative stocks are not allowed, the lower threshold is fixed at $b = 0$.

The rest of this chapter looks at the inventory model in detail. In Section 8.1 the model is described and the value function is shown to be bounded above and below by functions that are piecewise linear. In Section 8.2 a condition is developed that insures that an optimal policy involves exercising both upward and downward control and that there is a unique inaction region. In Section 8.3 the functions $\hat{L}$, ψ, and Ψ are used to characterize the optimal policy and associated value function, and in Section 8.4 the Hamilton-Jacobi-Bellman equation is used. Many of the arguments here parallel those in Chapter 7, so the proofs are omitted or sketched only briefly. Long-run averages are described in Section 8.5, and several examples are discussed in Section 8.6. Throughout, the variable adjustment cost is assumed to be linear. Section 8.7 provides a discussion of why more general adjustment costs are difficult to incorporate.

8.1. An Inventory Model

Let $X(t)$ be a (μ, σ^2) Brownian motion with initial value $X(0) = x$. Changes in X represent net flows into or out of the inventory in the absence of control. As noted above, the manager can also augment or reduce the stock by discrete amounts, interpreted as purchases or sales on a secondary market. Since holding costs at any date depend on the current stock, it is convenient to formulate the problem using the stock as the single state variable. Let $Z(t)$ be the stochastic process for the stock.

The manager's problem is to choose the (random) dates $0 \leq T_1 \leq T_2 < \ldots \leq T_i < \ldots$ at which control is exercised and, for each date T_i, the (possibly random) level z_i to which the stock is adjusted. As in the menu cost model, $\gamma = \{(T_i, z_i)\}_{i=1}^{\infty}$ is an *impulse control policy* if

    i. $0 \leq T_1 \leq T_2 < \ldots \leq T_i < \ldots$ are stopping times; and
    ii. z_i is $\mathfrak{F}_{T_i}$-measurable, all i, all ω.

Let Γ be the set of all impulse control policies.

Given an impulse control policy γ, the stochastic process for the inventory $Z(t)$ is

$$Z(t) = z_i + \left[X(t) - X(T_i) \right], \quad t \in [T_i, T_{i+1}), i = 0, 1, 2, \dots, \text{ all } \omega, \quad (8.1)$$

where $x_0 = 0$ and $T_0 = 0$. Thus, over each interval $[T_i, T_{i+1})$ the inventory $Z(t)$ is a Brownian motion with parameters (μ, σ^2). Note that the size of the adjustment at T_i is

$$y_i = z_i - Z(T_i), \quad i = 1, 2, \dots.$$

Let $h(z)$ denote the (flow) holding cost when the stock is z, let $C(y)$ denote the cost of adjusting the stock by the increment y, and let r be the (constant) interest rate. The following assumption is used throughout.

Assumption 8.1. i. $r, \sigma^2 > 0$;

ii. h is continuous and weakly convex; it is differentiable except possibly at $z = 0$; and it is strictly decreasing on $\mathbf{R}_-$ and strictly increasing on $\mathbf{R}_+$, with $h(0) = 0$;

iii.

$$C(y) = \begin{cases} C_0 + Py, & \text{if } y > 0, \\ 0, & \text{if } y = 0, \\ c_0 + py, & \text{if } y < 0, \end{cases}$$

$$\text{where } C_0, c_0 > 0, \ P \geq 0, \text{ and } P \geq p.$$

Both the fixed and variable components of adjustment costs can differ for upward and downward adjustments. The fixed costs C_0 and c_0, interpreted as the time of the manager or a transaction fee, are strictly positive for both types of adjustment. The value $P \geq 0$ is the unit cost of adding to the stock, and if $p > 0$, then p is the unit revenue from reducing the stock. In this case the restriction $P \geq p$ is needed so that the system is not a money pump. If $p < 0$, then $|p| > 0$ is the unit cost of disposing of excess inventory, and the restriction $P \geq p$ does not bind. The menu cost model is the special case where the two fixed costs are the same, $C_0 = c_0 > 0$, and there are no proportional costs, $P = p = 0$.

For any initial state z_0 and any impulse control policy $\gamma = \{(T_i, z_i)\}_{i=1}^{\infty}$, let $H(z_0; \gamma)$ denote the expected discounted value of total costs:

$$H(z_0; \gamma) \equiv \mathrm{E}_{z_0} \left\{ \int_{T_0}^{T_1} e^{-rt} h[Z(t)] dt \right.$$

$$\left. + \sum_{i=1}^{\infty} \left[e^{-rT_i} C\left[z_i - Z(T_i) \right] + \int_{T_i}^{T_{i+1}} e^{-rt} h[Z(t)] dt \right] \right\},$$

where $Z(t)$ is as in (8.1). The assumptions on γ, h, and C insure that $H(z_0; \gamma)$ is well defined for all z_0 and γ (although it may be equal to ∞). Define the value function

$$v(z) \equiv \inf_{\gamma \in \Gamma} H(z; \gamma), \quad \text{all } z.$$

The following result puts bounds on v.

Proposition 8.1. Under Assumption 8.1, v is bounded above and below by functions that are continuous and piecewise linear.

Proof. Clearly v is bounded below by

$$H_L(z) = \begin{cases} 0, & \text{if } z \leq 0, \\ \min\{0, -pz\}, & \text{if } z > 0. \end{cases}$$

For an upper bound choose any $a < 0 < A$ and let $\hat{\gamma}_0$ be the policy

$$T_i = \min\{t > T_i: Z(t) \notin (a, A)\},$$

$$z_i(\omega) = 0, \quad i = 1, 2, \ldots, \text{ all } \omega.$$

The expected discounted cost of the policy $\hat{\gamma}_0$ for the initial condition $z = 0$ is

$$H(0; \hat{\gamma}_0) = E_0 \left\{ \sum_{i=1}^{\infty} \left[\int_{T_{i-1}}^{T_i} e^{-rt} h\,(Z(t))\,dt + e^{-rT_i} C\left[0 - Z(T_i)\right] \right] \right\},$$

where $T_0 = 0$. Define

$$D_0 \equiv \max\{h(a), h(A)\},$$

$$D_1 \equiv \max\{C_0 - Pa, c_0 - pA\},$$

$$d \equiv E_0\left[e^{-rT_1}\right] < 1,$$

and note that

$$H(0; \hat{\gamma}_0) \leq \frac{1}{r}D_0 + \frac{d}{1-d}D_1$$

is finite. For any $z \neq 0$ the policy of adjusting immediately to $\hat{z} = 0$ and then using the policy $\hat{\gamma}_0$ is feasible. Call this policy $\hat{\gamma}$, and note that $H(z; \hat{\gamma}) \leq H_U(z)$, all z, where

$$H_U(z) \equiv H(0; \hat{\gamma}_0) + \max\{C_0, c_0\} - \begin{cases} Pz, & \text{if } z \leq 0, \\ pz, & \text{if } z > 0. \end{cases}$$

Hence H_U is an upper bound on v. ∎

The Principle of Optimality then suggests that v (and only v) satisfies the Bellman equation

$$v(z) = \inf_{T \geq 0, z'} \mathrm{E}_z \left\{ \int_0^T e^{-rt} h(Z(t)) dt \right. \tag{8.2}$$
$$\left. + e^{-rT} \left[C \left(z' - Z(T) \right) + v(z') \right] \right\}, \quad \text{all } z.$$

As with the menu cost model, the assumption that the underlying process $X(t)$ for the uncontrolled stock is a Brownian motion is critical for writing the problem in this form. If X were some other diffusion, its increments would depend on the date t or the state $X(t)$ of the process. Consequently, after the first adjustment the increments to the process $Z(t)$ would depend on $X(t)$. Only for a Brownian motion is the distribution of future increments independent of the past and unvarying over time. (Of course, if the underlying process X is a geometric Brownian motion, the problem can be formulated in terms of $\ln X$.)

8.2. Preliminary Results

It is useful to begin by considering the conditions under which an optimal policy involves exercising control. The argument here is more complicated than the one for the menu cost model. In particular, the presence of a proportional adjustment cost means that additional restrictions on h are required.

Let $v_P(z)$ be the expected discounted value of total costs over an infinite horizon if the initial value for the stock is z and no control is exercised. Recall from Section 7.2 that

$$v_P(z) \equiv \mathrm{E}_z \left[\int_0^\infty e^{-rt} h \left(Z(t) \right) dt \right]$$
$$= \frac{1}{J} \left[\int_0^\infty e^{-R_2 u} h(z + u) du + \int_{-\infty}^0 e^{-R_1 u} h(z + u) du \right], \quad \text{all } z, \tag{8.3}$$

where $R_1 < 0 < R_2$ and $J > 0$ are as in Section 5.2.

The idea behind the proof that control is exercised is as follows. Purchasing a unit of inventory at $t = 0$ has an annualized cost of rP, and it changes the holding cost at each date $t > 0$ by $h'(Z(t))$. The expected net change in the flow cost at any future date, $\mathrm{E}_{z_0} \left[h'(Z(t)) + rP \right]$, depends on the distribution of the stock $Z(t)$ at that date. Recall that under Assumption 8.1 h is weakly convex and is decreasing for $z < 0$. Suppose $\lim_{z \to -\infty} h'(z) + rP < 0$. If the initial stock $z_0 < 0$ is large in absolute value, then for some $\varepsilon > 0$,

$$\mathrm{E}_{z_0} \left[h'(Z(t)) + rP \right] < -\varepsilon,$$

at least until t is very large. Thus, for a long period of time the reduction in holding costs, the term $E_{z_0}[h'(Z(t))] < 0$, outweighs the annualized purchase price, $rP > 0$, by at least ε. The term $E_{z_0}[h'(Z(t)) + rP]$ may be positive for t sufficiently large, however, so an additional restriction is needed to insure that the integral of these terms is finite. Then, because the interest rate is positive, they can be downweighted to an arbitrarily small value by choosing $|z_0|$ sufficiently large.

The following assumption insures that the optimal policy involves exercising control at both thresholds.

Assumption 8.2. The holding cost h satisfies

$$\lim_{z \to \infty} h'(z) + rp > 0 \quad \text{and} \quad \lim_{z \to -\infty} h'(z) + rP < 0,$$

and the integrals

$$I_1 = \int_0^\infty e^{-R_2 \xi} h'(\xi)d\xi \quad \text{and} \quad I_2 = \int_{-\infty}^0 e^{-R_1 \xi} h'(\xi)d\xi$$

are finite.

Proposition 8.2. If Assumption 8.1 holds, then an optimal policy involves exercising both upward and downward control.

Proof. Suppose to the contrary that upward control is never exercised. Then $\lim_{z \to -\infty}[v(z) - v_P(z)] = 0$. In addition, h is convex and satisfies Assumption 8.2. Hence there exist $\delta, \varepsilon > 0$, and $y < 0$ such that

$$|v(\zeta) - v_P(\zeta)| < \delta,$$

$$h'(\zeta) + rP < -\varepsilon, \quad \text{all } \zeta < y. \tag{8.4}$$

Consider an upward adjustment from z to $z + a$, with $z < z + a < y$. Since by hypothesis control is not exercised, for any such z and a

$$v(z) \le C_0 + Pa + v(z + a).$$

Hence the first line in (8.4) implies

$$0 \le C_0 + Pa + v_P(z + a) - v_P(z) + 2\delta$$

$$= C_0 + \int_z^{z+a} [v'_P(\zeta) + P] d\zeta + 2\delta.$$

Use (8.3) to write these conditions as

$$0 \le C_0 + \frac{1}{J} \int_z^{z+a} \int_{-\infty}^0 e^{-R_1 u} \left[h'(\zeta + u) + rP \right] du d\zeta$$

$$+ \frac{1}{J} \int_z^{z+a} \int_0^\infty e^{-R_2 u} \left[h'(\zeta + u) + rP \right] du d\zeta + 2\delta. \tag{8.5}$$

Consider the first integral in (8.5). Since $\zeta + u < z + a + 0 < y$, it follows from the second line in (8.4) that this term is

$$< -\frac{\varepsilon}{J} \int_z^{z+a} \int_{-\infty}^0 e^{-R_1 u} du d\zeta$$

$$= \frac{\varepsilon}{J} \frac{a}{R_1}.$$

Since $R_1 < 0$ this term is negative, and it can be made arbitrarily large in absolute value by choosing a large. The second integral in (8.5) is

$$< \frac{a}{J} \int_0^\infty e^{-R_2 u} \left[h'(z + a + u) + rP \right] du$$

$$< \frac{a}{J} \int_{-(z+a)}^\infty e^{-R_2 u} \left[h'(z + a + u) + rP \right] du$$

$$= \frac{a}{J} e^{R_2(z+a)} \int_0^\infty e^{-R_2 \xi} \left[h'(\xi) + rP \right] d\xi,$$

where the first line uses the fact that h is convex, the second uses the fact that $z + a < 0$ and $h'(\zeta) < 0$ for $\zeta < 0$, and the third uses the change of variable $\xi = z + a + u$. Under Assumption 8.2 the integral in the last line is finite, and since $R_2 > 0$ and $z + a < 0$, the whole term can be made arbitrarily small by choosing $|z|$ large. Hence for $z < z + a < y < 0$, with $|z|$, $a > 0$ sufficiently large, (8.5) fails, contradicting the assumption no control is exercised as $z \to -\infty$.

A similar argument applies for downward control. ∎

The next result establishes that the optimal policy involves critical values $b^* < 0 < B^*$ describing a single inaction region (b^*, B^*). The optimal policy requires adjusting immediately if the state lies outside (b^*, B^*).

Proposition 8.3. Under Assumptions 8.1 and 8.2 there exist critical values $b^* < 0 < B^*$, with $|b^*|$, $B^* < \infty$, such that the unique optimal stopping time in (8.2) is $T = 0$ for $z \notin (b^*, B^*)$ and is $T = T(b^*) \wedge T(B^*)$ for $z \in (b^*, B^*)$.

Proof. The argument, which uses the convexity of h, parallels the proof of Proposition 7.3. ∎

8.3. Optimizing: A Direct Approach

The next goal is to characterize the optimal thresholds b^*, B^* and return points q^*, Q^*. As in the option and menu cost models, there are two approaches. In this section a direct approach employing the functions $\hat{L}$, ψ, and Ψ is used, and in Section 8.4 the Hamilton-Jacobi-Bellman equation is used.

For any $b < z < B$, define the stopping time $T = T(b) \wedge T(B)$ and recall that

$$w(z, b, B) \equiv E_z\left[\int_0^T e^{-rs} h(Z(s))ds\right]$$

$$= \int_b^B \hat{L}(\zeta; z, b, B)h(\zeta)d\zeta,$$

$$\psi(z, b, B) \equiv E_z\left[e^{-rT} \mid Z(T) = b\right] \Pr_z[Z(T) = b],$$

$$\Psi(z, b, B) \equiv E_z\left[e^{-rT} \mid Z(T) = B\right] \Pr_z[Z(T) = B],$$

where $\hat{L}$, ψ, and Ψ are described in detail in Chapter 5, and $E_z[\cdot]$ denotes an expectation conditional on the initial value z.

For any fixed policy (b, B, q, Q), let $F(z, b, B, q, Q)$ denote the associated return, given the initial state z. Then F satisfies the Bellman-type equation

$$F(z, b, B, q, Q) = \begin{cases} m + P(b - z), & z \le b, \\ w(z, b, B) + \psi(z, b, B)m \\ \quad + \Psi(z, b, B)M, & z \in (b, B), \\ M + p(B - z), & z \ge B. \end{cases} \tag{8.6}$$

where

$$m \equiv C_0 + P(q - b) + F(q, b, B, q, Q),$$

$$M \equiv c_0 + p(Q - B) + F(Q, b, B, q, Q).$$

The firm's problem is to choose b, B, q, Q to minimize F, so

$$v(z) = \min_{b,B,q,Q} F(z, b, B, q, Q). \tag{8.7}$$

The optimal policy is characterized by first-order conditions. Here, as in the menu cost model, the conditions for the thresholds b and B are equivalent to smooth pasting.

Lemma 8.4. Let Assumptions 8.1 and 8.2 hold.

  i. Fix any m, M, P, and $\hat{b} < B$. If

$$w_b(z, \hat{b}, B) + \psi_b(z, \hat{b}, B)m + \Psi_b(z, \hat{b}, B)M - \psi(z, \hat{b}, B)P = 0. \quad (8.8)$$

holds for any $z \in [\hat{b}, B)$, then it holds for all $z \in [\hat{b}, B)$, and in addition

$$w_z(\hat{b}, \hat{b}, B) + \psi_z(\hat{b}, \hat{b}, B)m + \Psi_z(\hat{b}, \hat{b}, B)M = -P.$$

 ii. Fix any m, M, p, and $b < \hat{B}$. If

$$w_B(z, b, \hat{B}) + \psi_B(z, b, \hat{B})m + \Psi_B(z, b, \hat{B})M - \Psi(z, b, \hat{B})p = 0. \quad (8.9)$$

holds for any $z \in (b, \hat{B}]$, then it holds for all $z \in (b, \hat{B}]$, and in this case

$$w_z(\hat{B}, b, \hat{B}) + \psi_z(\hat{B}, b, \hat{B})m + \Psi_z(\hat{B}, b, \hat{B})M = -p.$$

Proof. The argument parallels the proof of Lemma 7.4. ∎

Lemma 8.4 implies that the optimal thresholds b^* and B^* are independent of the current state. In addition, since q^* is chosen to minimize m and Q^* to minimize M, the optimal return points are also independent of the current state. As always, these facts are immediate consequences of the Principle of Optimality.

The following result uses Lemma 8.4 to characterize the optimum.

Proposition 8.5. Let Assumptions 8.1 and 8.2 hold. If b^*, B^*, q^*, Q^* attain the minimum in (8.7), then

$$
\begin{aligned}
w_z(b^*) + \psi_z(b^*)m^* + \Psi_z(b^*)M^* + P &= 0, \\
w_z(B^*) + \psi_z(B^*)m^* + \Psi_z(B^*)M^* + p &= 0,
\end{aligned}
\quad (8.10)
$$

$$
\begin{aligned}
w_z(q^*) + \psi_z(q^*)m^* + \Psi_z(q^*)M^* + P &= 0, \\
w_z(Q^*) + \psi_z(Q^*)m^* + \Psi_z(Q^*)M^* + p &= 0,
\end{aligned}
\quad (8.11)
$$

where m^*, M^* are the unique pair satisfying

$$
\begin{aligned}
m^* &= C_0 + P(q^* - b^*) + w(q^*) + \psi(q^*)m^* + \Psi(q^*)M^*, \\
M^* &= c_0 + p(Q^* - B^*) + w(Q^*) + \psi(Q^*)m^* + \Psi(Q^*)M^*.
\end{aligned}
\quad (8.12)
$$

Proof. Suppose b^*, B^*, q^*, Q^* describe an optimal policy. Then

$$
v(z) = \begin{cases}
m^* + P(b^* - z), & z \le b^*, \\
w(z, b^*, B^*) + \psi(z, b^*, B^*)m^* & \\
\quad + \Psi(z, b^*, B^*)M^*, & z \in \left(b^*, B^*\right), \\
M^* + p(B^* - z), & z \ge B^*.
\end{cases}
\tag{8.13}
$$

where m^* and M^* are as in (8.12). A necessary condition for the optimality of b^* is (8.8), and as shown in Lemma 8.4 that condition holds if and only if the first equation in (8.10) holds. A similar argument for B^* using (8.9) establishes that the second equation in (8.10) holds. The conditions in (8.11) are necessary for minima at q^* and Q^*. ∎

Proposition 8.5 characterizes the optimal policy b^*, B^*, q^*, Q^* as the solution to the system of four equations (8.10)–(8.11), with m^* and M^* defined by (8.12). This system of six equations in six unknowns provides a straightforward characterization of the optimum, and the resulting value function is in (8.13). As before, however, there is also another route to the solution.

8.4. Using the Hamilton-Jacobi-Bellman Equation

The optimal policy and value function can also be characterized by using the Hamilton-Jacobi-Bellman (HJB) equation, together with the appropriate boundary and optimality conditions. Proposition 8.6 states the result formally.

Proposition 8.6. Let Assumptions 8.1 and 8.2 hold. If b^*, B^*, q^*, Q^* describe an optimal policy, and v is the optimized value function, then
   i. v satisfies

$$
\begin{aligned}
rv(z) &= h(z) + \mu v'(z) + \tfrac{1}{2}\sigma^2 v''(z), & z &\in \left(b^*, B^*\right), \\
v(z) &= m^* + P(b^* - z), & z &\le b^*, \\
v(z) &= M^* + p(B^* - z), & z &\ge B^*;
\end{aligned}
\tag{8.14}
$$

   ii. v and v' are continuous at b^*,

$$
\lim_{z \downarrow b^*} v(z) = m^*, \quad \text{and} \quad \lim_{z \downarrow b^*} v'(z) + P = 0;
\tag{8.15}
$$

   iii. v and v' are continuous at B^*,

$$
\lim_{z \uparrow B^*} v(z) = M^*, \quad \text{and} \quad \lim_{z \uparrow B^*} v'(z) + p = 0;
\tag{8.16}
$$

iv. q^* and Q^* satisfy

$$v'(q^*) + P = 0, \quad \text{and} \quad v'(Q^*) + p = 0, \tag{8.17}$$

where m^* and M^* are as in (8.12).

Proof. The argument parallels the proof of Proposition 7.6. ∎

Corollary. Let $b < q < Q < B$ be an arbitrary policy, and let $F(\cdot, b, B, q, Q)$ be the function in (8.6). Then F satisfies (8.14), and it is continuous in z at b and B.

As in the menu cost model the solution can be reverse engineered from the conditions above. For an arbitrary policy $b < q < Q < B$ the function $F(\cdot, b, B, q, Q)$ can be found by using (8.14), the value matching conditions in (8.15) and (8.16), and the values m, M satisfying the linear system in (8.12). Among all such functions, the optimized value function v in addition satisfies the smooth pasting conditions in (8.15) and (8.16) and the optimal return conditions in (8.17).

The following exercise deals with cases in which upward control is never exercised. A similar result holds if downward control is never exercised.

Exercise 8.1. Suppose Assumption 8.2 fails. In particular, suppose that

$$\lim_{z \to -\infty} h'(z) + rP \ge 0,$$

so $b^* = -\infty$. Show that (8.15) is replaced with

$$\lim_{z \to -\infty} \left[v(z) - v_P(z) \right] = 0,$$

$$\lim_{z \to -\infty} v'(z) + P \ge 0.$$

The next result shows that the optimal return points q^* and Q^* are unique. The argument is similar to the one in the proof of Proposition 7.7.

Proposition 8.7. Under Assumptions 8.1 and 8.2,

$$\min_{z \in (b, B)} \left[v(z) + Pz \right]$$

has a unique solution q^*, and

$$\min_{z \in (b, B)} \left[v(z) + pz \right]$$

has a unique solution Q^*.

Proof. Suppose to the contrary that $v(z) + Pz$ has two local minima. Then there is a local maximum between them: there exist $q_1 < q_2 < q_3$ such that

$$v'(q_2) + P = 0, \qquad v''(q_2) \leq 0,$$

$$v'(q_i) + P = 0, \qquad v''(q_i) \geq 0, \quad i = 1, 3.$$

Then it follows from (8.14) that

$$rv(q_2) \leq h(q_2) - \mu P,$$

$$rv(q_i) \geq h(q_i) - \mu P, \quad i = 1, 3.$$

Hence

$$h(q_2) - h(q_i) \geq r [v(q_2) - v(q_i)]) \geq r P(q_i - q_2), \quad i = 1, 3,$$

contradicting the assumption that h is single troughed. Hence $v(z) + Pz$ has only one local minimum, at q^*. A similar argument applies for Q^*. $\blacksquare$

Note that on (b^*, B^*) the value function has a convex region flanked by concave regions, and outside that interval it is linear. Thus there are two points where $v'' = 0$, one in the interval (b^*, q^*) and one in (Q^*, B^*), and v can take three shapes, depending on the sign of p.

These three possibilities are displayed in Figure 8.1, which shows value functions for the sale prices $p = -0.2$, 0, and 0.2. The holding cost is the same in all three cases, $h(z) = h_0 \left(e^{\|\eta\|z} - 1 \right)$, with $h_0 = 1$ and $\eta = 0.2$, and the other parameters are fixed at $\mu = 0$, $\sigma = 1$, $r = 0.05$, and $C_0 = c_0 = P = 1$. The small circles on each value function indicate the optimal policy. Recall that if $p > 0$, then p is the unit revenue from reducing the stock, and if $p < 0$, then $|p|$ is the unit cost of reducing the stock. Hence the value function v, which represents expected discounted costs, shifts downward as p increases. In addition, the linear portion of the value function above the threshold B^* has slope p, so that slope changes sign with p.

8.5. Long-Run Averages

As in the model with fixed costs only, long-run averages can be described in terms of the functions θ, τ, and L defined at the beginning of Chapter 5. In settings with a large number of decision makers subject to i.i.d. shocks, these averages also represent the (stationary) cross-sectional distribution.

Let v and $1 - v$ denote the long-run fraction of adjustments that are from b^* and from B^*, respectively. Since each adjustment from b^* is to q^* and each one from B^* is to Q^*, it follows that v and $1 - v$ are also the fractions of starts from q^* and from Q^*. Let $T = T(b^*) \wedge T(B^*)$ and recall that

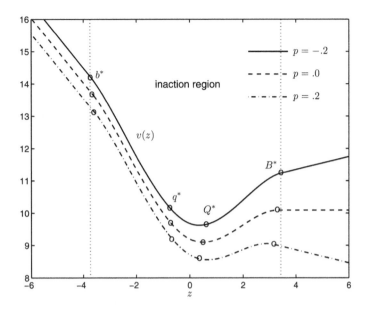

Figure 8.1. *Value functions for the inventory model for $p = -0.2$, $p = 0$, and $p = 0.2$. The holding cost is $h(z) = h_0(e^{\|\eta\|z} - 1)$, with $h_0 = 1$ and $\eta = 0.2$, and the other parameters are $\mu = 0$, $\sigma = 1$, $r = 0.05$, and $C_0 = c_0 = P = 1$.*

$$\theta(z, b^*, B^*) \equiv \text{Pr}_z\left[Z(T) = b^*\right]$$

is the probability that the lower threshold is reached first, conditional on the initial state $Z(0) = z$. Hence ν satisfies

$$\nu\theta(q^*) + (1 - \nu)\,\theta(Q^*) = \nu,$$

so

$$\nu = \frac{\theta(Q^*)}{1 - \theta(q^*) + \theta(Q^*)}.$$

Next recall that

$$\tau(z, b^*, B^*) = \text{E}_z\left[T(b^*) \wedge T(B^*)\right]$$

is the expected value of the stopping time T, conditional on the initial state z. Since ν and $1 - \nu$ are the shares of starts from q^* and Q^*, the average length of time between adjustments in the long run is

$$\bar{\tau} = v\tau(q^*) + (1 - v)\,\tau(Q^*).$$

The expected number of adjustments per unit time is then $1/\bar{\tau}$, and of these the proportion v are at the lower threshold. Hence the average control exercised per unit time at the lower threshold is $\left(q^* - b^*\right)v/\bar{\tau}$, and the average control exercised at the upper threshold is $\left(Q^* - B^*\right)(1 - v)/\bar{\tau}$.

Finally, recall the (undiscounted) expected local time function $L(\cdot\,; z, b^*, B^*)$. The stationary density $\bar{\pi}(\cdot)$ is the weighted average of $L(\cdot\,; q^*, b^*, B^*)$ and $L(\cdot\,; Q^*, b^*, B^*)$, with weights v and $1 - v$, normalized by the average duration:

$$\bar{\pi}(\zeta) = \frac{1}{\bar{\tau}}\left[vL(\zeta; q^*, b^*, B^*) + (1 - v)\,L(\zeta; Q^*, b^*, B^*)\right], \quad \zeta \in \left(b^*, B^*\right).$$

8.6. Examples

In this section several examples are studied in more detail. The first two are specializations of the inventory model that assume linear holding costs. The first has a lower threshold fixed at $b = 0$, while the second allows negative stocks. The third example is an investment model with two state variables, an exogenous shock that is a geometric Brownian motion and a capital stock that can be adjusted. The return is a homogeneous function of the two states, so the problem can be written in terms of their ratio. The "fixed" cost in this example is that part or all of the current capital stock must be scrapped when new capital is purchased. The fourth example is an investment model that involves only upward adjustment. In addition, upward control is exercised only if the state is not too low. Below the adjustment region there is a second inaction region.

8.6.1. An Inventory Problem with b = 0

The inventory problem studied in Harrison, Selke, and Taylor (1983) specializes the model above in two ways: the lower threshold is fixed at $b = 0$, and the holding cost is linear. Thus, $h(z) = Hz$, where $H, z > 0$, and Assumption 8.2 requires $H/r > -p$. Hence the HJB equation takes the form

$$rv(z) = Hz + \mu v'(z) + \tfrac{1}{2}\sigma^2 v''(z), \quad z \in \left(0, B^*\right).$$

A particular solution to this equation is

$$f(z) = \frac{H}{r}\left(z + \frac{\mu}{r}\right),$$

so the value function has the form

$$v(0) = C_0 + Pq^* + v(q^*),$$

$$v(z) = \frac{H}{r}\left(z + \frac{\mu}{r}\right) + D_1 e^{R_1 z} + D_2 e^{R_2 z}, \quad z \in \left(0, B^*\right),$$

$$v(z) = c_0 + p(Q^* - z) + v(Q^*), \qquad z \geq B^*,$$

where D_1, D_2 are constants. These constants and the policy parameters q^*, Q^*, B^* are determined by the value matching conditions

$$\lim_{z \downarrow 0} v(0) = C_0 + Pq^* + v(q^*),$$

$$\lim_{z \uparrow B^*} v(z) = c_0 + p(Q^* - B^*) + v(Q^*);$$

the smooth pasting condition at B^*

$$\lim_{z \uparrow B^*} v'(z) = -p;$$

and the optimal return conditions at q^* and Q^*

$$v'(q^*) = -P,$$

$$v'(Q^*) = -p.$$

Since the lower threshold is exogenously fixed rather than optimally chosen, smooth pasting does not hold at that point.

Exercise 8.2. (a) Explain carefully how D_1, D_2, q^*, Q^*, and B^* can be determined from the five conditions above.

(b) Sketch the optimal policy function.

(c) How do q^*, Q^*, and B^* vary with H, p, and P?

8.6.2. Cash Management

The cash management problem studied in Constantinides and Richard (1978) is similar to the preceding example, except that negative stocks are allowed, the lower threshold is chosen optimally, and the holding cost function is *piecewise* linear with a kink at $z = 0$. The interpretation is as follows. Consider a firm that holds a cash reserve, as well as various interest-bearing assets. The firm's revenues flow into the reserve, and those funds are used to pay operating and other costs. The state variable $Z(t)$ is the size of the cash reserve, and in the absence of control $Z(t)$ is a Brownian motion with drift μ and variance $\sigma^2 > 0$.

The cash reserve does not earn interest, so the firm has an incentive to keep the reserve small by moving funds into and out of interest-bearing assets. Doing so entails transaction costs, which can be thought of as brokers' fees. These fees, which may be different for movements into and out of the cash reserve, have fixed and proportional components. Thus the adjustment cost parameters are $p < 0$ and C_0, c_0, $P > 0$. The holding costs are piecewise linear:

$$h(z) = \begin{cases} \eta z, & \text{if } z < 0, \\ Hz, & \text{if } z > 0, \end{cases}$$

where $\eta < 0$ is the cost of holding negative balances, that is, of drawing on a line of credit, and $H > 0$ is the opportunity cost of holding positive cash balances. The interest rate is $r > 0$.

Clearly Assumption 8.1 holds. Assumption 8.2 requires that in addition

$$-\eta/r > P \quad \text{and} \quad H/r > -p.$$

The first inequality states that the present discounted value of drawing on the line of credit forever, $-\eta/r$, exceeds the proportional cost of adding to the cash reserve. The second states that the present discounted value of holding an extra unit of reserves forever, H/r, exceeds the unit cost of moving cash out of the reserve.

Note that there are three interest rates in this problem, $-\eta$, H, and r. They are, respectively, the (borrowing) rate on a line of credit, the (lending) rate earned on short-term assets, and the rate at which the firm discounts future returns. Hence it makes sense to assume $H \le r \le -\eta$, although this is not required.

The HJB equation for this problem is

$$rv(z) = h(z) + \mu v'(z) + \tfrac{1}{2}\sigma^2 v''(z), \quad z \in (b^*, B^*),$$

where h is as above. It is easy to verify that

$$f(z) = \begin{cases} (\mu/r + z)\,\eta/r, & z \in (b^*, 0), \\ (\mu/r + z)\,H/r, & z \in (0, B^*), \end{cases}$$

are particular solutions to the two branches. The homogenous solutions have the usual form, so the value function is

$$v(z) = \begin{cases} v(b) + (b^* - z)\,P, & z \le b^*, \\ \eta\mu/r^2 + \eta z/r + d_1 e^{R_1 z} + d_2 e^{R_2 z}, & z \in (b^*, 0), \\ H\mu/r^2 + Hz/r + D_1 e^{R_1 z} + D_2 e^{R_2 z}, & z \in [0, B^*), \\ v(B) + (B^* - z)\,p, & z \ge B^*. \end{cases}$$

where d_1, d_2, D_1, D_2 are constants that must be determined. There are four constants here instead of the usual two, but v and v' must be continuous at $z = 0$, which provides two additional restrictions.

It remains to determine the four constants and the optimal policy b^*, B^*, q^*, Q^*. The value matching, smooth pasting, and optimal return conditions provide six equations:

$$v(b^*) - v(q^*) + P\left(b^* - q^*\right) = C_0,$$

$$v(B^*) - v(Q) + p\left(B^* - Q^*\right) = c_0,$$

$$\lim_{z \downarrow b^*} v'(z) + P = 0,$$

$$\lim_{z \uparrow B^*} v'(z) + p = 0,$$

$$v'(q^*) + P = 0,$$

$$v'(Q^*) + p = 0.$$

In addition, continuity of v and v' at $z = 0$ requires

$$0 = \frac{H - \eta}{r}\frac{\mu}{r} + \left(D_1 - d_1\right) + \left(D_2 - d_2\right),$$

$$0 = \frac{H - \eta}{r} + R_1\left(D_1 - d_1\right) + R_2\left(D_2 - d_2\right).$$

These eight equations determine the eight unknowns.

Notice that since the optimal return points q^* and Q^* could be both positive, both negative, or of opposite sign, there are three possibilities.

Exercise 8.3. (a) Suppose that $q^* < 0 < Q^*$. Write the system of eight equations as three subsystems: three involving b^*, q^*, d_1, d_2; three involving B^*, Q^*, D_1, D_2; and two involving d_1, d_2, D_1, D_2. How are these conditions altered if $q > 0$? If $Q < 0$?

(b) Describe how the solution can be calculated numerically with an algorithm that iterates between the two sets of three equations, using the pair involving d_1, d_2, D_1, D_2 to connect them.

(c) Describe how to calculate the long-run fraction of adjustments at each threshold, the expected time between adjustments, the average control exercised at each threshold, and the stationary density for the cash reserve.

Figure 8.2 displays v, v', and the optimal policy for a case where the holding costs and adjustment costs are symmetric and $\mu = 0$. The value function is single troughed with a minimum at $z = 0$, and the thresholds and return points are symmetric around that point.

Figure 8.3 displays the effect of introducing a positive drift, $\mu > 0$. The value function is still single troughed, but the inaction region is no longer symmetric. It gets wider at both ends, and the right side is elongated. In

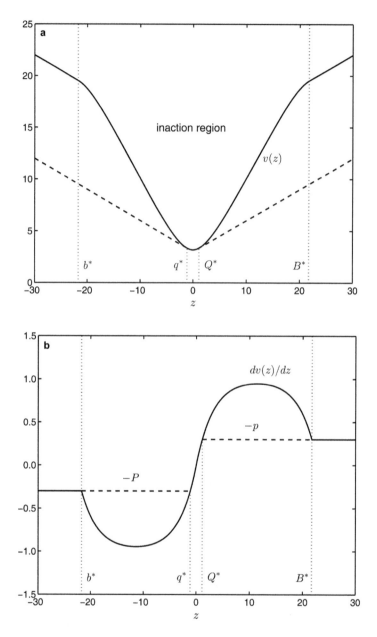

Figure 8.2. (a) The value function and (b) its derivative for the cash management problem with the baseline parameters $\mu = 0$, $\sigma = 1$, $r = -\eta = H = 0.05$, $C_0 = c_0 = 10$, and $P = -p = 0.3$. The optimal policy is $B^* = -b^* = 21.7$ and $Q^* = -q^* = 1.1$.

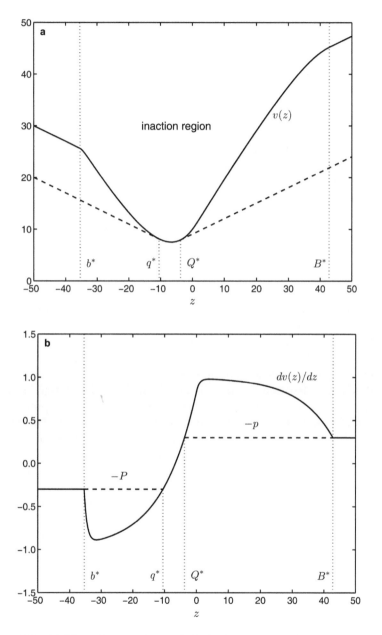

Figure 8.3. (a) The value function and (b) its derivative for the cash management problem with $\mu = 0.5$ and the baseline values for the other parameters. The optimal policy is $b^* = -35.4$, $q^* = -10.5$, $Q^* = -3.7$, and $B^* = 42.8$.

addition, both return points shift downward to accommodate the positive drift. For the indicated parameter values $Q^* < 0$.

8.6.3. Replacing Computer Equipment

In this example an investment model is studied that is representative of a large class of models with several common features: two state variables, an exogenous shock that is a geometric Brownian motion, an endogenous stock that can be adjusted, a return function that is homogeneous of degree one in the two states, a "fixed" adjustment cost λK that is proportional to the old stock, and a proportional cost $P\left(K' - K\right)$ that is linear in the size of the adjustment. The main features of the solution depend only on these assumptions, which encompass a number of interesting special cases. The example here has $\lambda = P$.

Consider the problem facing a firm that must decide when to replace its computer hardware. The usefulness of the computer system depends on the capacity of the hardware K, and the sophistication of the software X. The (flow) return from operating the system is $F(X, K)$, where F is continuously differentiable, strictly increasing, strictly quasi-concave, and displays constant returns to scale.

Hardware depreciates at a constant rate $\delta > 0$, and software quality X is a geometric Brownian motion with drift $\mu > 0$ and variance $\sigma^2 > 0$. For simplicity, ignore the costs of adopting new software.

When new hardware is purchased all of the old hardware must be scrapped, and it has no salvage value. The unit cost of new equipment, P, is constant. Thus, if a system of capacity K is scrapped and replaced with one of capacity K', the total cost is PK'. There is no explicit fixed cost of replacing the system. Instead, the fact that the old hardware must be scrapped plays the role of a fixed cost, one that increases proportionately with K. All returns and costs are discounted at the constant interest rate $r > 0$.

Let $V(K_0, X_0)$ be the value from following an optimal policy, given the initial state $K_0, X_0 > 0$. The Bellman equation for the firm's problem involves choosing a first stopping time T and a random variable K', where the latter is the hardware capacity of the new system:

$$V(K_0, X_0) = \max_{T, K'} \mathbb{E}\left[\int_0^T e^{-rt} F[K(t), X(t)]dt + e^{-rT}\left\{V[K', X(T)] - PK'\right\}\right]$$

$$\text{s.t.} \quad dK = -\delta K dt,$$

$$dX = \mu X dt + \sigma X dW, \quad 0 \le t < T,$$

given $K(0) = K_0$ and $X(0) = X_0$.

Since the return function and constraints are homogeneous of degree one, so is the value function V. To exploit homogeneity, define $x \equiv X/K$, $f(x) \equiv F(1, x)$, and $v(x) \equiv V(1, x)$. Note that $K(t) = e^{-\delta t} K_0$, $0 \le t < T$, and $x' = X(T)/K'$. Hence

$$K' = \frac{X(T)}{x'} = K(T)\frac{x(T)}{x'} = e^{-\delta T} K_0 \frac{x(T)}{x'}.$$

Substituting into the above expression for $V(K_0, X_0)$ gives the intensive form of the Bellman equation:

$$v(x_0) = \max_{T, x'} E_{x_0} \left[\int_0^T e^{-\eta t} f(x(t))dt + e^{-\eta T} x(T)\frac{v(x') - P}{x'} \right]$$

$$\text{s.t.} \quad dx = (\mu + \delta) x dt + \sigma x dW, \quad 0 \le t < T,$$

where $\eta \equiv r + \delta$.

Exercise 8.4. (a) Describe the qualitative form of the optimal policy. That is, when is control exercised and what is the nature of the control?

(b) Can the functions $\hat{L}$, ψ, and Ψ be used to find the solution? If so, what are the relevant first-order conditions? If not, explain why not.

(c) What is the HJB equation for the intensive form of the problem? How does the fact that x is a *geometric* Brownian motion affect that equation? What are particular and homogeneous solutions?

(d) Characterize the value function outside the inaction region. What are the value matching conditions?

(e) What are the smooth pasting conditions, and what condition characterizes the optimal return point(s)?

(f) How does the optimal policy change with an increase in μ?

(g) Suppose that when new capital is purchased, only part of the old capital must be scrapped. Let $1 - \omega$ be the fraction that is scrapped, so ωK is the fraction that is retained, where $\omega \in [0, 1)$. How does this change modify the intensive form of the Bellman equation?

8.6.4. Product Quality

Consider a firm whose profit flow depends on how well its product is matched to market tastes. Tastes change over time, so match quality evolves while the product is unchanged. Let X denote match quality, and assume that in the absence of intervention X is a Brownian motion with drift $\mu < 0$ and variance $\sigma^2 > 0$. The profit flow $\pi(X)$ is a function of match quality. Assume π is continuously differentiable, strictly increasing, bounded below by $\underline{\pi} = 0$, and bounded above by $\overline{\pi} > 0$. In addition, π has a single inflection point x_I, so π is strictly convex below x_I and strictly concave above x_I.

Match quality can be improved by changing the product. Assume that the cost of such a change has both fixed and variable components. In particular, let

$$C(y) = C_0 + Py, \quad C_0, P > 0,$$

be the cost of improving the match by $y > 0$.

Given the initial state x, the firm's problem is to choose an impulse control policy for making product improvements. The Bellman equation for the firm's problem is

$$v(x) = \max_{T,x'} E_x \left[\int_0^T e^{-rt} \pi(X(t)) dt + e^{-rT} \left\{ C_0 + P \left[x' - x(T) + v(x') \right] \right\} \right],$$

where T is a stopping time and x' is the quality of the match after the improvement.

Let $v_P(x)$ denote the expected discounted returns from operating forever without improving the product, given the initial state x.

Exercise 8.5. (a) Sketch π and v_P. Describe precisely conditions under which never adjusting is and is not an optimal policy.

In the rest of the problem assume that the optimal policy involves exercising control.

(b) Describe the qualitative form of the optimal policy, the stopping rule, and the rule governing product improvements. Is there more than one inaction region? Explain why or why not.

(c) Write the optimal value function v as an integral over states inside each inaction region. What is v in the region(s) where control is exercised immediately?

(d) Write the HJB equation for this problem. What are the boundary conditions?

(e) Characterize the optimal policy and the associated value function v as sharply as possible.

(f) Explain briefly how an increase in the absolute value of the drift, $\mu < 0$, affects the optimal policy and the value function.

8.7. Strictly Convex Adjustment Costs

The assumption that the variable cost of control is linear in the size of the adjustment is very natural for the inventory interpretation of the model, and it is also convenient mathematically. A strictly concave function would be awkward for the usual reasons in a minimization problem. A strictly convex function would imply that a large adjustment might be accomplished more cheaply by incurring the fixed cost more than once and making the change in two or more small increments rather than a single large one.

This possibility could be accommodated by defining a function that describes the least-cost way of adjusting:

$$\hat{C}(y) \equiv \begin{cases} \min_{n=1,2,\ldots} nC(y/n), & \text{if } y \neq 0, \\ 0, & \text{if } y = 0, \end{cases}$$

and then using $\hat{C}$ instead of C in the analysis. Note that $\hat{C}$ has a kink at each point where the number of adjustments changes. But a large adjustment could occur only at $t = 0$, and even then only if the initial stock were far outside the inaction region. All later adjustments would be made at the boundary of the inaction region, in a single step. Hence the kinked portion of the cost function $\hat{C}$ would not come into play after the initial adjustment.

Notes

An early treatment of the inventory problem is in Scarf (1960), and many variations have been studied subsequently. Alvarez and Lippi (2007) use a stochastic version of a Baumol-Tobin model similar to the inventory model in Sections 8.1–8.5 to study cash withdrawals by consumers. The first two examples in Section 8.6 are from Harrison, Selke, and Taylor (1983) and Constantinides and Richard (1978). The homogeneity argument in the investment model of the third example is like those in Alvarez and Stokey (1998).

Aggregate models of investment in settings with fixed costs at the firm level have also been studied. For example, see Bertola and Caballero (1990), Caballero and Engel (1999), Fisher and Hornstein (2000), and Bachmann, Caballero, and Engel (2006). See Caballero (1999) for an excellent survey and further references.

Investment at the plant level is very "lumpy" and hence very unlike the smooth behavior posited for the representative firm in a standard real business cycle model. This discrepancy has raised the question of whether incorporating heterogeneous firms with fixed costs of investment would change the behavior of aggregate investment in such models and thus alter the fluctuations they produce. Thomas (2002), Khan and Thomas (2003, 2007), and Gourio and Kashyap (2007) have all explored this issue. As in aggregate models of price adjustment, the mix of responses at the intensive and extensive margins—the size of adjustments and the number of firms adjusting—is important.

9

Models with Continuous
Control Variables

IN THE MENU cost and inventory models of Chapters 7 and 8 the only actions taken by the decision maker are discrete adjustments of the state variable. But the methods used in those problems can be extended to allow an additional feature as well, continuously chosen control variables that affect the evolution of the state between adjustments and also enter the return function directly. Because the state variable no longer evolves as a Brownian motion between adjustments, the functions $\hat{L}$, ψ, and Ψ are not useful in these settings. The optimal policy and value function can still be characterized with the Hamilton-Jacobi-Bellman equation, however. Moreover, numerical solutions of that equation can be calculated with standard ODE packages. The model of housing consumption and portfolio choice studied in Grossman and Laroque (1990) provides an illustration.

Consider a consumer whose only consumption is the service flow from a durable, her house, and whose only income is the return on her financial assets. Housing has interest and maintenance costs, where the latter is interpreted as offsetting depreciation. In addition housing affects the set of portfolios that are allowed. Specifically, the consumer is required to hold a minimum equity level in the house that is a fixed fraction of its value. This constraint reflects the fact that the purchase of a house typically requires a minimum down payment. The consumer may also hold additional wealth as housing equity, and she holds a mortgage on the remaining balance, if any. Wealth that is not tied up in the house is allocated between two financial assets, one safe and one risky. The riskless asset pays a fixed interest rate, while the risky asset has a stochastic return with fixed mean and variance. The rate of return on the riskless asset is assumed to be the same as the mortgage interest rate, so holding the riskless bond is equivalent to holding equity in her house.

The consumer makes two decisions, about housing consumption and about the allocation of her portfolio between safe and risky assets. Portfolio adjustment is costless and is carried out continuously, but the consumer can adjust her consumption flow only by selling her old house and buying a new one. This transaction involves paying a cost that is proportional to the size of the old house, interpreted as agents' commissions and other moving costs. Hence the consumer adjusts her housing consumption infrequently. Only if her consumption flow—the value of her house—is sufficiently large or small relative to her total wealth does she make a transaction.

Because of the adjustment cost, housing wealth and financial wealth are not perfect substitutes. Thus, the model has two state variables. If the return function—the consumer's utility function—has a certain homogeneity property, however, her decision problem can be written in an intensive form that involves only a ratio. In particular, the utility function must have the homogeneous form $u(K) = K^{1-\theta}/(1 - \theta)$, where $\theta > 0$. Under this assumption the optimized value function is also homogeneous, and the optimal policy functions depend only on the ratio of total wealth to housing wealth. Hence that ratio can serve as the single state variable in the reformulated problem.

The optimal policy for housing transactions is characterized by three critical values for that ratio, upper and lower thresholds and a return point between them. The region between the two thresholds is an inaction region: while the ratio lies in the interior of this region the consumer keeps her current house. When the ratio reaches either threshold, or if the initial condition lies outside the inaction region, the consumer immediately sells her old house and purchases a new one. When she makes a transaction, she chooses the new house so that the ratio of her total wealth to housing wealth, net of the transaction cost, is equal to the return value. One goal is to determine how these three critical values vary with parameters of the problem—the transaction cost, asset returns, and preference parameters.

In addition the consumer adjusts her portfolio of assets. This adjustment is continuous while the state variable remains inside the inaction region, and it is discrete when a new house is purchased. A second goal is to determine, for fixed parameters, how the optimal portfolio changes as a function of the state variable inside the inaction region, and a third goal is to determine how the entire portfolio decision shifts with changes in the parameters of the problem.

The rest of the chapter is organized as follows. In Section 9.1 the problem without transaction costs is analyzed. In this case the consumer can continuously and costlessly adjust her housing as well as her portfolio. This model is interesting as a baseline for comparisons and for developing parameter restrictions. It is also useful as a starting point for computing solutions for the model with transaction costs. The problem with transaction costs is set up in Section 9.2, and a normalized version formulated in terms of a single state variable, a ratio, is developed. In Section 9.3 the solution is characterized with the Hamilton-Jacobi-Bellman equation, and an algorithm for computing the solution is sketched. Section 9.4 looks at several extensions: exogenous moves, nondurable consumption, logarithmic utility, and a special case that adds several assumptions and uses a different state variable. In the last case the solution can be characterized with $\hat{L}$, ψ, and Ψ.

9.1. Housing and Portfolio Choice with No Transaction Cost

Let Q denote the consumer's total wealth and K the value of her house. The price of housing is constant, and the service flow from a house is equal to its value. For now there is no adjustment cost, so the consumer can adjust K continuously and costlessly.

There are two assets, one safe and one risky. Assume that short sales of the risky asset are not allowed, and let $A \geq 0$ be the consumer's holding of the risky asset. Then $Q - A$ is wealth in safe assets. The mortgage interest rate is the same as the return on the bond, so holdings of the safe asset are the sum of equity in the house and bond holdings. If $Q - A \leq K$, the entire amount can be interpreted as equity in the house. Let $\epsilon \in (0, 1]$ be the (exogenously given) minimal equity the consumer is required to hold in her house. Then the constraint on her portfolio is $Q - A \geq \epsilon K$. That is, her wealth in safe assets must be at least ϵ times the value of her house.

Let $r > 0$ be the riskless rate of return, let $\mu > r$ and $\sigma^2 > 0$ be the mean and variance of the return on the risky asset, and let $\delta \geq 0$ be the maintenance cost per unit of housing. Then given K and A, the law of motion for total wealth is

$$dQ = \left[A\mu + (Q - A - \epsilon K) r - (1 - \epsilon) r K - \delta K \right] dt + A\sigma dZ$$

$$= \left[rQ + (\mu - r) A - (r + \delta) K \right] dt + A\sigma dZ, \qquad (9.1)$$

where Z is a Wiener process. The four terms in square brackets in the first line represent returns from risky assets, returns from safe assets, mortgage payments, and the cost of maintenance, respectively. The second line expresses this sum as portfolio returns minus interest and depreciation on the house.

The consumer's instantaneous utility function has the constant elasticity form $U(K) = K^{1-\theta}/(1 - \theta)$, and she discounts future utility at the constant rate $\rho > 0$. Given $Q_0 > 0$, the consumer's problem is to choose $\{K(t), A(t)\}$ to solve

$$\max \mathrm{E}_0 \left[\int_0^\infty e^{-\rho t} \frac{K(t)^{1-\theta}}{1 - \theta} dt \right]$$

$$\text{s.t.} \quad K(t) \in [0, Q(t)/\epsilon],$$

$$A(t) \in [0, Q(t) - \epsilon K(t)],$$

and the law of motion for wealth in (9.1).

The following assumption summarizes the parameter restrictions thus far.

Assumption 9.1.

$$0 < \epsilon \le 1, \qquad \delta \ge 0,$$

$$0 < r < \mu, \qquad \sigma^2 > 0,$$

$$\theta > 0, \ \theta \ne 1, \quad \rho > 0.$$

The case $\theta = 1$, which represents $U(K) = \ln K$, can be treated along similar lines and is considered in Section 9.4.3.

Since the constraints—including the law of motion for wealth—are homogeneous of degree one in (Q, K, A) and the return function is homogeneous of degree $1 - \theta$, the optimal policy has the form $K = k^* Q$, $A = a^* Q$, where k^* and a^* are constants.

For any policy $K = kQ$ and $A = aQ$ with fixed k, a, total wealth $Q(t)$ in (9.1) is a geometric Brownian motion with drift and variance

$$m(k, a) \equiv r + (\mu - r) a - (r + \delta) k,$$

$$s^2(k, a) \equiv a^2 \sigma^2.$$

In this case

$$E_0 \left[Q(t)^{1-\theta} \right] = Q_0^{1-\theta} e^{\Gamma(k,a)t}, \quad \text{all } t,$$

where

$$\Gamma(k, a) \equiv (1 - \theta) \left[m(k, a) - \theta \tfrac{1}{2} s^2(k, a) \right],$$

and the consumer's problem can be written as

$$\max_{\substack{k \in [0, 1/\epsilon] \\ a \in [0, 1-\epsilon k]}} \frac{k^{1-\theta}}{1 - \theta} Q_0^{1-\theta} \int_0^\infty e^{-\rho t} e^{\Gamma(k,a)t} dt. \tag{9.2}$$

The integral in (9.2) is finite if and only if $\rho > \Gamma(k, a)$. If $0 < \theta < 1$, then $k^{1-\theta}/(1 - \theta) > 0$. In this case the parameters must be restricted so that $\rho > \Gamma(k, a)$ for all feasible k, a, thus insuring expected discounted utility is finite along every feasible path. If $\theta > 1$, then $k^{1-\theta}/(1 - \theta) < 0$. In this case the parameters must be restricted so that $\rho > \Gamma(k, a)$ for at least one feasible

k, a, insuring that expected discounted utility is finite along at least one feasible path.

Lemmas 9.1 and 9.2 describe the optimal portfolio when $\rho > \Gamma$ and restrictions insuring that this inequality holds. Note that if $0 < \theta < 1$ the consumer's goal is to maximize $\rho - \Gamma(k, a)$, while if $\theta > 1$ her goal is to minimize it. In either case, then, her objective is to maximize $\Gamma(k, a)/(1 - \theta)$. Let

$$p = \frac{\mu - r}{\sigma^2} \tag{9.3}$$

denote the inverse "price" of risk, the expected excess return $\mu - r$ on the risky asset over the variance. Under Assumption 9.1 p is strictly positive. Lemma 9.1 describes the optimal portfolio share in the risky asset, $\alpha(k)$, for arbitrary (fixed) k.

Lemma 9.1.   Under Assumption 9.1 for any $0 \le k \le 1/\epsilon$ the solution to the problem

$$\max_{a \in [0, 1 - \epsilon k]} \frac{\Gamma(k, a)}{1 - \theta}$$

is

$$\alpha(k) = \begin{cases} 1 - \epsilon k, & \text{if } p/\theta > 1 - \epsilon k, \\ p/\theta, & \text{if } p/\theta \le 1 - \epsilon k. \end{cases} \tag{9.4}$$

Proof.   Note that

$$\Gamma_a(k, a) = (1 - \theta) \left[(\mu - r) - \theta a \sigma^2 \right]$$

$$= (1 - \theta) \sigma^2 (p - \theta a) .$$

If $0 < \theta < 1$ the objective is to maximize $\Gamma(k, a)$. In this case $\Gamma_{aa} < 0$, so Γ is concave. Since $\Gamma_a(k, 0) > 0$ there cannot be an optimum at $a = 0$. If $p/\theta > 1 - \epsilon k$, then

$$\Gamma_a(k, 1 - \epsilon k) = (1 - \theta) \sigma^2 \left[p - \theta (1 - \epsilon k) \right] > 0,$$

so the optimum is at a corner, $\alpha(k) = 1 - \epsilon k$. Otherwise the optimal portfolio is interior and satisfies $\Gamma_a = 0$, so

$$\alpha(k) = p/\theta.$$

Hence the optimal portfolio is as in (9.4).

If $\theta > 1$ the objective is to minimize $\Gamma(k, a)$. In this case Γ is convex, and the arguments above hold with a sign change. ∎

Lemma 9.1 says that unless the consumer has a house of maximal size, $k = 1/\epsilon$, and hence has no discretionary wealth to allocate, the share of wealth in the risky asset is strictly positive. For consumers who are sufficiently risk averse (high θ) the solution is interior, at $a = p/\theta$. For these consumers the share of wealth in the risky asset is increasing in μ and decreasing in r, σ^2, and θ. For consumers who are sufficiently risk tolerant (low θ) the constraint $1 - \epsilon k$ binds and the solution is at a corner. For the latter group, housing services have an a extra cost, at the margin. In addition to the interest and maintenance costs, $r + \delta$, an increase in housing services involves an incremental portfolio distortion. Notice that the constraint $a \leq 1 - \epsilon k$ comes into play even if $\epsilon = 0$, reflecting the fact that sufficiently risk-tolerant consumers would like to take a short position in the safe asset.

The next assumption insures that $\rho > \Gamma(k^*, a^*)$.

Assumption 9.2. If $0 < \theta < 1$,

$$\rho > (1 - \theta) \times \begin{cases} (\mu - \theta\sigma^2/2), & \text{if } p/\theta > 1, \\ (r + p^2\sigma^2/2\theta), & \text{if } p/\theta \leq 1. \end{cases}$$

Lemma 9.2. Under Assumptions 9.1 and 9.2,

$$\rho > \Gamma(k, a), \begin{cases} \text{all feasible } k, a, & \text{if } 0 < \theta < 1, \\ \text{some feasible } k, a, & \text{if } \theta > 1. \end{cases}$$

Proof. Suppose $0 < \theta < 1$. Then

$$\frac{d}{dk}\Gamma(k, \alpha(k)) = -(1 - \theta)(r + \delta) + (1 - \theta)\sigma^2 [p - \theta\alpha(k)]\alpha'(k)$$

$$\leq -(1 - \theta)(r + \delta)$$

$$< 0, \tag{9.5}$$

where the second line uses the facts $p - \theta\alpha(k) \geq 0$ and $\alpha'(k) \leq 0$. Hence for any $\epsilon \geq 0$,

$$\rho > \Gamma(0, \alpha(0)) \geq \Gamma(k, \alpha(k)) \geq \Gamma(k, a), \quad \text{all feasible } (k, a),$$

where the first inequality uses Assumption 9.2, the second uses (9.5), and the third uses the fact that $\alpha(k)$ maximizes $\Gamma(k, a)$.

If $\theta > 1$, then since $r > 0$, for $a = 0$ and all k sufficiently small,

$$\rho > 0 > (1 - \theta)[r - (r + \delta)k] = \Gamma(k, 0). \quad \blacksquare$$

Finally, consider the consumer's choice of housing services. Lemma 9.2 implies that the integral in (9.2) is finite for all feasible k, a if $0 < \theta < 1$, and is finite for some feasible k, a if $\theta > 1$. In either case the maximized value in (9.2) is finite and has the form $W(Q_0) = Q_0^{1-\theta} w^*$, where

$$w^* \equiv \max_{k \in [0, 1/\epsilon]} \left[\frac{k^{1-\theta}}{1-\theta} \frac{1}{\rho - \Gamma[k, \alpha(k)]} \right],$$

and $\alpha(k)$ is as in (9.4).

Exercise 9.1. Let $k^*(\theta)$ and $\alpha[k^*(\theta); \theta]$ denote the optimal policy for a consumer with risk aversion θ. Show that there is a threshold $\hat{\theta}$ with the property that the portfolio constraint $a \leq 1 - \epsilon k$ binds for this consumer at that point if and only if $\theta < \hat{\theta}$.

9.2. The Model with Transaction Costs

Suppose now that the consumer must pay a transaction cost of λK when she sells her house, where $\lambda > 0$. Because the transaction cost applies only to K, total wealth Q is no longer a sufficient state variable to describe the consumer's position. Two state variables are needed, (Q, K) or some other (equivalent) pair.

It is convenient to assume that the transaction cost λ is no greater than the consumer's minimal equity position ϵ in her house. This assumption insures that she can always afford to sell her house. Assume in addition that the consumer's initial wealth is sufficient to pay the transaction cost for the initial house.

Assumption 9.3. $0 < \lambda \leq \epsilon$, and $Q_0 > \lambda K_0$.

At dates when a housing transaction is made the consumer's total wealth after the purchase equals her wealth before the sale, net of the transaction cost. At other dates wealth grows stochastically, as before, and the value of the house is constant.

Let Q_0, K_0 denote the consumer's initial total wealth and housing wealth. The consumer chooses (i) a sequence of stopping times $\{T_i\}$ when she sells her old house and buys a new one, (ii) a sequence of random variables $\{K_i\}$, the value of the new house when she transacts, and (iii) a stochastic process $A(t)$ for her portfolio at all dates. Given Q_0, K_0, a policy $\gamma = \left\{ (T_i, K_i,)_{i=1}^{\infty}, A(\cdot) \right\}$ is feasible if it satisfies

$$0 \leq A(t) \leq Q(t) - \epsilon K_{i-1}, \quad t \in [T_{i-1}, T_i), \ i = 1, 2, \ldots,$$

$$K_i \leq Q_i/\epsilon, \qquad\qquad\qquad\qquad i = 1, 2, \ldots,$$

where $T_0 = 0$ and

$$dQ = \left[rQ + (\mu - r)\,A - (r + \delta)\,K_{i-1}\right]dt + A\sigma\,dZ,$$

$$t \in (T_{i-1}, T_i), \quad i = 1, 2, \ldots,$$

$$Q_i = Q(T_i) - \lambda K_{i-1}, \qquad\qquad i = 1, 2, \ldots.$$

Let $\Gamma(Q_0, K_0)$ be the set of all policies that are feasible from Q_0, K_0, and for any $\gamma \in \Gamma(Q_0, K_0)$, let

$$H(Q_0, K_0; \gamma) = \mathrm{E}_0\left[\int_{T_0}^{T_1} e^{-\rho t}\frac{K_0^{1-\theta}}{1-\theta}dt + \sum_{i=1}^{\infty}\int_{T_i}^{T_{i+1}} e^{-\rho t}\frac{K_i^{1-\theta}}{1-\theta}dt\right]$$

denote the expected discounted utility of the consumer. Define the maximized value

$$V(Q_0, K_0) \equiv \sup_{\gamma \in \Gamma(Q_0, K_0)} H(Q_0, K_0; \gamma).$$

Notice that one feasible policy is to transact immediately, setting $A(t) \equiv 0$, purchasing the maximum size house that can be maintained forever, and never transacting again. Since the maintenance cost must be paid, the maximum affordable house is

$$\hat{K} \equiv \frac{r}{\delta + r}\left(Q_0 - \lambda K_0\right).$$

This policy delivers finite lifetime utility, and it places a lower bound on what the consumer can attain. The value when there is no transaction cost provides an upper bound.

Hence under Assumptions 9.1 and 9.2, $V(Q_0, K_0)$ is finite for any initial conditions. This fact suggests that the Principle of Optimality holds, so the consumer's problem can be written in the recursive form

$$V(Q_0, K_0) = \max_{\{A(t)\}, T, K'} \mathrm{E}_0\left[\int_0^T e^{-\rho t}\frac{K_0^{1-\theta}}{1-\theta}dt + e^{-\rho T}V(Q', K')\right] \qquad (9.6)$$

s.t. $\quad 0 \le A(t) \le Q(t) - \epsilon K_0,$

$$dQ = \left[rQ + (\mu - r)\,A - (r + \delta)\,K_0\right]dt + A\sigma\,dZ, \quad t \in (0, T),$$

$$K' \le Q'/\epsilon,$$

$$Q' = Q(T) - \lambda K_0,$$

where T is a stopping time.

As in the problem without transaction costs, homogeneity of the return function and the constraints in (9.6) imply homogeneity of the value and policy functions. Hence the problem can be formulated in terms of one state variable, a ratio. A convenient choice is $q = Q/K$, the ratio of total wealth to housing wealth. Define $a = A/Q$ as before, and note that

$$K' = \frac{Q'}{q'} = \frac{q(T) - \lambda}{q'} K.$$

Hence the Bellman equation (9.6) can be written as

$$v(q_0) = \max_{\{a(t)\}, T, q'} E_0 \left[\int_0^T \frac{1}{1 - \theta} e^{-\rho t} dt + e^{-\rho T} \left(\frac{q(T) - \lambda}{q'} \right)^{1 - \theta} v(q') \right] \quad (9.7)$$

$$\text{s.t.} \quad 0 \le a(t) \le 1 - \epsilon/q(t),$$

$$dq = \left[rq + (\mu - r) aq - (r + \delta) \right] dt + aq\sigma dZ, \quad t \in (0, T),$$

$$q' \ge \epsilon,$$

where $v(q_0) \equiv V(q_0, 1)$.

Two properties of the optimal policy follow directly from (9.7). First, it clearly requires a transaction if the ratio of total wealth to housing wealth q is sufficiently large. Therefore, since q cannot fall below ϵ, the optimal stopping time has the form

$$T = T(b) \wedge T(B), \quad \text{for some } \epsilon \le b < B < \infty.$$

In addition, the optimal return point does not depend on the state $q(T)$ when the adjustment is made. Here, as in the menu cost model, the only cost of adjustment is a fixed cost. Hence the optimal return point S, is the same for upward and downward adjustments.

In contrast to the problems considered in Chapters 6–8, here the state variable q is not a Brownian motion or a geometric Brownian motion. Indeed, here a continuous decision variable $a(t)$ appears in the law of motion for q. Hence the functions $\hat{L}$, ψ, and Ψ are not useful for analyzing (9.7). The Hamilton-Jacobi-Bellman equation can still be used, however, both to characterize the solution analytically and to compute it numerically.

9.3. Using the Hamilton-Jacobi-Bellman Equation

First consider the state space. There is no upper bound on q, but the portfolio constraint implies that ϵ is a lower bound. If $\epsilon > \lambda$ the appropriate state space is $[\epsilon, \infty)$, and $b^* = \epsilon$ is a possibility. If $\lambda = \epsilon$ the consumer is bankrupt at $q = \epsilon$, so the appropriate state space is (ϵ, ∞), and b^* is necessarily interior.

A solution consists of a value function $v(q)$ defined on the state space, thresholds $b^* < S^* < B^*$ defining an inaction region and a return point, and a portfolio policy $a(q)$ defined on (b^*, B^*). The function v satisfies the Hamilton-Jacobi-Bellman (HJB) equation for (9.7) on the inaction region and is defined by the value from immediate adjustment outside that region. Value matching and smooth pasting hold at the two thresholds, and an optimality condition holds at the return point. The novel feature is a maximization inside the HJB equation, reflecting the fact that the portfolio is adjusted continuously. It is convenient to define the function

$$H(q) = (q - \lambda)^{1-\theta}, \quad q \ge \epsilon,$$

for normalizing the continuation values.

Proposition 9.3. Under Assumptions 9.1–9.3 the solution has the following properties:

i. v satisfies

$$\rho v(q) = \frac{1}{1-\theta} + \max_{a \in [0, 1-\epsilon/q]} \left\{ \left[rq + (\mu - r)\, aq - (r + \delta) \right] v'(q) \right.$$

$$\left. + \frac{1}{2}\sigma^2 (aq)^2\, v''(q) \right\}, \quad q \in (b^*, B^*), \tag{9.8}$$

$$v(q) = H(q)M^*, \qquad\qquad\qquad q \notin (b^*, B^*), \quad (9.9)$$

where

$$M^* \equiv \max_S \frac{v(S)}{(S)^{1-\theta}}; \tag{9.10}$$

ii. v and v' are continuous at b,

$$\lim_{q \downarrow b^*} v(q) = H(b^*)M^*, \tag{9.11}$$

$$\lim_{q \downarrow b^*} v'(q) \ge H'(b^*)M^*, \quad \text{with equality if } b^* > \epsilon;$$

iii. v and v' are continuous at B,

$$\lim_{q \uparrow B^*} v(q) = H(B^*)M^*, \tag{9.12}$$

$$\lim_{q \uparrow B^*} v'(q) = H'(B^*)M^*;$$

iv. the return point S^* attains the maximum in (9.10),

$$v(S^*) = H(S^* + \lambda)M^*. \tag{9.13}$$

Note that M^* is the continuation value for a consumer who has just sold her house and has total wealth of unity after paying the transaction cost.

It follows from (9.8) that $a(q)$ satisfies the first-order condition

$$pv'(q) + a(q)qv''(q) \geq 0, \quad \text{with equality if } a(q) < 1 - \epsilon/q,$$

where $p = (\mu - r)/\sigma^2$ is defined in (9.3). Since $v' > 0$, it follows that $a(q) > 0$, all q, so the nonnegativity constraint never binds. The equity constraint may bind, however, so

$$a(q) = \min \left\{ \frac{p}{\Theta(q)}, 1 - \epsilon/q \right\}, \tag{9.14}$$

where

$$\Theta(q) \equiv \frac{-qv''(q)}{v'(q)} \tag{9.15}$$

is the local coefficient of relative risk aversion for the value function. Thus the portfolio rule in (9.14) is like the one in (9.4) except that the relevant coefficient of risk aversion—which in both cases is the one for the value function—is variable here.

Establishing further properties of the solution analytically is difficult, but calculating solutions numerically is fairly easy. A method that works well is the following procedure, which iterates on the values M_n, S_n, b_n, B_n and the functions v_n, a_n.

Fix the parameters $\mu, \sigma^2, r, \rho, \theta, \delta, \lambda, \epsilon$. Suppose that a candidate portfolio rule $a_n(q)$ is given. Write the HJB equation as

$$v''(q) = \frac{2}{[s_n(q)q]^2} \left[\rho v(q) - m_n(q)v'(q) - \frac{1}{1-\theta} \right], \tag{9.16}$$

where

$$m_n(q) \equiv \left[r + (\mu - r) a_n(q) \right] q - (r + \delta),$$

$$s_n(q) \equiv \sigma a_n(q).$$

To solve this second-order equation with a standard ODE package, define the stacked function $F(q) = [v(q), v'(q)]$, with derivatives

$$dF_1(q) = F_2(q),$$

$$dF_2(q) = \frac{2}{[s_n(q)q]^2} \left[\rho F_1(q) - m_n(q) F_2(q) - \frac{1}{1-\theta} \right].$$

For notational simplicity drop the subscript n. At each step, given $a(q)$ and M, S, b, B, choose an interval $\left[\underline{b}, \overline{B} \right]$ that contains $[b, B]$ and grids $\{M_i\}_{i=1}^{I}$ and $\{S_j\}_{j=1}^{J}$ around M and S. For each pair (M_i, S_j) solve the ODE backward from S_j to $\underline{b}$ and forward from S_j to $\overline{B}$. For both solutions use the initial condition implied by (9.10) and (9.13),

$$F(S_j) = \left[v(S_j), v'(S_j) \right]$$

$$= \left[H(S_j + \lambda) M_i, \quad H'(S_j + \lambda) M_i \right].$$

Then select the thresholds b_{ij} and B_{ij} that minimize a weighted sum of the errors in the value matching and smooth pasting conditions in (9.11) and (9.12), and check that the range $[\underline{b}, \overline{B}]$ is large enough so that the choices are not constrained. After the thresholds and errors for all pairs (M_i, S_j) have been calculated, select the pair $(\hat{\imath}, \hat{\jmath})$ with the smallest total error.

Define $(M_{n+1}, S_{n+1}, b_{n+1}, B_{n+1}) = (M_{n\hat{\imath}}, S_{n\hat{\jmath}}, b_{n\hat{\imath}\hat{\jmath}}, B_{n\hat{\imath}\hat{\jmath}})$ and update $[\underline{b}, \overline{B}]$. To calculate the functions v_{n+1}, a_{n+1}, solve the ODE once more, with initial conditions $M_{n\hat{\imath}}, S_{n\hat{\jmath}}$ and range $[\underline{b}, \overline{B}]$, with a fixed and rather fine grid for q, call it the vector q_{n+1}^v. The solution to the ODE consists of two vectors containing the functions v_{n+1} and v'_{n+1} evaluated at the points in q_{n+1}^v. Use (9.14)–(9.16) to construct vectors containing v''_{n+1}, Θ_{n+1}, and a_{n+1} evaluated at these points.

The pair of vectors (q_{n+1}^v, a_{n+1}) describes the next approximation to the optimal policy function. Notice that this function must be defined on the interval $[\underline{b}, \overline{B}]$, not just $[b_{n+1}, B_{n+1}]$. Also notice that the ODE solver must have access to (q_{n+1}^v, a_{n+1}), perhaps by passing them as global variables.

For the initial iteration use the solution to the problem with no transaction cost as a starting point. That solution consists of the normalized value w^*, the ratio k^* of housing wealth to total wealth, and the portfolio ratio a^*. Use the constant function $a_0(q) = a^*$ for the portfolio policy, and use $M_0 = w^*$, $S_0 = 1/k^*$ to locate the grids for M and S. There is little to guide the initial choices for $\underline{b}$ and $\overline{B}$ except to require $b_0 < S_0$ and $B_0 > S_0$.

Note that the interval $[\underline{b}, \overline{B}]$ serves only to insure that the ODE is solved over a wide enough range, one that contains $[b, B]$. The interval $[\underline{b}, \overline{B}]$ should not be too wide, however, since the ODE behaves badly if it is calculated too far outside the range where it is meaningful.

Iterate in this fashion until the errors in the value matching and smooth pasting conditions are small and the value and policy functions have converged to the desired degree of accuracy. Since the problem with no transaction cost provides good initial guesses for a, S_0, and M_0, the procedure converges quickly. After the final iteration, solve the ODE once more on (b^*, B^*). Then construct the final policy function a^* as in the earlier stages, and use (9.9) to extend v outside (b^*, B^*).

Figures 9.1 and 9.2 display iterates of the value and policy functions for an example with the parameter values,

$$\mu = 0.70, \quad \sigma = 0.1655, \quad r = 0.01,$$
$$\rho = 0.04, \quad \theta = 2.0,$$
$$\delta = 0.05, \quad \lambda = 0.10, \quad \epsilon = 0.15.$$

The parameters μ, σ, and r describing asset returns are from Kocherlakota (1996). The preference parameters ρ and θ are within the range that is standard in the macro literature. The maintenance cost $\delta = 0.05$ is a little higher than the usual depreciation rate for structures, to allow for property taxes and other minimal operating expenses. Commissions for real estate agents are typically around 5–6% of the transaction value, and estimates of other costs—time spent searching, moving costs, and the like—are estimated to be around 4–5%, so $\lambda = 0.10$ is a reasonable figure for the transaction cost. The equity constraint of $\epsilon = 0.15$ is the typical down payment required for a single-family house.

Figure 9.1 shows the first two iterations in the approximation. Figure 9.1a shows the functions v_0 and v_1, return points S_0 and S_1, and thresholds b_1 and B_1. The function $v_0(q) = q^{1-\theta} w^*$ is the value function for a consumer who faces no transaction cost, and $S_0 = 1/k^*$ is the optimal ratio of total wealth to housing wealth for that consumer. Outside the inaction region the value functions are

$$v_n(q) = H(q)M_n, \quad q \notin (b_n, B_n),$$

where M_n is the normalized continuation value from S_n. Thus, $M_0 = w^*$. The initial thresholds b_0 and B_0 (not shown) are simply guesses.

The transaction cost reduces the consumer's welfare, so $v_1 < v_0$. In addition, the fact that transactions are costly favors asset accumulation over current consumption, so the consumer chooses a higher ratio of total wealth to housing wealth when transacting, $S_1 > S_0$. Figure 9.1b shows the derivatives v_0' and v_1' of the approximate value functions.

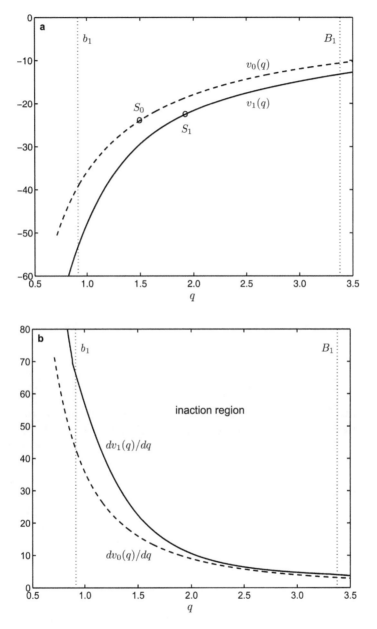

Figure 9.1. *The first two approximations of (a) the value function and (b) its derivative for the housing model. The parameter values are $\mu = 0.07$, $\sigma = 0.1655$, $r = 0.01$, $\rho = 0.04$, $\delta = 0.05$, $\epsilon = 0.15$, and $\lambda = 0.10$.*

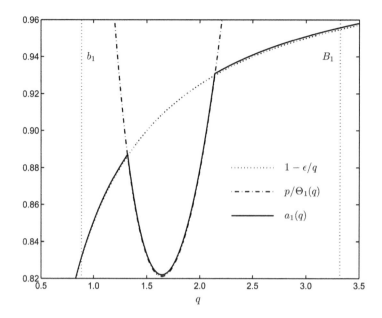

Figure 9.2. *Construction of the first approximation of the portfolio policy.*

Figure 9.2 shows the construction of the approximate policy function a_1. The dotted curve, which is increasing, is the equity constraint $1 - \epsilon/q$. The broken curve, which is U-shaped, is the unconstrained portfolio $p/\Theta_1(q)$ based on v_1. The minimum of these two, the solid curve, is the function $a_1(q)$.

Notice that the transaction cost makes the consumer more risk averse in the middle of the inaction region and more risk tolerant as q approaches either transaction threshold. Thus, for the parameter values in this example, the equity constraint binds only near the thresholds.

Figure 9.3 shows three approximate policy functions. The dashed line is the constant portfolio $a_0(q) = a^*$ from the model with no transaction cost. The broken line is the function a_1 from Figure 9.2, and the solid line is the function a_2 from the next iteration. There is a modest difference between a_0, which is constant at about 0.90, and a_1, which varies between 0.82 and 0.96. There is very little difference between a_1 and a_2. The critical values b_2, B_2, S_2 are slightly higher than b_1, B_1, S_1. Further iteration produces negligible changes.

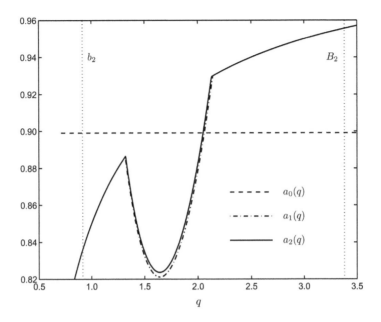

Figure 9.3. *The first three iterates of the approximate policy function.*

9.4. Extensions

In this section several extensions of the housing model are studied as exercises. The first exercise adds exogenous moves, the second adds nondurable consumption, and the third treats the case $\theta = 1$, log utility. The fourth treats a similar model that adds three assumptions and uses a slightly different state variable. With these changes the state variable is a geometric Brownian motion, and the solution can be characterized using $\hat{L}$, ψ, and Ψ.

9.4.1. Exogenous Moves

Suppose there are involuntary as well as voluntary moves. Specifically, suppose there is a Poisson shock with arrival rate κ. If this shock arrives the consumer is required to move and must pay the transaction cost.

Exercise 9.2. Derive the HJB equation for the model with the exogenous shock.

9.4.2. Nondurable Consumption

Suppose that in addition to housing there is a composite nondurable good C. Assume the consumer's instantaneous preferences involve a constant elasticity of substitution (CES) aggregator:

$$F(C, K) = \begin{cases} \left[\omega C^{1-\zeta} + (1 - \omega) K^{1-\zeta} \right]^{1/(1-\zeta)}, & \zeta \neq 1, \\ C^{\omega} K^{1-\omega}, & \zeta = 1, \end{cases}$$

where $\omega \in [0, 1)$ is the relative weight on nondurables, and $1/\zeta$ is the elasticity of substitution. As before her intertemporal utility function is homogeneous of degree $1 - \theta$,

$$E_0 \left[\int_0^\infty e^{-\rho t} \frac{\{F[C(t), K(t)]\}^{1-\theta}}{1 - \theta} dt \right].$$

Exercise 9.3. Write the normalized form for the consumer's problem. What is the associated HJB equation?

9.4.3. Log Utility

Consider the housing model with $\theta = 1$, so that $U(K) = \ln K$.

Exercise 9.4. (a) Write the consumer's problem for the case with no transaction cost and show that the optimal policy has the form $K(t) = kQ(t)$, $A(t) = aQ(t)$, all t.
(b) Show that for any k, a, $\ln Q(t)$ is a Brownian motion with parameters

$$m(k, a) = r + (\mu - r) a - (r + \delta) k - \tfrac{1}{2}a^2\sigma^2,$$

$$s^2(a) = a^2\sigma^2.$$

Show that

$$E_0 [\ln Q(t)] = \ln Q_0 + m(k, a)t, \quad \text{all } t,$$

and

$$E_0 \left[\int_0^\infty e^{-\rho t} \ln K(t)dt \right] = \frac{1}{\rho} \left(\ln Q_0 + \ln k \right) + \frac{1}{\rho^2} m(k, a).$$

Hence the value of a consumer with initial wealth Q_0 is

$$W(Q_0) = \frac{1}{\rho} \ln Q_0 + w^*,$$

where

$$w^* \equiv \max_{\substack{k \in [0, 1/\epsilon] \\ a \in [0, 1 - \epsilon k]}} \left[\frac{1}{\rho} \ln k + \frac{1}{\rho^2} m(k, a) \right].$$

(c) Show that Lemma 9.1 holds for $\theta = 1$. Find restrictions on ρ, r, μ, σ^2, δ that insure w^* is finite. Characterize k^*, the optimal ratio of housing wealth to total wealth.

(d) Write the Bellman equation for the problem with a transaction cost, using Q, K as state variables, the analog of (9.6). Write the intensive form of that problem, the analog of (9.7). What is the state variable for that problem?

(e) Write the HJB equation corresponding to the intensive form of the Bellman equation. What are the boundary and optimality conditions?

9.4.4. A Special Case: $\epsilon = 1$, $\delta = 0$, and Fixed $\hat{a}$

In this section three additional assumptions are imposed: no mortgage is allowed, $\epsilon = 1$; there is no maintenance cost, $\delta = 0$; and the share of financial (nonhousing) wealth in the risky asset is constant. In addition, a different state variable is used for the analysis. These changes make the law of motion for the state variable a geometric Brownian motion, so the solution can be found using the functions $\hat{L}$, ψ, and Ψ.

For $\epsilon = 1$, financial wealth is $X = Q - K$. Define the ratios

$$x \equiv \frac{X}{K} = \frac{Q - K}{K} = q - 1,$$

$$\hat{a} \equiv \frac{A}{X} = \frac{A}{Q - K} = a \frac{q}{q - 1},$$

so x is the ratio of financial wealth to housing wealth, and $\hat{a}$ is the share of financial wealth (not total wealth) held in the risky asset. The following assumption is used in this section.

Assumption 9.4. $\epsilon = 1$, $\delta = 0$, and $\hat{a} \in [0, 1]$ is fixed.

Exercise 9.5. (a) Show that under Assumption 9.4 x is a geometric Brownian motion with mean $\hat{\mu} = r + (\mu - r)\hat{a}$ and variance $\hat{\sigma}^2 = (\hat{a}\sigma)^2$.

Using x as the state variable the Bellman equation (9.7) can be written as

$$v(x_0) = \max_{T, x' \geq 0} \mathbf{E}\left[\int_0^T \frac{1}{1-\theta} e^{-\rho t} dt \right. \tag{9.17}$$

$$\left. + e^{-\rho T} \left(\frac{x(T) + 1 - \lambda}{x' + 1} \right)^{1-\theta} v(x') \right]$$

$$\text{s.t.} \quad dx = \hat{\mu} x dt + \hat{\sigma} x dZ,$$

where $v(x)$ is the maximized value of a consumer who has housing wealth of unity and financial wealth x. Define

$$h(x) \equiv (x + 1 - \lambda)^{1-\theta}$$

for the scaling factor after a transaction.

The optimal stopping time in (9.17) takes the form $T = T(d) \wedge T(D)$, where d and D are thresholds for the new state variable. Hence (9.17) can be written as

$$v(x) = \max_{d, D, x'} \left\{ w(x) + [\psi(x) h(d) + \Psi(x) h(D)] \frac{v(x')}{h(x' + \lambda)} \right\}, \tag{9.18}$$

where $w(x, d, D)$, $\psi(x, d, D)$, and $\Psi(x, d, D)$ are as defined at the beginning of Chapter 5 and the arguments d, D have been suppressed.

The return function here is the constant function $1/(1 - \theta)$. This fact has two implications. First, the value of never transacting is the value of consuming forever the services of a house of size one. That is,

$$w(x, 0, \infty) = v_P(x) = \int_0^\infty \frac{1}{1-\theta} e^{-\rho t} dt = \frac{1}{1-\theta} \frac{1}{\rho} \equiv \Omega.$$

Under Assumption 9.4 this strategy is always feasible: there is no maintenance cost, $\delta = 0$, and the consumer owns the house, $\epsilon = 1$, so there is no interest cost. The fact that the return function is a constant also implies that for any d, D,

$$w(x) = \mathbf{E}_x \left[\int_0^T \frac{1}{1-\theta} e^{-\rho t} dt \right]$$

$$= [1 - \psi(x) - \Psi(x)] \Omega.$$

Define

$$m^* \equiv \max_{s'} \frac{v(s')}{h(s' + \lambda)}, \tag{9.19}$$

and note that the value from transacting in state x is $h(x)m^*$.

Exercise. (b) Show that $h(x)m^*$ is strictly increasing in x for $\theta < 1$ and $\theta > 1$.

First consider the question of whether control is necessarily exercised. Setting $d = 0$ means the consumer never downsizes her house, and setting $D = \infty$ means she never upgrades. The next exercise shows that the consumer always upgrades her house if the ratio of her financial wealth to housing wealth is sufficiently high.

Exercise. (c) Show that $D^* < \infty$.

The optimal policy can be characterized by the first-order conditions for (9.18) and (9.19). The condition for d^* is an inequality, however. If the transaction cost λ is large the lower threshold may be $d^* = 0$. In this case the consumer prefers to stay in her current house and avoid the transaction cost when the ratio of her financial wealth to housing wealth is low. As usual, the conditions for the thresholds can be written as smooth pasting conditions.

Exercise. (d) Show that if d^*, D^*, s^* is an optimal policy, then

$$w_x(d^*) + \left[\psi_x(d^*)h(d^*) + \Psi_x(d^*)h(D^*)\right] m^* \geq h'(d^*)m^*,$$

$$\text{with equality if } d^* > 0,$$

$$w_x(D^*) + \left[\psi_x(D^*)h(d^*) + \Psi_x(D^*)h(D^*)\right] m^* = h'(D^*)m^*,$$

$$w_x(s^*) + \left[\psi_x(s^*)h(d^*) + \Psi_x(s^*)h(D^*)\right] m^* = h'(s^* + \lambda)m^*,$$

where

$$m^* = \frac{1 - \psi(s^*) - \Psi(s^*)}{h(s^* + \lambda) - \psi(s^*)h(d^*) - \Psi(s^*)h(D^*)}\Omega.$$

The solution can also be characterized by using the HJB equation associated with (9.17). Note that since x is a geometric Brownian motion, the terms $v'(x)$ and $v''(x)$ in the HJB equation are multiplied by x and x^2, respectively, so

$$\rho v(x) = \frac{1}{1 - \theta} + \hat{\mu} x v'(x) + \tfrac{1}{2}\hat{\sigma}^2 x^2 v''(x), \quad x \in (d, D). \tag{9.20}$$

$$v(x) = h(x)m^*, \qquad\qquad x \notin (d, D).$$

Exercise. (e) What are the value matching, smooth pasting, and optimal return conditions for (9.20)?

9.4.5. Replacing Computer Hardware, Revisited

Consider again the model of replacing computer hardware in Section 8.6.3. Suppose there is a proportional cost γ to adopting software improvements, so the cost of adopting the increment dX is γdX. In addition, suppose that the firm has the option not to adopt software improvements as soon as they appear.

Exercise 9.6. Explain briefly how this change can be incorporated in the HJB equation.

Notes

The housing model studied here is from Grossman and Laroque (1990). See Alvarez and Stokey (1998) for a discussion of recursive problems with homogeneous value functions.

Flavin and Nakagawa (2004) and Stokey (2008) analyze versions of the housing model that include nondurable consumption as well. Marshall and Parekh (1999) use a model in which the adjustment cost applies to total consumption to study the equity premium puzzle.

Smith, Rosen, and Fallis (1988) estimate the transaction cost for housing to be about 10%, and Flavin and Nakagawa (2004), Siegel (2005), and Cocco (2005) all find empirical evidence that adjustment costs are important for explaining the behavior of housing consumption. Both Chetty and Szeidl (2004) and Kullmann and Siegel (2005) find empirical evidence of state-dependent risk aversion, and Martin (2003) finds evidence that nondurable consumption adjusts at the time of a move.

Caballero (1990) looks at the time series implications of the type of slow or lagged adjustment generated by fixed costs for durable goods purchases. Caballero (1993) and Caplin and Leahy (1999) study models of aggregate durable purchases in settings in which individuals experience both idiosyncratic and aggregate shocks. Eberly (1994) simulates a model with many consumers who experience idiosyncratic shocks and compares it with evidence on new car purchases.

See Chetty and Szeidl (2007) for a model with adjustment costs that lead to a value function with convex regions.

Part III

Instantaneous Control Models

10

Regulated Brownian Motion

CONSIDER THE FOLLOWING purely mechanical description of a stock. In the absence of any regulation, the flows into and out of the stock are exogenous and stochastic, and the cumulative difference between the inflows and outflows is described by a Brownian motion X. There are fixed values b, B, with $b < B$. The stock is not allowed to rise above B or to fall below b. An automatic regulator exercises control when the stock reaches either threshold, increasing or decreasing the stock by just enough to keep it inside the interval $[b, B]$.

For example, the inflow can be interpreted as production, the outflow as sales, and the stock as an inventory held as a buffer between the two. Then $dX(t)$ is the excess of production over sales at date t, with $dX(t) < 0$ when demand exceeds production. B is the capacity for carrying inventory, and it is natural to take b to be zero. Control exercised at B is interpreted as the disposal of goods on a secondary market, and control exercised at b as the purchase of goods from a backstop supplier.

To begin, the costs and benefits from these activities can be set aside: there is no objective function and no decisions are made. The first goal is to describe the control exercised at each threshold and the resulting process for the regulated stock, given arbitrary values for b, B. More precisely, fix $b < B$, and suppose $x_0 = X(0) \in [b, B]$. Let $L(t)$ and $U(t)$ denote the cumulative control the regulator has exercised at the lower and upper boundaries, respectively, by date t. The regulated stock at any date is then

$$Z(t) = X(t) + L(t) - U(t), \quad \text{all } t. \tag{10.1}$$

$L(t)$ and $U(t)$ are stochastic processes, and (L, U, Z) have the following properties:

    i. L and U are continuous and nondecreasing, with $L_0 = U_0 = 0$;
    ii. $Z(t)$ defined by (10.1) satisfies $Z(t) \in [b, B]$, all t;

    iii. $L(t)$ increases only when $Z(t) = b$, and $U(t)$ increases only when $Z(t) = B$.

Thus, the first goal is to define L and U in terms of the exogenous process X.

    With definitions of L and U in hand, decision problems can then be studied. In the inventory problem and in other economic applications, the values b, B are chosen to minimize the expected discounted sum of various costs, given a (constant) interest rate $r > 0$. Three types of costs can be incorporated: a unit cost for adding to the stock at the lower threshold, a unit cost for decreasing the stock at the upper threshold, and a strictly convex carrying cost. To describe them the following definitions are useful. Fix $r > 0$, $b < B$, and an initial value $Z(0) = z \in [b, B]$. Define

$$\alpha(z, b, B; r) \equiv \mathrm{E}_z \left[\int_0^\infty e^{-rs} dL \right],$$

$$\beta(z, b, B; r) \equiv \mathrm{E}_z \left[\int_0^\infty e^{-rs} dU \right], \tag{10.2}$$

$$\Pi(A; z, b, B; r) \equiv \mathrm{E}_z \left[\int_0^\infty e^{-rs} 1_A(Z(s)) ds \right], \quad A \in \mathfrak{B}_{[b, B]},$$

where $\mathrm{E}_z [\cdot]$ denotes an expectation conditional on the initial condition, 1_A is the indicator function for the set A, and $\mathfrak{B}_{[b, B]}$ denotes the Borel subsets of $[b, B]$. Then $\alpha(z, b, B; r)$ is the expected discounted value of control exercised at the lower threshold, $\beta(z, b, B; r)$ is an analogous expression for control at the upper threshold, and $\Pi(A; z, b, B; r)$ is the expected discounted occupancy measure. Let $\pi(\cdot, z, b, B; r)$ denote the expected discounted local time associated with Π. Then the expected costs for adjusting the stock at the two boundaries are proportional to α and β, and the expected carrying cost is an integral involving π.

    If $r = 0$ the integrals in (10.2) diverge. Nevertheless long-run averages can be calculated, the expected control exercised per unit time at each threshold and the stationary distribution. These averages are useful for characterizing aggregate behavior. In particular, if there is a continuum of i.i.d. agents of measure one, each described by the same regulated process, then the stationary density π represents the (constant) cross-sectional distribution, and α and β represent the (constant) level of aggregate control exercised at the boundaries.

    Notice that this model is similar to the one studied in Chapter 8 except that there are no fixed costs of adjustment. Thus, it can be viewed as the limiting case as the fixed costs go to zero. As the fixed costs fall, the decision maker chooses to make more frequent and smaller adjustments, so the return points are closer to the thresholds. That is, the sizes of the optimal upward and downward adjustments, $|q - b|$ and $|Q - B|$, shrink to zero as the fixed costs go to zero. In the limit, instead of discrete jumps, the adjustments take the form of "regulation" at the two thresholds that is just sufficient to keep the process from exiting the inaction region.

The rest of this chapter is organized as follows. One-sided and two-sided regulators are developed in Section 10.1. Explicit formulas for α, β, and π are developed in Section 10.2 for the discounted case, $r > 0$, and in Section 10.3 for the undiscounted case, $r = 0$. Section 10.4 contains an example, a simple inventory model, that shows how these formulas can be used.

10.1. One- and Two-Sided Regulators

Suppose there is only a lower threshold, b, and the initial condition is $X(0) = X_0 \geq b$. The regulator triggers inflows when the stock is at b. Define the stopping time T_0 as the first date when $X(t) = b$, and note that

$$L(t) = \begin{cases} 0, & t \leq T_0, \text{ all } \omega, \\ b - \min_{s \in [0,t]} X(s), & t > T_0, \text{ all } \omega. \end{cases} \quad (10.3)$$

Clearly $L(t)$ is continuous and nondecreasing, $L(0) = 0$, and L is strictly increasing at t only if $t > T_0$ and $X(t) = \min_{s \in [0,t]} X(s)$. The stock at any date is

$$\begin{aligned} Z(t) &= X(t) + L(t) \\ &= \begin{cases} X(t), & t \leq T_0, \text{ all } \omega, \\ b + [X(t) - \min_{s \in [0,t]} X(s)], & t > T_0, \text{ all } \omega, \end{cases} \\ &\geq b, \quad \text{all } t \geq 0, \end{aligned}$$

and L is strictly increasing only when $Z(t) = b$. Hence L in (10.3), $U \equiv 0$, and Z as above satisfy conditions (i)–(iii).

Similarly, suppose there is only an upper threshold, B, and the initial condition is $X(0) = X_0 \leq B$. The regulator triggers outflows when the stock is at B. Define the stopping time T_1 as the first date when $X(t) = B$, and note that

$$U(t) = \begin{cases} 0, & t \leq T_1, \text{ all } \omega, \\ \max_{s \in [0,t]} X(s) - B & t > T_1, \text{ all } \omega. \end{cases} \quad (10.4)$$

Clearly $U(t)$ is continuous and nondecreasing, $U(0) = 0$, and U is strictly increasing at t only if $t > T_1$ and $X(t) = \max_{s \in [0,t]} X(s)$. The stock at any date is

$$Z(t) = X(t) - U(t)$$

$$= \begin{cases} X(t), & t \le T_1, \quad \text{all } \omega, \\ B - [\max_{s \in [0,t]} X(s) - X(t)], & t > T_1, \quad \text{all } \omega, \end{cases}$$

$$\le B, \quad \text{all } t \ge 0,$$

and U is strictly increasing at t only if $Z(t) = B$. Hence U in (10.4), $L \equiv 0$, and Z as above satisfy conditions (i)–(iii).

Now suppose there are two boundaries, $b < B$, and $X_0 \in [b, B]$. Construction of the stochastic processes $U(t)$ and $L(t)$ proceeds by induction.

The basic idea is to define successive blocks of time so that during each block control is exercised at only one of the boundaries, and the threshold at which control is exercised alternates between successive blocks. Within each block the increments to U or L—but only one of them—are defined using (10.3) or (10.4). The end of the block, the point at which regulation switches to the other threshold, is a stopping time. Thus the construction defines a sequence of stopping times $0 \le T_0 < T_1 < T_2 < \ldots < T_n < \ldots$ with the property that there is an initial block of the form $[0, T_0]$ or $[0, T_1]$ during which no control is exercised, and subsequently control is exercised only at b over "even" blocks—those of the form $(T_{2i}, T_{2i+1}]$—and only at B over "odd" blocks—those of the form $(T_{2i+1}, T_{2i+2}]$. Notice that $T_0, T_1, \ldots$, are not the only times when the regulated process reaches the thresholds. The process may reach b multiple times during any even block, and it may reach B multiple times during any odd block.

If $T(b) < T(B)$ let

$$T_0 = T(b),$$
$$U(t) = L(t) = 0, \quad t \in [0, T_0), \tag{10.5}$$

so no control is exercised during $[0, T_0)$ and $Z(T_0) = b$. If $T(B) < T(b)$ let

$$T_0 = 0, \qquad T_1 = T(B),$$
$$U(t) = L(t) = 0, \quad t \in [0, T_1), \tag{10.6}$$

so no control is exercised during $[0, T_1)$ and $Z(T_1) = B$. In either case, the construction of U, L, and Z is identical over all subsequent odd and even blocks, so it suffices to look at a typical block of each type.

Consider a typical even block, starting at T_{2i}, with $Z(T_{2i}) = b$. The idea is to construct processes $\hat{X}_{2i}$, $\hat{L}_{2i}$, and $\hat{Z}_{2i}$, each having as its argument a re-initialized time variable $s = t - T_{2i}$. These functions are used to define the next stopping time, T_{2i+1}, and to construct L and Z over the interval $[T_{2i}, T_{2i+1})$.

Define

$$\hat{X}_{2i}(s) \equiv b + \left[X(T_{2i} + s) - X(T_{2i}) \right], \quad s \geq 0, \text{ all } \omega.$$

Notice that $\hat{X}_{2i}(0) = b$, and $\hat{X}_{2i}$ has increments identical to those of X. Define

$$\hat{L}_{2i}(s) \equiv b - \min_{\tau \in [0,s]} \hat{X}_{2i}(\tau),$$

$$\hat{Z}_{2i}(s) \equiv \hat{X}_{2i}(s) + \hat{L}_{2i}(s), \quad s \geq 0, \text{ all } \omega.$$

Define the stopping time $\hat{S}_{2i+1}$ as the first time $\hat{Z}_{2i}(s)$ reaches the threshold B. Then for the original process let

$$T_{2i+1} = T_{2i} + \hat{S}_{2i+1},$$

$$U(t) = U(T_{2i}), \tag{10.7}$$

$$L(t) = L(T_{2i}) + \hat{L}_{2i}(t - T_{2i}), \quad t \in (T_{2i}, T_{2i+1}], \text{ all } \omega,$$

and use (10.1) to define $Z(t)$. During an even block of time no control is exercised at the upper threshold, so $U(t)$ is constant. The additional control exercised at the lower threshold is described by $\hat{L}_{2i}$.

Next consider a typical odd block, starting at T_{2i+1} with $Z(T_{2i+1}) = B$. Define

$$\hat{X}_{2i+1}(s) \equiv B + \left[X(T_{2i+1} + s) - X(T_{2i+1}) \right], \quad s \geq 0, \text{ all } \omega.$$

Notice that $\hat{X}_{2i+1}(0) = B$, and $\hat{X}_{2i+1}$ has increments identical to those of X. Define

$$\hat{U}_{2i+1}(s) \equiv \max_{\tau \in [0,s]} \hat{X}_{2i+1}(\tau) - B,$$

$$\hat{Z}_{2i+1}(s) \equiv \hat{X}_{2i+1}(s) - \hat{U}_{2i+1}(s), \quad s \geq 0, \text{ all } \omega.$$

Define the stopping time $\hat{S}_{2i+2}$ as the first time $\hat{Z}_{2i+1}$ reaches the threshold b. Then for the original process let

$$T_{2i+2} = T_{2i+1} + \hat{S}_{2i+2},$$

$$U(t) = U(T_{2i+1}) + \hat{U}_{2i+1}(t - T_{2i+1}), \tag{10.8}$$

$$L(t) = L(T_{2i+1}), \quad t \in (T_{2i+1}, T_{2i+2}], \text{ all } \omega,$$

and use (10.1) to define $Z(t)$. During an odd block of time $L(t)$ is constant, and additional control at the upper threshold is described by $\hat{U}_{2i+1}$.

Continue in this fashion, alternating blocks of time. Figure 10.1 displays a sample path with a block of each type. Panel **a** shows the paths for $X(t)$

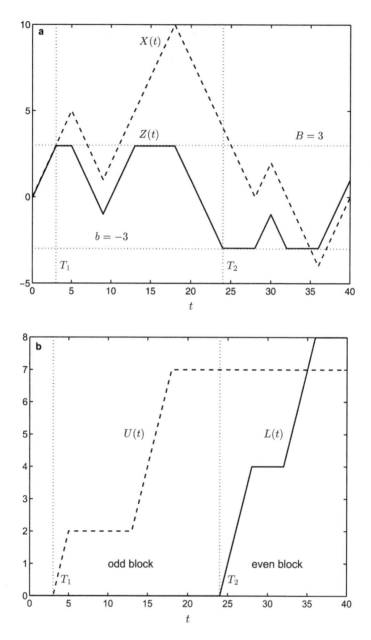

Figure 10.1. (a) Sample path for a regulated Brownian motion, and (b) cumulative control $U(t)$ and $L(t)$ exercised at the upper and lower thresholds.

and $Z(t)$, and panel **b** shows the corresponding paths for $U(t)$ and $L(t)$. To summarize, the argument above establishes the following result.

Proposition 10.1. For any $b < B$ and any Brownian motion X with $X(0) = x_0 \in [b, B]$, the unique functions satisfying conditions (i)–(iii) are $U(t)$ and $L(t)$ defined by (10.5)–(10.8) and $Z(t)$ defined by (10.1).

10.2. Discounted Values

Let b, B and X, U, L, Z be as in Section 10.1, with $X(0) = Z(0) = z \in [b, B]$, and fix an interest rate $r > 0$. In this section expressions are developed for the functions defined in (10.2): the expected discounted value of control exercised at each threshold, $\alpha(z, b, B; r)$ and $\beta(z, b, B; r)$, and the expected discounted local time function $\pi(\cdot; z, b, B; r)$ for the regulated process. These functions are useful for studying problems in which a decision maker is choosing the thresholds b and B to minimize an objective function involving proportional costs of control at each threshold and holding costs that depend on the stock Z.

The main tool for this purpose will be Ito's lemma, Theorem 3.3. Recall that if $\hat{\mu}(Z)$ and $\hat{\sigma}(Z)$ are the infinitesimal parameters of the process Z, then $\hat{\mu}(Z)ds + \hat{\sigma}(Z)dW = dZ$ and $\hat{\sigma}^2(Z)ds = \left[(dZ)^2\right]$. Hence for a constant discount rate $r \geq 0$, Ito's lemma states that if the function $f : [b, B] \to \mathbf{R}$ is twice continuously differentiable and $Z(0) = z$, then for any $t \geq 0$,

$$e^{-rt}f(Z(t)) = f(z) - r \int_0^t e^{-rs}f(Z)ds + \int_0^t e^{-rs}f'(Z)dZ$$

$$+ \frac{1}{2}\int_0^t e^{-rs}f''(Z)\,(dZ)^2, \quad \text{all } \omega.$$

(10.9)

The argument here involves taking the expected value of this equation, so expressions are needed for $E[dZ]$ and $E\left[(dZ)^2\right]$. The resulting version of (10.9) can then be specialized, and for judicious choices of f it delivers closed-form solutions for α, β, and π.

Since $Z = X - U + L$, it is straightforward that

$$E\,[dZ] = E\,[dX - dU + dL]$$

$$= \mu ds - E\,[dU] + E\,[dL].$$

$E\left[(dZ)^2\right]$ can be evaluated by taking a sequence of discrete approximations, like those in Sections 2.4 and 2.8, to the processes X, U, L, Z.

For $n = 1, 2, \ldots$, let the nth process for Z take values on a grid with $n + 1$ evenly spaced points on $[b, B]$. The nth process has step size h_n, time increment Δ_n, and probability p_n defined by

$$h_n = \frac{B-b}{n}, \qquad \Delta_n = \left(\frac{h_n}{\sigma}\right)^2, \qquad p_n = \frac{1}{2}\left(1 + \frac{\mu}{\sigma^2}h_n\right).$$

Over each time interval Δ_n, the increment to the unregulated process is $\Delta X = h_n$ with probability p_n and $\Delta X = -h_n$ with probability $1 - p_n$, so the mean and variance of each approximating process for X match those of the original. In addition $\Delta U = h_n$ if $Z = B$ and $\Delta X = h_n$, and $\Delta L = h_n$ if $Z = b$ and $\Delta X = -h_n$. Otherwise $\Delta U = \Delta L = 0$. Hence

$$
\begin{aligned}
\mathrm{E}\left[(\Delta Z)^2\right] &= \mathrm{E}\left[(\Delta X - \Delta U + \Delta L)^2\right] \\
&= \mathrm{E}\left[(\Delta X)^2 + (\Delta U)^2 + (\Delta L)^2 - 2\Delta X \Delta U + 2\Delta X \Delta L\right] \\
&= \mathrm{E}\left[(\Delta X)^2\right] - \mathrm{E}\left[(\Delta U)^2\right] - \mathrm{E}\left[(\Delta L)^2\right],
\end{aligned}
$$

where the second line uses the fact that $\Delta U \Delta L \equiv 0$ and the third uses the fact that $\Delta X = \Delta U$ if $\Delta U > 0$ and $\Delta X = -\Delta L$ if $\Delta L > 0$. For the nth process,

$$\mathrm{E}\left[(\Delta U)^2 \mid Z = B\right] = p_n h_n^2.$$

Since $\Pr\left[Z = B\right]$ is of order $1/n$ or, equivalently, of order h_n, it follows that

$$\frac{1}{\Delta_n}\mathrm{E}\left[(\Delta U)^2\right] \simeq \frac{1}{\Delta_n}p_n h_n^3 \simeq p_n h_n,$$

where $\simeq$ means "has the same order as." Hence this term goes to zero as $n \to \infty$. An analogous argument applies for ΔL, so

$$\mathrm{E}\left[(dZ)^2\right] = \mathrm{E}\left[(dX)^2\right] = \sigma^2 ds.$$

Since f, f', and f'' are continuous, they are bounded on $[b, B]$. Hence for any $r > 0$ the integrals in (10.9) are bounded as $t \to \infty$. Take the limit, take the expected value conditional on the initial condition $Z(0) = z$, and note that the term on the left vanishes to obtain

$$
\mathrm{E}_z\left[\int_0^\infty e^{-rs}\left\{rf(Z) - \mu f'(Z) - \tfrac{1}{2}\sigma^2 f''(Z)\right\}ds\right]
$$

$$
= f(z) + f'(b)\mathrm{E}_z\left[\int_0^\infty e^{-rs}dL\right] - f'(B)\mathrm{E}_z\left[\int_0^\infty e^{-rs}dU\right],
$$

where the last two terms use the fact that dL is positive only if $Z = b$ and dU is positive only if $Z = B$.

The expected values on the right are simply $\alpha(z)$ and $\beta(z)$ and, by Theorem 3.7, the expected value on the left can be written as an integral over states involving the function π. Hence for any twice differentiable function f,

$$\int_b^B \left[rf(\zeta) - \mu f'(\zeta) - \tfrac{1}{2}\sigma^2 f''(\zeta) \right] \pi(\zeta, z) d\zeta$$

$$= f(z) + f'(b)\alpha(z) - f'(B)\beta(z).$$

The rest of the argument involves choosing functions f of a particular form. Specifically, note that for functions of the form $f(\zeta) = e^{\lambda \zeta}$, with $\lambda \neq 0$,

$$\left(r - \mu\lambda - \tfrac{1}{2}\sigma^2 \lambda^2 \right) \int_b^B e^{\lambda \zeta} \pi(\zeta, z) d\zeta = e^{\lambda z} + \lambda e^{\lambda b}\alpha(z) - \lambda e^{\lambda B}\beta(z). \quad (10.10)$$

Propositions 10.2–10.4 use (10.10) to characterize α, β, and π.

Let $R_1 < 0 < R_2$ denote the roots of the quadratic $\left(r - \mu\lambda - \tfrac{1}{2}\sigma^2 \lambda^2 \right) = 0$, and let

$$\Delta = e^{R_2 B} e^{R_1 b} - e^{R_1 B} e^{R_2 b}.$$

Proposition 10.2. Fix $\left(\mu, \sigma^2 \right)$, $r > 0$, and $b < B$. Then

$$\alpha(z, b, B; r) = \frac{1}{\Delta} \left(\frac{e^{R_1 B} e^{R_2 z}}{R_2} - \frac{e^{R_2 B} e^{R_1 z}}{R_1} \right),$$

$$\beta(z, b, B; r) = \frac{1}{\Delta} \left(\frac{e^{R_1 b} e^{R_2 z}}{R_2} - \frac{e^{R_2 b} e^{R_1 z}}{R_1} \right), \qquad z \in [b, B]. \quad (10.11)$$

Proof. For $\lambda = R_1, R_2$, the term on the left in (10.10) is zero. Hence

$$\begin{pmatrix} e^{R_1 B} & -e^{R_1 b} \\ e^{R_2 B} & -e^{R_2 b} \end{pmatrix} \begin{pmatrix} \beta(z) \\ \alpha(z) \end{pmatrix} = \begin{pmatrix} e^{R_1 z}/R_1 \\ e^{R_2 z}/R_2 \end{pmatrix}, \qquad z \in [b, B],$$

and α and β are as in (10.11). ∎

Proposition 10.3. Fix $\left(\mu, \sigma^2 \right)$, $r > 0$, and $b < B$. Then

$$\pi(\zeta; b, b, B; r) = \frac{e^{R_1 b} e^{R_2 b}}{r\Delta} \left[R_2 e^{R_2(B-\zeta)} - R_1 e^{R_1(B-\zeta)} \right],$$

$$\pi(\zeta; B, b, B; r) = \frac{e^{R_1 B} e^{R_2 B}}{r\Delta} \left[R_2 e^{R_2(b-\zeta)} - R_1 e^{R_1(b-\zeta)} \right], \qquad \zeta \in [b, B]. \quad (10.12)$$

Proof.   For $z = b$ the term on the right in (10.10) is

$$\frac{e^{\lambda b}e^{R_1 b}e^{R_2 b}}{\Delta}\left[e^{R_2(B-b)} - e^{R_1(B-b)} + \frac{\lambda e^{R_1(B-b)}}{R_2} - \frac{\lambda e^{R_2(B-b)}}{R_1}\right.$$

$$\left. -e^{\lambda(B-b)}\frac{\lambda}{R_2} + e^{\lambda(B-b)}\frac{\lambda}{R_1}\right]$$

$$= \frac{e^{\lambda b}e^{R_1 b}e^{R_2 b}}{\Delta}\left[\frac{R_1 - \lambda}{R_1}\left[e^{R_2(B-b)} - e^{\lambda(B-b)}\right]\right.$$

$$\left. -\frac{R_2 - \lambda}{R_2}\left[e^{R_1(B-b)} - e^{\lambda(B-b)}\right]\right].$$

Also note that

$$r - \lambda\mu - \frac{1}{2}\sigma^2\lambda^2 = r\left(\frac{R_1 - \lambda}{R_1}\right)\left(\frac{R_2 - \lambda}{R_2}\right).$$

Use these facts in (10.10) to obtain

$$\int_b^B \pi(\zeta;b,b,B;r)e^{\lambda(\zeta-b)}d\zeta$$

$$= \frac{e^{R_1 b}e^{R_2 b}e^{\lambda(B-b)}}{r\Delta}\left[\frac{R_2}{R_2 - \lambda}\left[e^{(R_2-\lambda)(B-b)} - 1\right] - \frac{R_1}{R_1 - \lambda}\left[e^{(R_1-\lambda)(B-b)} - 1\right]\right]$$

$$= \frac{e^{R_1 b}e^{R_2 b}e^{\lambda(B-b)}}{r\Delta}\int_b^B\left[R_2 e^{(R_2-\lambda)(B-\zeta)} - R_1 e^{(R_1-\lambda)(B-\zeta)}\right]d\zeta$$

$$= \frac{e^{R_1 b}e^{R_2 b}}{r\Delta}\int_b^B\left[R_2 e^{R_2(B-\zeta)} - R_1 e^{R_1(B-\zeta)}\right]e^{\lambda(\zeta-b)}d\zeta.$$

Since this equation holds for any $\lambda \neq 0$, $\pi(\zeta;b)$ is as in (10.12). An analogous argument applies for $z = B$. ∎

Let ψ, Ψ, and J be as defined in Chapter 5. The next result then follows immediately.

Proposition 10.4.   Fix (μ, σ^2), $r > 0$, and $b < B$. Then for any $z \in [b, B]$,

$$\pi(\zeta; z, b, B; r) = \frac{1}{J} e^{R_i(z-\zeta)} + \psi(z) \left[\pi(\zeta; b) - \frac{1}{J} e^{R_2(b-\zeta)} \right] \tag{10.13}$$

$$+ \Psi(z) \left[\pi(\zeta; B) - \frac{1}{J} e^{R_1(B-\zeta)} \right], \quad i = \begin{cases} 1, & \text{if } b \le \zeta \le z, \\ 2, & \text{if } z \le \zeta \le B, \end{cases}$$

Proof. Fix $z \in (b, B)$ and define the stopping time $T = T(b) \wedge T(B)$. The function $\pi(\cdot; z)$ is the sum of three parts, one representing time before T and two representing time after T, for stops at b and at B. Hence

$$\pi(\zeta; z) = \hat{L}(\zeta; z) + \psi(z)\pi(\zeta; b) + \Psi(z)\pi(\zeta; B), \quad \text{all } \zeta \in [b, B],$$

where $\hat{L}(\zeta; z, b, B; r)$ is expected discounted local time before T. Recall from Section 5.6 that

$$\hat{L}(\zeta; z) = \frac{1}{J} \left[e^{R_i(z-\zeta)} - \psi(z) e^{R_2(b-\zeta)} - \Psi(z) e^{R_1(B-\zeta)} \right],$$

$$i = \begin{cases} 1, & \text{if } b \le \zeta \le z, \\ 2, & \text{if } z \le \zeta \le B, \end{cases}$$

establishing the claim. ∎

Notice from (10.13) that $\pi(\zeta; z)$ is everywhere continuous, but it has a kink at $\zeta = z$. Hence $\pi_z(\zeta; z)$ has a jump at $\zeta = z$,

$$\lim_{\zeta \uparrow z} \pi_z(\zeta; z) - \lim_{\zeta \downarrow z} \pi_z(\zeta; z) = \frac{R_1 - R_2}{J}, \quad \text{all } \zeta, z \in [b, B]. \tag{10.14}$$

Also note that the results in Propositions 10.2–10.4 continue to hold if one of the thresholds grows without bound, as $b \to -\infty$ or $B \to \infty$.

The following exercise provides an alternative way to write π.

Exercise 10.1. Show that if $b > -\infty$, then

$$\pi(\zeta; z) = \alpha(z) \frac{1}{J} \left[R_2 e^{R_2(b-\zeta)} - R_1 e^{R_1(b-\zeta)} \right], \quad \zeta \in [b, z].$$

Show that if $B < +\infty$, then

$$\pi(\zeta; z) = \beta(z) \frac{1}{J} \left[R_2 e^{R_2(B-\zeta)} - R_1 e^{R_1(B-\zeta)} \right], \quad \zeta \in [z, B].$$

Note that since $\alpha(z) \to 0$ and $e^{R_1(b-\zeta)} \to +\infty$ as $b \to -\infty$, the first expression must be interpreted carefully if there is no lower threshold. The same is true for the second expression if there is no upper threshold.

The next two results show that the derivatives of α, β, and π have certain properties. As the inventory example in Section 10.4 shows, these properties are useful in applications where the thresholds b and B are chosen to optimize an objective function.

Proposition 10.5.   Fix (μ, σ^2), $r > 0$, and $b < B$. Then the ratios

$$\frac{\alpha_b(z)}{\pi(b;z)}, \quad \frac{\beta_b(z)}{\pi(b;z)}, \quad \frac{\pi_b(\zeta;z)}{\pi(b;z)}, \quad \zeta \in [b, B],$$

$$\frac{\alpha_B(z)}{\pi(B;z)}, \quad \frac{\beta_B(z)}{\pi(B;z)}, \quad \frac{\pi_B(\zeta;z)}{\pi(B;z)}, \quad \zeta \in [b, B],$$

are independent of z, for $z \in (b, B)$.

Proof.   Exercise 10.1 shows that

$$\pi(b;z) = \alpha(z) \frac{1}{J}(R_2 - R_1).$$

For the first claim note that

$$\alpha_b(z) = -\alpha(z)\frac{\Delta_b}{\Delta}.$$

For the second note that

$$\beta_b(z) = \frac{1}{\Delta^2}\frac{1}{R_1 R_2}\left[\Delta\left(R_1^2 e^{R_1 b} e^{R_2 z} - R_2^2 e^{R_2 b} e^{R_1 z}\right)\right.$$

$$\left. -\Delta_b\left(R_1 e^{R_1 b} e^{R_2 z} - R_2 e^{R_2 b} e^{R_1 z}\right)\right]$$

$$= \frac{1}{\Delta^2}\frac{1}{R_1 R_2}\left[\left(e^{R_2 B} e^{R_1 b} - e^{R_1 B} e^{R_2 b}\right)\left(R_1^2 e^{R_1 b} e^{R_2 z} - R_2^2 e^{R_2 b} e^{R_1 z}\right)\right.$$

$$\left. -\left(R_1 e^{R_2 B} e^{R_1 b} - R_2 e^{R_1 B} e^{R_2 b}\right)\left(R_1 e^{R_1 b} e^{R_2 z} - R_2 e^{R_2 b} e^{R_1 z}\right)\right]$$

$$= \frac{1}{\Delta^2}\frac{(R_2 - R_1)}{R_1 R_2}e^{R_1 b} e^{R_2 b}\left[R_1 e^{R_1 B} e^{R_2 z} - R_2 e^{R_2 B} e^{R_1 z}\right]$$

$$= \frac{1}{\Delta}(R_2 - R_1)\, e^{R_1 b} e^{R_2 b}\alpha(z).$$

For the third use the result in Exercise 10.1. For $\zeta < z$,

$$\frac{\pi_b(\zeta;z)}{\pi(b;z)} = \frac{\alpha_b(z)}{\alpha(z)} + \frac{R_2^2 e^{R_2(b-\zeta)} - R_1^2 e^{R_1(b-\zeta)}}{R_2 e^{R_2(b-\zeta)} - R_1 e^{R_1(b-\zeta)}},$$

and the claim follows from the first result. For $\zeta > z$,

$$\frac{\pi_b(\zeta; z)}{\pi(b; z)} = \frac{\beta_b(z)}{\pi(b; z)} \frac{1}{J} \left[R_2 e^{R_2(B-\zeta)} - R_1 e^{R_1(B-\zeta)} \right],$$

and the claim follows from the second result.

Similar arguments establish the other three claims. ∎

These results have a very natural interpretation. For example, note that $\alpha_b(z)$ is the effect of a change in b on the expected discounted control exercised at b, given the current state z. The first result states that this value is proportional to $\pi(b; z)$, the expected discounted local time at b given the current state z. That is, conditional on arriving at b, the effect of changing b is always the same. Changing the current state z alters only the arrivals at b. The other results have similar interpretations.

Proposition 10.6. Fix (μ, σ^2), $r > 0$, and $b < B$. Then the functions α, β, and π satisfy

$$\alpha_b(z) = \alpha(z)\alpha_{zz}(b), \qquad \alpha_B(z) = \beta(z)\alpha_{zz}(B),$$

$$\beta_b(z) = \alpha(z)\beta_{zz}(b), \qquad \beta_B(z) = \beta(z)\beta_{zz}(B),$$

$$\pi_b(\zeta; b) = \alpha(b)\pi_{zz}(\zeta; b), \quad \pi_B(\zeta; B) = \beta(B)\pi_{zz}(\zeta; B), \quad \text{all } \zeta \in [b, B].$$

Proof. Use the expressions for α and β in (10.11) to get

$$\alpha_b(z) = -\frac{\Delta_b}{\Delta}\alpha(z) = \alpha(z)\alpha_{zz}(b),$$

and

$$\beta_b(z) = \frac{1}{\Delta^2} \left[\left(\frac{R_1 e^{R_2 z} e^{R_1 b}}{R_2} - \frac{R_2 e^{R_1 z} e^{R_2 b}}{R_1} \right) \left(e^{R_2 B} e^{R_1 b} - e^{R_1 B} e^{R_2 b} \right) \right.$$

$$\left. - \left(\frac{e^{R_2 z} e^{R_1 b}}{R_2} - \frac{e^{R_1 z} e^{R_2 b}}{R_1} \right) \left(R_1 e^{R_2 B} e^{R_1 b} - R_2 e^{R_1 B} e^{R_2 b} \right) \right]$$

$$= \frac{R_2 - R_1}{\Delta^2} e^{R_1 b} e^{R_2 b} \left(\frac{e^{R_2 z} e^{R_1 B}}{R_2} - \frac{e^{R_1 z} e^{R_2 B}}{R_1} \right)$$

$$= \alpha(z)\beta_{zz}(b),$$

establishing the first two claims. Then use the expressions for π in Exercise 10.1 to find that for $z < \zeta$,

$$\pi_{zz}(\zeta; b) = \beta_{zz}(b)\frac{1}{J}\left[R_2 e^{R_2(B-\zeta)} - R_1 e^{R_1(B-\zeta)}\right],$$

$$\pi_b(\zeta; z) = \beta_b(z)\frac{1}{J}\left[R_2 e^{R_2(B-\zeta)} - R_1 e^{R_1(B-\zeta)}\right].$$

The third claim then follows from the second. Similar arguments establish the other three claims. ∎

These results also have natural interpretations. The first three state that the effects of a change in b on the expected discounted control exercised at b and at B and on the expected discounted local time at any level, given the current state z, are all proportional to $\alpha(z)$. Since $\alpha(z)$ measures arrivals at b, given the current state, this interpretation makes sense: the change in b matters only when the process arrives at b. What is slightly surprising is the form of the second term on the right side in each expression. In the first, for example, it is $\alpha_{zz}(b)$ rather than $\alpha_z(b)$.

Figure 10.2 displays the functions α, β, and π. Panel **a** shows $\alpha(\cdot)$ and $\beta(\cdot)$ as functions of the initial value z for a process with positive drift. For the same process panel **b** shows $\pi(\cdot; z)$ as a function of ζ, for $z = -2, 0, 2$. The positive drift in z makes all these functions asymmetric. Note that the area under each of the three curves in panel b is equal to $1/r$.

10.3. The Stationary Distribution

To characterize the stationary distribution for Z one cannot simply take the limits in (10.2) as $r \to 0$, since all of the integrals diverge. Instead, for $r = 0$ the analogs of α, β, and π must be defined in a slightly different way. The first step is to construct a new set of time blocks for Z, defined so that ex ante they are similar and taken together they cover the entire history of the process.

Fix an initial condition $Z(0) = z \in [b, B]$, and consider the sequence of stopping times $0 = \tau_0 < \tau_1 < \tau_2 < \ldots \to \infty$ defined as

$$\tau_{n+1} = \min\{t > \tau_n \mid Z(t) = z, \text{ and } Z(s) = b,$$

$$Z(s') = B, \text{ for some } \tau_n < s, s' \le t\}.$$

Thus, each stopping time is defined by requiring $Z(t)$ to reach each threshold, b and B, at least once and then to return to the initial state z. Each of these stopping times is finite with probability one, and

$$Z(\tau_n(\omega)) = z, \quad \text{all } \omega, \text{ all } n.$$

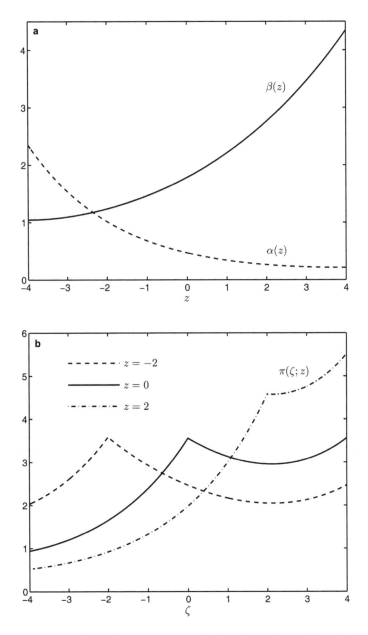

Figure 10.2. *For a Brownian motion regulated at $b = -4$ and $B = 4$, (a) the expected discounted control at each threshold $\alpha(z)$ and $\beta(z)$, as functions of the initial state z, and (b) the expected discounted local time $\pi(\zeta; z)$ for $z = -2, 0, 2$. The parameter values are $\mu = 0.1$, $\sigma = 1$, and $r = 0.05$.*

If the initial value is $Z(0) = b$ or B, these blocks are formed by aggregating the blocks defined in Section 10.1 into pairs.

Fix z, let $\tau = \tau_1$, and define

$$\alpha_0(z, b, B) = \frac{\mathrm{E}_z[L(\tau)]}{\mathrm{E}_z(\tau)},$$

$$\beta_0(z, b, B) = \frac{\mathrm{E}_z[U(\tau)]}{\mathrm{E}_z(\tau)},$$

$$\Pi_0(A; z, b, B) = \frac{\mathrm{E}_z[m(A, \tau)]}{\mathrm{E}_z(\tau)}, \quad A \in \mathcal{B}_{[b,B]},$$

where $m(A, \tau)$ is the (undiscounted) occupancy measure for the set A up to τ, as discussed in Section 3.5. The value α_0 is the expected control per unit time exercised at the lower threshold over $[0, \tau]$, and β_0 is an analogous expression for control at the upper threshold. The function $\Pi_0(\cdot; z)$ normalizes the occupancy measure so that $\Pi_0([b, B]; z) \equiv 1$. Let π_0 be the density for Π_0.

As with the discounted values, the undiscounted values α_0, β_0 and the density π_0 can be calculated by making use of (10.9) for particular functions f. Recall that (10.9) holds for any t and for any twice differentiable function f. In particular, note that $t = \tau$ implies $Z(\tau) = Z_0 = z$. Since $r = 0$, (10.9) then implies

$$0 = \int_0^\tau f'(Z)dZ + \frac{1}{2}\int_0^\tau f''(Z)\,(dZ)^2.$$

Then substitute for dZ and $(dZ)^2$, take the expectation, and rearrange terms to get

$$0 = \mathrm{E}_z\left[\int_0^\tau \left\{\mu f'(Z) + \frac{1}{2}\sigma^2 f''(Z)\right\} ds\right]$$
$$+ f'(b)\mathrm{E}_z\left[\int_0^\tau dL\right] - f'(B)\mathrm{E}_z\left[\int_0^\tau dU\right],$$

where the last terms use the fact that dL is positive only if $Z = b$ and dU is positive only if $Z = B$. Writing the first integral in terms π_0, and the second and third in terms of α_0 and β_0, gives

$$0 = \int_b^B \left[\mu f'(\zeta) + \tfrac{1}{2}\sigma^2 f''(\zeta)\right] \pi_0(\zeta)d\zeta + f'(b)\alpha_0 - f'(B)\beta_0. \quad (10.15)$$

Note that a_0, β_0, and π_0 do not depend on z.

The next result provides an important fact about α_0, β_0, and π_0: they describe the long-run stationary distribution.

Proposition 10.7.   Let $Z(t)$ be a regulated Brownian motion on $[b, B]$, with initial value $z \in [b, B]$. Then as $t \to \infty$,

$$\frac{1}{t} \mathrm{E}_z\, [L(t)] \to \alpha_0,$$

$$\frac{1}{t} \mathrm{E}_z\, [U(t)] \to \beta_0,$$

$$\mathrm{Pr}_z\{Z(t) \in A\} \to \Pi_0(A), \quad \text{all } A \in \mathcal{B}_{[b, B]}.$$

For a proof see Harrison (1985, pp. 87–89).

Equation (10.15) holds for any f. As before, judicious choices for f produce explicit solutions for α_0, β_0, and π_0.

Proposition 10.8.   If $\mu \neq 0$, then

$$\alpha_0 = \frac{\mu e^{\delta b}}{e^{\delta B} - e^{\delta b}},$$

$$\beta_0 = \frac{\mu e^{\delta B}}{e^{\delta B} - e^{\delta b}}, \tag{10.16}$$

$$\pi_0(\zeta) = \frac{\delta e^{\delta \zeta}}{e^{\delta B} - e^{\delta b}}, \quad \text{all } \zeta \in [b, B],$$

where $\delta = 2\mu/\sigma^2$. If $\mu = 0$, then

$$\alpha_0 = \beta_0 = \frac{\sigma^2}{2\,(B - b)},$$

$$\pi_0(\zeta) = \frac{1}{B - b}, \quad \text{all } \zeta \in [b, B]. \tag{10.17}$$

Remark.   If $\mu \neq 0$, π_0 is the density for a truncated exponential distribution with parameter δ. If $\mu = 0$, π_0 is the uniform density.

Proof.   Since π_0 integrates to unity, for $f(\zeta) = \zeta$, (10.15) implies

$$0 = \mu + \alpha_0 - \beta_0, \tag{10.18}$$

and for $f(\zeta) = e^{\lambda \zeta}$, $\lambda \neq 0$, it implies

$$0 = \left(\mu + \tfrac{1}{2}\sigma^2 \lambda\right) \int_b^B e^{\lambda \zeta} \pi_0\,(\zeta)\, d\zeta + \alpha_0 e^{\lambda b} - \beta_0 e^{\lambda B}. \tag{10.19}$$

Suppose $\mu \neq 0$. For $\lambda = -\delta = -2\mu/\sigma^2$ the first term in (10.19) is zero, so

$$\alpha_0 e^{-\delta b} - \beta_0 e^{-\delta B} = 0.$$

Combine this fact and (10.18) to obtain the expressions for α_0 and β_0 in (10.16). Then use these expressions in (10.19) to find that

$$\int_b^B e^{\lambda \zeta} \pi_0 \left(\zeta \right) d\zeta = \frac{\delta}{\lambda + \delta} \frac{e^{(\lambda + \delta) B} - e^{(\lambda + \delta) b}}{e^{\delta B} - e^{\delta b}}, \quad \text{all } \lambda \neq -\delta,$$

so π_0 is as claimed.

If $\mu = 0$, (10.18) implies $\alpha_0 = \beta_0$, and for $f(z) = z^2/2$, (10.15) implies

$$\tfrac{1}{2} \sigma^2 = \alpha_0 \left(B - b \right),$$

so α_0 and β_0 are as in (10.17). Then substitute these expressions into (10.19) to obtain

$$\int_b^B e^{\lambda \zeta} \pi_0(\zeta) d\zeta = \frac{1}{\lambda} \frac{e^{\lambda B} - e^{\lambda b}}{B - b}, \quad \text{all } \lambda \neq 0,$$

so π_0 is as claimed. ∎

Figure 10.3 shows α_0, β_0, and π_0, for fixed σ, b, and B. Panel **a** shows α_0 and β_0, plotted as functions of the drift parameter μ, for positive values of that parameter. Since $b = -B$, these functions are symmetric around $\mu = 0$. A stronger upward drift raises β_0 and reduces α_0. Panel **b** shows the stationary density $\pi_0(\zeta)$, plotted for $\zeta \in [b, B]$ for three values of the drift parameter, $\mu = 0, 0.125$, and 0.25. A stronger upward drift tilts the density toward higher values.

Notice that if the drift is nonzero, these expressions continue to hold if there is only one threshold, the one in the direction of the drift. Specifically, suppose $\mu < 0$. Then $\delta < 0$, so for any finite b, the limits as $B \to \infty$ are

$$\alpha_0 = -\mu, \quad \beta_0 = 0, \quad \pi_0(\zeta) = -\delta e^{\delta(\zeta - b)}, \quad \zeta \geq b.$$

Similarly, $\mu > 0$ implies $\delta > 0$, so for any finite B, the limits as $b \to -\infty$ are

$$\alpha_0 = 0, \quad \beta_0 = \mu, \quad \pi_0(\zeta) = \delta e^{\delta(\zeta - B)}, \quad \zeta \leq B.$$

Exercise 10.2. Suppose that a large number of warehouses carry inventories of a certain product. Each warehouse has a net inflow (supply minus demand) that is a Brownian motion with mean μ and variance $\sigma^2 > 0$. Each warehouse has capacity $B > 0$. Stocks cannot be negative, so each warehouse must buy or sell additional units of the product to keep the stock between

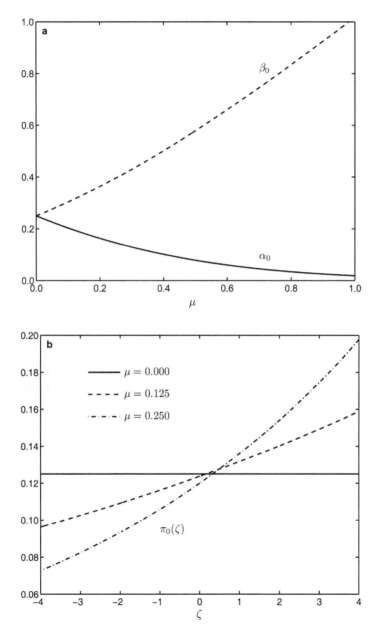

Figure 10.3. For a Brownian motion regulated at $b = -4$ and $B = 4$, (a) the expected control per unit time α_0 and β_0 as functions of the drift μ, and (b) the stationary density $\pi_0(\zeta)$, for various drift parameters. The diffusion parameter is $\sigma = 2$.

$b = 0$ and $B > 0$. Each does this in a continuous way, so the stock at each warehouse is a regulated Brownian motion, regulated at $b = 0$ and $B > 0$.

(a) Describe the stationary distribution of inventories across warehouses.

(b) Describe the stationary level of purchases by warehouses (a flow) to keep stocks from going negative and of sales by warehouses (also a flow) that have reached capacity.

10.4. An Inventory Example

The inventory model in Harrison and Taskar (1983) illustrates how these results can be used. Consider a manager who controls an inventory and wants to minimize the expected discounted value of holding costs plus adjustment costs. The holding cost $h(z)$ is a flow that depends on the size of the stock. Assume h is continuously differentiable and (weakly) convex, with a minimum at some finite value z_m.

In addition, there are proportional costs of adjusting the stock in either direction. Specifically, the cost of upward control is P and the cost of downward control is p, with

$$P > 0 \quad \text{and} \quad P > p.$$

If $p > 0$, then p is interpreted as the unit revenue when the manager sells excess inventory. If $p \leq 0$, then $-p$ is the unit cost of disposing of excess inventory. Although p may take either sign, $p < P$ is required to make the problem interesting. If $p > P$, infinite profits can be earned by buying inventory at the price P and selling it p. If $p = P$, then since there are no fixed costs, total costs are minimized by the (trivial) policy of keeping the stock constant at the level z_m that minimizes holding costs.

Finally, assume that there exist values $z_1 < z_m < z_2$ such that

$$h'(z_1) + rP < 0 \quad \text{and} \quad h'(z_2) - rp > 0,$$

where $r > 0$ is the interest rate. This assumption insures that it is useful to exercise control when the stock is sufficiently high or low. The first inequality implies that a small increase in the stock reduces holding costs net of the annuitized purchase price if z is below z_1. The second implies that a small reduction in the stock reduces holding costs net of the annuitized disposal price if z is above z_2.

In the absence of control the unregulated inventory $X(t)$ is a (μ, σ^2) Brownian motion. Suppose the manager chooses a policy of regulating the inventory at fixed upper and lower thresholds. Then the regulated stock is $Z(t) = X(t) + L(t) - U(t)$, where $L(t)$ and $U(t)$ are the total control exercised at the two thresholds by date t.

For any thresholds b, B, let $F(z, b, B)$ denote the expected discounted value of total costs if the inventory is regulated at those thresholds, given the initial stock $Z(0) = z$. Then

$$F(z, b, B) = E_z \left[\int_0^\infty e^{-rt} \left[h(Z)dt + PdL - pdU \right] \right] \qquad (10.20)$$

$$= \int_b^B \pi(\zeta; z)h(\zeta)d\zeta + \alpha(z)P - \beta(z)p, \quad z \in [b, B],$$

where the functions π, α, and β depend on b and B. If the initial stock z is less than b, a cost of $P(b - z)$ is incurred immediately to bring the stock up to b, and if the initial stock exceeds B a cost of $p(B - z)$ is incurred to bring it down to B. Hence

$$F(z, b, B) = \begin{cases} P(b - z) + F(b, b, B), & \text{if } z < b, \\ p(B - z) + F(B, b, B), & \text{if } z > B. \end{cases} \qquad (10.21)$$

For any b, B, the function F describes the value to the decision maker of adopting that (arbitrary) policy.

The optimal thresholds b^*, B^* minimize total cost, given z. Hence necessary conditions for the optimal policy, given z, are

$$0 = F_b(z, b^*, B^*) \qquad (10.22)$$

$$= \int_{b^*}^{B^*} \pi_b(\zeta; z)h(\zeta)d\zeta - \pi(b^*; z)h(b^*) + \alpha_b(z)P - \beta_b(z)p$$

and

$$0 = F_B(z, b^*, B^*) \qquad (10.23)$$

$$= \int_{b^*}^{B^*} \pi_B(\zeta; z)h(\zeta)d\zeta + \pi(B^*; z)h(B) + \alpha_B(z)P - \beta_B(z)p.$$

Since all of the functions in (10.22) and (10.23) are known, this pair of equations provides one method for characterizing the optimal policy.

The following proposition points out an important fact about these conditions.

Proposition 10.9. If the first-order condition in (10.22) holds for any $z \in [b^*, B^*]$, then it holds for all $z \in [b^*, B^*]$. Similarly, if (10.23) holds for any $z \in [b^*, B^*]$, then it holds for all $z \in [b^*, B^*]$.

Proof. Since $\pi(b^*; z) > 0$, (10.22) can be written as

$$h(b^*) = \int_{b^*}^{B^*} \frac{\pi_b(\zeta; z)}{\pi(b^*; z)} h(\zeta)d\zeta + \frac{\alpha_b(z)}{\pi(b^*; z)}P - \frac{\beta_b(z)}{\pi(b^*; z)}p.$$

By Proposition 10.5, the right side is independent of z, establishing the first claim. A similar argument establishes the second. ∎

This result is not surprising, as it simply confirms that the Principle of Optimality holds. That is, suppose the current inventory is z and the optimal thresholds are b^*, B^*. If the stock evolves to $z' \neq z$ and the optimization problem is solved again, the choice of thresholds should be unchanged: b^* and B^* should still be optimal.

The optimal policy can also be characterized by using the Hamilton-Jacobi-Bellman (HJB) equation. The usual perturbation argument suggests that $F(\cdot, b, B)$ satisfies that equation for $z \in (b, B)$, for any b, B. Proposition 10.10 verifies that fact directly. In addition, it is clear from (10.21) that F is continuous at b and B, for any choice of thresholds. Proposition 10.10 establishes that the same is true for the derivative F_z, but that F_{zz} is continuous at these points only for the optimal thresholds b^*, B^*. The proof involves evaluating the derivatives F_z and F_{zz}. For this step it is crucial to keep in mind the fact that $\pi(\zeta; z)$ has a kink at $\zeta = z$, so π_z has a jump. Thus, for any b, B, differentiating (10.20) twice gives

$$F_z(z, b, B) = \int_b^z \pi_z(\zeta; z)h(\zeta)d\zeta + \int_z^B \pi_z(\zeta; z)h(\zeta)d\zeta$$
$$+ \alpha_z(z)P - \beta_z(z)p, \tag{10.24}$$

$$F_{zz}(z, b, B) = \int_b^B \pi_{zz}(\zeta; z)h(\zeta)d\zeta - \frac{R_2 - R_1}{J}h(z)$$
$$+ \alpha_{zz}(z)P - \beta_{zz}(z)p, \quad \text{all } z \in (b, B), \tag{10.25}$$

where the second derivative uses the result in (10.14).

Proposition 10.10. For any b, B, the function $F(\cdot, b, B)$ defined in (10.20) and (10.21) satisfies the HJB equation

$$rf(z) = h(z) + \mu f'(z) + \tfrac{1}{2}\sigma^2 f''(z), \tag{10.26}$$

on the open interval (b, B). In addition,

    i. F_z is continuous at b and B, for any b, B;
    ii. F_{zz} is continuous at b if and only if (10.22) holds;
    iii. F_{zz} is continuous at B if and only if (10.23) holds.

Proof. Homogeneous solutions to (10.26) have the form

$$H(z) = a_1 e^{R_1 z} + a_2 e^{R_2 z},$$

where a_1 and a_2 are arbitrary constants, and $R_1 < 0 < R_2$ are the roots of the quadratic $\frac{1}{2} R^2 \sigma^2 + R\mu - r = 0$. Hence $\alpha(z)$ and $\beta(z)$ are homogeneous solutions, as is $\pi(\zeta; z)$, all $\zeta \in (b, B)$. Thus (10.20), (10.24), and (10.25) together imply that for $f = F(\cdot, b, B)$ the only nonhomogeneous terms in (10.26) are $h(z)$ on the right side and the term in F_{zz} (see (10.25)) that involves $h(z)$. Since

$$\frac{\sigma^2}{2} \frac{R_2 - R_1}{J} = 1,$$

these terms cancel, establishing the first claim.

For (i), use (10.11) and (10.12) to find that for any b, B,

$$\alpha_z(b, b, B) = -1, \qquad \beta_z(b, b, B) = 0,$$
$$\alpha_z(B, b, B) = 0, \qquad \beta_z(B, b, B) = 1,$$

and

$$\pi_z(\zeta; b, b, B) = 0, \quad \pi_z(\zeta; B, b, B) = 0, \quad \text{all } \zeta \in (b, B).$$

Evaluate (10.24) and use these facts to find that

$$\lim_{z \downarrow b} F_z(z, b, B) = -P, \quad \lim_{z \uparrow B} F_z(z, b, B) = -p,$$

which agrees with the derivatives of (10.21) at b and B.

For (ii), recall from Exercise 10.1 that if $b > -\infty$,

$$\pi(b; z) = \alpha(z) \frac{1}{J} (R_2 - R_1), \quad \text{all } z.$$

Evaluate (10.25) at $z = b$, and use this fact to find that $F_{zz}(b, b, B) = 0$ if and only if

$$\int_b^B \pi_{zz}(\zeta; b) h(\zeta) d\zeta - \frac{\pi(b; z)}{\alpha(z)} h(b) + \alpha_{zz}(b) P - \beta_{zz}(b) p = 0.$$

By Proposition 10.6, this condition holds if and only if (10.22) holds.

For (iii) use an analogous argument at B. ∎

Proposition 10.10 shows that the optimal thresholds b^*, B^* and the value function $v(\cdot) \equiv F(\cdot, b^*, B^*)$ are characterized by:

i. v satisfies the HJB equation

$$rv(z) = h(z) + \mu v'(z) + \tfrac{1}{2}\sigma^2 v''(z),$$

on (b^*, B^*), and outside that interval

$$v(z) = \begin{cases} P(b^* - z) + v(b^*), & \text{if } z < b^*, \\ p(B^* - z) + v(B^*), & \text{if } z > B^*; \end{cases}$$

ii. the smooth pasting conditions hold,

$$\lim_{z \downarrow b^*} v'(z) = P, \quad \lim_{z \uparrow B^*} v'(z) = p;$$

iii. the super contact conditions hold,

$$\lim_{z \downarrow b^*} v''(z) = 0, \quad \lim_{z \uparrow B^*} v''(z) = 0.$$

Figure 10.4 displays the solution for an example with the exponential holding cost function

$$h(z) = \begin{cases} h_0 e^{\eta z}, & z \ge 0, \\ h_0 e^{\delta z}, & z < 0, \end{cases}$$

and the parameter values

$$\begin{array}{llll} r = 0.05, & \mu = -0.2, & \sigma = 0.5, & h_0 = 1.0, \\ \eta = 0.6, & \delta = -0.4, & P = 1.0, & p = -0.2. \end{array}$$

Thus, holding positive inventory is slightly more expensive than holding backorders, $\eta > |\delta|$; the stock tends to drift downward in the absence of control, $\mu < 0$; and disposing of inventory entails a modest cost, $p < 0$. Panel **a** shows the annualized cost function $h(z)/r$, and panel **b** shows the value function and optimal thresholds b^*, B^*. For this example expected discounted holding costs are infinite if no control is exercised.

Exercises 10.3–10.5 look at several variations on a similar problem with a quadratic holding cost and a lower threshold fixed at $b = 0$.

Exercise 10.3. Consider a manager regulating an inventory. In the absence of control the inventory is a Brownian motion with parameters (μ, σ^2). The inventory is not allowed to be negative, and the holding cost is $h(z) = h_0 z^2$. Additions to the inventory can be purchased for $P > 0$, and excess inventory

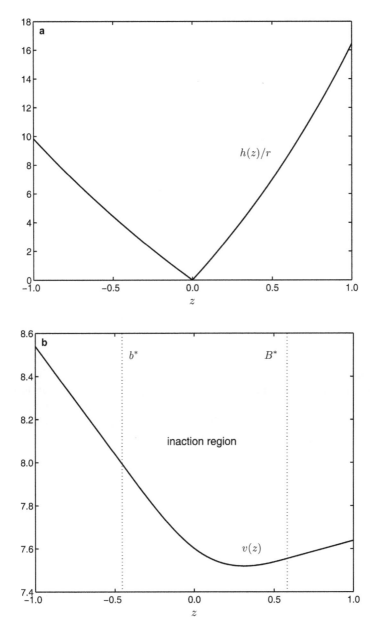

Figure 10.4. *(a) The annualized cost function and (b) value function for the inventory model. The parameter values are* $\mu = -0.2$, $\sigma = 0.5$, $r = 0.05$, $\eta = 0.6$, $\delta = -0.4$, $h_0 = 1$, $P = 1$, *and* $p = -0.2$. *The optimal thresholds are* $b^* = 0.454$ *and* $B^* = 0.58$.

can be sold for p, where $0 < p < P$. The interest rate $r > 0$ is constant over time. The manager's problem is to minimize the expected discounted value of total costs.

(a) Write the HJB equation.

(b) What are particular and homogeneous solutions for this equation?

(c) What are the boundary conditions for the HJB equation, and what is the value function outside the inaction region?

(d) Describe the expected purchases and sales per unit time under the optimal policy.

Exercise 10.4. Suppose that the manager has two inventories of the type in Exercise 10.3, with identical parameters (μ, σ^2) and independent shocks. If the two stocks are merged, the holding cost for the merged inventory Y is $H(Y) = 2h(Y/2)$, and the flows into and out of the merged inventory are the sum of the flows for the individual inventories.

(a) Describe carefully the relationship between the HJB equations for the single and merged inventories. Are the particular and homogeneous solutions the same or different? What about the boundary conditions?

(b) Are expected purchases and sales per unit time for the merged inventory twice what they are for a single inventory? Explain briefly.

Exercise 10.5. Consider a manager who looks after a large number (a continuum) of inventories, each of the type in Exercise 10.3, and all with mutually independent shocks. Assume there is unit mass of these inventories. There is no secondary market, but the manager can transfer goods among the various inventories. Shipping is costly, however. Assume that the cost takes an "iceberg" form: for each unit of goods that leaves one inventory, only $0 < \lambda < 1$ arrives at the destination.

(a) What condition is needed to insure that total inflows into inventories are equal to total outflows net of "iceberg" costs?

(b) Show that if $\lambda < 1$, this condition cannot hold if $\mu \leq 0$. Show that if $\mu > 0$ it can hold, and explain how the manager can make the flows match.

(c) For fixed λ, how does the expected discounted value of holding costs change with μ?

Notes

The treatment of regulated Brownian motion in Sections 10.1–10.3 follows Harrison (1985, Chapters 2 and 5), and the inventory model in Section 10.4 is from Harrison and Taskar (1983). The language here also follows Harrison. As he notes in his introduction, the term *reflected Brownian motion*, while standard among mathematicians, is less descriptive. Dumas (1991), who coined the term *super contact condition*, has a nice discussion of the relationship between impulse and instantaneous control problems.

11

Investment: Linear and Convex Adjustment Costs

A VARIETY OF investment problems can be analyzed using models similar to the inventory model in Section 10.4. Several examples are studied below to illustrate some of the features that can be incorporated and the types of solutions that result. All of the examples have a similar structure for the revenue function, but they make different assumptions about investment costs.

Consider a firm whose revenue flow at any date, net of wages, materials, and other variable costs, depends on its capital stock and a random variable describing demand. Demand is a geometric Brownian motion or a more general diffusion. The firm's problem is to choose the investment policy that maximizes the expected discounted value of net revenue minus investment costs.

If investment is completely reversible, in the sense that the purchase and sale prices for capital are equal, and there are no nonprice adjustment costs, the model produces Jorgensen's (1963) result: at each date the capital stock is adjusted to equate the (ever-changing) marginal revenue product of capital with the (constant) user cost of capital.

But the framework can also accommodate two types of frictions. The first is a wedge between the purchase and sale prices for capital goods, as in the inventory model in Section 10.4. Recall that in that model the optimal policy consisted of two thresholds, b and B. The open interval (b, B) was an inaction region, and outside that interval the optimal policy involved adjusting immediately to the nearest threshold. In particular, a discrete adjustment was required at date $t = 0$ if the initial condition was outside $[b, B]$. After an initial discrete adjustment, if needed, the optimal policy involved regulating the process at each threshold, so the state remained inside the interval.

If the price of capital is the only cost and the purchase and sale prices differ, the optimal policy in the investment model has a similar structure.

The only difference is that the thresholds $b(X)$ and $B(X)$ are functions of demand. But the optimal policy still involves an initial discrete adjustment if the initial capital stock K_0 is outside the interval $\left[b(X_0), B(X_0)\right]$. Thereafter the stock is regulated at the two thresholds, and the open interval between those thresholds is an inaction region where the firm neither invests nor disinvests.

A second friction can also be incorporated, a strictly convex cost of adjustment in addition to the price. This cost can be thought of as representing the time of managers or the disruption to production in the existing plant. Recall that in the framework with lump-sum fixed costs, mathematical tractability required that the variable cost be linear, for the reasons discussed in Section 8.7. Here there are no fixed costs, so those arguments do not apply.

If the purchase and sale prices for capital differ, then there are still threshold functions $b(X)$ and $B(X)$ defining an inaction region, given demand. But with strictly convex adjustment costs discrete investment is not an option. Investment is necessarily a flow, and adjustment is continuous when the capital stock is outside the interval $[b(X), B(X)]$. If the capital stock is less than $b(X)$ the firm invests at a rate that depends on the distance from the threshold: the farther from the threshold, the faster the rate of investment. Similarly, if the capital stock exceeds $B(X)$ the firm disinvests at a rate that depends on the distance from the threshold.

Thus, in the presence of a convex adjustment cost the model delivers the conclusion from Tobin's (1969) q theory, as modified by Hayashi (1982) and Abel (1985): investment is an increasing function of q, the marginal value of installed capital. Specifically, the rate of investment is positive if q is sufficiently high, zero if q is in an intermediate range, and negative if q is sufficiently low. Of course, the state can lie in the region outside $[b(X), B(X)]$ only over some initial period. Once the state enters the interval $[b(X), B(X)]$, investment or disinvestment at the boundaries prevents it from exiting.

The intermediate region shrinks to a single point if the cost of investment varies smoothly with the rate of investment, as happens if the purchase and sale prices for capital are equal and the adjustment cost function is smooth at zero. With no adjustment cost this model is the one in Jorgensen (1963). The third region, the disinvestment region, disappears if the sale price is zero or if the adjustment cost exceeds the sale price of capital. That is, investment is in essence irreversible—disinvestment never occurs—if the adjustment cost for disinvestment is sufficiently large or the sale price for capital sufficiently small.

Since labor is subject to the same types of adjustment costs these models can also be interpreted as descriptions of hiring and firing decisions. Indeed adjustment costs may be even more important for labor than for capital, since labor is a bigger fraction of total costs.

The rest of the chapter is organized as follows. Section 11.1 sets out a model that allows different purchase and sale prices for capital goods, but has no other costs. Section 11.2 adds strictly convex adjustment costs, and Section 11.3 looks at two special cases. The first, which has a profit function that is linear in capital, equal purchase and sale prices for capital, and a quadratic adjustment cost, produces a closed-form solution. This model is the one in Abel and Eberly (1997). The second, which has profit and adjustment cost functions that are homogeneous of degree one, allows the problem to be written in terms of a single state variable, a ratio. In Section 11.4 the homogeneous model is studied more closely under the assumption that there is no adjustment cost and capital has no resale value. Thus, investment is irreversible. In Section 11.5 a second shock is added to that model, a stochastic price for investment goods. The resulting model is the one in Bertola and Caballero (1994). In Section 11.6 a model of a two-sector economy is sketched.

11.1. Investment with Linear Costs

In this section and the next, several versions of a basic investment model are presented. All have the same structure for demand, but the investment costs have different forms. None is analyzed in detail. The only goal is to see how various components of the investment cost affect the qualitative nature of the optimal policy.

Consider a firm choosing a path for gross investment to maximize the expected discounted value of operating profits net of investment costs. Let $K(t)$ denote the firm's capital stock and $X(t)$ denote demand. The revenue function $\Pi(K, X)$ is time invariant and subsumes the cost of labor and other variable inputs. The following assumption will be maintained throughout the chapter.

Assumption 11.1. Π is twice continuously differentiable and strictly increasing, and is weakly concave in its second argument, with $\Pi(0, X) = 0$ and $\Pi_{XK} > 0$.

Thus profits are increasing and strictly concave in the capital stock, and both total and marginal profits increase with demand.

Demand X is a diffusion,

$$dX = \mu(X)dt + \sigma(X)dW, \tag{11.1}$$

where W is a Wiener process. For example, X might be a geometric Brownian motion or an Ornstein-Uhlenbeck process. The interest rate $r > 0$ is

constant, and a joint restriction involving r and the growth rate of demand is
also needed, to insure that for any initial conditions the expected discounted
value of future profits is finite. The exact form of this restriction depends
on Π and the stochastic process X, and specific cases will be discussed as
they arise.

Suppose that new investment goods can be purchased at the price $P > 0$,
and old capital goods can be sold at the price $p \geq 0$. Assume the sale price
is less than the purchase price, $p < P$. The assumption that $p \geq 0$ is without
loss of generality. Since capital always has a positive marginal product, the
firm would never pay to dispose of capital goods. Hence investment behavior
is identical for all $p \leq 0$.

For now suppose that there are no other costs, so the adjustment costs
are linear, as in Chapter 10. There are two state variables here rather than
one, but the arguments developed in Chapter 10 can be adapted.

Let $L(t)$ denote cumulative gross investment up to date t and $U(t)$
denote cumulative gross disinvestment. Then $\{L(t), t > 0\}$ and $\{U(t), t > 0\}$
are nondecreasing stochastic processes of the type discussed in Chapter 10.
Capital depreciates at the constant rate $\delta \geq 0$, so the stochastic process for
the capital stock is

$$dK(t) = dL(t) - dU(t) - \delta K(t)dt. \tag{11.2}$$

The firm's objective is to maximize expected discounted revenue net of
investment costs. Hence its problem is

$$V(K_0, X_0) = \max_{\{L(t),U(t) \ t \geq 0\}} E_0 \left[\int_0^\infty e^{-rt} \{\Pi[K(t), X(t)]dt \tag{11.3} \right.$$

$$\left. - PdL(t) + pdU(t)\} \right],$$

where the maximization is over nondecreasing functions.

Since the return function Π is increasing and concave in K, for each
X, and is increasing in X, a direct argument can be used to show that
the optimal investment policy has the following form. It is defined by two
continuous increasing functions $b(X)$ and $B(X)$, with $b \leq B$. Given any
value X for demand, if the capital stock is below the lower threshold—
if $K < b(X)$—the firm immediately purchases enough capital to bring the
stock up to $b(X)$. If the stock exceeds the upper threshold—if $K > B(X)$—
the firm immediately sells off enough capital to bring the stock down to
$B(X)$. If the capital stock lies inside the interval $(b(X), B(X))$ the firm
neither invests nor disinvests. Hence the set

$$S \equiv \{(K, X) : b(X) < K < B(X)\} \tag{11.4}$$

is an inaction region. After an initial discrete adjustment, if necessary, the firm invests when the state reaches the lower boundary $b(X)$ and disinvests when it reaches the upper boundary $B(X)$. In both cases just enough control is exercised so that the state does not leave the set $\overline{S}$, the closure of S.

The goal is to characterize the optimal thresholds b and B, and the associated value function V. The arguments from Chapter 10 can be applied.

Fix any continuous thresholds b and B, define the set S as in (11.4), and let V be the associated value function. When the state is in S there is no investment or disinvestment, so the usual argument can be used to approximate the right side of (11.3) as the return over a small interval Δt plus the expected discounted continuation value. For the continuation value use a second-order Taylor series approximation to

$$\frac{1}{1+r\Delta t}\mathrm{E}\left[V(K_0+\Delta K, X_0+\Delta X)\right],$$

using (11.1) and (11.2) to approximate ΔX and ΔK, and employing Ito's lemma (Theorem 3.3) after the expectation is taken. The terms V_{KX} and V_{KK} in the approximation have higher order than Δt and can be dropped, so the resulting Hamilton-Jacobi-Bellman (HJB) equation is

$$rV(K, X) = \Pi(K, X) - \delta K V_K + \mu V_X + \tfrac{1}{2}\sigma^2 V_{XX}. \qquad (11.5)$$

Outside the set $\overline{S}$ the firm adjusts immediately to the boundary of S, so the value function in this region is

$$V(K, X) = \begin{cases} V[b(X), X] - P[b(X) - K], & K < b(X), \\ V[B(X), X] + p[K - B(X)], & K > B(X). \end{cases}$$

Hence V satisfies value matching along both thresholds.

Finally, the argument in Proposition 10.10 implies that for arbitrary thresholds the smooth pasting conditions also hold,

$$\lim_{K\uparrow b(X)} V_K(K, X) = P,$$
$$\lim_{K\downarrow B(X)} V_K(K, X) = p, \qquad (11.6)$$

and that for the optimal thresholds b^*, B^* the super contact conditions hold as well,

$$\lim_{K\uparrow b^*(X)} V_{KK}(K, X) = 0,$$
$$\lim_{K\downarrow B^*(X)} V_{KK}(K, X) = 0. \qquad (11.7)$$

Thus the solution can be found by solving the HJB equation in (11.5) and then using (11.6) and (11.7) to determine certain constants and the optimal thresholds.

It follows from (11.6) that the set S can also be written as

$$S = \{(K, X) \mid V_K(K, X) \in (p, P)\}. \tag{11.8}$$

Thus, investment is zero if the marginal value of capital V_K lies inside the open interval (p, P). In this case the marginal value of capital is too low to justify further investment but too high to justify disinvestment.

The functions $b^*(X)$ and $B^*(X)$ divide K-X space into three regions. Figure 11.1 displays an example in which V is homogeneous of degree one, so b^* and B^* are rays, and the inaction set S is a cone. In the region above S the marginal value of capital is less than p, and the firm disinvests. In the region below S the marginal value of capital exceeds P and the firm invests.

Figure 11.1 is useful for thinking about what happens as the sale price p changes. As p increases disinvesting becomes more attractive. The upper threshold B^* rotates clockwise, expanding the disinvestment region and shrinking the inaction region. The prospect of disinvesting on better terms

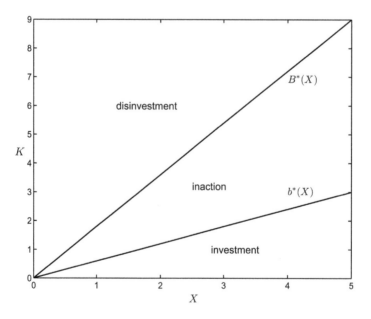

Figure 11.1. *The inaction region for the investment model when $V(X, K)$ is homogeneous of degree one.*

also makes investment more attractive, so b^* rotates counterclockwise, expanding the investment region and further shrinking the inaction region. The upper threshold converges to the lower one as $p \uparrow P$. If investment is costlessly reversible—if $p = P$—the two thresholds coincide and the inaction region is a ray. This case is examined in detail below.

As p falls all these effects are reversed: the upper boundary B^* rotates counterclockwise, the lower boundary b^* rotates clockwise, and the inaction region expands on both sides. As $p \downarrow 0$ the upper boundary converges to the vertical axis, and the disinvestment region vanishes for $p = 0$. This case is examined in detail in Sections 11.4 and 11.5.

Recall the classic version of this problem with equal sale and purchase prices for capital, $p = P$. The optimal policy involves equating the marginal product of capital Π_K with its user cost $(r + \delta)P$. To relate this condition with those in (11.6) and (11.7), note that for any paths $\{L(t)\}$ and $\{U(t)\}$ for investment and disinvestment, (11.2) implies

$$P\,[dL(t) - dU(t)] = P\,[\delta K\,dt + dK(t)].$$

Substitute this expression into (11.3) to write the firm's problem in terms of $\{K(t)\}$ only,

$$V(K_0, X_0)$$

$$= \max_{\{K(t)\}} \mathrm{E}_0 \left[\int_0^\infty e^{-rt} \{\Pi[K(t), X(t)] - \delta P K(t)\}\,dt - P \int_0^\infty e^{-rt}dK(t) \right]$$

$$= \mathrm{E}_0 \left[\int_0^\infty e^{-rt} \max_{\{K(t)\}} \{\Pi[K(t), X(t)] - (r + \delta)\,PK(t)\}\,dt \right] + PK_0,$$

where the last line uses an integration by parts. The first-order condition for the restated problem is

$$\Pi_K[K(t), X(t)] = (r + \delta)\,P, \quad \text{all } t,$$

equating the marginal product of capital with its user cost, as in Jorgensen (1963).

Notice that the value function in this case has the form $V(K_0, X_0) = v(X_0) + PK_0$. The term $v(X_0)$, which depends only on current market conditions, represents the value of a start-up firm—one that has no initial capital—while the term PK_0 is the market value of the initial capital stock of an incumbent firm.

11.2. Investment with Convex Adjustment Costs

Suppose that in addition to the price of capital, investing or disinvesting entails a strictly convex adjustment cost. This cost can be thought of as representing the time of managers or the disruption to current production. Let $\gamma(I, K) \geq 0$ denote the adjustment cost, which may depend on the capital stock as well as on the investment flow I. The total cost of investing at the rate I is then

$$C(I, K) = \begin{cases} \gamma(I, K) + PI, & \text{if } I > 0, \\ 0, & \text{if } I = 0, \\ \gamma(I, K) + pI, & \text{if } I < 0. \end{cases}$$

The following restrictions on γ are used.

Assumption 11.2.   i. For any $K > 0$, $\gamma(\cdot, K)$ is continuously differentiable and strictly convex, with a minimum at $\gamma(0, K) = 0$, and with

$$\lim_{I \to -\infty} \gamma_I(I, K) + p < 0; \tag{11.9}$$

 ii. for any I, $\gamma(I, \cdot) \geq 0$ is continuous, weakly decreasing, and weakly convex in K.

Thus, for any K, the function $\gamma(\cdot, K)$ is U-shaped, with a minimum at $\gamma(0, K) = 0$. The assumption that γ is differentiable at $I = 0$ is without loss of generality. If γ has a kink at that point, p and P can be redefined to absorb the kink, and the adjustment cost function redefined so that it is smooth. Two functional forms for γ that satisfy Assumption 11.2 are $\gamma(I, K) = g(I)$ and $\gamma(I, K) = Kg(I/K)$, where $g(\cdot)$ is U-shaped, smooth, and strictly convex, with a minimum at $g(0) = 0$.

With convex adjustment costs, there cannot be impulses of investment. Investment must be a flow, so the law of motion for the capital stock is

$$dK(t) = [I(t) - \delta K(t)] dt, \tag{11.10}$$

where $I(t)$ can take either sign. The firm's objective is to choose a stochastic process $\{I(t)\}$, given the initial conditions (K_0, X_0). Hence its problem is

$$V(K_0, X_0) = \max_{\{I(t),\ t \geq 0\}} \mathrm{E}_0 \left[\int_0^\infty e^{-rt} \{ \Pi[K(t), X(t)] \tag{11.11} \right.$$
$$\left. - C[I(t), K(t)] \} dt \right],$$

where the law of motion for X is as before, in (11.1).

The right side of (11.11) can be approximated, as before, over a small interval Δt, using (11.10) for dK. The new feature here is that the cost of investment, a flow, is part of the current return. Hence the HJB equation for (11.11) is

$$rV(K, X) = \Pi(K, X) - \delta K V_K + \mu V_X + \tfrac{1}{2}\sigma^2 V_{XX} \qquad (11.12)$$

$$+ \max_I \left[I V_K - C(I, K) \right],$$

and it holds everywhere, not just inside the inaction region.

The optimal investment policy, call it $I^*(K, X)$, solves the maximization problem in the final term in (11.12). Thus qualitative properties of the optimal policy can be determined without detailed information about V. Indeed, the only properties of V needed in what follows are that the marginal value of capital V_K is positive, strictly decreasing in K, and strictly increasing in X. That is, $V_K > 0$, $V_{KK} < 0$, and $V_{KX} > 0$. Assume that V has these properties, inherited from Π, and note that strict concavity in K is a strengthening of Assumption 11.1.

To simplify the notation, fix K and suppress it as an argument of C, and consider the maximization problem from (11.12),

$$\max_I \left[I V_K - C(I) \right]. \qquad (11.13)$$

The function C is continuous and convex, and it is smooth except possibly at the origin. Optimization requires equating the marginal value of capital with the marginal cost of investment, if possible, choosing I so that $V_K = C'(I)$. Several facts about the optimal policy follow immediately.

Since $V_K > 0$, the optimal policy involves investing only at rates for which the marginal cost C' is positive. Any positive rate of investment satisfies this requirement, but (11.9) implies that $C'(I) < 0$ for $I < 0$ and $|I|$ sufficiently large. Hence only a finite range of negative investment rates satisfy the requirement. In particular, there are two possibilities.

If $p = 0$, then C has its minimum at $I = 0$. In this case disinvesting is always costly: there is no revenue from the sale of capital goods and the adjustment cost is positive. Hence disinvestment never occurs. The viable range for investment is $I \in [0, +\infty)$, and the corresponding range for marginal cost is $[P, +\infty)$. The solution to (11.13) is then

$$I^* = 0 \qquad\qquad \text{if } V_K \leq P,$$

$$I^* > 0 \text{ satisfying } V_K = C'(I^*), \quad \text{if } V_K > P.$$

Alternatively, if $p > 0$, then C has its minimum at the point $\underline{I} < 0$ defined by

$$C'(\underline{I}) = \gamma'(\underline{I}) + p = 0.$$

At this point the marginal adjustment cost $|\gamma'(\underline{I})|$ exactly offsets the revenue p from the sale of additional capital. At any rate of disinvestment faster than $\underline{I}$ both the net revenue from disinvesting and the remaining capital stock could be strictly increased by disinvesting at a slower pace. Hence disinvestment rates below $\underline{I}$ are never chosen. The viable range for investment is $(\underline{I}, \infty)$, and the corresponding range for marginal cost is $(0, \infty)$.

Marginal cost does not necessarily take values on the entire range $(0, \infty)$, however. In particular, if $p < P$, then marginal cost C' jumps at $I = 0$. The resulting gap creates an inaction region, as before. Thus, if $0 < p \leq P$ the solution to (11.13) is

$$I^* \in \left(\underline{I}, 0\right) \text{ satisfying } V_K = C'(I^*), \quad \text{if } 0 < V_K < p,$$

$$I^* = 0, \qquad\qquad\qquad\qquad\qquad\qquad \text{if } p \leq V_K \leq P,$$

$$I^* > 0 \text{ satisfying } V_K = C'(I^*), \qquad \text{if } V_K > P.$$

Since C is strictly convex, the optimal investment rate $I^*(K, X)$ is unique. The interval $\left[p, P\right]$ is an inaction region where investment is zero, and outside this interval the rate of investment is strictly increasing in V_K. If $p = P$ the inaction region is a single point.

The inaction region S is still defined as in (11.8), and the presence of a convex adjustment cost does not change its qualitative shape. Thus X-K space can still be divided into three regions, as in Figure 11.1.

What the adjustment cost does change is the behavior of investment outside the inaction region. In the absence of adjustment costs, impulses of investment are used to adjust the capital stock if $V_K \notin [p, P]$. In the presence of adjustment costs, investment is a continuous flow, with the rate of investment or disinvestment depending on how far V_K is from P or p. Thus the model with adjustment costs delivers the type of behavior described in modern q theory: investment is an increasing function of the marginal value of installed capital.

Figure 11.2 displays an example with different purchase and sale prices for investment goods, $1 = p < P = 4$, and a quadratic adjustment cost, $\gamma(I) = I^2/2$. Panel **a** shows the cost function C, which is continuous and convex with a minimum at $\underline{I} = -1$ and a kink at $I = 0$. Panel **b** shows marginal cost C', which increases from 0 to ∞ as I increases from $\underline{I}$ to ∞ and is continuous except at $I = 0$. At $I = 0$ it jumps from p to P, creating the inaction region for V_K. The regions for disinvestment and investment are indicated.

Figure 11.2 is also useful for thinking about what happens as p changes. As p increases, the portion of the cost function C below $I = 0$ shifts downward, and the point $\underline{I}$ where the minimum is attained moves to the left. The

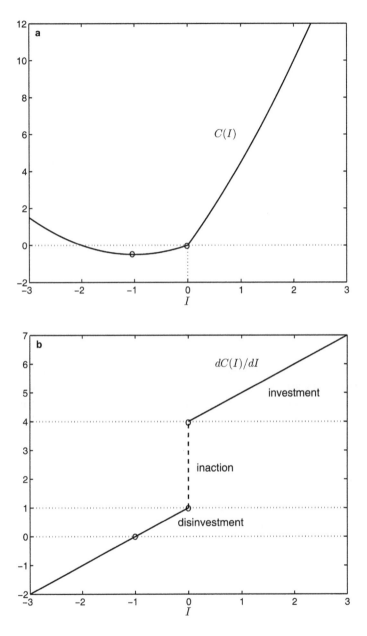

Figure 11.2. *(a) The total adjustment cost and (b) marginal adjustment cost for the investment model. The sale and purchase prices are $p = 1$ and $P = 4$, and the adjustment cost is $\gamma(I) = I^2/2$.*

portion of the marginal cost function C' below $I = 0$ shifts upward. The kink in C and the jump in C' shrink, with both vanishing when $p = P$.

As p falls, all those effects are reversed. The point $\underline{I}$ where the minimum is attained moves to the right, toward $I = 0$, and the range where $C' > 0$ shrinks, vanishing when $p = 0$.

Note that marginal cost is linear in the example only because the adjustment cost is quadratic. In general, marginal cost C' can be any function that is strictly increasing and is continuous except possibly at $I = 0$.

This model can be used to address a variety of specific questions. As an example, the next exercise asks whether increased uncertainty raises or lowers investment.

Exercise 11.1. (a) Let $\Pi(K, X) = XK^\beta$, where $0 < \beta < 1$, and $\ln(X) = Z$, where Z is an Ornstein-Uhlenbeck process with parameter $\alpha > 0$. Assume there are no adjustment costs and the purchase and sale prices for capital are equal, so $C(I, K) = IP$, all I. Show that an increase in α increases the average level of the capital stock.

(b) How does the answer in part (a) change if there are quadratic adjustment costs, $\gamma(I, K) = \gamma_0 I^2$?

11.3. Some Special Cases

The model developed in the previous sections can be specialized in various ways. Two cases are sketched below. The first imposes linearity to obtain a value function that is additively separable. Further specializing, by imposing quadratic adjustment costs and equal purchase and sale prices for capital, then leads to an exact solution. The second case imposes homogeneity to reduce the dimensionality of the problem. This model is further specialized in Section 11.4—eliminating the adjustment cost, setting $p = 0$, and using an isoelastic return function—to obtain another exact solution.

Suppose the return per unit of capital is independent of the firm's size, so the profit function is linear in capital. This assumption is sensible as a model of a small firm that takes prices for its inputs and outputs to be exogenous stochastic processes and always operates at full capacity.

Specifically, let

$$\Pi(K, X) = XK.$$

Notice that assuming the return per unit of capital is simply X is without loss of generality. If instead it were $\pi(X) = X$, one could define a new stochastic process $\hat{X} \equiv \pi(X)$ so the return function would be $\hat{X}K$. As the next exercise shows, linearity of the profit function in capital implies the value function is also linear in capital.

Exercise 11.2. Let $\hat{K}(t) = K(t) - K_0 e^{-\delta t}$ be the difference between the firm's total capital stock at date t and the depreciated capital held from date 0.

(a) Show that

$$d\hat{K}(t) = \left[I(t) - \delta \hat{K}(t) \right] dt,$$

with $\hat{K}_0 = 0$.

(b) Use $\hat{K}$ to show that the value function has the form

$$V(K, X) = w(X)K + V(0, X).$$

(c) Obtain an explicit expression for the function w. What is its interpretation?

(d) Show that if X is a geometric Brownian motion with parameters (μ, σ^2), then $w(X) = \eta X$, where $\eta \equiv 1/(r + \delta - \mu)$.

A closed-form solution can be obtained if this model is further specialized. Assume the price of investment goods, $P > 0$, is the same for purchases and sales, and let the adjustment cost be quadratic, so the cost of investment is

$$C(I) = PI + \tfrac{1}{2} \gamma I^2, \quad \text{all } I,$$

where $\gamma > 0$. As shown in Exercise 11.2 the value function has the form

$$V(K, X) = \eta X K + G(X), \tag{11.14}$$

and under the assumptions here the HJB equation (11.12) specializes to

$$rV = XK - \delta K V_K + \mu X V_X + \tfrac{1}{2} \sigma^2 X^2 V_{XX}$$
$$+ \max_I \left[V_K I - PI - \tfrac{1}{2} \gamma I^2 \right]. \tag{11.15}$$

Exercise 11.3. (a) What is the optimal investment rate I^* in terms of K and X? Explain why it has the form it does. When is $I^* = 0$?

(b) Use (11.14) to write V_K, V_X, and V_{XX} in terms of G and its derivatives, and substitute the resulting expressions in (11.15) to get

$$\frac{1}{2} \sigma^2 X^2 G'' + \mu X G' - rG + \frac{1}{2\gamma} (\eta X - P)^2 = 0, \quad \text{all } X.$$

Solutions of this ODE have the form

$$G(X) = G_p(X) + c_1 X^{R_1} + c_2 X^{R_2},$$

where G_p is a particular solution, $R_1 < 0 < R_2$ are roots of the quadratic $r - \mu R - \frac{1}{2}\sigma^2 R(R-1) = 0$, and c_1, c_2 are constants.

(c) Show that there is a particular solution that is a quadratic,

$$G_p(X) = g_0 + g_1 X + \tfrac{1}{2}g_2 X^2.$$

Solve for the coefficients in terms of the parameters $P, \gamma, r, \mu, \sigma^2, \eta$. What parameter restriction is needed to insure $g_1 > 0$? When is $g_2 > 0$ and when < 0? What is the reasoning?

(d) Use the limiting behavior of G as $X \to 0$ and as $X \to \infty$ to show that $c_1 = c_2 = 0$.

At some point disinvestment is limited by the fact that the firm's capital stock cannot be negative, but obtaining the closed-form solution requires ignoring the nonnegativity constraint on capital. If demand is growing, $\mu > 0$, and initial demand X_0 exceeds the critical value at which investment is zero, then the nonnegativity constraint will seldom be violated. The value and policy functions here can be interpreted as describing such a firm.

Another useful special case exploits homogeneity. Suppose the profit and adjustment cost functions are homogeneous of degree one,

$$\Pi(K, X) = X\pi(K/X),$$

$$\gamma(I, K) = Kg(I/K);$$

and the demand shock X is a geometric Brownian motion,

$$\frac{dX}{X} = \mu dt + \sigma dW.$$

In addition, define the piecewise linear function

$$\rho(I) = \begin{cases} PI, & I \geq 0, \\ pI, & I < 0. \end{cases}$$

The firm's problem can then be written as

$$V(K_0, X_0) = \max_{\{I(t)\}} \mathrm{E}_0\left[\int_0^\infty e^{-rt}\{X\pi(K/X) \right. \tag{11.16}$$

$$\left. - K\left[\rho(I/K) + g(I/K)\right]\}dt\right]$$

$$\frac{dK}{K} = \left(\frac{I}{K} - \delta\right)dt,$$

$$\frac{dX}{X} = \mu dt + \sigma dW,$$

and the associated HJB equation is

$$rV = X\pi(K/X) - \delta K V_K + \mu X V_X + \tfrac{1}{2}\sigma^2 X^2 V_{XX}$$
$$+ \max_I \left\{ V_K I - K \left[\rho(I/K) + g\,(I/K) \right] \right\}, \tag{11.17}$$

where V and its derivatives are evaluated at $(K/X, 1)$. This second-order PDE can be written as an ODE by exploiting homogeneity.

The return function and constraints in (11.16) are homogeneous of degree one in (K, X, I). Hence V is homogeneous of degree one in (K, X), and the optimal policy is homogeneous in the sense that if the stochastic process I^* is optimal for the initial conditions (K_0, X_0), then for any $\lambda > 0$ the process λI^* is optimal for the initial conditions $(\lambda K_0, \lambda X_0)$.

Define the ratios $k \equiv K/X$ and $i \equiv I/K$, and the intensive form of the value function $v(k) \equiv V(k, 1)$, $k \geq 0$. Then

$$V(K, X) = Xv(K/X), \quad \text{all } K, X,$$

so

$$V_K = v', \qquad V_X = v - kv', \qquad V_{XX} = k^2 \frac{1}{X} v''.$$

Substituting for V and its derivatives in (11.17) gives the HJB equation in the intensive form,

$$(r - \mu)\,v = \pi(k) - (\delta + \mu)\,kv' + \tfrac{1}{2}\sigma^2 k^2 v'' + k \max_{i \geq 0} \left[v'i - \rho(i) - g(i) \right].$$

The coefficient on v in the normalized HJB equation is $(r - \mu)$. Assume that $r > \mu$, so that this coefficient is positive. Note that for this homogeneous model the inaction region in K-X space is a cone, as shown in Figure 11.1.

The homogeneous model can be further specialized in various ways. The next section looks at a special case with an isoelastic profit function, $\pi(k) = \pi_0 k^\alpha$; no adjustment costs, $g = 0$; and a zero sale price for capital, $p = 0$.

11.4. Irreversible Investment

This section examines the case in which investment is irreversible in the sense that $p = 0$. Capital has no resale value, so it is never worthwhile to disinvest. The data analyzed in Ramey and Shapiro (2001) suggest that this assumption is realistic, at least for some industries.

In addition assume that there are no adjustment costs, $\gamma(I, K) = 0$, so the only cost of investment is the purchase price of the new capital goods, $P > 0$.

The homogeneity argument in Section 11.3 requires X to be a geometric Brownian motion and requires the profit function Π to be homogeneous of degree one. Assume in addition that the profit function has the form $\pi(K, X) = K^\alpha X^{1-\alpha}$, where $0 < \alpha < 1$.

Since there are no adjustment costs, this model is a specialization of the one in Section 11.1, and since $p = 0$ the firm never disinvests. Hence its problem is to choose a nondecreasing stochastic processes $\{L(t), \ t \geq 0\}$ describing cumulative gross investment. That is, given an initial condition (K_0, X_0) the firm's problem is

$$V(K_0, X_0) \equiv \max_{\{L(t)\}} \mathrm{E}_0 \left\{ \int_0^\infty e^{-rt} \left[K^\alpha(t) X^{1-\alpha}(t) dt - P dL(t) \right] \right\} \quad (11.18)$$

$$dK = dL - \delta K dt,$$

$$dX = \mu X dt + \sigma X dW.$$

As shown in Section 11.1, the optimal policy is defined by a threshold function $b(X)$. If $K < b(X)$ the firm makes a discrete investment of size $b(X) - K$, so below the threshold the value function is

$$V(K, X) = V[b(X), X] + P[b(X) - K], \quad K < b(X).$$

Thereafter investment is just sufficient to keep K from falling below $b(X)$. Hence there may be a discrete investment at $t = 0$ if the initial capital stock K_0 is low relative to initial demand X_0. In this case $L(0) > 0$ represents an initial investment that raises the capital stock immediately to $b(X_0)$. Discrete investments are not required at later dates, however.

The region above $b(X)$ in X-K space is the inaction region. In this region the value function satisfies the HJB equation associated with (11.18),

$$rV = K^\alpha X^{1-\alpha} - \delta K V_K + \mu X V_X + \tfrac{1}{2}\sigma^2 X^2 V_{XX}, \quad K > b(X).$$

The argument in Section 11.3 can be applied to replace this PDE with an ODE.

Note that the optimal threshold has the form $b(X) = b^* X$, where the constant b^* must be determined. Define the ratio $k(t) \equiv K(t)/X(t)$ and the function $v(k) \equiv V(k, 1)$, and write the HJB equation in the intensive form,

$$(r - \mu) v = k^\alpha - (\delta + \mu) k v' + \tfrac{1}{2}\sigma^2 k^2 v'', \quad k > b^*. \quad (11.19)$$

Assume that $r > \mu$, so the coefficient on v is positive. The interest rate must exceed the drift in demand to insure that the firm has finite value. In the region where the firm makes discrete investments

$$v(k) = v(b^*) + P\left(b^* - k\right), \quad k < b^*.$$

Clearly value matching holds at $k = b^*$.

All solutions to (11.19) have the form

$$v(k) = v_P(k) + a_1 h_1(k) + a_2 h_2(k), \quad k > b^*,$$

where v_P is any particular solution, and $h_i(k)$, $i = 1, 2$, are homogeneous solutions. The following exercise finds an explicit solution.

Exercise 11.4.   (a) Show that a particular solution is

$$v_P(k) = \frac{1}{\eta} k^\alpha,$$

where

$$\eta \equiv (r - \mu) + \alpha \, (\delta + \mu) - \alpha \, (\alpha - 1) \tfrac{1}{2}\sigma^2,$$

and $r > \mu$ implies $\eta > 0$.

(b) Show that $v_P(k_0)$ is the value of a firm with initial conditions $K_0 = k_0$ and $X_0 = 1$ that never invests.

(c) Show that the homogeneous solutions are $h_i(k) = k^{R_i}$, $i = 1, 2$, where R_1, R_2 are the roots of the quadratic

$$0 = (r - \mu) + (\delta + \mu) \, R - \tfrac{1}{2}\sigma^2 R \, (R - 1).$$

Show that the assumption $r > \mu$ insures the roots are real and of opposite sign. Label them $R_1 < 0 < R_2$.

Therefore, all solutions to (11.19) can be written as

$$v(k) = \frac{1}{\eta} k^\alpha + a_1 k^{R_1} + a_2 k^{R_2}, \quad k > b^*,$$

where the constants a_1 and a_2 must be determined.

Since there is no upper threshold,

$$\lim_{k \to \infty} \left(v(k) - \frac{1}{\eta} k^\alpha \right) = 0,$$

reflecting the fact that as $k \to \infty$, the time until investment is positive becomes arbitrarily long, with probability arbitrarily close to one. Since $R_1 < 0 < R_2$, this condition holds if and only if $a_2 = 0$. Let R (without a subscript) denote the negative root, so the value function has the form

$$v(k) = \begin{cases} k^\alpha/\eta + a_1 k^R, & k \geq b^*, \\ v(b^*) - P \left(b^* - k \right), & 0 \leq k < b^*. \end{cases}$$

It remains to determine a_1 and b^*.

Exercise 11.5. (a) Use the smooth pasting condition, $\lim_{k \downarrow b*} v'(k) = P$, to find that

$$a_1 = \frac{1}{R} \left[P \left(b^* \right)^{1-R} - \frac{\alpha}{\eta} \left(b^* \right)^{\alpha - R} \right].$$

(b) Use the super contact condition, $\lim_{k \downarrow b*} v''(k) = 0$, to find that

$$b^* = (AP)^{1/(\alpha-1)}, \tag{11.20}$$

where

$$A \equiv \frac{\eta}{\alpha} \frac{1-R}{\alpha - R}. \tag{11.21}$$

The effect of changes in the parameters μ, σ^2, and others on investment can be determined by looking at their effect on A and hence on b^*. Consider the effect of increasing the variability of demand. Note from (11.20) that an increase in the variance σ^2 lowers the threshold b^* if and only if it increases A. Recall that

$$\eta = r + \alpha \delta - (1 - \alpha) \mu + \alpha (1 - \alpha) \tfrac{1}{2} \sigma^2,$$

and define

$$R \equiv \frac{1}{\sigma^2} (m - D).$$

$$D \equiv \left[m^2 + 2\sigma^2 (r - \mu) \right]^{1/2},$$

$$m \equiv \delta + \mu + \tfrac{1}{2} \sigma^2,$$

Write A, η, m, D, and R as functions of σ^2 and use (11.21) to find that

$$\frac{A'}{A} = \frac{\eta'}{\eta} + \frac{(1 - \alpha) R'}{(1 - R) (\alpha - R)}.$$

Clearly $\eta' > 0$, so the first term is positive. The second is also positive if $R' > 0$.

Exercise 11.6. Show that

$$R' = \frac{(D - m)}{2D\sigma^2} \left(\frac{D - m}{\sigma^2} + 1 \right) > 0.$$

Thus, when investment is irreversible a higher variance σ^2 leads to a lower investment threshold b^*. That is, the optimal policy allows the ratio of the capital stock to demand to fall farther before triggering positive investment. In the irreversible case greater uncertainty reduces investment.

In the perfectly flexible environment, one with $p = P$, increasing the variability of demand has no effect. To see this, recall from Section 11.1 that with perfect flexibility the optimal policy requires at all times equating the marginal product of capital with its user cost. For a homogenous return function this requires a constant ratio $k = K/X$ of capital to demand. Call the optimal ratio for the flexible environment k^f. For the profit function here, k^f satisfies

$$\pi'(k^f) = \alpha \left(k^f\right)^{\alpha-1} = (r + \delta)\, P.$$

Note that k^f does not involve σ^2. Thus, in the flexible case greater uncertainty has no effect on the choice of k^f.

Finally, notice that the threshold for the perfectly flexible environment is the same as the one for the irreversible environment with $\sigma^2 = 0$. To see this, note that as $\sigma^2 \to 0$,

$$R \to -\frac{r - \mu}{\delta + \mu}, \qquad A \to \frac{r + \delta}{\alpha},$$

so $b^* \to k^f$. Thus, in the irreversible case $b^* = k^f$ when $\sigma^2 = 0$. Hence in the absence of demand shocks irreversibility has no effect on the threshold. Consequently irreversibility has an effect on the realized path for investment if and only if the initial ratio is too high, $K_0/X_0 > k^f$. For an initial condition of this type the firm sells capital at date 0 if $p = P$. If $p = 0$ the firm simply waits for depreciation and growth in demand to raise the marginal product of capital. Thereafter its investment is identical to what it would be in the reversible case.

Thus, if $\sigma^2 = 0$ investment in the two cases is identical after an initial period whose length depends on K_0. Increasing the variance reduces investment in the irreversible environment and leaves it unchanged in the flexible environment. Hence for a fixed variance $\sigma^2 > 0$, the investment threshold is lower in the irreversible environment. In this sense irreversibility reduces the incentives to invest.

Exercise 11.7. How does an increase in the drift parameter μ affect b^*?

11.5. Irreversible Investment with Two Shocks

The model in the previous section can be modified to allow a stochastic price for investment goods as well as stochastic demand. In particular, suppose that P is also a geometric Brownian motion. For now suppose that the processes X and P are independent.

In this case, as before, the value function V is homogeneous of degree one in (K, X) and the optimal policy involves investing if K/X is below a threshold. The new element here is that the threshold, call it $\kappa(P)$, depends on the current price of investment goods. Thus the optimal policy has the following form. If $K/X < \kappa(P)$, use an impulse of investment to bring the ratio up to $\kappa(P)$. Thereafter regulate K/X at the (stochastic) threshold $\kappa(P)$. The goal is to characterize the function $\kappa(P)$ and the value function.

The value function is now

$$V(K_0, X_0, P_0) = \max_{\{L(t)\}} E_0 \left[\int_0^\infty e^{-rt} \left[K^\alpha(t) X^{1-\alpha}(t) dt - P(t) dL(t) \right] \right]$$

$$dK = -\delta K dt + dL,$$

$$dX = \mu_x X dt + \sigma_x X dW_x,$$

$$dP = \mu_p P dt + \sigma_p P dW_p,$$

where W_x and W_p are independent Wiener processes and the maximization is over nondecreasing functions $L(t) \geq 0$. The associated HJB equation is

$$rV = K^\alpha X^{1-\alpha} - \delta K V_K + \mu_x X V_X + \tfrac{1}{2}\sigma_x^2 X^2 V_{XX}$$

$$+ \mu_p P V_P + \tfrac{1}{2}\sigma_p^2 P^2 V_{PP}, \quad K/X > \kappa(P),$$

where the independence of the shocks implies that the term involving V_{XP} has zero expectation. The argument that V is homogeneous of degree one in (K, X) is as before, so

$$V(K, X, P) = Xv(K/X, P),$$

where $v(k, P) \equiv V(k, 1, P)$.

Exercise 11.8.   (a) Show that the intensive form of the HJB equation is

$$\left(r - \mu_x\right) v = k^\alpha - \left(\delta + \mu_x\right) kv_k + \tfrac{1}{2}\sigma_x^2 k^2 v_{kk} + \mu_p P v_P + \tfrac{1}{2}\sigma_p^2 P^2 v_{PP}.$$

(b) Show that the function $v_P(k) = k^\alpha/\eta$ is a particular solution of this equation and that it has the same interpretation as before.

(c) Show that homogeneous solutions have the form

$$h(k, P) = c_0 P^\omega k^\lambda,$$

where (ω, λ) satisfy

$$0 = - \left(r - \mu_x\right) - \left(\delta + \mu_x\right) \lambda + \tfrac{1}{2}\sigma_x^2 \lambda (\lambda - 1) + \mu_p \omega + \tfrac{1}{2}\sigma_p^2 \omega (\omega - 1). \quad (11.22)$$

As $k \to \infty$ optimal investment is zero, with high probability, for a long time. This is true for any P, so

$$\lim_{k \to \infty} \left(v(k, P) - \frac{k^\alpha}{\eta} \right) = 0, \quad \text{all } P,$$

which implies that the homogeneous solution(s) must have $\lambda < 0$. A similar argument applies with P and k reversed, so

$$\lim_{P \to \infty} \left(v(k, P) - \frac{k^\alpha}{\eta} \right) = 0, \quad \text{all } k,$$

and the homogeneous solution(s) must have $\omega < 0$ as well.

Conjecture that there is only one homogeneous term. Then the value function has the form

$$v(k, P) = \begin{cases} k^\alpha/\eta + c_0 P^\omega k^\lambda, & k \ge \kappa(P), \\ v\left[\kappa(P), P\right] - P\left[\kappa(P) - k\right], & k < \kappa(P), \end{cases} \quad (11.23)$$

and the smooth pasting and super contact conditions determine the function $\kappa(P)$ and the constants ω, $\lambda < 0$, and $c_0 > 0$.

Smooth pasting requires $v_k(\kappa(P), P) = P$, all P, so

$$\frac{\alpha}{\eta} \left[\kappa(P)\right]^{\alpha-1} + \lambda c_0 P^\omega \left[\kappa(P)\right]^{\lambda-1} = P, \quad \text{all } P. \quad (11.24)$$

For $\lambda c_0 \ne 0$ this condition holds if and only if the functions of P in each term agree and the coefficients on the two terms on the left sum to one.

Exercise 11.9. (a) Show that (11.24) implies

$$\kappa(P) = \kappa_0 P^{1/(\alpha-1)},$$
$$\omega = \frac{\lambda - \alpha}{1 - \alpha}, \quad (11.25)$$

where κ_0 is a constant that must be determined.

(b) Show that (11.22), with ω as in (11.25), implies that $\lambda < 0$ must satisfy the quadratic

$$0 = \tfrac{1}{2}s^2\lambda^2 - \left(\delta + h + \tfrac{1}{2}s^2\right)\lambda - (r - \mu_p - h), \quad (11.26)$$

where

$$s^2 = \sigma_x^2 + \frac{\sigma_p^2}{(1-\alpha)^2},$$

$$h = \mu_x - \frac{\mu_p}{1-\alpha} + \frac{\sigma_p^2}{2}\frac{\alpha}{(1-\alpha)^2}.$$

Show that if $r > \mu_p + h$ the roots of the quadratic in (11.26) are real and of opposite sign.

(c) Show that discounted profits are infinite if $r \le \mu_p + h$.

It remains to determine the constants c_0 and κ_0 in (11.23) and (11.25). The coefficients on the three terms in (11.24) must satisfy

$$\frac{\alpha}{\eta}\kappa_0^{\alpha-1} + \lambda c_0 \kappa_0^{\lambda-1} = 1,$$

which puts one restriction on (c_0, κ_0). In addition, the super contact condition $v_{kk} = 0$ implies

$$(\alpha - 1)\frac{\alpha}{\eta}\kappa_0^{\alpha-1} + (\lambda - 1)\lambda c_0 \kappa_0^{\lambda-1} = 0.$$

Combine these two equations to find that

$$\kappa_0 = \left(\frac{\eta}{\alpha}\frac{1-\lambda}{\alpha-\lambda}\right)^{1/(\alpha-1)},$$

$$c_0 = -\frac{1}{\lambda}\frac{1-\alpha}{\alpha-\lambda}\left(\frac{\eta}{\alpha}\frac{1-\lambda}{\alpha-\lambda}\right)^{(1-\lambda)/(\alpha-1)}.$$

Note that the function $\kappa(P)$ in (11.25) has the same form as b^* in (11.20), with λ in place of R.

If the price of capital goods changes over time, either deterministically or stochastically, and capital can be sold at the purchase price P, then the user cost of capital must be adjusted for expected capital gains. Since $E[dP]/dt = \mu_p P$, the user cost formula is

$$\pi'(k^f) = \alpha\left(k^f\right)^{\alpha-1} = (r + \delta - \mu_p)\,P,$$

and the solution requires

$$r + \delta > \mu_p.$$

The price of capital goods cannot be expected to rise so fast that it is profitable to hoard them for later resale.

The model can also accommodate correlation in the shocks affecting X and P. Suppose X and P are geometric Brownian motions with increments

$$\frac{dX}{X} = \mu_x dt + \sigma_x' dW, \quad \frac{dP}{P} = \mu_p dt + \sigma_p' dW,$$

where W_1 and W_2 are independent Wiener processes, $W' = (W_1, W_2)$, and $\sigma_i' = (\sigma_{i1}, \sigma_{i2})$, $i = x, p$, are vectors. Thus there are two independent shocks and two channels through which they can operate, and both shocks can operate through both channels.

Exercise 11.10. Show that

$$\frac{1}{dt} E\left[dW' \sigma_i \sigma_j' dW\right] = \sigma_i' \cdot \sigma_j \equiv \sigma_{ij}, \quad i, j = x, p.$$

How must the HJB equation be modified to accommodate this specification for the shocks?

11.6. A Two-Sector Economy

Consider an economy consisting of two sectors, "widgets" and other goods. Let C_1 denote consumption of widgets and C_2 consumption of other goods. The representative consumer has preferences

$$E_0\left[\int_0^\infty e^{-\rho t} \frac{1}{1-\sigma} \left\{U[C_1(t), C_2(t)]\right\}^{1-\sigma} dt\right],$$

where the function U is strictly increasing, strictly quasi-concave, and homogeneous of degree one, and $\sigma > 0$, $\sigma \neq 1$.

Output in each sector is produced using sector-specific capital as the only input, and each technology is linear. The technology in the widget sector is deterministic, and without loss of generality the productivity parameter can be set to unity. Output in this sector can be used only for consumption, so

$$C_1(t) = K_1(t).$$

The technology in sector 2 is stochastic. Specifically, the productivity parameter X in this sector is a diffusion,

$$dX = \mu(X)dt + \sigma(X)dW,$$

where W is a Wiener process. Output in this sector can be used for consumption or for investment in either sector. Hence

$$C_2 dt + dL_1 - dU_1 + dL_2 - dU_2 = X K_2 dt,$$

where L_i and U_i denote cumulative gross investment and disinvestment in sector i. Both capital stocks depreciate at the rate $\delta > 0$, so

$$dK_i = dL_i - dU_i - \delta K_i \, dt, \quad i = 1, 2.$$

Consider a social planner who makes all the consumption and investment decisions for the economy. In particular, consider two environments.

First consider an economy in which investment is costlessly and instantaneously reversible. That is, the existing capital stock can be allocated freely between the two sectors at any date or turned into consumption goods.

Exercise 11.11. (a) Formulate the social planner's problem. Show that the value function $v(K_1, K_2, X)$ for this problem depends on the capital stocks through their sum, $K = K_1 + K_2$.

(b) Show that the value function is homogeneous of degree $1 - \sigma$ in K.

(c) Characterize the optimal consumption and investment policies as sharply as you can.

Next consider an economy in which investment in sector 1 is irreversible. That is, $U_1 \equiv 0$.

(d) Formulate the social planner's problem. In what region of the state space does the value function $v(K_1, K_2, X)$ depend on K_1 and K_2 only through their sum?

(e) Show that the value function is homogeneous of degree $1 - \sigma$ in (K_1, K_2).

(f) Characterize the optimal consumption and investment policies as sharply as you can.

Notes

Section 11.1 draws on Abel and Eberly (1994), Section 11.2 on Abel and Eberly (1997), and Sections 11.3 and 11.4 on Bertola and Caballero (1994).

The literature on investment under uncertainty is vast. See Abel (1983, 1985) for early contributions connecting uncertainty and the structure of investment costs with q theory. See Caballero (1999) for an excellent survey of the literature and many references.

The effect of irreversibility on the investment decisions of a single firm has been studied extensively since Arrow (1968). Among the early contributions are MacDonald and Siegel (1985, 1986), Pindyck (1988),

Dixit (1992, 1995), and Abel and Eberly (1999). Pindyck (1991) provides
an excellent overview and many references.

Caplin and Leahy (1993) look at learning and the incentive to delay in
a model with irreversible investment, and Leahy (1993) introduces compe-
tition in a model with irreversibility and asks which aspects of an individual
firm's behavior are altered. Abel and Eberly (1996) and Abel et al. (1996)
look at setups in which investment is reversible but costly.

Kogan (2001, 2004) uses a general equilibrium model with multiple
sectors, idiosyncratic shocks, and irreversible investment to study aggregate
investment, aggregate output, and asset prices. Veracierto (2002) analyzes
an aggregate model with irreversibilities to assess their role in business
cycles.

Techniques similar to those studied in this chapter have been used to
study labor markets with hiring and firing costs. For example, see Bentolila
and Bertola (1990); Caballero, Engel, and Haltiwanger (1997); and Campbell and Fisher (2000a,b). Moscarini (2005) uses related methods to study a
model of job matching, and Alvarez and Shimer (2008) use them to analyze
a version of the Lucas and Prescott (1974) "islands" model.

Part IV

Aggregation

12
An Aggregate Model with Fixed Costs

AGGREGATE MODELS IN which individual agents face fixed adjustment costs fall into two broad categories. In the first agents are subject to idiosyncratic shocks, and the shocks can be modeled as i.i.d. across agents. The law of large numbers then implies that once a stationary cross-sectional distribution of shocks and endogenous states has been reached, economic aggregates are constant over time. If the initial distribution is the stationary one aggregates are constant from the outset. Thus in settings with a large number of agents and idiosyncratic shocks, constructing tractable aggregate models is relatively straightforward.

In the second type of model some or all of the shocks are aggregate shocks. In this type of setting the law of large numbers is not helpful, and analytical results are much harder to obtain. Nevertheless, they are sometimes available for special cases. The trick is to find particular assumptions that lead to a stationary distribution, so that the entire cross-sectional distribution is not required as a state variable. (Alternatively, computational methods that describe the evolution of the entire distribution have also been pursued successfully.)

Two aggregate versions of the menu cost model of Chapter 7 are studied here to illustrate possibilities of the second type. Recall that in the menu cost model the exogenous shocks experienced by individual firms are shocks to an economywide price index. Thus aggregate versions of that model fall into the second category. Nevertheless, some special cases have been identified that are tractable analytically.

Before proceeding it is useful to recall the questions these models are designed to address. First and foremost are questions about the real effects of monetary policy. Specifically, the goal is to study the hypothesis that monetary policy has real effects in the short run because nominal prices are sticky in the short run. Money is neutral in the longer run, affecting only the rate of inflation, because prices are flexible in the longer run, adjusting in a way that accommodates monetary policy.

One of the first important lessons of the menu cost literature is that it is dangerous to ask about the effects of fixed costs by taking a frictionless economy in equilibrium, adding frictions, and then asking about the effect of an exogenous shock or a policy measure. The answer is quite different from the one delivered by modeling an ongoing world with frictions. The behavior of rational agents—and hence of economic aggregates as well—in response to any particular sequence of exogenous shocks depends on the stochastic process generating the shocks, not just the realizations. The effect of a big shock in a setting where big shocks are rare may be quite different from its effect in a setting where such shocks are commonplace. Rational agents adapt their behavior in response to changes in their environment, and aggregates reflect those adaptations.

In addition, the menu cost literature illustrates the importance of how adjustment is modeled. For this issue it is useful to think of the aggregate response to any change in the money supply in terms of two components: the average size of adjustments among firms that change their prices—the intensive margin—and the fraction of firms that change—the extensive margin.

Some sticky price models have time-dependent rules describing when firms change prices. These rules take two forms. In the first, a firm is allowed to change its price only at exogenously specified fixed dates. Typically these dates are assumed to be evenly spaced for any single firm and to be evenly distributed across firms. Thus the same fraction of firms is adjusting at each point in time. In the second, opportunities for any particular firm to change its price have Poisson arrivals. Hence these arrivals are independent of the firm's own price, the aggregate price level, and other aspects of the environment. The arrivals are independent across firms, so as before the same fraction of firms is adjusting at any point in time.

Under a time-dependent rule of either sort a change in monetary policy—an increase in the average growth rate, for example—can be accommodated only by changes in the size of the adjustments by firms that the timing rule selects as adjusters. Thus over any time interval a money supply that is growing more rapidly draws responses from the same fraction of firms as one that is growing more slowly. The firms that adjust make larger changes, but over any time interval the same fraction of firms *fail* to respond when money growth is faster. Hence the aggregate response is altered only through changes on the intensive margin. Under time-dependent rules there is no adjustment on the extensive margin.

In menu cost models of the type analyzed in Chapter 7, in which both the size and timing of price adjustments are chosen by rational decision makers, a change in the money growth rule elicits responses on both margins. In response to an increase in the average rate of money growth firms adjust more frequently, in addition to making larger changes when they adjust. Thus the aggregate price level responds to a change in monetary policy through changes on the extensive margin as well as the intensive margin.

This reasoning makes one suspect that monetary non-neutralities will be substantially smaller in menu cost models than in models with time-dependent pricing rules. It also highlights the difficulty of accurately assessing the effects of policy changes in time-dependent models, since one important avenue of response is closed off.

The rest of this chapter looks at an aggregate version of the menu cost model from Chapter 7. In particular, two economies are examined, identical except for the monetary policy in place. In the first economy the money supply process is monotone, and in this setting shocks to the money supply have no effect. This model is from Caplin and Spulber (1987). In the second the (log) money supply follows a Brownian motion with zero drift, and here the effect of an increment in the money supply depends on the state of the economy when the shock arrives. Specifically, a monetary expansion may lead to an increase in output, and will do so more strongly if initial output is low. A monetary expansion may also lead to price increases and will do so more strongly if initial output is high. Both effects are reversed for a monetary contraction. Thus the model delivers a positive correlation between money and output: it displays a Phillips curve. This model is from Caplin and Leahy (1997).

The second model also illustrates an outcome that can occur in other settings as well, an endogenous aggregate that behaves like a regulated Brownian motion. The behavior of individual agents allows the aggregate—here it is aggregate real balances—to track an exogenous process—here it is nominal balances—up to a certain threshold. After that threshold is reached the actions of individual firms—here their price adjustments—prevent the process from crossing the threshold.

Some of the methods described in this chapter may also prove useful for studying other aggregates—investment demand, labor markets, housing demand, and so on. A few such models based on sticky or lumpy adjustment at the micro level have been studied, but these areas are as yet largely unexplored.

The rest of this chapter is organized as follows. In Section 12.1 the basic model is described. In Section 12.2 it is studied under the assumption that the money supply process is monotone, and for these policies money is neutral even in the short run. In Section 12.3 the same economy is studied under the assumption that the log money supply is a Brownian motion with zero drift. This economy displays a short-run Phillips curve, although money is still neutral in the long run. In this section firms are assumed to follow price adjustment rules of the type studied in Chapter 7, but with exogenously specified thresholds. In Section 12.4 the behavior of individual firms is studied more closely. Firms are assumed to have a target price that depends on real balances in a certain way and a loss function that is quadratic in the deviation from this target. Under these assumptions the model is shown to have a unique equilibrium in the sense that profit-maximizing behavior by firms is consistent with the aggregate behavior of the price level and real balances. Section 12.5 shows that the price target postulated in Section 12.4 can be justified with a standard model of consumer demand. The quadratic loss function can be viewed as an approximation to the true function, which is convex.

12.1. The Economic Environment

There is a continuum of monopolistically competitive, price-setting firms indexed by $i \in [0, 1]$, facing identical demand and cost conditions. Money and prices are measured in (natural) logs throughout. Let

$M(t) = $ (log) money supply,
$P_i(t) = $ (log) nominal price of firm i,
$P(t) = H(\{P_i\}) = $ (log) aggregate price index,
$p_i(t) = P_i(t) - P(t) = $(log) relative price of firm i,
$m(t) = M(t) - P(t) = $ (log) real money balances.

Assume throughout that the function $H(\cdot)$ used to calculate the aggregate price index depends only on the cumulative distribution function for the prices of individual firms, and that it is log-linearly homogeneous in the sense that

$$H(\{P_i + a\}) = H(\{P_i\}) + a. \tag{12.1}$$

That is, if the distribution of (log) prices shifts by the constant a, then the aggregate price index shifts by a. Most price indexes have this property. Note that (12.1) implies the average of the (log) relative prices is identically zero,

$$H(\{p_i\}) = H(\{P_i - P\}) \equiv 0.$$

At any date t the economy is completely described by the aggregate state variables $[M(t), \{P_i(t)\}]$, the money supply, and the distribution of prices across firms. In all of the models analyzed here, however, the distribution of relative prices is contrived—for tractability—to be invariant. Hence the pair $[M(t), P(t)]$ or $[m(t), P(t)]$ suffices for the aggregate state.

In this chapter firms follow price adjustment policies similar to those analyzed in Chapter 7, except that the firm's target price depends on real balances m as well as the aggregate price index P. The target price is determined by profit maximization, with real balances entering because they affect aggregate expenditure. The argument developing the target price is spelled out in Section 12.5. To characterize adjustment behavior in the presence of a fixed cost, a quadratic loss function for deviations of price from the target is assumed. This loss function can be viewed as a second-order approximation to the true loss function, which is convex.

The main ingredients for the model in Section 12.5 are consumers with Dixit-Stiglitz preferences $\int x_i^{1-\theta} di$, $0 < \theta < 1$, over the continuum of differentiated products; firms with production costs of the isoelastic form $c(x) = c_0 x^\xi / \xi$, $\xi > 1$, where x is the firm's output level and $c(x)$ is total cost; and total consumer expenditures that are proportional to money balances at each date. As shown in Section 12.5, under these assumptions the profit-maximizing relative price for each firm is

$$p_i^*(t) = b + \eta m(t), \tag{12.2}$$

where b and $\eta \in (0, 1)$ are constants that depend on the parameters θ, ξ, c_0. The corresponding nominal price is

$$P_i^*(t) = P(t) + b + \eta \left[M(t) - P(t) \right]$$
$$= b + (1 - \eta) P(t) + \eta M(t),$$

so in a frictionless world the firm adjusts $(1 - \eta)$-for-one to changes in the aggregate price level and η-for-one to changes in nominal balances. Notice that since $0 < \eta < 1$ the pricing game exhibits strategic complementarity: firm i raises its nominal price when $P(t)$ rises.

To begin the analysis, briefly consider the behavior of an economy in which there are no menu costs. As noted above the homogeneity property in (12.1) implies that the average of the relative prices is identically zero. In a frictionless world all firms adjust price continuously to keep profits at a maximum. Hence all firms set the same price, and consequently the distribution of relative prices is a point mass at zero,

$$p_i(t) = 0, \quad \text{all } i, \text{ all } t.$$

It then follows from (12.2) that the (constant) equilibrium level of real balances in the frictionless world is

$$m(t) = m^* \equiv -b/\eta, \quad \text{all } t.$$

In the absence of adjustment costs all firms adjust their prices one-for-one to changes in the money supply. Hence the aggregate price level also moves one-for-one, and real balances are constant. Consequently, output and profits are identical across firms and constant over time, and

$$x_i(t) = \bar{x}, \quad \pi_i(t) = \bar{\pi}, \quad \text{all } i, \text{ all } t,$$

where $\bar{x}$ and $\bar{\pi}$ are also the aggregates.

For the economy with menu costs it is convenient to define $\varepsilon(t)$ to be the deviation of real balances from m^*,

$$\varepsilon(t) \equiv m(t) - m^*. \tag{12.3}$$

Using (12.3) and the definition of m^*, the profit-maximizing relative price in (12.2) is

$$p_i^*(t) = \eta \varepsilon(t). \tag{12.4}$$

Notice that if real balances exceed m^*, the target price exceeds zero: every firm would prefer to have a relative price that exceeds the average.

To motivate adjustment behavior in a world with menu costs, note that the deviation of the firm's relative price from its target level is

$$\alpha_i(t) \equiv p_i(t) - p^*(t)$$

$$= p_i(t) - \eta \varepsilon(t).$$

Assume the firm's loss, the reduction in its profits, is a quadratic function of this deviation,

$$L(\alpha_i) = \gamma \alpha_i^2 = \gamma \left(p_i - \eta \varepsilon \right)^2, \quad \gamma > 0. \tag{12.5}$$

The quadratic form can be viewed as an approximation to the true function, which is convex. There is also an assumption, implicit in (12.5), that the same loss function applies for any level of real balances ε.

Notice the relationship between the average price level and real balances. A firm charging a price $P_i = P$ equal to the aggregate price index has a relative price of $p_i = 0$. If $\varepsilon(t) > 0$, so real balances $m(t)$ exceed m^*, then this "average" firm has a relative price that is below the profit-maximizing value in (12.4). That is, its deviation from its target is negative,

$$\alpha_i = 0 - \eta \varepsilon(t) = -\eta \left[m(t) - m^* \right] < 0.$$

Looked at the other way around, the fact that prices are low, on average, is what makes real balances high.

Finally, to close the model assume that the level of aggregate (real) expenditure, call it $\tilde{e}$, is proportional to the level of real balances $\tilde{m}$,

$$\tilde{e} = v_0 \tilde{m} = v_0 \exp(m) = v_0 \exp(m^* + \varepsilon). \tag{12.6}$$

In general, firm i's output depends on its relative price p_i, aggregate real balances $m^* + \varepsilon$, and the distribution of relative prices across other firms, $\{p_j\}$. But if the distribution of relative prices is constant, then its output depends only on p_i and ε,

$$x_i = \xi(p_i, \varepsilon), \quad \text{all } i.$$

As shown in Section 12.5, for the demand and cost structure here

$$\ln\left(x_i\right) = \ln\left(\tilde{e}\right) - \frac{1}{\theta} p_i$$

$$= \ln(v_0) + m^* + \varepsilon - \frac{1}{\theta} p_i, \quad \text{all } i, \tag{12.7}$$

where $\theta \in (0, 1)$ is the elasticity parameter in preferences. It follows as an accounting identity that aggregate output is equal to aggregate real expenditure.

12.2. An Economy with Monetary Neutrality

As shown in the previous section, in an economy with no menu costs all nominal values move immediately to offset increments in the money supply, so all relative values and real variables are constant over time and identical across firms. This section looks at a model in which all firms use (S, s) price adjustment rules, and the money supply is monotonically increasing. In this setting, too, monetary injections are immediately offset by price increases and hence have no effect on real balances or aggregate output. In contrast to the frictionless world, however, the distribution of prices and output across firms is nondegenerate, and individual firms experience fluctuations. This model is the one studied in Caplin and Spulber (1987).

The argument does not require constructing equilibrium policies, and it is left as an exercise to show that there is an equilibrium policy of the assumed type. It is also left as an exercise to show that the equilibrium (S, s) band becomes wider and the (constant) level of aggregate output is lower when average money growth is faster. Money growth does have aggregate effects in this model, but fluctuations in money growth do not cause fluctuations in output.

Suppose that firms face a fixed cost for changing price, and that all firms adopt the same (S, s) pricing rule. Suppose further that the money supply is monotonically increasing, so all price adjustments are in the upward direction. Finally, suppose that the initial distribution of prices is uniform on the (S, s) band. The following proposition characterizes the behavior of this economy.

Proposition 12.1. Suppose that for some $S > 0$,

    i. the initial distribution of relative prices across firms $\{p_i(0)\}$ is uniform on $[-S, +S]$;

    ii. each firm i uses a one-sided price adjustment policy, adjusting its relative price $p_i(t)$ from $-S$ to $+S$ when $p_i(t) = -S$; and

    iii. the (log) money supply $M(t)$ is continuous and nondecreasing.

Then real balances are constant over time:

$$M(t) - P(t) = M(0) - P(0), \quad \text{all } t;$$

and the distribution of relative prices $\{p_i(t)\}$ remains uniform on $[-S, +S]$ for all t.

Proof. Suppose that over a small increment of time Δt the money supply increases by

$$M(t + \Delta t) - M(t) = \Delta M.$$

Conjecture that the price index increases by the same amount,

$$P(t + \Delta t) - P(t) = \Delta P = \Delta M.$$

This change triggers price increases by firms with relative prices near $-S$. The number of adjusting firms is $\Delta M / 2S$, and each adjusts its price by $2S$, so the aggregate price index rises by ΔM, as conjectured. The adjusting firms make their changes continuously, so the distribution of relative prices $\{p_i(t)\}$ remains uniform on $[-S, +S]$. And since $\Delta P = \Delta M$, real money balances are unchanged. ∎

    Figure 12.1 illustrates the main idea of the proof. The adjusting firms are the small interval ΔM near $-S$, and each increases price by $2S$. Hence the increase in the aggregate price index is $\Delta M \times (1/2S) \times (2S) = \Delta M$, as conjectured, and since the adjustment is continuous the uniform distribution is preserved.

    In this economy the deviation of real balances from their level in the frictionless economy, $\varepsilon(t) = m(t) - m^* = \bar{\varepsilon}$, is constant over time. Hence the deviation of a firm's price from its target, $\alpha_i(t) = p_i(t) - \eta\varepsilon(t) = p_i(t) - \eta\bar{\varepsilon}$, changes only because of changes in its own relative price. A higher-than-usual rate of money growth, if it is brief enough so that firms do not change their price adjustment *rule*, feeds immediately into higher prices, with no real consequences. Aggregate output is constant, although individual firms experience fluctuating demand and profits as they cycle through various

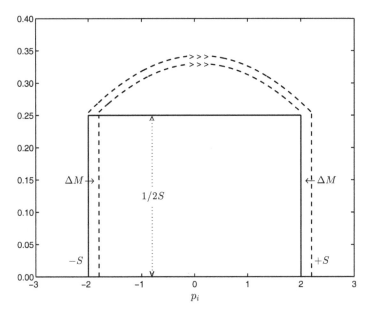

Figure 12.1. *Price adjustment in the Caplin-Spulber model.*

positions in the relative price distribution. In this economy short-run fluctuations in money growth do not lead to fluctuations in real balances or aggregate output.

But the mean rate of money growth (and possibly the variance as well) does affect both the price adjustment rule and the level of real balances. Hence it affects the cross-sectional dispersion of relative prices, the level of aggregate output, and the total resources devoted to price adjustment.

12.3. An Economy with a Phillips Curve

Proposition 12.1 shows that if money growth is always nonnegative, then even if the growth rate fluctuates it causes no fluctuations in aggregate output. In this section it is shown that if the money supply can fall as well as rise, fluctuations do occur.

The key to tractability is finding conditions under which the cross-sectional distribution of relative prices is stationary. The previous section suggests that a uniform distribution is an appealing candidate. But if firms use (S, s) price adjustment policies the resulting distribution remains uniform if and only if that policy has a special property. In this section firms are assumed to follow price adjustment policies of the required sort. In the next section it is shown that for appropriate initial conditions there exists an equilibrium in which those policies are profit maximizing.

In this section and the next the (log) money supply is assumed to be a Brownian motion. Proposition 12.2 then shows that if firms use the right kind of two-sided price adjustment policy, a uniform distribution of relative prices across firms is stationary, and excess real balances are a regulated Brownian motion confined within a band $[-B, +B]$ that is symmetric around zero. Money growth leads to changes in real balances—but no price changes—when excess real balances lie in $(-B, +B)$, and it can trigger inflation or deflation—with no change in real balances—if excess real balances are at $+B$ or $-B$. Since aggregate expenditure is equal to real balances, this economy has a short-run Phillips curve: faster money growth leads—at least sometimes—to an increase in aggregate output.

As before, let $\varepsilon(t) = m(t) - m^*$ be excess real balances, and suppose that each firm follows the following price adjustment policy, with $\alpha_i(t) = p_i(t) - \eta\varepsilon(t)$ as its state variable. If firm i's relative price is at its minimum, $p_i = -S$, and excess real balances are at their maximum, $\varepsilon = +B$, so $\alpha_i = -S - \eta B$ is at its lower bound, then the firm raises its relative price to $p_i' = +S$. This adjustment raises its state variable to $\alpha_i' = S - \eta B$. Symmetrically, if firm i's relative price is at its maximum, $p_i = +S$, and excess real balances are at their minimum, $\varepsilon = -B$, so that $\alpha_i = S + \eta B$, then the firm reduces its relative price to $p_i' = -S$.

Proposition 12.2 shows that if the money supply follows a Brownian motion and firms use this adjustment rule, then real balances follow a regulated Brownian motion with barriers $\pm B$.

Proposition 12.2. Let $M(t)$ be a Brownian motion with parameters (μ, σ^2), and define $\{P_i\}$, P, m, ε, $\{p_i\}$, and $\{\alpha_i\}$ as above. Assume that for some $S, B > 0$ and $\eta \in (0, 1)$,

i. the initial level of excess real balances satisfies $\varepsilon(0) \in [-B, +B]$;
ii. the initial distribution of relative prices across firms $\{p_i(0)\}$ is uniform on $[-S, +S]$; and
iii. each firm i uses a symmetric, two-sided price adjustment policy, adjusting its relative price p_i to $+S$ when $\alpha_i \leq -S - \eta B$ and to $-S$ when $\alpha_i \geq S + \eta B$.

Then

a. the distribution of relative prices $\{p_i(t)\}$ remains uniform on $[-S, +S]$, all t;
b. excess real balances $\varepsilon(t)$ are a regulated Brownian motion, regulated at $\pm B$.

Proof. Suppose $\varepsilon(0) \in (-B, +B)$. As long as $\varepsilon(t)$ remains in the open interval $(-B, +B)$, no firms adjust their prices. Hence the price index $P(t)$ does not change and the distribution of relative prices remains uniform on $[-S, +S]$. In this region increments to the money supply lead to one-for-one increments in real balances, so $m(t)$ and $\varepsilon(t)$ track $M(t)$.

Let $T = T(B) \wedge T(-B)$ be the first date when $\varepsilon(t)$ reaches $+B$ or $-B$. Consider sample paths where it first reaches $+B$. Further increases in money trigger price adjustments by the firms with the lowest relative prices. Consider these sample paths beyond date T. For any such path choose any time interval ΔT with the property that

$$M(T + s) - P(T) - m^* > -B, \quad \text{all } s \in [0, \Delta T],$$

so the money supply does not fall too far before $T + \Delta T$. Then $\varepsilon(T + s) > -B$, all $s \in [0, \Delta T]$, so no firms make downward price adjustments over this time interval. Let

$$\Delta_{\max} = \max_{0 \le s \le \Delta T} M(T + s) - M(T)$$

be the maximum increase in the money supply over this interval. After a net increase of $\Delta_{\max}$ all firms with initial relative prices $p_i(0) \in \left[-S, -S + \Delta_{\max} \right]$ have raised their prices by $2S$. Since the money supply is continuous, these price adjustments occur continuously. Thus the (uniform) distribution of prices $\{P_i(t)\}$ shifts to the right by $\Delta_{\max}$. Hence the aggregate price index P rises by $\Delta_{\max}$, and the distribution of relative prices $\{p_i\}$ remains uniform on $[-S, +S]$. At the end of this time interval excess real balances are

$$\varepsilon(T + \Delta T) = M(T + \Delta T) - P(T + \Delta T) - m^*$$
$$= M(T + \Delta T) - M(T) + M(T) - \left[P(T) + \Delta_{\max} \right] - m^*$$
$$= B + \Delta M - \Delta_{\max}$$
$$\le B,$$

so they do not exceed $+B$. This argument holds for any sample path that reaches $+B$ before $-B$, and for any ΔT such that $\varepsilon(T + \Delta T)$ remains above $-B$.

A similar argument applies when real balances reach $-B$, and for subsequent time intervals, establishing conclusions (a) and (b). ∎

Figure 12.2 displays a path for nominal balances $M(t)$ and the associated path for excess real balances $\varepsilon(t)$, with both initially at zero. The former can be any continuous function. The latter tracks changes in the former one-for-one as long as $\varepsilon(t)$ remains inside the interval $(-B, +B)$. If $\varepsilon(t)$

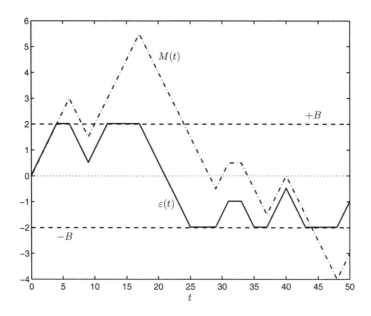

Figure 12.2. *Sample paths for nominal balances $M(t)$ and excess real balances $\varepsilon(t)$ in the Caplin-Leahy model.*

reaches either boundary it remains at that level until changes in $M(t)$ push it back inside the interval. Since aggregate output is equal to aggregate real expenditure, $\varepsilon(t)$ also describes the log deviation of aggregate output from its mean.

Figure 12.3 displays the behavior of the state variables ε and p_i. The distribution of p_i is always uniform on $[-S, +S]$, and excess real balances ε lie on the interval $[-B, +B]$.

While ε is in the interior of this interval no firms adjust their prices. That is, while $\varepsilon \in (-B, +B)$, all nominal and relative prices remain unchanged. In this region changes in money lead to one-for-one changes in real balances, moving ε back and forth within the interval.

When $\varepsilon = +B$ further increases in the money supply induce the firms with the lowest relative prices to adjust their prices upward. Specifically, firms with relative prices at $-S$ adjust those prices to $+S$, bringing them to the other end of the uniform distribution. In Figure 12.3 these (discrete) adjustments are indicated by the arrows along the broken curve. These changes are the same as those described in the proof of Proposition 12.1. As shown there, they raise the aggregate price level P by exactly the size of the

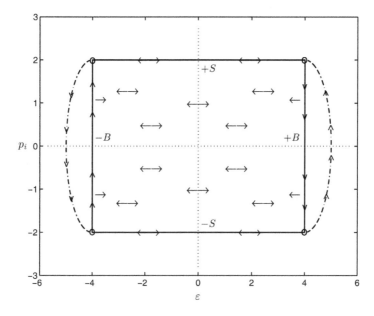

Figure 12.3. *Relative price p_i and excess real balances ε in the Caplin-Leahy model.*

increase in M. The increase in P reduces the relative prices $\{p_i\}$ of all firms that are not adjusting, and in addition implies that ε remains constant at $+B$. In Figure 12.3 these (continuous) changes in relative prices are indicated by the arrows along the solid vertical line at $\varepsilon = +B$.

When $\varepsilon = +B$, decreases in the money supply lead to one-for-one decreases in ε with no price changes. These changes in ε are indicated by arrows that point left along the boundary where $\varepsilon = +B$. Thus when $\varepsilon = +B$ increases in money cause price increases, with no change in real balances, and decreases in money reduce real balances, with no change in prices.

A symmetric argument applies when $\varepsilon = -B$.

The next section shows that if the money supply has zero drift, if $\mu = 0$, then for an appropriate choice of S and B the two-sided price adjustment policy postulated in Proposition 12.2 is an optimal policy for profit-maximizing firms.

12.4. Optimizing Behavior and the Phillips Curve

In Proposition 12.2 the behavior of firms is mechanical. In this section it is linked to profit maximization, so the economic environment must be described in more detail. Let $C > 0$ be the real (fixed) cost of price adjustment; $r > 0$ be the interest rate; η, γ be as described in Section 12.1, and $\mu = 0$ and $\sigma^2 > 0$ be the parameters of the money supply process. In this section it is shown that for any $r, \eta, \gamma, \sigma^2, C$ there exists a unique pair (S, B) with the property that if all firms except firm i adopt the price adjustment rule in condition (iii) of Proposition 12.2, then it is optimal for firm i to adopt that rule as well.

Suppose all firms except firm i use adjustment rule (iii). If $\varepsilon(t) = +B$ then increases in $M(t)$ lead to price increases by other firms, causing one-for-one increases in the price index $P(t)$. Consequently $\varepsilon(t)$ is unchanged and firm i's relative price p_i falls. Similarly, if $\varepsilon(t) = -B$ then decreases in $M(t)$ trigger price decreases by other firms, reducing $P(t)$. Hence $\varepsilon(t)$ is unchanged and firm i's relative price p_i rises. Otherwise changes in $M(t)$ trigger no price changes by other firms. Hence P remains constant, real balances increase one-for-one with M, and firm i's relative prices p_i is unchanged.

Consequently, as long as firm i is not adjusting its own nominal price, its relative price has increment

$$dp_i = 0 - dP = \begin{cases} -dM, & \text{if some firms adjust price,} \\ 0, & \text{if no firms adjust price,} \end{cases} \tag{12.8}$$

and real balances have increment

$$d\varepsilon = dM - dP = \begin{cases} 0, & \text{if some adjust,} \\ +dM, & \text{if none adjust.} \end{cases} \tag{12.9}$$

Hence as long as firm i is not adjusting its own nominal price,

$$d\alpha_i = dp_i - \eta d\varepsilon = \begin{cases} -dM, & \text{if some adjust,} \\ -\eta dM, & \text{if none adjust,} \end{cases}$$

where some adjust if $\varepsilon = +B$ and $dM > 0$, or if $\varepsilon = -B$ and $dM < 0$, and otherwise none adjust.

Since α_i does not have i.i.d. increments, the results in Chapter 7 do not apply. Nevertheless, the Hamilton-Jacobi-Bellman (HJB) equation for the firm's problem can be used to establish the desired result. The key idea is that the rule for relative price adjustments in condition (iii) of Proposition 12.2 displays two types of symmetry.

One type is obvious: if it is optimal to adjust the relative price to $+T$ when real balances are $+B$ and the relative price is $-S$ or lower, then it is optimal to adjust to $-T$ when real balances are $-B$ and the relative price is $+S$ or higher. This conclusion follows immediately from the symmetry of the loss function and the fact that the money supply process has zero drift. Firm i takes B as given, and its optimal policy displays the first type of symmetry for any B.

The key to establishing the desired result is a second type of symmetry: the adjustment policy has $T = S$. Establishing the existence of an equilibrium requires showing that for some B, a price adjustment strategy with $T = S$ is an optimal policy for firm i. The equilibrium is unique (within this class) if there is only one B with this property.

The argument has several steps. Lemma 12.3 characterizes the solution to firm i's HJB equation, given any $B > 0$. This step produces a value function, given B, and Lemmas 12.4 and 12.5 establish properties of the associated optimal policy function. Proposition 12.6 draws on these results to show that for any parameter values $r, \eta, \gamma, \sigma^2, C$ there exists a unique B that leads to an optimal policy with the required property.

Fix $r, \eta, \gamma, \sigma^2, C$, and consider a firm in an economy where the increments to its relative price and real balances are as in (12.8) and (12.9) as long as the firm takes no action. The firm's problem, given its initial state (p_{i0}, ε_0), is to choose a sequence of stopping times $\{T_k\}_{k=1}^{\infty}$ and random variables $\{\hat{p}_k\}_{k=1}^{\infty}$, where $\hat{p}_k$ is the relative price after the kth adjustment, to minimize the expected discounted value of its losses from mispricing, plus adjustment costs. Let $v(p_i, \varepsilon)$ denote the firm's value function. The state space for the problem is $D \equiv \mathbf{R} \times [-B, +B]$, and v satisfies the Bellman equation

$$v(p_i, \varepsilon) = \min_{T, \hat{p}} E \left\{ \int_0^T e^{-rt} \gamma \left[p_i(t) - \eta \varepsilon(t) \right]^2 dt \right.$$
$$\left. + e^{-rT} \left[v \left(\hat{p}, \varepsilon(T) \right) + C \right] \right\}, \tag{12.10}$$

where M is a Brownian motion and

$$dP = \begin{cases} dM, & \text{if } \varepsilon = +B \text{ and } dM > 0, \text{ or } \varepsilon = -B \text{ and } dM < 0, \\ 0, & \text{otherwise,} \end{cases}$$

$$dp_i = -dP,$$

$$d\varepsilon = dM - dP, \quad 0 \le t \le T.$$

The HJB equation for the value function in (12.10) is

$$rv(p_i, \varepsilon) = \gamma \left(p_i - \eta \varepsilon \right)^2 + \frac{1}{dt} E \left[dv \right], \tag{12.11}$$

where

$$dv = v_p dp_i + \tfrac{1}{2} v_{pp} \left(dp_i \right)^2 + v_\varepsilon d\varepsilon + \tfrac{1}{2} v_{\varepsilon\varepsilon} \left(d\varepsilon \right)^2 + v_{p\varepsilon} dp_i d\varepsilon.$$

The next lemma characterizes the solution to (12.11). Note that the value function v satisfies (12.11) only in the inaction region. Nevertheless it is useful to begin by constructing a function that satisfies (12.11) on all of D and then adjusting it in the regions where (12.11) does not hold.

Lemma 12.3. Fix $r, \eta, \gamma, \sigma^2$ and $B > 0$. Then the solution to the HJB equation (12.11) is

$$v(p_i, \varepsilon) = \left[a_0 + a_1 p_i + a_2 e^{-\beta p_i} \right] e^{\beta \varepsilon} + \left[a_0 - a_1 p_i + A_2 e^{\beta p_i} \right] e^{-\beta \varepsilon} \quad (12.12)$$

$$+ \frac{\gamma}{r} \left(p_i - \eta \varepsilon \right)^2 + \gamma \left(\frac{\eta \sigma}{r} \right)^2,$$

where

$$\beta = \sqrt{2r}/\sigma,$$

$$c_0 = \frac{2\gamma \, (\eta - 1)}{r},$$

$$a_1 = \frac{c_0/\beta}{e^{\beta B} + e^{-\beta B}},$$

$$a_0 = -\frac{1}{\beta} \left(a_1 + \frac{c_0 \eta B}{e^{\beta B} - e^{-\beta B}} \right),$$

and a_2, A_2 are arbitrary constants.

Proof. Clearly $dp_i d\varepsilon = 0$ and

$$dv = \begin{cases} -v_p dM + \frac{1}{2} v_{pp} (dM)^2, & \text{if } dP \neq 0, \\ +v_\varepsilon dM + \frac{1}{2} v_{\varepsilon\varepsilon} (dM)^2, & \text{if } dP = 0. \end{cases} \quad (12.13)$$

Let D^o denote the interior of D. The proof involves specializing dv for D^o and the two boundaries of D where $\varepsilon = \pm B$, and then using the specialized versions in (12.11).

On D^o, $dP = 0$. Since $E[dM] = 0$ and $E\left[(dM)^2 \right] = \sigma^2 dt$, in this region (12.13) implies

$$E\left[dv \right] = \frac{1}{2} \sigma^2 v_{\varepsilon\varepsilon} dt.$$

Hence on D^o (12.11) takes the form

$$rv(p_i, \varepsilon) = \gamma \left(p_i - \eta \varepsilon \right)^2 + \frac{1}{2} \sigma^2 v_{\varepsilon\varepsilon}. \quad (12.14)$$

For any p_i, this equation is a second-order ODE with solutions of the form

$$v(p_i, \varepsilon) = f(p_i)e^{\beta\varepsilon} + F(p_i)e^{-\beta\varepsilon} + \frac{\gamma}{r}\left(p_i - \eta\varepsilon\right)^2 + \gamma\left(\frac{\eta\sigma}{r}\right)^2, \quad (12.15)$$

where f and F are arbitrary functions of p_i. These functions can be characterized by looking at the boundaries of D where $\varepsilon = \pm B$.

Along the boundary where $\varepsilon = +B$, careful attention must be paid to the sign of dM. Let $z = \sigma\sqrt{dt} > 0$ denote the absolute size of the increment to nominal balances. If the nominal shock is positive, $dM = z$, some firms adjust their prices upward. Hence the aggregate price level rises, $dP = dM = z$, and real balances are unchanged, $d\varepsilon = 0$. In this case (12.13) implies

$$dv = -v_p z + \tfrac{1}{2}v_{pp}z^2.$$

If the nominal shock is negative, $dM = -z$, no firms adjust their prices. Hence the aggregate price level is unchanged, $dP = 0$, and real balances fall, $d\varepsilon = dM = -z$. In this case (12.13) implies

$$dv = -v_\varepsilon z + \tfrac{1}{2}v_{\varepsilon\varepsilon}z^2.$$

These two events are equally likely, so substituting into (12.11) gives

$$rv\left(p_i, B\right) = \gamma\left(p_i - \eta B\right)^2 + \frac{1}{dt}\frac{1}{2}\left[-v_p z + \frac{1}{2}v_{pp}z^2 - v_\varepsilon z + \frac{1}{2}v_{\varepsilon\varepsilon}z^2\right].$$

Then use (12.14) to obtain

$$\tfrac{1}{2}\left(v_{\varepsilon\varepsilon} - v_{pp}\right)z^2 + \left(v_p + v_\varepsilon\right)z = 0,$$

and take the limit as $z \to 0$ to conclude that along the boundary where $\varepsilon = +B$,

$$v_p(p_i, B) + v_\varepsilon\left(p_i, B\right) = 0. \quad (12.16)$$

The same argument, with the signs reversed, applies for $\varepsilon = -B$, so (12.16) also holds for $\varepsilon = -B$.

To characterize f and F, use (12.15) to obtain expressions for v_p and v_ε and evaluate (12.16) and the companion equation with $\varepsilon = -B$ to obtain

$$\begin{aligned}
\left(f' + \beta f\right)e^{\beta B} + \left(F' - \beta F\right)e^{-\beta B} &= c_0\left(p_i - \eta B\right), \\
\left(f' + \beta f\right)e^{-\beta B} + \left(F' - \beta F\right)e^{\beta B} &= c_0\left(p_i + \eta B\right).
\end{aligned} \quad (12.17)$$

Solutions of (12.17) have the form

$$f(p_i) = a_0 + a_1 p_i + a_2 e^{\lambda_2 p_i} + a_3 e^{\lambda_3 p_i} + \cdots,$$

$$F(p_i) = A_0 + A_1 p_i + A_2 e^{\lambda_2 p_i} + A_3 e^{\lambda_3 p_i} + \cdots,$$

where the constants $a_0, A_0, a_1, \ldots$ and the exponents λ_j must be determined. The constant and linear terms in f and F match the terms on the right side in (12.17), and the exponential terms satisfy homogeneous equations.

The terms that are linear in p_i imply

$$\beta \left(a_1 e^{\beta B} - A_1 e^{-\beta B} \right) = c_0,$$

$$\beta \left(a_1 e^{-\beta B} - A_1 e^{\beta B} \right) = c_0,$$

so $A_1 = -a_1$, and

$$a_1 = \frac{1}{\beta} \frac{c_0}{e^{\beta B} + e^{-\beta B}},$$

as claimed. The constant terms imply

$$\beta \left(a_0 e^{\beta B} - A_0 e^{-\beta B} \right) = -c_0 \eta B - a_1 \left(e^{\beta B} - e^{-\beta B} \right),$$

$$\beta \left(a_0 e^{-\beta B} - A_0 e^{\beta B} \right) = +c_0 \eta B - a_1 \left(e^{-\beta B} - e^{\beta B} \right),$$

so $A_0 = a_0$, and

$$a_0 = -\frac{1}{\beta} \left(a_1 + \frac{c_0 \eta B}{e^{\beta B} - e^{-\beta B}} \right),$$

as claimed.

Finally, the exponential terms in f and F must satisfy the homogeneous equations

$$\left(\lambda_j + \beta \right) a_j e^{\beta B} + \left(\lambda_j - \beta \right) A_j e^{-\beta B} = 0,$$

$$\left(\lambda_j + \beta \right) a_j e^{-\beta B} + \left(\lambda_j - \beta \right) A_j e^{\beta B} = 0.$$

Add and subtract these equations from each other to obtain

$$\left(\lambda_j + \beta \right) a_j + \left(\lambda_j - \beta \right) A_j = 0,$$

$$\left(\lambda_j + \beta \right) a_j - \left(\lambda_j - \beta \right) A_j = 0.$$

Hence there are exactly two terms of this form, one with $(\lambda_j, a_j, A_j) = (-\beta, a_2, 0)$ and one with $(\lambda_j, a_j, A_j) = (\beta, 0, A_2)$, where a_2 and A_2 are arbitrary constants. ∎

The value function has the form in (12.12) only inside the inaction region, where the HJB equation holds. For the firm's problem, given $B > 0$, it remains to determine the upper and lower boundaries of that region, call them $H(\varepsilon)$ and $h(\varepsilon)$; the return locus, call it $\tau(\varepsilon)$; and the constants a_2 and A_2.

Lemma 12.4. The boundaries of the inaction region $H(\varepsilon)$ and $h(\varepsilon)$ satisfy the value matching conditions

$$\lim_{p_i \uparrow H(\varepsilon)} v(p_i, \varepsilon) = v(\tau(\varepsilon), \varepsilon) + C, \tag{12.18}$$

$$\lim_{p_i \downarrow h(\varepsilon)} v(p_i, \varepsilon) = v(\tau(\varepsilon), \varepsilon) + C, \quad \text{all } \varepsilon \in [-B, +B],$$

and smooth pasting conditions

$$\lim_{p_i \uparrow H(\varepsilon)} v_p(p_i, \varepsilon) = 0, \tag{12.19}$$

$$\lim_{p_i \downarrow h(\varepsilon)} v_p(p_i, \varepsilon) = 0, \quad \text{all } \varepsilon \in [-B, +B].$$

The locus $\tau(\varepsilon)$ satisfies the optimal return condition

$$v_p(\tau(\varepsilon), \varepsilon) = 0, \quad \text{all } \varepsilon \in [-B, +B]. \tag{12.20}$$

Proof. Optimal repricing requires

$$\tau(\varepsilon) = \arg\min_{p'} v(p', \varepsilon), \quad \text{all } \varepsilon \in [-B, +B],$$

which requires (12.20).

Since the firm always has the option to reprice immediately,

$$v(p_i, \varepsilon) \le v(\tau(\varepsilon), \varepsilon) + C, \quad \text{all } p_i, \varepsilon,$$

with equality if the firm reprices. Thus, if v is convex in p_i, the inaction region is an interval around $\tau(\varepsilon)$, with boundaries defined by functions $h(\varepsilon) < \tau(\varepsilon) < H(\varepsilon)$ satisfying (12.18).

Finally, consider the firm's problem at $(h(\varepsilon), \varepsilon)$. The firm must be indifferent between adjusting its price immediately to $\tau(\varepsilon)$ or waiting for a small increment of time Δt and then deciding what to do. Suppose it waits. Over Δt, real balances rise or fall by $z = \sigma\sqrt{\Delta t}$, with equal probability. The firm then strictly prefers to adjust if real balances rise and to do nothing if they fall. Hence

$$(1+r\Delta t)\, v(h(\varepsilon), \varepsilon) - \gamma (h(\varepsilon) - \eta \varepsilon)^2 \,\Delta t$$

$$\approx \tfrac{1}{2}\, [v(h(\varepsilon), \varepsilon + z) + v(h(\varepsilon), \varepsilon - z)]$$

$$= \tfrac{1}{2}\, [v(h(\varepsilon) - x, \varepsilon + z) + v(h(\varepsilon), \varepsilon - z)],$$

where the last line uses the fact that the firm adjusts if real balances rise, so it is indifferent between having a relative price of $h(\varepsilon)$ or of $h(\varepsilon) - x$. Taking an approximation on the right that is second order in z and first order in x gives

$$\left[rv(h(\varepsilon), \varepsilon) - \gamma\, (h(\varepsilon) - \eta\varepsilon)^2\right] \Delta t$$

$$= \tfrac{1}{2}\left[-v_p x + v_\varepsilon z + \tfrac{1}{2}v_{\varepsilon\varepsilon}z^2 - v_\varepsilon z + \tfrac{1}{2}v_{\varepsilon\varepsilon}z^2\right]$$

$$= \tfrac{1}{2}\sigma^2 v_{\varepsilon\varepsilon}\Delta t - \tfrac{1}{2}v_p x.$$

Recall that (12.14) holds on the interior of the inaction region. Hence it holds as $p_i \downarrow h(\varepsilon)$. Use this fact to conclude that $v_p(h(\varepsilon), \varepsilon) = 0$, so the second line in (12.19) holds. Use a similar argument at $H(\varepsilon)$. ∎

Next, it is useful to note that the symmetry of v implies that the constants a_2, A_2 are equal and that τ, h, H are symmetric in a certain sense.

Lemma 12.5.   The function v in (12.12) satisfies $v(p_i, \varepsilon) = v(-p_i, -\varepsilon)$, all p_i, ε, if and only if $A_2 = a_2$. In this case

$$h(\varepsilon) = -H(-\varepsilon), \quad \tau(\varepsilon) = -\tau(-\varepsilon), \quad \text{all } \varepsilon \in [-B, +B]. \quad (12.21)$$

Proof.   The conclusion follows immediately from the symmetry of v. ∎

The results thus far describe the behavior of an individual firm i, taking B as given. To complete the argument it must be shown that for some B, in addition to the symmetry in (12.21), the firm's inaction region and return threshold satisfy

$$h(B) = \tau(-B) = -S \quad \text{and} \quad H(-B) = \tau(B) = S, \quad (12.22)$$

for some S. To determine B, S, and the constant a_2, use the value matching, smooth pasting, and optimal return conditions (12.18)–(12.20), evaluated at $\varepsilon = B$, with the equilibrium conditions in (12.22) imposed. That is,

$$v(-S, B) = v(+S, B) + C,$$
$$v_p(-S, B) = v_p(+S, B) = 0.$$

Using (12.12) for v and v_p, the resulting system of three equations is

$$-2Sa_1\left(e^{\beta B} - e^{-\beta B}\right) + a_2\left(e^{\beta S} - e^{-\beta S}\right)\left(e^{\beta B} - e^{-\beta B}\right) + \frac{4\gamma}{r}\eta SB = C,$$

$$a_1\left(e^{\beta B} - e^{-\beta B}\right) - \beta a_2\left[e^{-\beta S}e^{\beta B} - e^{\beta S}e^{-\beta B}\right] + \frac{2\gamma}{r}(S - \eta B) = 0,$$

$$a_1\left(e^{\beta B} - e^{-\beta B}\right) - \beta a_2\left(e^{\beta S}e^{\beta B} - e^{-\beta S}e^{-\beta B}\right) - \frac{2\gamma}{r}(S + \eta B) = 0,$$

$$(12.23)$$

where a_1 (from Lemma 12.3) is a function of B. The following proposition establishes the main result.

Proposition 12.6. For any $r, \eta, \gamma, C, \sigma^2$ there exist unique values (S^e, B^e) and a_2 satisfying (12.23).

Proof. Sum and difference the last two equations in (12.23) and rearrange the first to obtain

$$\left[a_2\left(e^{\beta S} - e^{-\beta S}\right) - 2a_1 S\right]\left(e^{\beta B} - e^{-\beta B}\right) = C - \frac{4\gamma}{r}\eta SB,$$

$$\beta a_2\left(e^{-\beta S} - e^{\beta S}\right)\left(e^{\beta B} + e^{-\beta B}\right) = \frac{4\gamma}{r}S,$$

$$\left[2a_1 - \beta a_2\left(e^{\beta S} + e^{-\beta S}\right)\right]\left(e^{\beta B} - e^{-\beta B}\right) = \frac{4\gamma}{r}\eta B.$$

Then use the second to eliminate

$$a_2 = \frac{4\gamma}{r\beta}\frac{S}{\left(e^{-\beta S} - e^{\beta S}\right)\left(e^{\beta B} + e^{-\beta B}\right)} \qquad (12.24)$$

to obtain

$$\frac{1-\eta}{\beta} + \eta B\frac{e^{\beta B} + e^{-\beta B}}{e^{\beta B} - e^{-\beta B}} = S\frac{e^{\beta S} + e^{-\beta S}}{e^{\beta S} - e^{-\beta S}},$$

$$B - \frac{1}{\beta}\frac{e^{\beta B} - e^{-\beta B}}{e^{\beta B} + e^{-\beta B}} = \frac{rC}{4\gamma\eta S}.$$

Define the function

$$\Omega(z) \equiv z\frac{e^z + e^{-z}}{e^z - e^{-z}},$$

and write this pair of equations as

$$\eta\left[\Omega(\beta B) - 1\right] = \Omega(\beta S) - 1, \tag{12.25}$$

$$B\left[1 - \frac{1}{\Omega(\beta B)}\right] = \frac{rC}{4\gamma\eta S}. \tag{12.26}$$

The function Ω is strictly increasing and asymptotically linear, and at $z = 0$ it takes the value unity and has a slope of zero. Hence (12.25) defines an upward-sloping locus in (S-B) space, call it $\Pi_1(S)$, that starts at the origin, and (12.26) defines a downward-sloping locus, call it $\Pi_2(S)$, that asymptotes to each axis. These curves intersect exactly once, as shown in Figure 12.4, defining the solution (S^e, B^e). The constant a_2 is then given by (12.24). ∎

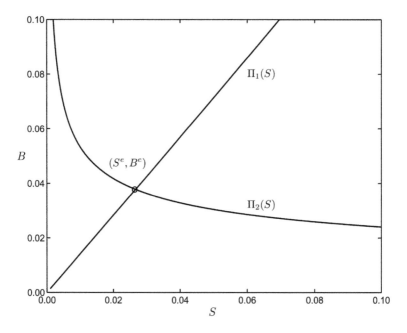

Figure 12.4. *Determination of the equilibrium (S^e, B^e) for the baseline parameters* $r = 0.05$, $\sigma = 0.03$, $\eta = 0.5$, $C = 0.001$, *and* $\gamma = 0.5$.

Proposition 12.6 establishes that for any $r, \eta, \gamma, C, \sigma^2$ there exists a unique (S^e, B^e) with the property that the behavior postulated in condition (iii) of Proposition 12.2 is profit maximizing for firms. The value function for any firm is as described in Lemma 12.3 in the firm's inaction region, the region where

$$p_i \in \big(h(\varepsilon), H(\varepsilon)\big), \quad \varepsilon \in [b, B].$$

Elsewhere the firm immediately adjusts its price, and its value is $v(p_i, \varepsilon) = v(\tau(\varepsilon), \varepsilon) + C$. The threshold functions h, H and the adjustment policy τ are as in Lemma 12.4, and these functions satisfy (12.22). The constant a_2 is in (12.24).

Figures 12.4–12.6 display the equilibrium for the parameter values

$$r = 0.05, \quad \sigma = 0.03, \quad \eta = 0.5,$$
$$C = 0.001, \quad \gamma = 0.5.$$

Figure 12.4 shows the functions $\Pi_1(S)$ and $\Pi_2(S)$, whose intersection determines (S^e, B^e), here equal to $(0.0266, 0.0378)$. Figure 12.5 shows the optimal policy functions h, H, τ. They are increasing and bowed slightly toward the ε-axis. In equilibrium discrete adjustments to p_i occur at only two points,

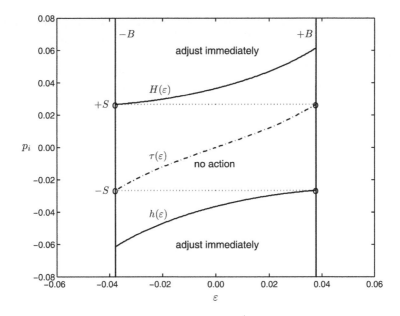

Figure 12.5. *The optimal price adjustment policy.*

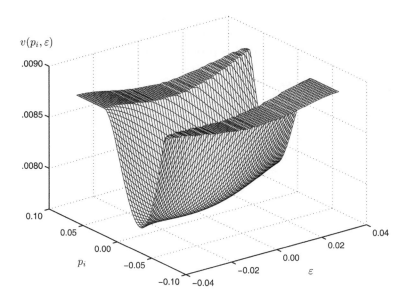

Figure 12.6. *The value function* $v(p_i, \varepsilon)$.

from $+S$ to $-S$ when $\varepsilon = -B$, and from $-S$ to $+S$ when $\varepsilon = +B$. The other parts of the policy functions can be interpreted as describing the optimal first adjustment by a single "deviant" firm that starts with an arbitrary relative price p_i.

Figure 12.6 shows the value function v. Recall from (12.10) that v measures foregone profits relative to a frictionless world. Cross sections, which hold real balances constant, are V-shaped. The flat shoulders are regions where adjustment is immediate, so the value is function is constant at $v(p_i, \varepsilon) = v(\tau(\varepsilon), \varepsilon) + C$.

The model also makes predictions about the frequency of price changes. After a price increase, a firm is at $(+S, +B)$. At this point, the money supply must either rise by $2S$ to trigger another price increase or fall by $2B$ to trigger a price reduction.

Exercise 12.1. Use an argument like the one in Exercise 5.3 to show that the average length of time between price changes for an individual firm is

$$\mathrm{E}\,[T] = \frac{4SB}{\sigma^2}.$$

Changes in the model's exogenous parameters affect three features of the equilibrium. The spread $2B$ in the long-run distribution of real balances measures the variability of output, the spread $2S$ in the cross-sectional price distribution measures price dispersion, and the frequency of price changes $1/\mathrm{E}[T]$ measures price variability. An increase in σ, the variability of money growth, should increase the band widths S and B, and it should also increase the frequency of price adjustment $1/\mathrm{E}[T]$. The ratio C/γ measures the cost of price adjustment relative to the loss from mispricing. Presumably an increase in C/γ increases S and B and hence reduces $1/\mathrm{E}[T]$. For the elasticity parameter η, recall that a firm's optimal nominal price is

$$P_i^* = \eta M + (1 - \eta)\, P.$$

For smaller η the firm cares more about its relative price and less about real balances. Presumably this fact leads to a wider band for real balances and a narrower one for relative price, increasing B and reducing S. In this model price changes are an investment, with costs that are immediate and returns that arrive in the future. Hence an increase in the interest rate r should make the firm less willing to change price, increasing B, S, and $\mathrm{E}[T]$. Establishing these results is left as an exercise.

Exercise 12.2.   (a) Show that an increase in σ increases S, B, and $1/\mathrm{E}[T]$.

   (b) Show that an increase in C/γ increases S, B, and $\mathrm{E}[T]$.

   (c) Show that a decrease in η increases B and reduces S. What is the effect on $\mathrm{E}[T]$?

   (d) Show that an increase in r increases S, B, and $\mathrm{E}[T]$.

In the model in this section prices rise only when output is at its maximum level, a result with a Keynesian flavor, since inflation occurs only at full employment. Since prices fall only when output is at its minimum, it follows that inflation and output are positively correlated. In addition, since inflation in the recent past indicates that output is near its maximum, and hence that the economy is susceptible to further inflation, the rate of inflation displays positive serial correlation.

A key feature of the economies in Propositions 12.1 and 12.2 is the uniform distribution of relative prices across firms. The models in Sections 12.2 and 12.3 display two very different circumstances under which the uniform distribution arises. The first rests on one-sided price adjustment by firms, the second on symmetric price adjustment. The first provides a good approximation to economies in which the mean rate of money growth is high relative to its variance. In such economies episodes during which the money supply falls far enough so that real balances reach their lower limit are rare. Thus price decreases are rare, and the uniform distribution is preserved. The second provides a good approximation to economies in which the variance of money growth is high relative to its mean.

The model studied in this section includes no idiosyncratic shocks to the demands or costs of individual firms. Idiosyncratic shocks of either sort give firms an incentive to adjust price even if the aggregate price level is constant. Thus in economies with low inflation such shocks give firms an opportunity to react to changes in the aggregate price level without incurring additional adjustment costs. Evidence on the frequency and pattern of retail price changes, which shows large price increases and decreases even during periods of low and stable inflation, suggests that such shocks are important. Indeed, in an economy with low inflation they are probably the impetus for most price changes. Adding idiosyncratic shocks makes the model analytically less tractable, but numerical solutions can be used to study its properties.

12.5. Motivating the Loss Function

This section develops a simple model that justifies the loss function and decision rule postulated in Section 12.1. There is a continuum of differentiated goods, $i \in [0, 1]$, each produced by a single firm. Suppose that the representative consumer has preferences of the Dixit-Stiglitz form for these goods,

$$u(x) = \int_0^1 x_i^{1-\theta} \, di, \quad 0 < \theta < 1.$$

Given prices $\{\tilde{P}_i\}$ and an expenditure level $\tilde{E}$, (in levels, not logs), the consumer chooses consumption $\{x_i\}$ to maximize his utility subject to the budget constraint

$$\int_0^1 \tilde{P}_i \, x_i \, di \le \tilde{E}.$$

Define the aggregate price index $\tilde{P}$ by

$$\tilde{P} \equiv \left[\int_0^1 \tilde{P}_i^{(\theta-1)/\theta} di \right]^{\theta/(\theta-1)}.$$

Notice that in log form this index satisfies the homogeneity condition in (12.1). Use this index to define relative prices and real expenditures by

$$\tilde{p}_i \equiv \frac{\tilde{P}_i}{\tilde{P}}, \quad \text{and} \quad \tilde{e} \equiv \frac{\tilde{E}}{\tilde{P}}.$$

The consumer's demand for product i depends only on its relative price $\tilde{p}_i$ and total real expenditures $\tilde{e}$. In particular,

$$x_i\left(\tilde{p}_i, \tilde{e}\right) = \tilde{e}\, \tilde{p}_i^{-1/\theta}, \quad \text{all } i,$$

so (12.7) holds.

Next consider the decision problem of a typical firm. Suppose that its (real) cost of production depends only on the quantity of output it produces. This assumption holds if the firm purchases an invariant mix of inputs from a large number of suppliers whose prices change continuously with the aggregate price level. Alternatively, it holds if labor is the only input, and the real wage is constant. Taking the latter route, suppose in particular that the labor required to produce x_i units of output is

$$c(x_i) = \frac{\rho_0 x_i^{\xi}}{\xi}, \quad \rho_0 > 0, \xi > 1.$$

Note that this cost function is strictly convex: returns to scale are strictly decreasing.

Assume the real wage w is constant. Then (real) profits are

$$\pi_i\left(\tilde{p}_i, \tilde{e}\right) = \tilde{p}_i x_i\left(\tilde{p}_i, \tilde{e}\right) - \frac{w\rho_0}{\xi}\left[x_i\left(\tilde{p}_i, \tilde{e}\right)\right]^{\xi}$$

$$= \tilde{e}\tilde{p}_i^{1-1/\theta} - \frac{w\rho_0}{\xi}\tilde{e}^{\xi}\tilde{p}_i^{-\xi/\theta}.$$

Hence the profit-maximizing relative price is

$$\tilde{p}_i^* = \rho_1 \tilde{e}^{\eta}, \tag{12.27}$$

where

$$\rho_1 \equiv \left(\frac{w\rho_0}{1-\theta}\right)^{\theta/(\theta+\xi-1)} \quad \text{and} \quad \eta \equiv \frac{\theta\,(\xi-1)}{\theta+\xi-1}.$$

Since $0 < \theta < 1$ and $\xi > 1$, it follows that $0 < \eta < 1$, so prices are strategic complements. Notice that constant returns to scale, $\xi = 1$, implies $\eta = 0$, so the profit-maximizing price is independent of aggregate real expenditures $\tilde{e}$. For the problem at hand, this case is not interesting.

So far the expenditure level of the consumer has been fixed. To close the model suppose that real expenditures are proportional to real money balances,

$$\tilde{e} = v_0 \tilde{m}, \tag{12.28}$$

as in (12.6). For example, suppose that the consumer faces a cash-in-advance constraint $\tilde{E} \leq v_0 \tilde{M}(t)$, where $v_0 > 0$ represents the (constant) velocity of money. If the cash-in-advance constraint always binds, then real expenditures have the form in (12.28).

In any case, if expenditures take the form in (12.28), then the optimal relative price in (12.27), in log form, is

$$p_i^* \equiv \ln \tilde{p}_i^* = b + \eta m, \qquad (12.29)$$

where

$$b \equiv \ln \rho_1 + \eta \ln v_0.$$

Note that (12.29) justifies (12.2). Finally, note that aggregate output is proportional to real balances,

$$x \equiv \int_0^1 \tilde{p}_i x_i \left(\tilde{p}_i, \tilde{e} \right) di$$

$$= \int_0^1 \tilde{e} \, \tilde{p}_i^{(\theta-1)/\theta} di$$

$$= \tilde{e} = v_0 \tilde{m},$$

where the last line uses (12.28).

Notes

The model in Section 12.2 is from Caplin and Spulber (1987) and the one in Sections 12.3 and 12.4 is from Caplin and Leahy (1991, 1997), although the analysis here is quite different. I thank Vladislav Damjanovic and Charles Nolan for pointing out an error in the analysis of the boundary conditions in an early version of Section 12.4 and showing how to correct it. See Damjanovic and Nolan (2007) for further results using this approach.

The literature on aggregate menu cost models is extensive. Mankiw (1985) introduced menu costs into an aggregate model that experiences a single unanticipated shock and showed that even a small shock can have large effects. Subsequent work by Caplin and Spulber (1987), Cabellero and Engel (1991, 1993), Caplin and Leahy (1991, 1997), Danziger (1999), and Dotsey, King, and Wolman (1999) studied the robustness of that conclusion. Three model features emerged as important for the conclusions: the nature of the monetary shocks, whether they have high mean or high variance; the presence or absence of idiosyncratic shocks, which provide another motive for price adjustment; and the nature of the price adjustment process, whether it is state dependent as implied by menu costs or time dependent as in Calvo (1983).

New Bureau of Labor Statistics data on the size and frequency of price adjustments in the United States have stimulated recent work. See Bils and Klenow (2004), Klenow and Kryvtsov (2008), and Nakamura and Steinsson (2007) for summaries of this evidence. It suggests that idiosyncratic shocks and other types of heterogeneity are important, and subsequent work has incorporated these features. Midrigan (2006), Golosov and Lucas (2007), Gertler and Leahy (2008), and Nakamura and Steinsson (2008) all develop calibrated computational models that include idiosyncratic as well as aggregate shocks but differ in other ways. Klenow and Kryvtsov (2008) compare the ability of various models to account for both the size and frequency of adjustments. They distinguish the intensive and extensive margins—the size of adjustments and the number of firms adjusting—and discuss the role of each in accommodating monetary shocks. Caballero and Engel (2007) further explore the role of these two margins in explaining the difference between time-dependent and state-dependent models of price adjustment.

A
Continuous Stochastic Processes

THIS APPENDIX CONTAINS background material on continuous stochastic processes in general and Wiener processes in particular.

A.1. Modes of Convergence

Let $(\Omega, \mathfrak{F}, P)$ be a probability space and $\{X_n\}_{n=1}^{\infty}$ a sequence of random variables on that space. There are several distinct notions of convergence for such a sequence. In addition there are several distinct names for each notion.

(a) Convergence with probability one

The sequence $\{X_n\}$ converges to the random variable X *with probability one* if

$$\Pr\left\{\lim_{n\to\infty} X_n = X\right\} = 1.$$

This type of convergence is also called *convergence almost surely (a.s.)* or *convergence almost everywhere (a.e.)*.

(b) Convergence in probability

The sequence $\{X_n\}$ converges to the random variable X *in probability* if for every $\varepsilon > 0$

$$\lim_{n\to\infty} \Pr\left\{|X_n - X| \le \varepsilon\right\} = 1.$$

This type of convergence is also called *convergence in measure*.

(c) Convergence in distribution

Let F_n be the cumulative distribution function (c.d.f.) for X_n, $n = 1, 2, \ldots$. The sequence $\{X_n\}$ converges to the random variable X *in distribution* (or the sequence $\{F_n\}$ converges to the c.d.f. F *in distribution*) if

$$\lim_{n \to \infty} F_n(a) = F(a), \quad \text{all } a \text{ for which } F \text{ is continuous.}$$

This type of convergence is also called *convergence in law* or *weak convergence*.

(d) Strong convergence

For $n = 1, 2, \ldots$, let μ_n be the probability measure on $\mathbf{R}$ defined by $\mu_n(A) = \Pr\{X_n \in A\}$, for any Borel set A. The sequence $\{\mu_n\}$ converges strongly to μ if

$$\lim_{n \to \infty} \mu_n(A) = \mu(A), \quad \text{all } A.$$

It can be shown that (a) $\Rightarrow$ (b) $\Rightarrow$ (c) and that (d) $\Rightarrow$ (c). But note that while the conclusion (a) $\Rightarrow$ (b) holds for a sequence of random variables $\{X_n\}$ defined on a probability space $(\Omega, \mathfrak{F}, P)$—or more generally, for a sequence of measurable functions $\{f_n\}$ defined on any measure space $(\Omega, \mathfrak{F}, \mu)$ where μ has finite total measure—it need not hold for spaces with infinite measure.

Also note a difference in type between the concepts in (a) and (b) versus those in (c) and (d). The definitions in (a) and (b) involve convergence of $\{X(\omega)\}$ for each ω, while those in (c) and (d) involve only the sequence of c.d.f.s (or, equivalently, of probability measures on $\mathbf{R}$) that these random variables induce. Thus, while (a) and (b) involve the underlying space $(\Omega, \mathfrak{F}, \mu)$, (c) and (d) do not. Indeed, the underlying space could change along the sequence.

Also note that if $(\Omega, \mathfrak{F})$ is any measurable space and $\{X_n\}_{n=1}^{\infty}$ is a sequence of measurable real-valued functions on it, there are two more notions of convergence.

(e) Pointwise convergence

The sequence $\{X_n\}$ *converges pointwise* to X if

$$\lim_{n \to \infty} X_n(\omega) = X(\omega), \quad \text{all } \omega \in \Omega.$$

That is, for every $\omega \in \Omega$ and every $\varepsilon > 0$ there exists $N(\omega, \varepsilon)$ such that

$$\left| X_n(\omega) - X(\omega) \right| < \varepsilon, \quad \text{all } n > N(\omega, \varepsilon).$$

(f) Uniform convergence

The sequence $\{X_n\}$ *converges uniformly* to X if for every $\varepsilon > 0$ there exists $N(\varepsilon)$ such that

$$\left|X_n(\omega) - X(\omega)\right| < \varepsilon, \quad \text{all } \omega \in \Omega, \text{ all } n > N(\varepsilon).$$

Clearly (f) $\Rightarrow$ (e) $\Rightarrow$ (a).

A.2. Continuous Stochastic Processes

Let $C = C[0, \infty)$ denote the space of continuous functions $X: [0, \infty) \to \mathbf{R}$. A *continuous stochastic process* on $[0, \infty)$ is one for which $X(\cdot, \omega) \in C[0, \infty)$, a.e. $\omega \in \Omega$. Thus, continuous stochastic processes can be constructed by starting with a probability space $(\Omega, \mathfrak{F}, P)$; defining a measurable mapping from $(\Omega, \mathfrak{F})$ to $(C, \mathbb{C})$, where $\mathbb{C}$ is a σ-algebra of subsets of C; and then defining an appropriate filtration.

The standard choice for the σ-algebra $\mathbb{C}$ is defined in terms of the following metric on C. Let

$$\rho(X, Y) \equiv \sum_{t=1}^{\infty} \frac{1}{2^t} \frac{\rho_t(X, Y)}{1 + \rho_t(X, Y)}, \tag{A.1}$$

where

$$\rho_t(X, Y) \equiv \sup_{t-1 < s \le t} |X(s) - Y(s)|, \quad X, Y \in C.$$

The idea is to divide time into unit intervals $[0, 1]$, $(1, 2]$, $(2, 3]$, $\ldots$, use the sup norm ρ_t on each interval, scale the resulting pieces so that each lies on $[0, 1]$, weight the tth component by $(1/2)^t$, and sum. The scaling ensures that the sum in (A.1) is finite. Indeed, $\rho(X, Y) \in [0, 1]$, all X, Y. Note that ρ is not a norm, however.

By definition, $X_k \to X$ in this metric if and only if

$$\text{for every } \varepsilon > 0 \text{ there exists } K(\varepsilon) > 0 \tag{A.2}$$

$$\text{such that } \rho(X_k, X) < \varepsilon, \quad \text{all } k > K(\varepsilon).$$

But (A.2) implies that

$$\text{for every } \varepsilon > 0 \text{ and } T > 0 \text{ there exists } N(\varepsilon, T) > 0 \tag{A.3}$$

$$\text{such that } \rho_t(X_k, X) < \varepsilon, \quad \text{all } t \le T, \text{ all } k > N(\varepsilon, T).$$

To see this, fix $\varepsilon > 0$, choose $K(\varepsilon)$ satisfying (A.2), and choose any $T > 0$. Define $\hat{\varepsilon} = 2^{-T}\varepsilon/(1+\varepsilon)$, and choose $\hat{K} > 0$ such that $\rho(X_k, X) < \hat{\varepsilon}$, all $k > \hat{K}$. Then

$$\frac{1}{2^t}\frac{\rho_t(X_k, X)}{1 + \rho_t(X_k, X)} \le \rho(X_k, X) < \hat{\varepsilon}, \quad \text{all } k > \hat{K}, \text{ all } t,$$

so

$$\rho_t(X_k, X) < \varepsilon, \quad \text{all } k > \hat{K}, \text{ all } t \le T.$$

The idea is that if it is possible to make the sum

$$\sum_{t=1}^{\infty} \frac{1}{2^t}\frac{\rho_t(X_k, X)}{1 + \rho_t(X_k, X)}$$

arbitrarily small in the tail of the sequence $\{X_k\}$, then for any T it is possible to make the first T components of the sum *uniformly* small.

Conversely, suppose (A.3) holds. Note that since $\rho_t/(1+\rho_t) < 1$, all t, it follows that

$$\sum_{t=T+1}^{\infty} \frac{1}{2^t}\frac{\rho_t(X, Y)}{1 + \rho_t(X, Y)} < \frac{1}{2^T}, \quad \text{all } X, Y.$$

Thus the sum of the tail terms beyond T in (A.1) can be made arbitrarily small, for any (X, Y), by choosing T large. Fix $\varepsilon > 0$, choose $T > 0$ such that $1/2^T < \varepsilon/2$, and choose $N > 0$ such that

$$\rho_t(X_k, X) < \frac{\varepsilon}{2}, \quad \text{all } k > N \text{ and } t \le T.$$

Then for all $k > N$,

$$\rho(X_k, X) = \sum_{t=1}^{T} \frac{1}{2^t}\frac{\rho_t(X_k, X)}{1 + \rho_t(X_k, X)} + \sum_{t=T+1}^{\infty} \frac{1}{2^t}\frac{\rho_t(X_k, X)}{1 + \rho_t(X_k, X)}$$

$$\le \sum_{t=1}^{T} \frac{1}{2^t}\frac{\varepsilon/2}{1 + \varepsilon/2} + \frac{1}{2^T}$$

$$\le \frac{\varepsilon/2}{1 + \varepsilon/2} + \frac{1}{2^T}$$

$$\le \frac{\varepsilon}{2} + \frac{\varepsilon}{2},$$

so (A.2) holds. Hence (A.2), which defines convergence in the metric ρ, is equivalent to (A.3), which defines convergence in the product topology on the space $[0, 1] \times (1, 2] \times (2, 3] \times \ldots$. Let $\mathbb{C}$ denote the σ-algebra generated by the open sets using the metric ρ.

Thus if $(\Omega, \mathfrak{F}, P)$ is a probability space, a continuous stochastic process can be defined by constructing a measurable mapping from $(\Omega, \mathfrak{F})$ to $(C, \mathbb{C})$. Because the mapping is measurable, the probability measure P on $(\Omega, \mathfrak{F})$ induces a probability measure Q on $(C, \mathbb{C})$. This property is important for the following reason. Let X be a stochastic process defined in this way, and consider any measurable, real-valued function of X. For two examples, choose any $T > 0$ and $a \in \mathbf{R}$; define A to be the subset of C consisting of sample paths with the property that $X(T)$ does not exceed a,

$$A \equiv \{X \in C : X(T) \leq a\};$$

and define B to be the set of sample paths with the property that $X(t)$ does not exceed a for any $t \leq T$,

$$B \equiv \{X \in C : X(t) \leq a, \quad \text{all } 0 \leq t \leq T\}.$$

Note that A and B are measurable sets: $A, B \in \mathbb{C}$. Hence the probabilities

$$Q(A) = P\{\omega \in \Omega : X(T, \omega) \leq a\} = \Pr\{X(T) \leq a\},$$

and

$$Q(B) = P\{\omega \in \Omega : M(T, \omega) \leq a\} = \Pr\{M(T) \leq a\},$$

where

$$M(T, \omega) \equiv \max_{s \in [0, T]} X(s, \omega),$$

are well defined. Since a was arbitrary, this result implies that distribution functions can be constructed for $X(T)$ and $M(T)$. A similar argument shows that the same is true for any measurable function of X.

A.3. Wiener Measure

To construct a stochastic process one must define a filtered space $(\Omega, \mathbb{F}, P)$ and a measurable function X. A canonical example of a continuous stochastic process is defined as follows. Let $\Omega = C$, and let

$$X(t, \omega) = \omega(t), \quad \text{all } \omega \in \Omega, \text{ all } t \geq 0.$$

For each $t \geq 0$, let $\mathfrak{F}_t$ be the smallest σ-algebra such that $X(t, \omega)$ is measurable, all $0 \leq s \leq t$, and let $\mathbb{F} = \{\mathfrak{F}_t, t \geq 0\}$. It can be shown that the smallest

σ-algebra containing all of the $\mathfrak{F}_t$s is $\mathfrak{F}_\infty = \mathbb{C}$. Choose any probability measure P on $(C, \mathbb{C})$. Then X is a stochastic process that is adapted to $(\Omega, \mathbb{F}, P)$. An important example is the following.

Theorem A.1 (Wiener's theorem). Let $(C, \mathbb{C})$ and X be as above. There exists a unique probability measure P on $(C, \mathbb{C})$ such that X is a Wiener process.

For a proof see Billingsley (1968, p. 62). The idea is to show that there exists a unique probability measure that has the required finite-dimensional distributions. This measure is called *Wiener measure*.

Exercise A.1. Let $W : \mathbb{R}_+ \times \Omega \to \mathbb{R}$ be a Wiener process on the filtered space $(\Omega, \mathbb{F}, P)$. Fix $k > 0$, and define $W^* : \mathbb{R}_+ \times \Omega \to \mathbb{R}$ by

$$W^*(t, \omega) = \frac{1}{\sqrt{k}} W(kt, \omega).$$

Show that there exists a filtration $\mathbb{F}^* = \{\mathfrak{F}_t^*\}$ such that W^* is a Wiener process on $(\Omega, \mathbb{F}^*, P)$. Describe the relationship between the filtrations $\mathbb{F} = \{\mathfrak{F}_t\}$ and $\mathbb{F}^* = \{\mathfrak{F}_t^*\}$.

A.4. Nondifferentiability of Sample Paths

The sample paths of a Brownian motion are continuous, but they are 'kinky' rather than smooth. More precisely, they are not differentiable. To understand why, it is useful to recall the notions of total and quadratic variation of a function and their relationship with differentiability.

 Let $f : [0, \infty) \to \mathbb{R}$ be a real-valued function. The *total variation* of f over $[0, T]$ is

$$\mathrm{TV} = \sup \left\{ \sum_{i=1}^{n} |f(t_i) - f(t_{i-1})| \right\},$$

where the sup is over finite partitions $0 = t_0 < t_1 < \cdots < t_n = T$. The *quadratic variation* of f over $[0, T]$ is

$$\mathrm{QV} = \lim_{n \to \infty} \sum_{j=1}^{2^n} \left[f\left(\frac{jT}{2^n}\right) - f\left(\frac{(j-1)T}{2^n}\right) \right]^2.$$

Recall the following two results from real analysis.

Theorem A.2. A function f has finite total variation on $[a, b]$ if and only if it can be written as the difference of two increasing functions. In this case $f'(X)$ exists for almost all $X \in [a, b]$ (Royden 1968, p. 100).

Theorem A.3. If f is continuous and has finite total variation, then its quadratic variation is zero.

In addition, there is the following fact about Brownian motion.

Theorem A.4. If X is a (μ, σ^2) Brownian motion, then over any finite interval $[S, S + T]$ it has quadratic variation $\mathrm{QV}(\omega) = \sigma^2 T$, for a.e. $\omega \in \Omega$.

It follows immediately from the latter two results that over any interval $[S, S + T]$ a Brownian motion has total variation $\mathrm{TV}(\omega) = \infty$ along almost every sample path. This property suggests that sample paths of a Brownian motion are not differentiable with respect to time, and this assertion is correct. See Breiman (1968, Theorem 12.25) for a proof.

Exercise A.2. Prove Theorem A.4 for the case $\mu = 0$, $\sigma^2 = 1$, and $S = 0$. That is, show that over any finite interval $[0, T]$, a Wiener process W has quadratic variation $\mathrm{QV}(\omega) = T$, for a.e. $\omega \in \Omega$.

Hint. Fix $T > 0$, and for each $n = 1, 2, \ldots$, define the random variables

$$\Delta_{j,n}(\omega) \equiv W\left(\frac{jT}{2^n}, \omega\right) - W\left(\frac{(j-1)T}{2^n}, \omega\right), \quad j = 1, \ldots, 2^n.$$

For each n, ω, the $\Delta_{j,n}$s are an i.i.d. sequence of random variables, each sequence having mean zero and variance $T/2^n$. Their sum,

$$Q_n(\omega) \equiv \sum_{j=1}^{2^n} \left[\Delta_{j,n}(\omega)\right]^2,$$

is an approximation to $\mathrm{QV}(\omega)$ over $[0, T]$.

Notes

See Billingsley (1968) and Chung (1974) for more detailed discussions of various modes of convergence, the space C, and Wiener measure. Becker and Boyd (1997) discuss continuous stochastic processes and describe some applications. See Harrison (1985, Chapters 1.1–1.3 and Appendix A) and Chung and Williams (1990, Chapter 4) for more detailed discussions of quadratic variation.

B

Optional Stopping Theorem

THIS APPENDIX CONTAINS proofs of the optional stopping results, Theorems 4.3 and 4.4. The proofs are for discrete time only, although the results hold for continuous-time processes as well. Here Z denotes a stochastic process that may have either a continuous or discrete time index ($t \in \mathbf{R}_+$ or $t = 0, 1, 2, \ldots$), and Z_k denotes a process for which $k = 0, 1, 2, \ldots$, must be discrete.

Continuous-time processes must have the following two properties, however: every sample path, at every date t, must be continuous from the right and must have a limit from the left. Since Brownian motions have sample paths that are continuous, they meet this requirement. Jump processes (for example, processes with Poisson arrival times) also meet it, if the usual convention is followed in defining the paths at the jump points. The continuous-time processes used here are assumed to have these properties.

B.1. Stopping with a Uniform Bound, $T \leq N$

One preliminary result is needed for the first proof. Lemma B.1 shows that the basic (in)equality involving expectations in the definition of a (sub)martingale is preserved for integrals over appropriate subsets of Ω.

Lemma B.1. Let Z be a (sub)martingale on the filtered probability space $(\Omega, \mathbb{F}, P)$. Then for any $s \leq t$,

$$\mathrm{E}\left[Z(s)I_A\right] (\leq) = \mathrm{E}\left[Z(t)I_A\right], \quad \text{all } A \in \mathfrak{F}_s.$$

Proof. For any $s \leq t$,

$$
\begin{aligned}
\mathrm{E}\left[I_A Z(s)\right] (\leq) &= \mathrm{E}\left\{I_A \, \mathrm{E}\left[Z(t) \mid \mathfrak{F}_s\right]\right\} \\
&= \mathrm{E}\left\{\mathrm{E}\left[I_A Z(t) \mid \mathfrak{F}_s\right]\right\} \\
&= \mathrm{E}\left[I_A Z(t)\right],
\end{aligned}
$$

where the first line uses the fact that Z is a (sub)martingale, the second uses the fact that A is $\mathfrak{F}_s$-measurable, and the last uses the law of total probability. ∎

Proof of Theorem 4.3. (Discrete time only) (i) Clearly $Z_{T \wedge k}$ is adapted to $(\Omega, \mathbb{F}, P)$, so to establish that it is a (sub)martingale it suffices to show that it satisfies the two properties in the definition, (4.1) and ((4.7) or) (4.2).

For each $k = 1, 2, \ldots$, the stopped process $Z_{T \wedge k}$ satisfies

$$
\mathrm{E}\left[\left|Z_{T \wedge k}\right|\right] (\leq) = \mathrm{E}\left[\sum_{i=1}^{k} |Z_i|\right] < \infty,
$$

where the second inequality follows from the fact that $\{Z_k\}$ is a (sub)martingale. Hence $Z_{T \wedge k}$ satisfies (4.1).

To show that $\{Z_{T \wedge k}\}$ satisfies ((4.7) or) (4.2), it suffices to show that for any $k < n$,

$$
\int_A \left(Z_{T \wedge n} - Z_{T \wedge k}\right) dP \; (\geq) = 0, \quad \text{all } A \in \mathfrak{F}_k. \tag{B.1}
$$

Fix $k < n$ and $A \in \mathfrak{F}_k$. For each $i = k, \ldots, n-1$, define the set $A_i \in \mathfrak{F}_i$ by

$$
A_i = A \cap [T > i] = A \cap [T \leq i]^c .
$$

Thus A_i is the subset of A where T has not occurred by date i.

For any $k < j \leq n$, if $\omega \in A$ and $T(\omega) = j$, then $\omega \in A_i$, $i = k, \ldots, j-1$, and $\omega \notin A_i$, $i = j, \ldots, n-1$. Hence

$$
\begin{aligned}
Z_{T \wedge n}(\omega) - Z_{T \wedge k}(\omega) &= Z_j(\omega) - Z_k(\omega) \\
&= \sum_{i=k}^{j-1} \left[Z_{i+1}(\omega) - Z_i(\omega)\right] \\
&= \sum_{i=k}^{n-1} \left[Z_{i+1}(\omega) - Z_i(\omega)\right] I_{A_i}.
\end{aligned}
$$

292 B. Optional Stopping Theorem

If $\omega \in A$ and $T(\omega) > n$, then $\omega \in A_i$, $i = k, \ldots, n-1$, so

$$Z_{T \wedge n}(\omega) - Z_{T \wedge k}(\omega) = Z_n(\omega) - Z_k(\omega)$$

$$= \sum_{i=k}^{n-1} \left[Z_{i+1}(\omega) - Z_i(\omega) \right] I_{A^i}.$$

Finally, if $\omega \in A$ and $T(\omega) \leq k$, then $\omega \notin A_i$, $i = k, \ldots, n-1$, and

$$Z_{T \wedge n}(\omega) - Z_{T \wedge k}(\omega) = 0$$

$$= \sum_{i=k}^{n-1} \left[Z_{i+1}(\omega) - Z_i(\omega) \right] I_{A^i}.$$

Hence

$$\int_A \left(Z_{T \wedge n} - Z_{T \wedge k} \right) dP = \sum_{i=k}^{n-1} \int_{A_i} \left(Z_{i+1} - Z_i \right) dP. \tag{B.2}$$

But since $A_i \in \mathfrak{F}_i$, all i, it follows from Lemma B.1 that

$$\int_{A_i} \left(Z_{i+1} - Z_i \right) dP \, (\geq) = 0, \quad i = k, \ldots, n-1.$$

Hence for a martingale each term in the sum on the right side of (B.2) is zero and for a submartingale each is nonnegative, and it follows that (B.1) holds. Since k and n were arbitrary, this establishes the result.

(ii) $T \leq N$ implies $T \wedge N = T$. Using this fact and setting $n = N$ in part (i) establishes the claim. ∎

B.2. Stopping with Pr $\{T < \infty\} = 1$

Part (ii) of Theorem 4.3 says that if Z is a martingale and $T \leq N$ is a bounded stopping time, then $E[Z(T)] = E[Z(0)]$. Theorem 4.4 extends this conclusion to cases where $\Pr\{T < \infty\} = 1$ but there is no upper bound on the stopping time. The main idea is as follows.

If Z is a martingale and T is a stopping time, then by Theorem 4.3 the stopped process satisfies

$$E[Z(0)] = E[Z(T \wedge t)] = E[Z(t)], \quad \text{all } t. \tag{B.3}$$

Taking limits in (B.3), it follows that

$$E[Z(0)] = \lim_{t \to \infty} E[Z(T \wedge t)] = \lim_{t \to \infty} E[Z(t)]. \tag{B.4}$$

Since $T < \infty$ means Pr $\{T < \infty\} = 1$, in this case

$$\lim_{t \to \infty} Z(T \wedge t) = Z(T), \quad \text{a.e.}$$

Thus if in addition $Z(T)$ is integrable and exchanging the order of the limit and the expectation in (B.4) is justified,

$$\mathrm{E}\,[Z(0)] = \lim_{t \to \infty} \mathrm{E}\,[Z(T \wedge t)] = \mathrm{E}\left[\lim_{t \to \infty} Z(T \wedge t)\right] = \mathrm{E}\,[Z(T)]. \quad (\text{B.5})$$

In the rest of this section conditions are established under which (B.5) holds.

For one easy case, note that if $Z(T \wedge t)$ is uniformly bounded or, more generally, if there exists a random variable $X \geq 0$ with $\mathrm{E}[X] < \infty$ and $|Z(T \wedge t)| \leq X$, all t, then the desired result follows from the Lebesgue dominated convergence theorem. Theorem 4.4 requires a little less, however. Its proof uses the following result, which involves a random variable X defined on $(\Omega, \mathfrak{F}_\infty, P)$.

Lemma B.2. Let X be a random variable with $\mathrm{E}[|X|] < \infty$, and let T be a stopping time with Pr $[T < \infty] = 1$. Then

$$\lim_{n \to \infty} \mathrm{E}\left[X I_{\{T > n\}}\right] = 0.$$

Proof. For any n,

$$\mathrm{E}\,[|X|] \geq \mathrm{E}\left[|X|\, I_{\{T \leq n\}}\right]$$

$$= \sum_{k=1}^{n} \mathrm{E}\left[|X|\,|\,T = k\right] \mathrm{Pr}\,\{T = k\}.$$

Since

$$\lim_{n \to \infty} \sum_{k=1}^{n} \mathrm{E}\left[|X|\,|\,T = k\right] \mathrm{Pr}\,\{T = k\} = \mathrm{E}\,[|X|],$$

it follows that

$$\lim_{n \to \infty} \mathrm{E}\left[|X|\, I_{\{T \leq n\}}\right] = \mathrm{E}\,[|X|].$$

Hence

$$\lim_{n \to \infty} \mathrm{E}\left[|X|\, I_{\{T > n\}}\right] = 0,$$

establishing the desired result as well. ∎

In the proof of Theorem 4.4 $Z(T)$ is the random variable of interest.

Proof of Theorem 4.4. Hypothesis (ii) implies that $Z(T)$ is integrable. Hence for any t,

$$\mathrm{E}\left[Z(T)\right] = \mathrm{E}\left[Z(T)I_{\{T \leq t\}}\right] + \mathrm{E}\left[Z(T)I_{\{T > t\}}\right]$$

$$= \mathrm{E}\left[Z(T \wedge t)\right] - \mathrm{E}\left[Z(t)I_{\{T > t\}}\right] + \mathrm{E}\left[Z(T)I_{\{T > t\}}\right].$$

Take limits as $t \to \infty$, and note that by Theorem 4.3

$$\lim_{t \to \infty} \mathrm{E}\left[Z(T \wedge t)\right] (\geq) = \mathrm{E}\left[Z(0)\right],$$

by hypothesis (iii) the second terms vanishes, and by Lemma B.2 the third term vanishes. ∎

Notes

The arguments in this appendix draw on Karlin and Taylor (1975, Chapter 6.3) and Billingsley (1995, Section 35).

References

Abel, A. B. 1983. Optimal investment under uncertainty. *American Economic Review* 73: 228–33.

———. 1985. A stochastic model of investment, marginal q, and the market value of the firm. *International Economic Review* 26: 305–22.

Abel, A. B., and J. C. Eberly. 1994. A unified model of investment under uncertainty. *American Economic Review* 84: 1369–84.

———. 1996. Optimal investment with costly reversibility. *Review of Economic Studies* 63: 581–593.

———. 1997. An exact solution for the investment and value of a firm facing uncertainty, adjustment costs, and irreversibility. *Journal of Economic Dynamics and Control* 21: 831–52.

———. 1999. The effects of irreversibility and uncertainty on capital accumulation. *Journal of Monetary Economics* 44: 339–77.

Abel, A. B., A. K. Dixit, J. C. Eberly, and R. S. Pindyck. 1996. Options, the value of capital, and investment. *Quarterly Journal of Economics* 111: 753–77.

Ahlin, C. R. 2001. Optimal pricing under stochastic inflation: State-dependent (s, S) policies. Working Paper 0127. Department of Economics, Vanderbilt University.

Alvarez, F., and F. Lippi. 2007. Financial innovation and the transactions demand for cash. NBER Working Paper 13416. National Bureau of Economic Research, Cambridge, Mass.

Alvarez, F., and R. Shimer. 2008. Search and rest unemployment. NBER Working Paper 13772. National Bureau of Economic Research, Cambridge, Mass.

Alvarez, F., and N. L. Stokey. 1998. Dynamic programming with homogeneous functions. *Journal of Economic Theory* 82: 167–89.

Arrow, K. J. 1968. Optimal capital policy with irreversible investment. In J. N. Wolfe, ed., *Value, capital and growth*. Chicago: Aldine Publishing Company.

Arrow, K. J., and A. C. Fisher. 1974. Environmental preservation, uncertainty, and irreversibility. *Quarterly Journal of Economics* 88: 312–19.

Bachmann, R., R. J. Caballero, and E. M. R. A. Engel. 2006. Lumpy investment in dynamic general equilibrium. Working paper, Massachusetts Institute of Technology, Cambridge.

Bartle, R. G. 1966. *The elements of integration.* New York: Wiley.

———. 1976. *Real analysis,* second edition. New York: Macmillan.

Becker, R. A., and J. H. Boyd III. 1997. *Capital theory, equilibrium analysis and recursive utility.* Malden, Mass.: Blackwell.

Bellman, R. 1957. *Dynamic programming.* Princeton, N.J.: Princeton University Press.

Bentolila, S., and G. Bertola. 1990. Firing costs and labour demand: How bad is Eurosclerosis? *Review of Economic Studies* 57: 381–402.

Bertola, G., and R. J. Caballero. 1990. Kinked adjustment costs and aggregate dynamics. In O. J. Blanchard and S. Fischer, eds., *NBER Macroeconomics Annual* 5, Cambridge, Mass.: MIT Press.

———. 1994. Irreversibility and aggregate investment. *Review of Economic Studies* 61: 223–46.

Billingsley, P. 1968. *Convergence of probability measures.* New York: John Wiley & Sons.

———. 1995. *Probability and measure,* third edition. New York: John Wiley & Sons.

Bils, M., and P. J. Klenow. 2004. Some evidence on the importance of sticky prices. *Journal of Political Economy* 112(5): 947–85.

Borodin, A. N., and P. Salminen. 2002. *Handbook of Brownian motion—Facts and formulae,* second edition. Boston: Birkhauser.

Breiman, L. 1968. *Probability.* Reading, Mass.: Addison-Wesley. Republished in 1992 by the Society for Industrial and Applied Mathematics, Philadelphia.

Brennan, M., and E. Schwartz. 1985. Evaluating natural resource investments. *Journal of Business* 58: 135–57.

Caballero, R. J. 1990. Expenditures on durable goods: A case for slow adjustment. *Quarterly Journal of Economics* 105: 727–43.

———. 1993. Durable goods: an explanation for their slow adjustment. *Journal of Political Economy* 101: 351–84.

———. 1999. Aggregate investment. In *Handbook of macroeconomics*, vol. 1B. J. B. Taylor and M. Woodford, eds. Amsterdam: Elsevier Science.

Caballero, R. J., and E. M. R. A. Engel. 1991. Dynamic (S, s) economies. *Econometrica* 59: 1659–86. Reprinted in Sheshinski and Weiss (1993).

———. 1993. Heterogeneity and output fluctuations in a dynamic menu-cost model. *Review of Economic Studies* 60: 95–119.

———. 1999. Explaining investment dynamics in U.S. manufacturing: A generalized (S, s) approach. *Econometrica* 67: 783–826.

————. 2007. Price stickiness in *Ss* models: New interpretations of old results. Cowles Foundation Discussion Paper 1603, Yale University, New Haven, Conn.

Caballero, R. J., E. M. R. A. Engel, and J. Haltiwanger. 1997. Aggregate employment dynamics: Building from microeconomic evidence. *American Economic Review* 87: 115–37.

Calvo, G. 1983. Staggered prices in a utility-maximizing framework. *Journal of Monetary Economics* 12: 383–98.

Campbell, J. R., and J. D. M. Fisher. 2000a. Aggregate employment fluctuations with microeconomic asymmetries. *American Economic Review* 90: 1323–45.

————. 2000b. Idiosyncratic risk and aggregate employment dynamics. NBER Working Paper 7936. National Bureau of Economic Research, Cambridge, Mass.

Caplin, A. S., and J. Leahy. 1991. State-dependent pricing and the dynamics of money and output. *Quarterly Journal of Economics* 106: 683–708. Reprinted in Sheshinski and Weiss (1993).

————. 1993. Sectoral shocks, learning, and aggregate fluctuations. *Review of Economic Studies* 60: 777–94.

————. 1997. Aggregation and optimization with state-dependent pricing. *Econometrica* 65: 601–25.

————. 1999. Durable goods cycles. NBER Working Paper 6987. National Bureau of Economic Research, Cambridge, Mass.

Caplin, A. S., and D. F. Spulber. 1987. Menu costs and the neutrality of money. *Quarterly Journal of Economics* 102: 703–25. Reprinted in Sheshinski and Weiss (1993).

Chetty, R., and A. Szeidl. 2004. Consumption commitments: Neoclassical foundations for habit formation. NBER Working Paper 10970. National Bureau of Economic Research, Cambridge, Mass.

————. 2007. Consumption commitments and risk preferences. *Quarterly Journal of Economics* 122: 831–77.

Chung, K. L. 1974. *A course in probability theory*, second edition. New York: Academic Press.

Chung, K. L., and R. J. Williams. 1990. *Introduction to stochastic integration*. Boston: Birkhauser.

Cinlar, E. 1975. *Introduction to stochastic processes*. Englewood Cliffs, N.J.: Prentice-Hall.

Cocco, J. F. 2005. Portfolio choice in the presence of housing. *Review of Financial Studies* 18: 535–67.

Constantinides, G. M., and S. F. Richard. 1978. Existence of optimal simple policies for discounted-cost inventory and cash management in continuous time. *Operations Research* 26: 620–36.

Cox, J. C., and S. A. Ross. 1976. The valuation of options for alternative stochastic processes. *Journal of Financial Economics* 3: 145–66.

Cox, J. C., S. A. Ross, and M. Rubinstein. 1979. Option pricing: A simplified approach. *Journal of Financial Economics* 7: 229–63.

Damjanovic, V., and C. Nolan, 2007. (S, s) pricing in a general equilibrium model with heterogeneous sectors. Working paper, University of St. Andrews, Fife, Scotland.

Danziger, L. 1999. A dynamic economy with costly price adjustments. *American Economic Review* 89: 878–901.

Davis, S. J., J. C. Haltiwanger, and S. Schuh. 1996. *Job creation and destruction.* Cambridge, Mass.: MIT Press.

Dixit, A. K. 1991a. Analytical approximations in models of hysteresis. *Review of Economic Studies* 58: 141–51.

———. 1991b. A simplified treatment of the theory of optimal regulation of Brownian motion. *Journal of Economic Dynamics and Control* 15: 657–73. Reprinted in Sheshinski and Weiss (1993).

———. 1992. Investment and hysteresis. *Journal of Economic Perspectives* 6: 107–32.

———. 1993. *The art of smooth pasting.* Oxon, U.K.: Routledge.

———. 1995. Irreversible investment with uncertainty and scale economies. *Journal of Economic Dynamics and Control* 19: 327–50.

Dixit, A. K., and R. S. Pindyck. 1994. *Investment under uncertainty.* Princeton, N.J.: Princeton University Press.

Doms, M. E., and T. Dunne. 1998. Capital adjustment patterns in manufacturing plants. *Review of Economic Dynamics* 1: 409–29.

Dotsey, M., R. G. King, and A. L. Wolman. 1999. State-dependent pricing and the general equilibrium dynamics of money and output. *Quarterly Journal of Economics* 114: 655–90.

Duffie, D. 1988. *Security markets: Stochastic models.* New York: Academic Press.

———. 1996. *Dynamic asset pricing theory.* Princeton, N.J.: Princeton University Press.

Dumas, B. 1991. Super contact and related optimality conditions. *Journal of Economic Dynamics and Control* 15: 675–85.

Eberly, J. C. 1994. Adjustment of consumers' durables stocks: Evidence from automobile purchases. *Journal of Political Economy* 102: 403–36.

Feller, W. 1968. *An introduction to probability theory and its applications,* vol. I, third edition. New York: John Wiley & Sons.

———. 1971. *An introduction to probability theory and its applications,* vol. II, second edition. New York: John Wiley & Sons.

Fisher, J. D. M., and A. Hornstein. 2000. (S, s) policies in general equilibrium. *Review of Economic Studies* 67: 117–46.

Flavin, M., and S. Nakagawa. 2004. A model of housing in the presence of adjustment costs: A structural interpretation of habit persistence.

NBER Working Paper 10458. National Bureau of Economic Research, Cambridge, Mass.

Fleming, W. H., and R. W. Rishel. 1975. *Deterministic and stochastic optimal control*. Berlin: Springer-Verlag.

Fleming, W. H., and H. Soner. 1993. *Controlled Markov processes and viscosity solutions*. New York: Springer-Verlag.

Gertler, M., and J. Leahy. 2008. A Phillips curve with an *Ss* foundation. *Journal of Political Economy* 116: 533–572.

Golosov, M., and R. E. Lucas. 2007. Menu costs and Phillips curves. *Journal of Political Economy* 115: 171-99.

Gourio, F., and A. K. Kashyap. 2007. Investment spikes: New facts and a general equilibrium exploration. *Journal of Monetary Economics* 54: 1–22.

Grossman, S. J., and G. Laroque. 1990. Asset pricing and optimal portfolio choice in the presence of illiquid durable consumption goods. *Econometrica* 58: 25–51.

Harrison, J. M. 1985. *Brownian motion and stochastic flow systems*. Malabar, Fla.: Robert E. Krieger Publishing Company. Republished by John Wiley & Sons, 1990.

Harrison, J. M., and M. I. Taskar. 1983. Instantaneous control of Brownian motion. *Mathematics of Operations Research* 8: 439–53.

Harrison, J. M., T. M. Selke, and A. J. Taylor. 1983. Impulse control of Brownian motion, *Mathematics of Operations Research* 8: 454–66.

Hayashi, F. 1982. Tobin's marginal and average *q*: A neoclassical interpretation. *Econometrica* 50: 213–24.

Henry, C. 1974. Option values in the economics of irreplaceable assets. *Review of Economic Studies, Symposium Issue* 41: 89–104.

Jorgensen, D. W. 1963. Capital theory and investment behavior. *American Economic Review* 53: 247–59.

Karatzas, I., and S. E. Shreve. 1991. *Brownian motion and stochastic calculus*, second edition. Berlin: Springer-Verlag.

Karlin, S., and H. M. Taylor. 1975. *A first course in stochastic processes*, second edition. New York: Academic Press.

———. 1981. *A second course in stochastic processes*. New York: Academic Press.

Kashyap, A. 1995. Sticky prices: new evidence from retail catalogs. *Quarterly Journal of Economics* 110: 245–74. Reprinted in Sheshinski and Weiss (1993).

Khan, A., and J. K. Thomas. 2003. Nonconvex factor adjustments in equilibrium business cycle models: Do nonlinearities matter? *Journal of Monetary Economics* 50: 331–60.

———. 2007. Idiosyncratic shocks and the role of nonconvexities in plant and aggregate investment dynamics. *Econometrica* forthcoming.

Klenow, P. J., and O. Kryvtsov. 2008. State-dependent or time-dependent pricing: Does it matter for recent U.S. inflation? *Quarterly Journal of Economics* 123(3): 863–904.

Kocherlakota, N. R. 1996. The equity premium: It's still a puzzle. *Journal of Economic Literature* 34: 42–71.

Kogan, L. 2001. An equilibrium model of irreversible investment. *Journal of Financial Economics* 6: 201–45.

———. 2004. Asset prices and real investment. *Journal of Financial Economics* 73: 411–32.

Krylov, N. V. 1995. *Introduction to the theory of diffusion processes*. Providence, R.I.: American Mathematical Society.

Kullman, C., and S. Siegel. 2005. Real estate and its role in household portfolio choice. Working paper, University of British Columbia, Vancouver, BC, Canada.

Lach, S., and D. Tsiddon. 1991. The behavior of prices and inflation: An empirical analysis of disaggregated price data. *Journal of Political Economy* 100: 349–89. Reprinted in Sheshinski and Weiss (1993).

Leahy, J. 1993. Investment in competitive equilibrium: The optimality of myopic behavior. *Quarterly Journal of Economics* 108: 1105–1133.

Lucas, R. E., Jr., and E. C. Prescott. 1974. Equilibrium search and unemployment. *Journal of Economic Theory* 7: 199–209.

MacDonald, R. L., and D. R. Siegel. 1985. Investment and the valuation of firms when there is an option to shut down. *International Economic Review* 26: 331–49.

———. 1986. The value of waiting to invest. *Quarterly Journal of Economics* 101: 707–27.

Mankiw, N. G. 1985. Small menu costs and large business cycles: A macroeconomic model of monopoly. *Quarterly Journal of Economics* 100: 529–37.

Marshall, David A., and Nayan G. Parekh. 1999. Can costs of consumption adjustment explain asset pricing puzzles? *Journal of Finance* 54: 623–654.

Martin, R. F. 2003. Consumption, durable goods, and transaction costs. International Finance Discussion Paper 756, Federal Reserve Board, Washington, D.C.

Midrigan, V. 2006. Menu costs, multi-product firms and aggregate fluctuations. Working paper, Federal Reserve Bank of Minneapolis, Minneapolis, Minn.

Moscarini, G. 2005. Job matching and the wage distribution. *Econometrica* 73: 481–516.

Nakamura, E., and J. Steinsson. 2007. Five facts about prices: A reevaluation of menu cost models. Working paper, Columbia University, New York.

———. 2008. Monetary non-neutrality in a multi-sector menu cost model. NBER Working Paper 14001. National Bureau of Economic Research, Cambridge, Mass.

Pindyck, R. S. 1988. Irreversible investment, capacity choice, and the value of the firm. *American Economic Review* 78: 969–85.

———. 1991. Irreversibility, uncertainty, and investment. *Journal of Economic Literature* 29: 1110–48.

Plehn-Dujowich, J. M. 2005. The optimality of a control-band policy. *Review of Economic Dynamics* 8: 877–901.

Ramey, V. A., and M. D. Shapiro. 2001. Displaced capital: A study of aerospace plant closings. *Journal of Political Economy* 109: 958–92.

Ross, S. M. 1983. *Stochastic processes.* New York: Wiley.

———. 1989. *Introduction to probability models,* fourth edition. Boston: Academic Press.

Royden, H. L. 1968. *Real analysis,* second edition. New York: Macmillan.

Scarf, H. 1960. The optimality of (S, s) policies in the dynamic inventory problem. In K. J. Arrow, S. Karlin, and P. Suppes, eds., *Mathematical methods in the social sciences,* 1959, Stanford, Calif.: Stanford University Press. Reprinted in Sheshinski and Weiss (1993).

Schachter, J. P., and J. J. Kuenzi. 2002. Seasonality of moves and the duration and tenure of residence: 1996. Population Division Working Paper Series 69, U.S. Census Bureau, Washington, D.C.

Sheshinski, E., and Y. Weiss. 1977. Inflation and costs of price adjustment. *Review of Economic Studies* 44: 287–303.

———. 1983. Optimum pricing policy under stochastic inflation. *Review of Economic Studies* 50: 513–29.

———, eds. 1993. *Optimal pricing, inflation, and the cost of price adjustment.* Cambridge, Mass.: MIT Press.

Siegel, S. 2005. Consumption-based asset pricing: Durable goods, adjustment costs, and aggregation. Working paper, Business School, University of Washington, Seattle, Wash.

Smith, L. B., K. T. Rosen, and G. Fallis. 1988. Recent developments in economic models of housing markets. *Journal of Economic Literature* 26: 29–64.

Stokey, N. L. 2008. Moving costs, nondurable consumption and portfolio choice. *Journal of Economic Theory* forthcoming.

Stokey, N. L., R. E. Lucas, with E. C. Prescott. 1989. *Recursive methods in economic dynamics.* Cambridge, Mass.: Harvard University Press.

Thomas, J. K. 2002. Is lumpy investment relevant for the business cycle? *Journal of Political Economy* 110: 508–34.

Tobin, J. 1969. A general equilibrium approach to monetary theory. *Journal of Money Credit and Banking* 1: 15–29.

Veracierto, M. L. 2002. Plant-level irreversible investment and equilibrium business cycles. *American Economic Review* 92: 181–97.

Vissing-Jorgensen, A. 2002. Towards an explanation of household portfolio choice heterogeneity: Nonfinancial income and participation cost structures. NBER Working Paper 8884. National Bureau of Economic Research, Cambridge, Mass.

Weisbrod, B. A. 1964. Collective-consumption services of individual-consumption goods. *Quarterly Journal of Economics* 78: 471–77.

Index

Page numbers for entries occurring in figures are followed by an *f* and those occurring in notes, by an *n*.

Abel, A. B., 226, 227, 248n, 249n
action region, 112, 116
adapted, to a filtration, 18
aggregate price index, 75, 129, 130, 144, 253, 256, 258, 260, 263, 266, 278
aggregate shocks, 2–3, 11, 196n, 253, 254, 281n
Ahlin, C. R., 152n
Alvarez, F., 175n, 196n, 249n
Arrow, K. J., 128n, 248n

Bachmann, R., 175n
Baumol-Tobin model, 175n
Bayesian learning, 56–57, 61, 66–67, 74
Becker, R. A., 288n
Bellman, R., 13n
Bellman equation, 4, 5, 11, 30, 33, 34; in an aggregate model, 267; in a housing model, 184, 193, 194; in inventory models, 157, 160, 172, 173, 174; in a menu cost model, 132, 136; in an option model, 109, 110, 113, 115
Bentolila, S., 249n
Bertola, G., 175n, 227, 248n, 249n
Billingsley, P., 25, 70, 74n, 287, 288n, 289
Bils, M., 12n, 152n, 281n
Borodin, A. N., 106n
Boyd, J. H., III, 288n
Breiman, L., 20, 28n, 74n, 288
Brennan, M., 128n
Brownian motion, 3, 5, 6, 12, 19–23, 27, 28n, 31, 35, 75–106; confidence bands for, 21f; Ito's lemma for, 37; Kolmogorov backward equation for, 48–49; Kolmogorov forward

equation for, 50–51; martingales based on, 53, 55, 58, 59–60, 61, 62; occupancy measure for, 41; ordinary differential equations for, 78, 87–88; random walk approximation of, 20–23; sample paths for, 75, 287–88, 289; strong Markov property of, 25; Tanaka's formula for, 43, 46. *See also* geometric Brownian motion; regulated Brownian motion
Bureau of Labor Statistics, U.S., 1, 12n, 281n
Bureau of the Census, U.S., 1, 2, 12n

Caballero, R. J., 175n, 196n, 227, 248n, 249n, 280n, 281n
Calvo, G., 281n
Campbell, J. R., 249n
capital gains, 30, 145, 246
Caplin, A. S., 196n, 249n, 254, 259, 280n
Caplin-Leahy model, 264f, 265f
Caplin-Spulber model, 261f
cash management model, 145–46, 167–72
c.d.f. *See* cumulative distribution function
central limit theorem, 23
CES aggregator. *See* constant elasticity of substitution aggregator
Chetty, R., 196n
Chung, K. L., 28n, 29n, 42, 46, 52n, 288n
Cinlar, E., 28n
Cocco, J. F., 196n
constant elasticity of substitution (CES) aggregator, 192
Constantinides, G.M., 167, 175n
continuous control variable, in a Hamilton-Jacobi-Bellman equation, 176–96

continuous stochastic process, 18, 284–86
continuous-time stochastic process, 12, 18, 25
convergence: almost everywhere (a.e.), 282; almost surely (a.s.), 282; in distribution, 283; in law, 283; in measure, 282; modes of, 282–84; in probability, 282; with probability one, 282
convergence theorem, martingale, 53, 70–74
convex adjustment costs: in impulse control models, 174–75; in instantaneous control models, 226, 227, in investment models, 232–36, 237–39
Cox, J. C., 128n
cumulative distribution function (c.d.f.), 48, 283

Damjanovic, V., 280n
Daniziger, L., 280n
Davis, S. J., 12n
depreciation, 153, 176, 178, 188, 237
diffusion parameters, 26, 148, 151f
diffusion, 12, 29n, 31, 78; defined, 25; infinitesimal parameters of, 26, 33, 38; martingales based on, 53, 58, 60; ordinary differential equations for, 98; properties of, 25–27; regular, 26
direct approach: in inventory models, 160–62; in menu cost model, 136–39; in an option model, 116–19
discounted local time, 42, 43, 76. *See also* expected discounted local time function
discounted occupancy measure, 42
discrete-time Markov process, 53, 57–58
disinvestment, 8, 226, 238, 240; convex adjustment costs and, 232, 233, 234; linear costs and, 228–29, 230–31; in a two-sector economy, 248
Dixit, A. K., 13n, 152n, 249n
Dixit-Stiglitz preferences, 257, 278
Doms, M. E., 12n
Dotsey, M., 280n
drift: of a Brownian motion, 19–20, 22, 25; of a diffusion, 26, 27; of a geometric Brownian motion, 39, 41; of an Ornstein-Uhlenbeck process, 28
Duffie, D., 13n, 128n
Dumas, B., 152n, 224n
Dunne, T., 12n

Eberly, J. C., 196n, 227, 248n, 249n

eigenfunction, 53, 58
eigenvalue, 57–58
eigenvector, 53, 57–58
Engel, E. M. R. A., 175n, 249n, 280n, 281n
excess real balances, 263, 264, 265f
exogenous moves, 178, 191
exogenous shocks, 11, 144, 166, 172, 191, 253, 254
expected discounted local time function ($\hat{L}$), 5, 12, 76, 78, 87, 93, 94–95, 96, 104, 106
expected discounted indicator functions (ψ, Ψ), 5, 12, 76, 78, 98, 103, 104, 106; properties and formulas, 82–87, 93–95, 103–5; regulated Brownian motion and, 208–9
expected local time function (L), 77, 91–93, 100, 164–66
extensive margin, 254–55

Fallis, G., 196n
family composition, 55–56, 61, 65–66
Fatou's lemma, 73
Feller, W., 28n
filtered probability space: defined, 18; stochastic integrals and, 34; stopping time on, 24; strong Markov property and, 25; Wiener measure and, 286, 287
filtration: defined, 18; in defining martingale, 53–57; in defining stopping time, 24; in defining strong Markov property, 25; Wiener measure and, 287
first-order Taylor series approximation, 30–31, 113
Fisher, A. C., 128n
Fisher, J. D. M., 175n, 249n
Flavin, M., 196n
Fleming, W. H., 51n

gambler's wealth, 53, 54–55, 61, 64–65, 68–69, 74
geometric Brownian motion, 5, 6–7, 12, 27, 31, 52n, 78, 86–87, 98; demand as, 225, 238; formulas for, 100–101, 104–6; in a housing model, 179, 184, 191, 193, 195; in inventory models, 166, 172, 173; in investment models, 10, 225, 227, 237, 238, 240, 243, 247; Ito's lemma for, 38–41; Kolmogorov backward equation for, 48, 49; Kolmogorov forward equation for, 50; martingales based on, 59; in a menu cost model, 129

Gertler, M., 281n
Golosov, M., 281n
Gourio, F., 175n
Grossman, S. J., 176, 196n

Haltiwanger, J., 12n, 249n
Hamilton-Jacobi-Bellman (HJB) equation, 6,
    10; in an aggregate model, 266, 267, 268,
    271; derivation of, 31–34, 88, 152n; for
    the housing model, 176, 178, 184–90, 191,
    192, 193, 195; for inventory models, 154,
    160, 162–64, 168, 173, 174, 220, 222, 224;
    for investment models, 229, 230, 233, 237,
    239, 240, 244, 247; Ito's lemma and, 38;
    for menu cost models, 130, 140–45, 146;
    for an option model, 109, 110, 119–25,
    127f
Harrison, J. M., 13n, 46, 51n, 106n, 153, 166,
    175n, 215, 218, 224n, 288n
Hayashi, F., 226
Henry, C., 128n
hiring and firing, 11, 226–27, 249n. *See also*
    job creation and destruction
HJB equation. *See* Hamilton-Jacobi-Bellman
    equation
holding costs, 9; in inventory models, 153,
    154, 155, 157, 158, 164, 166, 167, 168, 169,
    218, 222–24; in a menu cost model, 146;
    quadratic, 222–24
homogeneity of degree one, 7; in a housing
    model, 179; in inventory models, 172, 173;
    in investment models, 227, 230, 238, 239,
    240, 244, 247, 248
homogeneous solutions, of an ordinary
    differential equation, 93, 103; in inventory
    models, 168, 221, 224; in investment
    models, 241, 245; in a menu cost model,
    142; in an option model, 120
Hornstein, A., 175n
housing and portfolio choice model, 7–8,
    176–96

iceberg costs, 224
idiosyncratic shocks, 11, 77, 196n, 253, 278,
    280n, 281n
i.i.d. *See entries for* independently and
    identically distributed
impulse control models, 8, 12, 13n, 109–96
inaction region, 4, 7, 152n; in an aggregate
    model, 268, 271, 272, 275; in a housing
    model, 177, 185, 190; in instantaneous

control models, 8; in inventory models,
    154, 159, 166, 169, 173, 174, 175, 224, 225;
    in investment models, 229, 230–31, 233,
    234, 240; in a menu cost model, 129, 130,
    131, 135–36, 141, 142, 144, 145, 147, 148;
    in an option model, 112, 116; regulated
    Brownian motion and, 201
independent events, 18
independent families of sets, 18
independent random variables, 18–19
independently and identically distributed
    (i.i.d.) increments, 20, 25, 27, 39,
    266
independently and identically distributed
    (i.i.d.) random variables: in approximation
    of Brownian motion, 23; martingales and
    53, 58
independently and identically distributed
    (i.i.d.) shocks, 11, 77, 129–30, 144, 164,
    253
infinitesimal mean, 26
infinitesimal variance, 26
inflation, 254, 262, 277, 278
intensive margin, 254–55
inventory models, 8–10, 12, 153–75, 176,
    225; described, 154–57; examples, 166–
    74; Hamilton-Jacobi-Bellman equation for,
    154, 160, 162–64, 168, 173, 174, 220, 222,
    224; with a lower threshold fixed at zero,
    166–67; regulated Brownian motion and,
    201, 216–24
investment models, 1–2, 6–7, 10, 225–49;
    convex adjustment costs in, 226, 227,
    232–36; irreversible investments in (*See*
    irreversible investments); linear costs in,
    227–31; reversible investments in, 225,
    248; special cases, 236–39; two-sector
    economy and, 227, 247–48
irreversible investment, 10, 227, 239–43,
    248–49n; with two shocks, 243–47
Ito integral, 34
Ito's lemma, 12, 31, 43, 46, 87; definition and
    properties, 37–38; geometric Brownian
    motion and, 38–41; Kolmogorov backward
    equation and, 47; martingales and, 60;
    regulated Brownian motion and, 205

Jensen's inequality, 39, 62
job creation and destruction, 2, 11, 12n. *See
    also* hiring and firing
Jorgensen, D. W., 225, 226, 231

Karatzas, I., 51n
Karlin, S., 28n, 52n, 74n, 106n, 289
Kashyap, A., 152n, 175n
Khan, A., 175n
King, R. G., 280n
kinks, functions with, 31, 44, 91, 126, 167, 175, 209, 220, 232, 236
Klenow, P. J., 12n, 152n, 281n
Kocherlakota, N. R., 188
Kogan, L., 249n
Kolmogorov backward equation (KBE), 31, 47–49, 52n
Kolmogorov forward equation (KFE), 31, 50–51, 52n
Kolmogorov's inequality, 53, 62–63
Krylov, N. V., 51–52n
Kryvtsov, O., 12n, 152n, 281n
Kuenzi, J. J., 12n
Kullmann, C., 196n

labor, 226–27, 279. *See also* hiring and firing; job creation and destruction; wage offers
Lach, S., 152n
Laroque, G., 176, 196n
law of iterated expectations, 47
law of large numbers, 11, 253
law of total probability, 290
Leahy, J., 196n, 249n, 254, 280n, 281n
Lebesgue dominated convergence theorem, 292
Lebesgue measure, 41
linear costs, 227–31
Lippi, F., 175n
local time, 31, 41–43, 46, 52n, 100. *See also* discounted local time; expected discounted local time function; expected local time function
log utility, 178, 192–93
long-run averages, 11, 77; in inventory models, 154, 164–66; in a menu cost model, 130, 144; for regulated Brownian motion, 200
Lucas, R. E., 13n, 249n

MacDonald, R. L., 128n, 248n
Mankiw, N. G., 280n
Markov process, in constructing martingales, 53, 57–58
Markov property, strong, 24–25, 29n
Marshall, D. A., 196n

Martin, R. F., 196n
martingale convergence theorem, 53, 70–74
martingales, 12, 53–74; based on eigenvalues, 57–58; definition and examples, 53–57; optional stopping theorem for, 63–67, 291; sub- (*See* submartingales); super-, 53, 60–63; Wald (*See* Wald martingales)
mean reverting stochastic process, 27
menu cost model, 3, 6, 11, 12, 77, 129–52, 176, 253–55
Midrigan, V., 281n
monetary neutrality, 253–54, 259–61
money pump, 9, 155
Moscarini, G., 249n
mutually independent, 18–19

Nakagawa, S., 196n
Nakamura, E., 152n, 281n
no bubble condition, 123, 196
Nolan, C., 280n
nominal balances, 257, 263, 264f
nominal price, 75, 129, 130–31, 257, 264, 266, 277
nominal shocks, 269
nondurable consumption, 178, 192, 196n

occupancy measure, 12, 31, 45, 52n, 91, 100; discounted, 42; local time and, 41–43; for a regulated Brownian motion, 200, 214
ODE. *See* ordinary differential equation
optimal return condition: in an aggregate model, 271, 272; in a housing model, 184, 195; in inventory models, 163, 167, 169, 173; in a menu cost model, 141, 143
optional stopping theorem, 12, 53, 63–70, 74n, 78, 80; proofs, 289–93
option model, 109–28
ordinary differential equation (ODE), 6; for a Brownian motion, 78, 87–88; for a diffusion, 98; for a geometric Brownian motion, 39–41
Ornstein-Uhlenbeck (OU) process, 27, 78, 98; discrete approximation of, 27–28; formulas for, 101–2, 106; in investment models, 227, 236; Kolmogorov backward equation for, 48–49; Kolmogorov forward equation for, 50–51; in an option model, 125
outcome, in a probability space, 17

Parekh, N. G., 196n
partial differential equation (PDE), 47, 239, 240
Phillips curve, 254; economy with, 261–65; optimizing behavior and, 265–78
Pindyck, R. S., 13n, 248n, 249n
Plehn-Dujowich, J. M., 152n
pointwise convergence, 283
Poisson arrival time, 130, 145, 146, 191, 254, 289
portfolio policy, 2, 187–88, 190f
Prescott, E. C., 249n
price index. *See* aggregate price index
price stickiness, 1, 10–11, 12, 253, 254
Principle of Optimality, 5; in a housing model, 183; introduction of, 13n; in inventory models, 157, 161, 220; in a menu cost model, 132, 137
probability space, 17, 19; modes of convergence in, 282, 283. *See also* filtered probability space
productivity shocks, 2–3
product quality, 173–74

q theory, 234, 248n
quadratic adjustment cost, 234, 236, 237
quadratic holding cost, 222–24
quadratic loss function, 256, 257, 258
quadratic variation, 287

Ramey, V. A., 239
random variable, 17–18; convergence of a martingale to, 72–73; independent, 18–19, 54; independently and identically distributed, 23, 53, 58
random walk approximation, of Brownian motion, 20–23
real balances, 256–59, 259–61, 262–65, 266–67, 269, 272, 276–77, 279, 280
realization: of a random variable, 17; of a stochastic process, 18
reflected Brownian motion, 224n
regular diffusion, 26
regulated Brownian motion, 12, 199–224; in an aggregate model, 255, 262; discounted values for, 201, 205–12; in inventory models, 201, 216–24; one- and two-sided regulators, 201–5; stationary distribution for, 200, 212–18
relative price, 75–77; in an aggregate model,

256, 257, 259–67, 272, 276–80; in the Caplin-Leahy model, 265f; in a menu cost model, 129, 130–31, 144, 147, 148f
reversible investment, 225, 248
Richard, S. F., 167, 175n
Riemann integral, 33, 34, 36, 37
Rishel, R. W., 51n
risk aversion, 181, 182, 186, 190
riskless asset. *See* safe asset
risk tolerance, 7–8, 181, 190
risky asset, 176, 178, 180, 181, 193
Rosen, K. T., 196n
Ross, S. A., 128n
Ross, S. M., 28n
Royden, H. L., 287
Rubinstein, M., 128n

safe asset, 176, 178, 181
sale price, 225, 226, 228, 231, 234, 235f, 236
Salminen, P., 106n
salvage value: in an option model, 110, 111, 113–14, 115, 117, 120, 121, 125; in a replacement model, 172
sample path, 33, 286; of a Brownian motion, 75, 287–88, 289; defined, 18; of a diffusion, 25; integral along a, 42–43; for nominal and excess real balances, 263, 264f; nondifferentiability of, 287–88; of a regulated Brownian motion, 203, 204f; of a Wiener process, 19, 20
Scarf, H., 153, 175n
Schachter, J. P., 12n
Schuh, S., 12n
Schwartz, E., 128n
second-order Taylor series approximation, 6, 10, 119, 140, 229
Selke, T. M., 153, 166, 175n
Shapiro, M. D., 239
Sheshinski, E., 129, 152n
Shimer, R., 249n
Shreve, S. E., 51n
Siegel, D. R., 128n, 248n
Siegel, S., 196n
simple stochastic process, 35
Smith, L. B., 196n
smooth pasting condition, 6, 10, 12; in an aggregate model, 271, 272; in a housing model, 185, 187, 188, 195; in inventory models, 160, 163, 167, 169, 173, 222; in investment models, 229, 242, 245; in a

smooth pasting condition (*continued*)
    menu cost model, 141, 143; in an option
    model, 123, 124, 126
Soner, H., 51n
Spulber, D. F., 254, 259, 280n
state variables, 3, 7, 30; as regulated Brownian
    motion, 12
stationary density: Kolmogorov forward
    equation and, 50–51; for regulated
    Brownian motion, 200
stationary distribution, 11; for an Ornstein-
    Uhlenbeck process, 27–28; for a regulated
    Brownian motion, 200, 212–18
stationary transition function, 53, 57, 58
Steinsson, J., 152n, 281n
sticky prices. *See* price stickiness
stochastic integral, 12, 31, 34–37, 39–40
stochastic process, 12, 17–29; continuous,
    18, 284–86; continuous-time, 12, 18,
    25; defined, 17–18; mean reverting, 27;
    simple, 35
Stokey, N. L., 13n, 175n, 196n
stopping time, 4–5, 12, 29n, 42, 109;
    Brownian motion and, 75–76, 82, 84, 87,
    91; defined, 24; defined by thresholds,
    78–79; martingales and, 53, 63–70, 74n;
    regulated Brownian motion and, 201, 202,
    203, 212–18; strong Markov property and,
    24–25. *See also* optional stopping theorem
strictly convex adjustment costs, 173,
    174–75
strong convergence, 283
strong Markov property, 24–25, 29n
submartingale, 53, 70, 71, 72–73; definition
    and properties, 60–63; optional stopping
    theorem for, 63–66, 289–91
super contact condition, 10, 12; coining of
    term, 224n; in inventory models, 222; in
    investment models, 229, 242, 245, 246
supermartingale, 53, 60–63
Szeidl, A., 196n

Tanaka's formula, 31, 43–46, 52n
target price, 256–57, 258

Taskar, M. I., 218, 224n
Taylor, A. J., 153, 166, 175n
Taylor, H. M., 28n, 52n, 74n, 106n, 289
Taylor series approximation, 32; first-order,
    30–31, 113; second-order, 6, 10, 119, 140,
    229
Thomas, J. K., 175n
Tobin, J., 226
total variation, 287
Tsiddon, D., 152n
two-sector economy, 227, 247–48

uniform convergence, 284
upcrossing, 70–73

value matching condition, 6, 12; in an
    aggregate model, 271, 272; in a housing
    model, 185, 187, 188, 195; in inventory
    models, 167, 169, 173; in investment
    models, 241; in a menu cost model, 141,
    142–43; in an option models, 123, 125
variance, 19–20; calculation of, for a
    geometric Brownian motion, 39, 41; in the
    Hamilton-Jacobi-Bellman equation, 32;
    infinitesimal, 26
Veracierto, M. L., 249n
Vissing-Jorgensen, A., 12n

wage offers, 124–25
Wald martingales, 74, 106n; examples, 58–
    60; expected values for, 79–81; optional
    stopping theorem applied to, 78, 80
weak convergence, 283
wealth: gambler's, 53, 54–55, 61, 64–65,
    68–69, 74
Weisbrod, B. A., 128n
Weiss, Y., 129, 152n
Wiener measure, 286–87, 288n
Wiener process, 19–20
Wiener's theorem, 287
Williams, R. J., 42, 46, 52n, 288n
Wolman, A. L., 280n

zero expectation property, 36, 38, 40, 60

GPSR Authorized Representative: Easy Access System Europe - Mustamäe tee
50, 10621 Tallinn, Estonia, gpsr.requests@easproject.com

www.ingramcontent.com/pod-product-compliance
Ingram Content Group UK Ltd.
Pitfield, Milton Keynes, MK11 3LW, UK
UKHW042250300325
456820UK00002B/19